The Complete
NEW
TESTAMENT
STUDIES

The Complete
NEW TESTAMENT STUDIES

RUDOLF FRIELING

Floris Books

First published in German as *Christologische Aufsätze* (Vol 3)
and *Studien zum Neuen Testament* (Vol 4)
by Verlag Urachhaus, Stuttgart in 1982 and 1986
Some parts previously published in English
as *New Testament Studies* by Floris Books, Edinburgh in 1994
This expanded edition first published by Floris Books in 2021

See Sources and Translators, p. 531 for details of translators

© 1982, 1986 Verlag Urachhaus
English translation © 1995, 2021 Floris Books

All rights reserved. No part of this publication may be
reproduced without the prior permission of
Floris Books, Edinburgh
www.florisbooks.co.uk

British Library CIP Data available
ISBN 978-178250-735-2
Printed and bound by Gutenberg Press Limited, Malta

 Floris Books supports sustainable forest management by
printing this book on materials made from wood that
comes from responsible sources and reclaimed material

CONTENTS

Foreword ... 13

I
THE PATH OF CHRIST JESUS

1. Gospel ... 19
2. Growing Towards Death – Dying into New Life ... 25
3. From the Jordan Baptism to the Place of Skulls ... 32
   Baptism by water 32; The Jordan baptism 34; 'But I have a baptism to be baptised with ...' 34; The image of the Jordan baptism and of Golgotha 36; Above and below open to each other 37
4. The Son of God ... 40
5. The Sign of the Son of Man ... 48
6. Lord of the Elements ... 54
7. The Great 'Today' in the New Testament ... 61
8. 'Come to Me, All You ...' ... 66
9. He Wrote in the Earth ... 72
10. Christ at the Festival of Dedication of the Temple ... 78
    The Festival of Dedication of the temple 78; Solomon's Portico 80; 'I and the father are one' 80; The 'beautiful works' 82; 'You are gods' 82
11. Three Predictions of the Passion ... 86
12. Surrendering to Destiny ... 90

13	Christ Jesus' Prayers in Seclusion	95
	Flight on Sunday morning 96; The night of inspirations 97; The feeding of the five thousand 97; The transfiguration 98; The Lord's Prayer 99; Gethsemane 100	
14	Peter's Denial	102
	The prediction 102; The denial in Matthew and Mark 103; According to Luke 104; According to John 105; Easter sequel 107	
15	The Seven Words from the Cross	109
16	'Centre' in the Gospel of John	116
	At the Jordan 116; 'The middle of the festival' 117; 'And placed her in the midst' 118; And once again: 'the woman in the middle' 118; At Golgotha 119; The evening of Easter Sunday 119; The first Sunday after Easter 120	
17	The Seven Easter Stories in the Gospels	121
	The women at the grave 122; On the way to Emmaus 122; Easter evening 123; The appearance to Thomas 123; The mountain in Galilee 124; The Sea of Galilee 124; Ascension 124	
18	Walking with the Risen One: the Way to Emmaus	126
	The Risen One walks with the two disciples 126; He speaks with them 127; He thinks with them 129; Entering 131	
19	The Miraculous Draft of Fishes	133
20	Stages of resurrection	138
21	The Ascension of Christ	143
22	The Coming of the Son of Man	148

II
HEALINGS

23	Deeds of Power – Signs – Works	155
	Wonders 155; Deeds of power 158; Signs 159; Works 160	
24	The Healing Under the Opened Roof	162
25	The Healing of the Deaf and Mute Man	165

26	The Will to Be Healed	171
27	The Healings of the Blind in the Gospels	176
28	The Healing of the Man Born Blind (John 9)	181
	1. The healing 181; 2. The neighbours 183;	
	3. The Pharisees 184; 4. The parents 185; 5. The Pharisees	
	once more 185; 6. Christ reappears in the story 186;	
	7. Christ's concluding words 187	
29	The Raising of Lazarus	189

III
PARABLES

30	The Human Soul and the Good Earth	201
	Luke, the Marian evangelist 201; The parable of the good	
	earth 202; On listening 203; The counter-image: 'Think of	
	Lot's wife' 205	
31	Three Parables of Losing and Finding	208
	The shepherd and the lost sheep 209; The woman and the lost	
	coin 210; The father and the lost son 210; The triad of the	
	three parables 211	
32	The Parable of the Wedding Banquet	213
33	The Parable of the Great Banquet	220
34	The Workers in the Vineyard and their Payment	226
	What precedes it? 226; The parable 228; The parable becomes	
	transparent 229	
35	The Parable of the Wicked Tenants	232
36	The Rich Man and Death	240
37	Three Parables About Christ's Future Coming	245
	1. The wise and foolish maidens 245; 2. The talents 246;	
	3. The Last Judgment 247; Overview 248	
38	The Works of Charity	250
	Giving to eat and to drink 251; Taking in strangers and	
	clothing the naked 251; Visiting the sick and imprisoned 253	

IV
WITNESSES OF THE APOSTLES

39	Peter's Pentecost Address	257
40	Peter's Easter Night in the Year 44	263
41	The Martyr Stephen – the Day After Christmas *Stephen the Hellenist 270; The speech of Stephen 272; The countenance of an angel 272; The birth of Christ in the soul 274*	270
42	The Power of Transformation: Insights of St Paul *1. Transformation 277; 2. Reshaping 279; 3. Making completely anew 280*	277
43	Awaken, You Who Sleep!	283
44	God's Human Nature in Christ Jesus	289
45	Christianity's Potential for the Future	296
46	Father of Lights	302
47	The Seven Beatitudes of the Apocalypse	307
48	Life After Death and the Bible	315

V
SACRED NUMBER IN THE GOSPEL OF JOHN

49	Preliminary remarks	327
50	Three in the Utterances of Christ *The healing at the pool 333; The conversation with Nicodemus 335; The Festival of Dedication 337; The Greeks 339; Words on the cross 340; The resurrection 341; The appearance by the Sea of Galilee 345*	332
51	Seven in the Utterances of Christ *The first disciples 346; The Samaritan woman 348; Light and judgment 351; The healing of the blind man 354; The passion 359*	346

52 Trinitarian Formulations and Reiterations   362
    'The time of Passover was near' 362; Nicodemus 365;
    The three prayers to the Father 367; Pre-existence 372; '
    Where I am ...' 375; The ascension 376; The Adversary 380

53 The Trinity in the Structure of Single Sentences   384
    The Prologue 384; The conversation with
    Nicodemus 387; Some 'I am' sayings 388; Thirst and
    the Samaritan woman 391; Before Pilate 392

54 In Conclusion   394

VI
THE 'I AM UTTERANCES IN THE GOSPEL OF JOHN

55 The Twelvefold Nature of the I AM Utterances   401

VII
AGAPE – DIVINE LOVE IN THE FOURTH GOSPEL

56 Overview   411
57 The Agape of the Father   414
    1. The agape of the Father for the world 414; 2. The agape of
    the Father for the Son 417; 3. The agape of the Father for the
    disciples 428

58 The Agape of the Son   433
    1. The agape of the Son for his own 433; 2. The agape of the Son
    for the Father 445

59 The Agape of the Disciples   448
    1. The agape of the disciples for one another 448; 2. The agape
    of the disciples for Christ 452

60 Summary   459

VIII
THE TRANSFIGURATION

61 Preliminaries — 463
The transfiguration on the mountain 466

62 According to Luke — 469
The question put to the disciples 469; The transition to the transfiguration 470; Eight days later 471; Christ's praying 472; The transfigured countenance 473; The radiant garments 476; The two spirit figures 477; The spirit conversation 478; The changing consciousness of the disciples 481; The disappearance of the two spirit figures 483; Entering the cloud 484; The voice of heaven 485; The silence 486

63 According to Matthew — 488
Caesarea Philippi 488; The ascent 489; The high mountain 490; Metamorphosis 493; The sun 494; Cosmic aspects in Matthew's writing 495; Moses and Elijah 497; Peter 499; The luminous cloud 501; The fear of the disciples 503; 'Do not speak to anybody about this' 505; The conversation about Elijah 508

64 According to Mark — 510
Inspiration 510; Unearthly light 512; Elijah and Moses 514; The share of the three disciples 515; The overshadowing 516; The question of rising from the dead 517; The unique quality of Mark's report 520

65 Conclusion — 523
Looking at the Gospel of John 523; In conclusion 526

Bibliography — 529
Sources and Translators — 531
Index to Biblical References — 533
Index — 543

Quotations from the Bible are usually the author's own translations.

FOREWORD

The publication of this collection of articles and extended essays on a variety of New Testament themes will stand as a worthy memorial and fitting 'testament' to the theological scholarship and spiritual insight of Rudolf Frieling (1901–86), one of the original group of priests responsible for the founding of The Christian Community, a movement for religious renewal taking its inspiration and impulse from the work of Rudolf Steiner (1861–1925).

Frieling was just a young man of twenty-one when the Community was founded and had not yet finished his doctorate, but his talent and stature was soon recognised and he eventually became the leader (erzoberlenker) of The Christian Community, succeeding Friedrich Rittelmeyer and Emil Bock. He was to hold this position for twenty-five years.

Comparison between Frieling and Bock is singularly instructive and reveals the different strengths of these remarkable men. Whereas Bock approaches the Bible in what one might call a 'grand' manner, developing impressive, imaginative panoramas of the vast sweep of cosmic and human evolution, and writes in a style that is fluent and, on occasions, florid, Frieling prefers to focus on the investigation of the biblical text in a more concentrated exegetical manner. This gives his writing a certain denseness that is at first hard to penetrate, but perseverance will bring its own wonderful rewards.

It is an education in itself to see how Frieling can unpack the inner meaning and significance of a biblical word or phrase and place it in a context that is often surprising but which always feels right. Reading his masterly analyses of certain biblical passages, one realises the superficiality and lack of spiritual penetration of most orthodox commentaries. This meticulous attention to often the minutest detail of the text is made possible by a philological scholarship second to none and by a special feeling that Frieling possesses for the wholeness of the text he is examining.

Thus, not only does he adopt the traditional exegetical approach of seeking for parallels among the so-called synoptic gospels in order to illuminate a particular passage (what Frieling calls a 'horizontal' reading of the gospels). Such an approach, as Frieling himself points out, can lead to a fragmentation, an 'atomising', and a loss of the wholeness of the literary text. Rather,

> ... to complement the *horizontal* comparison, *vertical* reading must be cultivated, allowing each gospel to stand by itself ... to have its effect as a whole without the distraction of sideways glances to its synoptic neighbours. Then it becomes clear that ... one and the same event, described in like manner by all three synoptic gospel writers, assumes a different place value, depending on its position within that particular whole, and assumes a specific tone, depending on possible 'consonance'.

Frieling's astonishing analysis of the transfiguration event, contained in this volume, is a model of such an approach.

In an obituary, Michael Tapp summed up the achievement of Rudolf Frieling in a most moving way:*

> With Frieling his own modesty and apparent simplicity could almost disguise the depth and the penetration of his insights. He could create vivid images in a single sentence, often breaking into the inner substance of a word and laying it before the hearer in the simplest yet profoundest of ways. One always asked oneself, it's so simple, why couldn't I have thought of that? Of course, it is the kind of simplicity that only comes after all the complications have been worked through. It was not the kind of fundamentalistic simplicity which says 'all you need to do is believe in Jesus'. It was much more akin to the simplicity of John's gospel. Rudolf Frieling's

---

* *The Threshing Floor,* magazine of The Christian Community, February 1986.

achievement in showing the way forward to a new Christian spirituality is unique.

After having read this representative sample of Frieling's theological legacy, the reader will no doubt find Michael Tapp's words amply confirmed.

Tony Jacobs-Brown
July 1994

Note

The present edition has been greatly expanded to make it a comprehensive collection of Frieling's writings on the New Testament. The entire work has been re-edited and structured to match the German Volumes 3 and 4 of Frieling's collected works, *Gesammelte Schriften zum Alten und Neuen Testament*. Tony Jacob-Brown's Foreword has lost none of its relevance in the intervening quarter of century.

I
THE PATH OF CHRIST JESUS

I

GOSPEL

It is not uncommon to find that people associate the words evangel and evangelist with the angels.* You could say this is going too far etymologically speaking: 'evangel', like 'gospel', simply means 'good tidings', and even *angelos* (from which the second half of the word derives) primarily means 'messenger'. But then, an angel is also a messenger.

For people of ancient times this statement could also be reversed: the messenger is an angel. The basic facts of life were once experienced much more intensely, with all that lay behind them as well. What then is a messenger? Someone who throws a bridge between those who are separated in consciousness from each other. Many people in our own time know what this means: for example, if someone manages to get home with a message for his relations from some far distant prisoner. All human separations are simply consequences of the original separation of human consciousness from the all-embracing divine consciousness into something narrowly circumscribed of its own. With this original separation is connected the fact that we are isolated, 'scattered, each to his own home' (Jn 16:32). The human being, imprisoned in his private individual ego, no longer has an immediate knowledge of what goes on in the divine world – nor of what goes on in the souls of his fellow men. People therefore find it exciting and 'inexplicable' when this barrier appears to be raised somewhere and a human being shows a direct knowledge about something remote from

---

* The German language uses the Latin form *Evangelium* for 'gospel'. The meaning, 'good tidings', is the same, but it will soon become clear to the reader that the whole tenor of Rudolf Frieling's argument is coloured by this particular form of the word. For this reason, the less commonly used English word 'evangel' has occasionally been used instead of 'gospel' in this chapter. *(Translator)*.

them without any means of external communication. Something like this is only 'inexplicable' as long as we start from the idea that the private, individual consciousness common today was the original state of affairs.

Explaining something means reducing it to such facts as are obvious in themselves and whose evidence satisfies the desire to understand. The history of philosophy shows what difficulties we get into if we take today's 'normal' isolation as if it were a self-evident fact. Then the question arises of how to relate to anything outside ourselves. The truth is, however, that the all-embracing divine consciousness is the original state of things. Ultimately, the world comes from *one* divine root, so from the start it is something obvious, self-revelatory, that everyone knows about everyone. The isolation, the enclosure in private, circumscribed consciousness, only later took shape out of this original unity. It is not the knowledge that reaches into the 'beyond', not 'telepathy', that is alarming and inexplicable; it is far more of a riddle how man is able to shut himself up to such an extent within himself. The knowledge of all about all *would* really be something self-evident, needing no clarification, since it is part of the clarity of the all-embracing divine consciousness. What is puzzling and not self-evident is that we do *not* know about each other directly.

This isolated consciousness, far removed from universal sympathy, is the consequence of the Fall. We have separated ourselves from God. We therefore no longer know directly about God and his heavens, about our fellow human beings or the inner life of other creatures. Significantly, the first denial in the Bible of that original knowledge about, and feeling for, each other is expressed by the one who murdered his brother. 'I do not know; am I my brother's keeper?' (Gn 4:9). For the first time someone said, 'I do not know.'

Christ's redemptive deed is to lead the isolated human being out of his prison, and, moreover, with the qualities of personal responsibility and individual freedom made perfect. This breaking down of the limitation of knowing only himself is achieved in the sign of the *Holy Spirit*. Through this extension of consciousness the human being comes into contact with the spiritual world above him, with the *angels*. This in turn allows him to make the first steps in the direction of universal knowledge and universal sympathy, just as on the other hand he can sink into the world below him, into the animal and bestial.

Experience of the Holy Spirit and of angels are therefore intimately connected. So it happens that in the New Testament the Holy Spirit is sometimes represented by the angel. Christ makes this clear (according to Lk 9:26) when he speaks of the threefold glory of his coming again. It will be associated with a new perception of the divine threefoldness, 'when he comes in his [the Son's] glory and the glory of the Father and of the holy angels'. Also in Paul we find: 'In the presence of God and of Christ Jesus and of the elect angels' (1Tm 5:21).

Meeting a messenger on earth is an image of this meeting with angels in a more extended state of consciousness. So from the very beginning the word *angelos* (messenger) also carried with it the sense of 'angel'.

We find the angel-messenger at the very beginning of the gospel where the angel speaks to Mary and Joseph. First of all there is the *Christmas story*. The actual Christmas events do not lie within the field of 'normal' imprisoned consciousness, which can perceive only that a child is born. What primarily makes Christmas 'Christmas' is on the level of angelic consciousness: 'to you is born this day a Saviour.' The Christmas message is in the strictest sense an angelic message – *evangel*. It calls for the lifting of the soul above the usual state, opening it towards heaven, to the supersensible. Otherwise there is no true Christmas.

Divine Providence obviously finds it important that this higher, supersensible knowledge is not borne exclusively by angels. That is not enough. Salvation is only complete when those for whom it occurs can become conscious of it. From the beginning, Providence sets a high value on the fact that those to be saved are thus 'included' – even if there is only just a minimal awareness on the part of very few human beings. The few in whom the angelic announcement finds a hearing deputise for the whole of humanity. In them humanity turns its eyes heavenward, even when total blindness for the crucial event is otherwise universal.

This is also true of the *baptism in the Jordan*. The Christ now finally walks on the earthly plane and enters fully into the human vehicle prepared for him, but for humanity imprisoned in its deep soul-sleep this decisive event does not exist – except for one man: John the Baptist. As the 'witness to the light' he is the opened eye of humanity, its deputising member, fully conscious, fully awake. Moreover, this witnessing is part of the event itself, not only an addition to it.

Where is the angel element here? The appearance of the Baptist is announced by the evangelist with the citation: 'Behold, I send my angel before you.' Icons picture the Baptist with mighty wings; he acquires the stature of an angel. At the same time, however, he also decidedly belongs to humanity. 'There was a man ... whose name was John.' Man and angel merge in John. Sharing the consciousness of angels enables him to see what simply does not exist for other human beings. According to the gospel, only John, apart from Jesus, saw heaven open and the dove descend (Jn 1:34). The first promise given to Christ's disciples was that they should wake into this angelic awareness of heaven being open (Jn 1:51). But it appears that this promise referred to a future time, for the disciples' awareness failed again and again. This is particularly noticeable as the event of Golgotha draws near. What happens in the *garden of Gethsemane* is so tragic because the disciples are inwardly no longer able to follow. They sink into dullness, overpowered by the excessive demand for wakefulness. The necessary minimum of human empathy that Christ expects from at least the three chosen disciples is lacking. The angel therefore has to step in alone and – taking man's place – give Christ the strength that should have come from the disciples' watching and praying with him.

Have people ever really thought how the evangelists could actually describe what Christ experienced after he left the sleepers behind him? There was certainly no further opportunity when the Lord could have told them – as long as he walked in his mortal body. It can therefore only be a case of supersensible knowledge. What is told of Christ's agony in Gethsemane is again exclusively 'evangel', a message of the angels from the supersensible world.

It is only on *Good Friday* that human testimony is again evident. The disciple 'whom the Lord loved' stands beneath the cross and bears witness to what he has seen (Jn 19:35). At the baptism it is John the Baptist, and here at Golgotha it is the other John who, as the opened eye of humanity, is part of the event together with the three Marys.

Then the *resurrection* is such a mighty event – like an intrusion of the Last Day into our own time – that it takes place beyond human awareness. The event itself is without witness, but the result is visible. The disciples do not perceive the resurrection itself but rather the Risen One – and this only gradually. On Easter morning they are able to see only the negative: the empty tomb. As long as human eyes were unseeing, the Easter message was borne alone in the consciousness of the angels until it could be shared by man. 'He has risen' – once more, as at Christmas, an angelic message from the supersensible world. Finally, the disciples themselves share in the visionary consciousness, with differing degrees of certainty (Mt 28:17). At Easter, the angel message can finally be confirmed by man. The angel's 'He has risen' is answered by the testimony of the disciple, 'The Lord has risen indeed' (Lk 24:34). Man can from now on be called 'witness to his resurrection' (Ac 1:22).

In the fullest sense this comes only after the great spiritual strengthening of *Pentecost*. It is indeed remarkable that during those forty Easter days when the Risen One walked with them, the disciples, despite this unique experience, did not yet proclaim it to the rest of the world. Their experience that 'the Lord has risen indeed' had its strength, for the time being, only within the sheltered inner circle of those who thought and felt the same; it was not yet equal to the cold breath of the rest of the world. But at Pentecost it had reached that stage. By the working of the Holy Spirit the disciples suddenly became preachers who were able to fire the hearts of those standing outside their experience.

In contrast to Christmas and Easter, Pentecost appears to lack the angel element. The appearances of the Risen One introduced by angels come to an end with the two angels of the ascension – but where are the angels at Pentecost? On this occasion the disciples' consciousness has, by the gifts of the Holy Spirit, so far merged with that of the angels that the angels as it were no longer need to be specially visible and audible. They appear and speak in the spirit-filled disciples who now themselves have become proclaimers of the gospel – evangelists.

The legend of the Holy Grail describes how the Grail was borne by a group of angels before it found a worthy human keeper in Titurel. This indicates that, for a time, Christian consciousness on earth had so darkened that once again, as in Gethsemane, the angels deputised for man and had to harbour in their higher spheres the supersensible knowledge of the continued working of the deed of redemption.

Christianity must therefore gain a new insight. The word 'evangel', gospel, will lose its meaning more and more if it does not again acquire the very definite sense of an expansion and raising of human consciousness.

2

GROWING TOWARDS DEATH – DYING INTO NEW LIFE

MATTHEW 1:1–17

As we watch the astonishing phenomenon of spring, a new wave of life rising from the death of winter, we may well recall Goethe's words about 'dying to become'. Life, in its new growth and development, conquers death. And yet all this fresh, burgeoning life will likewise fade again. In the same way, in the human realm, the first breath of a newborn baby also heralds the inexorable reality of an eventual last breath. Does this saying about dying into new life therefore only have passing truth, like spring, and is it not constrained and limited by autumn? Surely 'dying to become' must be set against the equal truth of our growing towards death. And should we not actually admit an imbalance here, since the earth as a whole, after all, is bound sooner or later to come to an end? Basically it seems that death's scale-arm is longer, and it would be apt to reverse Goethe's maxim and interpret the world more truthfully as a place where we only 'become to die'.

If we reflect on this, we can lend a new ear to a chapter in the Bible that most readers tend to overlook – Chapter 5 of Genesis, which lists a sequence of generations. Following the tales of Cain and Abel, and the Fall, this chapter returns to the creation of man in the image of God. In most English translations it begins, 'This is the book of the generations of Adam.' Luther's translation begins, 'Book of the "begettings" of Adam'. The Hebrew word *tholedoth* in fact means both 'begettings' and 'births', as developmental stages of ongoing life with which the first human being was endowed by the Creator. The expression 'book' is not what we usually mean nowadays in the literary sense, but a record or account, as in bookkeeping. It is a record of the ten patriarchs before the Flood, from Adam to Noah. Thus it is one of those 'lists of generations' that Bible readers may well regard as very dry parts of the Holy Scriptures. And yet precisely such arid texts can also allow us to experience something particular.

Here it is said of Adam: 'And Adam was 130 years of age, and begot a son in his own likeness and image, and called him Seth. And the days of Adam after he had begotten Seth were 800 years and he begot sons and daughters so that all the days that Adam lived were 930 years; and he died.' (Gn 5:3–5).

From Seth onwards, this pattern of begettings is given in slightly abbreviated form, but then retained unchanged for the whole sequence up to Noah: 'Seth was 105 years old, and begot Enosh. Thereafter he lived 807 years and begot sons and daughters so that his whole age was 912 years; and he died' (5:6–8). Continual repetition of this pattern of begettings, or sirings, by the ancient patriarchs can give us a sense of how the legacy of original, paradisal life force that survived the Fall flows on through all these awakenings of ever new human lives on earth. At the same time, the phrase that concludes each generation returns time and again, the monotony of its continual repetition conjuring a power of inevitability: 'and he died' – *wayyamoth*. Since the Fall, death has entered the narrative. The Snake cunningly announces, 'You will not certainly die.' Death took a while to arrive, but slowly it did so: 'and he died ... and he died ... and he died ...' No other list of generations in the Bible reaches the proportions of this monumental announcement of death.

But the terrible monotony of 'died ... died ... died' *is* interrupted at a single place: in the case of Enoch, the seventh patriarch. The account referring to him initially follows the familiar pattern: when he was such and such an age, he begot a son and thereafter he lived a certain number of years and begot sons and daughters so that his whole age was so and so many years. But the concluding phrase is missing. Instead, emphasised through repetition, at 5:22 and 5:24, it is said that he 'walked with God'. When we get to Abraham later, we hear how he walked *before* God (17:1), but Enoch – and this same phrase is used a third and last time of Noah (6:9) – walks *with* God. He is not only a creature, a created being, but in his inner nature he stands beside the Creator himself and walks 'with' him. In other words, in the case of Enoch, we encounter something vast and indeed egregious, which the text only hints at in very sparing, reticent words. These words conceal the mystery more than they disclose it. God 'took' him, and he 'was no more', no longer present on earth, but present instead, it seems, in God. This is like a faint memory of truly antediluvian times: the path out of incarnation was once again found without death, under very special circumstances where the strongest connection with God, allied with higher powers of grace, was able to dematerialise the death-pregnant body of substance. The circumstances surrounding Enoch's passing remained unique, deeply rooted in the past, yet at the same time bright with the radiance of future promise. The otherwise invariable and inevitable 'and he died' is here audibly suppressed, and commences again in the generations following Enoch (5:25).

What is intimated and prefigured in Enoch was fulfilled in Christ, in his overcoming of death through the resurrection and ascension.

In the New Testament too, in the evangelists Matthew and Luke, we find a list of generations. Having developed a sense of the expressive power, the distinctive mode inherent in the list of the ancient patriarchs in the 'book of Adam', we will then also be able to experience something in the seemingly so dry and unedifying list of generations as given by the evangelists.

The singular form of Luke's index of generations lies in the fact that he runs it backwards from Jesus to Adam, and beyond the latter as far as to God himself. No fewer than 76 names are given to reach back to God, in each case the name only, without the least interjection or interruption. Most English translations have erased the radical nature of this stylised litany by adding each time 'the son of'. This is not present in the original text, where only the names are found, in the genitive case each time, thus: 'of Joseph, of Heli, of Matthat ... of Adam' (3:23–38). The 'genitive', as its name already tells us, is connected with begetting and descent. With the phrase that Adam was 'of God', Luke reaches the genitive of genitives.

All these entirely uninterrupted genitives that lead from 'Jesus' back to the primordial genitive 'of God', are sustained by a dynamic impetus. It is as if the longing awoken by the figure of Jesus for the pure, paradisal origin of the human being lends wings to this reverse path through the sequence of ancestors.

The index of ancestors with which Matthew opens his gospel

and – though he did not know this when he wrote it – the whole of the New Testament, has a quite different feeling for the reader. Matthew starts with Abraham and leads on through three times fourteen generations to Christ. Unlike Luke, he does not simply list the names but appends a separate phrase to each ancestor: 'Abraham begot Isaac, Isaac begot Jacob, Jacob begot Judas ...' In this way each name is given twice, firstly in the accusative case as object of the sentence (Isaac begot *Jacob*), and secondly in the nominative case as subject (*Jacob,* for his part, begot Judas). And between the accusative and the nominative form there is, in each case, a small, reflective pause.

In Luke, we read through the long sequence of names on the wing, as it were, rather like passing many stations in a fast train, their names flying by scarcely noticed. In Matthew, on the other hand, we are reminded of a journey that unfolds in a leisurely tempo. We stop at each station and stay there a moment. In this way, Matthew allows us to feel the historical weight of each name, and occasionally he interjects a special remark as well. Very striking, though, is the continual repetition of the word 'begot' *(egēnnesen)*. If we keep to the versions that simply say 'Joseph begot Jesus' (1:16) – here clearly finding no contradiction with the action of the Holy Spirit, which belongs to a different level* – then this 'begot' sounds no fewer than forty times. Such a lengthy and compact sequence cannot be found anywhere else in the Bible. The only comparison is with the monotonous repetition of the phrase 'and he died' in the 'Book of Adam'. There the power of death holds sway, of which Paul says that it 'reigned like a king' due to the Fall of Adam (Rom 5:17). It is true that the Genesis text does speak each time of begetting, but death has the last word. Matthew, writing *after* the event of Golgotha, does not mention death but, in the forty *egēnnesen* he celebrates the miracle of earth life's continuing regeneration – the son born ever anew and repeatedly repulsing the sole sway of death. This suppression of death, albeit only in a preliminary form through the begetting of new human beings, sounds in Matthew like a prelude to the still higher and final overcoming of death to which he then turns.

---

* For details see Lauenstein, *Der Messias,* p. 137.

Matthew writes his list in conscious reference to the litany of deaths in the register of ancient patriarchs. This is apparent from the fact that he includes the formula of the Old Testament 'Book of the generations of Adam' (Gn 5:1) in the first words of his gospel. It begins: 'Book of the generation of Jesus Christ' or in Greek: *Biblos genéseōs,* which is exactly the same as the Greek translation of the beginning of the fifth chapter of Genesis. In other words, Matthew expressly takes up this form of words, except that in place of Adam, he names the new Adam, Jesus Christ.

These very first words of Matthew point far beyond their apparent, overt meaning. The birth of Jesus is here only the prelude to a sequence of events that culminate in the events of Golgotha, and in resurrection and ascension: a sequence necessary in its entirety in order to enable Christ to make the transition from his previous, solely heavenly existence into his omnipresence within earthly humanity. The words of the Resurrected One, 'See, I am with you' (Mt 28:20), mark the conclusion to these events that, as a whole, appear as a single great birth. Born now into earthly humanity, he says, in a sense: 'And now I have arrived with you, now I am *here.*' The initial words of the Gospel of Matthew, in the actual form of their text, are thus a kind of superscription over all the Jesus Christ events, which represent a great, overarching birth.

As such, we find ourselves in full accord with the view of the first Christians. In his Pentecost address, Peter interprets the resurrection as a 'soothing of the birth pangs of death' (in the original not only 'pains' as often in translations, but expressly 'birth pains', Ac 2:24). This is the fulfilment of the 'birth of Jesus Christ'. In the same way, Paul sees a birth in the resurrection, applying the phrase 'today I have begotten you' to the Easter event (Ac 13:33).

If we discern, in the sequence of events that we can summarise as the Mystery of Golgotha, the actual birth of Christ, leading us beyond the birth of Jesus, then an enigma of the register in Matthew is solved. To Matthew who, as a tax-collector or publican, must have learned arithmetic, an arithmetical error has been attributed: he speaks of thrice fourteen generations, but in the third group leading up to Jesus, he gives only thirteen names. One generation too few.

The register speaks forty times of the generative power that repeatedly limits the sway of death. But how is this in the case of Jesus? It is not said of him that 'he begot'. Does death triumph after all, therefore, at the end of the series of ancestors, since the last-named dies childless? Does this very noticeable 'missing generation' not point to the step change that leads on from the birth of Jesus to the actual birth of Christ, fulfilled only after Golgotha? It would not really have been possible to say, 'and Jesus begot Christ,' and yet it was only through Jesus that the real birth of Christ could occur. True, the series of begettings does not continue in the accustomed manner in the case of Jesus. Yet this is not because death had the last word, but because, in this single human being, death was finally vanquished in an entirely new way. Death is here overcome not by virtue of a child who perpetuates the life of the father as the latter succumbs to death. Rather in the body of Jesus, death is conquered at the resurrection 'there and then', within one and the same human being. Generation and birth are raised to a higher level. The death-delaying 'generation' referred to forty times does not cease with Jesus but culminates in the resurrection, which, as Paul sees it, fulfils the words 'today I have begotten you' that resounded already at the Jordan baptism as recounted by Luke.*

If we stay in the 'horizontal' trajectory of natural events, then 'becoming to die' does hold true. But if we elevate ourselves to the huge reality that in Jesus Christ this line was raised from the horizontal to a higher level of deathless life, then the 'dying to become' can uplift us; and then the full, concealed truth of these words comes into their own.

This does not mean that earthly birth is therefore in any way diminished in value. That our souls immerse themselves at birth in the realm where we grow towards death is the prerequisite for us becoming fully human. It is after all only by participating in earth experience, and being delivered up to death, that these souls of ours can fully absorb the strength of the deed of redemption at Golgotha, which occurred not in heaven but on earth. The first part of these occurrences involved the Christ inclining out of free grace to the 'becoming to die', and passing through death in the body of Jesus so

---

* The voice of God that is given often as, 'You are my son, in you I am well pleased' (Lk 3:22), is rendered in older, more reliable form as, 'You are my son, today have I begotten you.'

as to overcome it 'there and then' from within, thus raising the human being to the level of death-conquering 'rebirth'. For our part, by experiencing and suffering our growing towards death in all humility, we make ourselves ready for the evolution towards Christ, whose fulfilment will be 'rebirth' into a higher form of existence in which life has the last word.

3

FROM THE JORDAN BAPTISM TO THE PLACE OF SKULLS

In olden times, when people spoke of the four elements, they had something quite different in mind from the elements that science acknowledges today. We could best compare what they meant with states of matter. Solid, fluid, airy and fiery were four different states that could not only be observed outwardly but were at the same time linked to inner experiences. At that time the human soul was still to a high degree 'wide open to the world', it could slip into qualities and conditions and, in the process, pass through various modes of self-experience, of inward 'moods'.

We still have a sense of what a 'heavy heart' means. To feel 'frozen' by great suffering, or 'turned to stone', does not need an explanation. Likewise, we understand what is meant if the 'ice breaks' and the atmosphere 'warms up'. Such idiomatic sayings still waken a response in us, and are the echoes of a time when such outward-inward experiences of the elements worked in us a great deal more vigorously.

Baptism by water

Historians have undertaken research into various aspects of the social context of early Christianity. They have found that in the Middle East at that particular time, cleansing baths and ritual washing played an important role, and not only amongst the Essenes in Qumran. Judaism, for instance, introduced water baptism for heathens converting to the faith. Around the time of Christ, there must have been a strong, widespread sense that people had become disastrously alienated from the worlds of their heavenly origins, and that cleansing and purification was needed. But in these cleansing rites, water, with its capacity to clean the body, was not employed only in a moral and allegorical manner as 'sensory' metaphor. The outward-inward capacity of qualitative experience also played into this.

We can refer to the solid element as 'earth'. Within it, earthly nature closes itself off in self-contained fashion. Water is not something earthly in this exclusive sense, for in it the earthly realm opens itself to powers streaming in from the cosmos. If you water a plant you can observe how the fine etheric life forces employ water as their medium. They cannot gain direct purchase on coarse-grained, solid matter but they can infiltrate it upon the paths of fluidity. Rudolf Meyer expresses the effect of those ancient water rites by saying that, through them, people 'felt how the finer life forces, always at risk of withering, were brought into movement, thus stimulating an etheric flow throughout the body.'*

Though the Jordan baptism had its completely distinctive character, we must also understand it in this context of widespread water rites. While in late (Second Temple) Judaism the capacity to feel nature's qualities had receded a great deal, making way for a more intellectual or abstract morality within religion, nevertheless the picture of John who baptised by immersing people in the streaming Jordan river, still testifies to language of elemental power.

The Baptist was aware that his actions were preliminary and could only achieve a small amount. No doubt his baptism sought to enable people to open their consciousness upward, and prepare them for supersensible impressions, 'so that he would be revealed in Israel, I came to baptise with water' (Jn 1:31); and yet this upward opening of earthbound souls needed to be carried further, towards the higher conditions of air (the word for air was synonymous with spirit) and ultimately of fire. For this elevation and enhancement of his baptism by water, John awaited the 'stronger One'.

---

* Meyer, *Die Wiedergewinnung des Johannes-Evangeliums*, p. 46.

The Jordan baptism

When Jesus approached him, amongst others who sought baptism, the Baptist felt it inappropriate that he, John, should baptise Jesus. And yet he did so, and it became evident that in this unique and special instance, baptism acquired a different meaning, and had a different effect. For the others, baptism loosened and opened a condition of soul too fixed and earthly. When Jesus was baptised, the opposite direction became significant, 'from above downward'. Water after all can mediate in both directions. The heavens opened and from super-earthly worlds divinity descended into earthly humanity. It seemed as if the element of water had in some way helped God to take hold of the earthly body.

There are icons in which the blue currents of the Jordan rise up high around the body of Jesus and surround him in something like a water veil, giving expression in simple yet brilliant iconography to the mediating role of the water element in this unique occurrence. The descending divinity could not so easily have entered the moribund, earth-hardened body. But this death-body was pervaded by the subtle etheric life organisation, which had an intimate connection with water. It could be invoked and activated, therefore, by water baptism especially, and in this way could help the divine gain purchase upon the earth. But a further three years were still needed for him to find his way fully through the living element of the etheric into the actual body of earth, so as to pass through the experience of death that awaited him within this mortal human sheath.

'But I have a baptism to be baptised with ...'

On his last, decisive travels to Jerusalem, Christ speaks of the fire that he came to earth to ignite. But at the same time he knows the condition governing the fulfilment of this fire-kindling. 'But I have a baptism to be baptised with, and how I am constrained until it is fulfilled' (Lk 12:50). *Another* baptism therefore, besides the Jordan baptism?

Being narrowly constrained or oppressed is certainly not the usual fear of death. The original text says roughly, 'how I am hard pressed'.

The starting point for the others receiving baptism at the time, was to loosen and release them from all too narrow imprisonment in the body. For the one coming from above, this was the very destination of his descent. Out of grace he wishes to absorb human death on earth into his very differently fashioned divine, heavenly experience. At the baptism in the Jordan he accomplished the decisive connection with the destined body, but the consequence of taking on this body only becomes manifest in death at Golgotha. Thus Golgotha is the other baptism, *after* the Jordan event, and one that still awaits him, and is bound up with the constriction of earthly death experience. Through this baptism, God is plunged into and 'consecrated' to a world that hitherto was a realm most alien to him.

Thus the three years are a passage towards death, and this journey has its stations. From the accounts in the gospels we gain the sense that in the first period the element of water plays a particular role. To begin with, Christ likes to tarry beside the Sea of Galilee. Capernaum, beside this lake, is in fact 'his town' (Mt 4:13, 9:1). Sometimes he preaches to the crowds on the shore from a boat. Again and again he crosses the lake. He causes the miraculous draft of fishes (Lk 5:1–9) and calms a tempest on the waters. He feeds the crowd gathered on its banks and walks upon its surface. This lake is an emblem of the Galilee period. The Gospel of John, on the other hand, is primarily characterised by the stony, dead landscape around Jerusalem in which the decisive events are to unfold. But John, too, tells of the water vessels filled to the brim at Cana in Galilee. The gospel gives us the phrase about being born of water and the breath of spirit. It tells of the well of the Samaritan woman, and then, in the region of Jerusalem, of the Pool of Bethesda, which is stirred into motion by an angel, and of the healing Pool of Siloam. It is as if the Christ felt the element of water as beneficent, making his existence on earth gentler and easier, more heavenly and agreeable, and helpful to his work.

The closer we come to the end, the more the water motif recedes. It returns once more, shortly before his death, during the Last Supper: the man with the water jug who shows the way, and the washing of the feet. But then everything becomes mercilessly hard, like the wood of the cross, like the rock of the place of skulls. The blue lake of Galilee is now far away. Only after the resurrection will its hour come again.

The image of the Jordan baptism and of Golgotha

The two baptisms through which Christ passes – the Jordan baptism and that other, which constrains him – each have their own distinctive imagery.

The Jordan event is marked by the element of flow and fluidity. The earthly body of Jesus is encircled by streaming currents, and the seer's gaze beholds his upper part too, projecting from the water, enveloped in an etheric water veil. The predominance here of something not entirely earthly, of life's affinity with heaven, corresponds to the influx of the supersensible. Above, the heavens open. From the loftiest heights, as if from the flaming love-fire of God, the words 'my beloved son' resound. As if embodying the spirit breathing light, the white dove appears. We are told that not only Jesus but John too perceived these supersensible events.

It is surely not by chance that this moment, informed so decisively by the supersensible, is related in other accounts besides those of the gospels. Today, these tend to be simply disregarded as the work of 'pious imagination' embellishing the tale by steeping it in legend. But we should allow for the fact that these mythical traits do not testify to arbitrary fantasy but to a certain power of perception. There are even manuscripts of the Gospel of Matthew in which the wording runs: 'And when he was baptised, a great light shone all around from the water.' In the apocryphal Gospel of the Ebionites, we read: 'And straightaway a great light illumined the whole place.' Justin the Martyr, around the mid-second century, reports a 'fire that was kindled in the Jordan'. Later Syrian accounts speak of clouds of light, of angelic choirs singing praise, of heavenly fragrances wafting in. But let us confine ourselves to the vision of light and fire in the waters of the Jordan. Rudolf Steiner once described how the seer, on awakening in the morning – when the soul and spirit that was 'outside' the body enters it and in doing so first passes through the flowing etheric realm of the life organism – can perceive something like a burning element immersing itself in water. Fire immersing itself in water: this is clearly an archetypal experience that can manifest wherever incarnation occurs. As Goethe's *Faust* has it, 'fire in water' is the 'great adventure'. In his hymn to the four elements, which concludes his Classical Walpurgis Night scene, he writes: 'Hail to the waves enveloped in sacred fire! Hail to the water! Hail to the fire! Hail to the rare adventure!' Here, embodiment is occurring. Homunculus, the artificially engendered 'little man', is to assume embodiment:

> Now it flames, now it flashes, already it pours
> What fiery wonder transfigures the waves ...
> And all around everything's surrounded by fire ...

Certainly, this is not of the same order as the event of the Jordan baptism, which truly involves no 'little man' who must fracture his glassy isolation in order to flourish in full, living embodiment. It is not a 'little man' but the archetype of the true human being that is borne downward to the Jordan baptism by the Son of God. This is spirit-soul of the loftiest and most sublime nature which, to quote Novalis, 'dives into the flood of life'. Yet the pictorial language – fire shining out within water – is the same.

Only through this immersion in the etheric life body of the earthly human being does the Godhead take its way into ever deeper embodiment in the death-body. The picture of Golgotha is now entirely governed by this body of death, which becomes the sole focus of our gaze. The picture of Golgotha is subject to the element of 'earth'. No heavens open. No light from above. No voice of God from the heights. Darkness envelops the cross. Instead of the streaming river we have the rock of the place of skulls, the dead wood of the cross, and the death-body exposed and spread upon it in torment. No veil of enveloping, resonant water but physical nakedness. 'I thirst'.

How different the two pictures are!

Above and below open to each other

No heavens open over Golgotha. Instead – after death has been accomplished – the earth opens: 'And see, the curtain in the temple was torn ... and the earth was shaken, and the rocks were sundered, and the graves opened' (Mt 27:51f). In the Jordan account, almost the same words are used – of tearing and sundering, except that there it is the heavens which were torn open (Mk 1:10). Until then, the higher worlds had been 'closed' to the earth. Late Judaism had been compelled to come to terms with the fact that direct revelation through the mouths of prophets had for centuries fallen silent. Heavens and earth, in consequence of the Fall, seemed to have entirely parted company, and could no longer be fruitful to each other. Revelation from above no longer came to self-encapsulating, earthly human beings. God-alienated earth existence no longer brought forth fruits which the higher world might have harvested.

Isaiah's yearning cry (64:1), 'Oh, that you would rend the heavens and come down,' was answered at the Jordan baptism. The upper world began to open once again to earth existence. Through the death at Golgotha, Christ enters the ossified earth world and bursts asunder its encrusted nature in his passage through death. The sundered rocks and the opening graves are the counterpart to the opening of the heavens. And now the earth can begin again to open productively to the higher world. The evangelist Matthew, in whose account of the passion we find the words about the rocks and graves, continues thus: 'and many bodies of the saints that slept arose, and came out of the graves after his resurrection and went into the holy city and appeared to many.' The earth enters upon a new phase: by virtue of the Christ sacrifice it is to be regained for the heavens. And this starts by a confirmation and affirmation of everything valuable that has, despite the Fall, nevertheless existed upon earth hitherto, which is included in, and integrated into, the new Easter event. Without the deed of Christ, all the achievements of the former 'saints' would not have succeeded in halting the downward trajectory. The good that could have been offered to the upper world through the right conduct of earthly human beings would have been sealed forever under the lids of tombs. But now Christ's deed means that none of this was in vain. The 'resurrection potential', until now concealed in the earth, can be integrated into the newly emerging world in the light of the great resurrection of Christ. In the phrase 'the holy city' we can already hear a faint and as yet far-off prelude to the motif of the heavenly Jerusalem.

In the heavenly Jerusalem, as the Christian seer beheld it on Patmos, the 'new heaven' and the 'new earth' flow into one. Upper and lower, now no longer living at odds with one other but opening to each other, are both rejuvenated. The earth, grown old, made fruitful from above, becomes the 'new earth'. The heaven grown old, now absorbing the due yields of earth existence, becomes the 'new heaven'.

In the hymn to the elements by Goethe which we mentioned earlier, 'earth' is characterised by the grave. But this grave must surely contain a secret good, for otherwise the call to the earth element, 'Hail, you crypts full of mystery!' could not resound. Such a call of praise would be meaningless if there were no hope of resurrection. We find the same word 'crypt' in Novalis: in his *Spiritual Songs* he sings of the now Christ-pervaded earth element: 'Everywhere from crypts, new life, new blood springs forth.'

When the blood of the Redeemer flowed to earth on Golgotha, the God had undergone that other, anxious and constricting baptism that, *after* the Jordan baptism, loomed for him with its fearful and constricting passage. In the blood imbued with divine love-fire that flowed to earth, the fire that Christ longed to kindle and set aflame on earth found its beginning. From then on, earthly existence has hope again. 'Hail, you crypts full of mystery!'

4

THE SON OF GOD

A PATTERN IN THE FABRIC OF THE GOSPEL OF MATTHEW

When we speak of a 'text', we are probably not always aware that this word originally meant a 'fabric' or 'weft' – related to the word 'textile'. The text of the gospels could be regarded, in fact, as a fabric in the full meaning of the word, with its resonances of craft and artistry. Out of the deeds and sufferings of Jesus Christ, each of the four evangelists wove his own particular text in which the words and configurations of words are formed into unique and distinctive patterns.

One such pattern of meaning becomes apparent when we look at passages in which the phrase the 'Son of God' is found in Matthew.

At the Jordan baptism, God's words about his 'beloved son' descend from heavenly heights (Mt 3:17). These words stand like a mighty heading over the whole of the rest of his account, through to the death and resurrection: 'This is my beloved son, in whom I reveal myself.' But now, as events unfold, it is a matter of these words meeting with a response, an echo, from human beings on earth. For Christ's work to become fruitful depends, in a sense, on human beings becoming aware of who it is that has come to them, and whom they are here encountering.

The first echo of the voice from heaven of which Matthew tells us, does not however come from the mouth of a human being. While humanity still lies in its deep sleep of unconsciousness, and does not even 'dream' that the most sublime divine being has come to visit it, the adversarial powers, with their capacities of supersensible discernment, have already grasped what is happening. They intervene and seek to divert the process of redemption that is now underway.

4. THE SON OF GOD

In the desert the Tempter approaches the God-become-man. His first words sound like a caricature, an aping of the sublime voice of God, 'If you are God's son' (4:3). The Tempter knows he will get nowhere by questioning whether God really said this, for the phrase 'my beloved son' is unshakeably planted in Christ's consciousness. But he might just possibly be induced to draw the wrong conclusions from this lofty consciousness. The second temptation, too, that Matthew reports, starts with 'If you are God's son' (4:6). But the same phrase is lacking in the temptation that Matthew reports as the third – the Tempter's offer of world rulership: 'If you fall down and pray to me'. Part of the distinctive quality of the fabric is that the 'missing' third utterance of the phrase is, as we will see, made good at the end of the gospel.

After the events of the Jordan baptism, reaching far into the supersensible, and the subsequent temptation, Matthew presents the unfolding work on earth of Christ within Jesus of Nazareth. Here it becomes apparent that the disciples see in him a unique master and teacher, and also reverently refer to him as 'Lord', and yet knowledge of his divine status has not yet dawned on them.

At one point they are close to this realisation. While crossing the Sea of Galilee by night, they experience how he calms the tempest; how, with commanding gestures, he orders the elemental powers whipped up by demonic forces to be stilled. The question rises in the souls of the disciples as to what sort of man it is who can do such a thing. In Matthew, unlike in Mark and Luke, the question is not simply 'Who is this man?' but its very nature already reveals an intimation of something out of the ordinary: *'What kind* of man is this?' (8:27).

We do not have to wait long for an answer, but need only read on to the very next sentence. Again, eerily, the reply does not come from humankind but from the adversarial powers. After calming the storm, Christ lands with the disciples at the further, eastern shore of the lake. Towards him rush two demonically possessed souls who lead a subhuman, underworld existence there. These possessed people – or rather the evil spirits indwelling them – cry out, 'What have we to do with you, you Son of God?' (8:29). They know that one stands before them who has the power to end their sway over humankind.

But the clairvoyant perception in the demons' cry clearly makes no impact yet on the disciples' awareness. They hear it, but do not comprehend it. What they have heard first dwells in the depths of their souls, below the threshold of consciousness.

A certain period has to pass before a knowledge of Christ awakening in the disciples' souls works its way closer to the light. Once again, as in the calming of the storm, this comes about during a night-time experience upon the lake. In those ancient times, the capacity for supersensible experiences could be drawn forth from people more easily than is the case today. By leaving 'terra firma' behind and entrusting themselves to the waves, it became possible for their daytime 'object consciousness' to loosen, especially if this happened at night. Night, with its darkness, extinguishes the world of clearly delineated objects and favours the entry into a different mode of consciousness. In their night-time passage over the lake, which is once again stirred up by storm, the disciples become able to behold supersensibly – for this is what was involved when they perceive Christ walking upon the waters. They experience him as spirit being in his ether form. They also hear his voice uttering the words 'I AM'. In this 'I AM' lies concealed the secret of the name of God. The disciples gain an impression that Christ is something quite other than the rabbi from Nazareth.

Matthew adds to this an unforgettable episode. Only he relates how Peter leaves the boat and also, for a moment, walks upon the water – until the on-rolling waves make him fearful and he begins to sink. Christ grasps him by the hand and saves him. The whole account is characterised by the motifs of 'sea voyage' and 'night'. The wonderful account of Peter sinking should not be taken at the mundane level of outer, material life, in which case it would resemble a miracle. In fact the story describes an actual occurrence, but one that belongs to a different plane. Peter attempts to live too in that other world in which Christ walks weightless on the waters of flowing, etheric forces. He tries to take first steps into a different form of consciousness and existence. But he has overestimated his capacities, and shows that he is not ready for these different conditions.

This whole night-time occurrence ends, in the account by Matthew (14:33), with 'those in the ship falling down before him in worship and saying, "Truly, you are the Son of God".'

Does this mean that this knowledge has really now dawned

4. THE SON OF GOD

on them fully? A little while later comes the well-known scene at Caesarea Philippi, where Peter, replying to the question 'And who do you say that I am?' avows, 'You are the Christ, the Son of the living God' (Mt 16:16). An attentive reader of the gospel will wonder here why this avowal could be so special and striking, given that the disciples have already previously worshipped him on the boat. Do they not have this knowledge already? It is hardly surprising that critical scholars, who tackle the gospel with their modern logic and rational coherence, point here to an inconsistency. Surely this represents a slip-up on the part of the evangelist? If Peter's avowal at Caesarea Philippi is to have weight and significance, then the same avowal from all the disciples during the boat journey cannot have preceded it. But they do not consider that the two avowals could have occurred at two different levels of consciousness. The one by no means need exclude the other.

Let us take an example that naturally does not come close to the one we are considering but can nevertheless give us an inkling of what I mean: we all know the nature of dream experiences. They may be very striking – and yet they very commonly slip away swiftly and evade our efforts to remember. With this in mind, we can imagine how difficult it could be to 'bring to shore' impressions of a supersensible nature from the sea of flowing experiences and integrate them into our ordinary awareness. Then it can happen that we 'know' something, but at the same time do not. When the disciples discerned the Son of God on board the ship and worshipped him, their insight into his being was that of a clairvoyant waking dream – close to awakening but not yet shining clearly within their ordinary daytime consciousness.

As Peter walks near Caesarea Philippi, this knowledge, hitherto subliminal, awoke within his bright day consciousness. That it was to him that this happened is no doubt connected with the fact that he had engaged more strongly than the others with the supersensible occurrences during the voyage across the lake, and had at least attempted those 'first steps'. His experience of that night was therefore more pronounced, and what had hitherto rested as knowledge in the depths of his soul could rise fully into the light of awareness.

But really fully into the light? Did full human consciousness of the Son of God already come to full human consciousness with this avowal by Peter? Again and again it shocks us as we read on to find how the same Peter is met soon afterwards by the terrible phrase, 'Get behind me, Satan' (16:23) – the same phrase that Christ spoke at the temptation (Mt 4:10). Why is this? Immediately after making his avowal, Peter was first granted a lofty acknowledgement, 'Blessed are you.' Straight after this, Christ passes on to the first announcement of his forthcoming suffering: that the Son of God must now suffer and die as the Son of Man. Peter disputes this: 'Lord, far be it for this to happen to you' (16:22). He cannot grasp the thought that it lies in the nature and being of the Son of God to seek human suffering and death upon the path of self-sacrifice. He thinks that the glory of rulership belongs to Christ, not humiliation, and therefore finds himself in the domain of the third temptation, 'You can rule the world if you ally yourself with the Adversary.' In uttering that first 'Get behind me,' Christ was already signing his own death sentence, choosing the path of defenceless suffering. In saying, 'Lord, far be it for this to happen to you,' Peter is, without wishing or knowing it, making himself into the mouthpiece of the Adversary, and this is why Christ so swiftly dismisses him.

So is Peter now the 'blessed' one, or is he Satan? We have to learn to distinguish different strata of the soul in one and the same person. In making his avowal, Peter was speaking from the divine Father-Ground of his being, and is worthy of the blessing he receives. He goes on being so. But he is at the same time worthy of rejection in so far as he succumbs. The second 'Get you behind me' is in fact not spoken to Peter but to the Adversary who at that moment came to utterance through Peter. In Peter he found a point of entry since, despite Peter's avowal, part of his soul remains in the dark, not yet fully illumined. And so his avowal of faith remains incomplete, in the same way that his attempt at walking on the water could not be accomplished.

And yet, though Peter's avowal is not yet fully mature and illumined, it is nevertheless sufficiently positive to enable him to participate a week later in the experience of the transfiguration. It means something – and not only for himself – that he was able to utter this declaration at all. It means something too for the higher world which, through this advance in human consciousness, can now respond with a new revelation. The temporal period of 'one week later' is at the same time the expression of an inner relationship between avowal and transfiguration. Upon a mountain, Peter, with two other disciples, is granted vision of the solar figure and form of Christ, and granted hearing of the voice of God which, as at the Jordan baptism, again utters the mystery of his 'beloved Son' (Mt 17:5). But at the transfiguration, too, we are reminded of the darkness that is still present in Peter. 'Without knowing what he says,' he speaks, 'It is good for us to be here. Let us build shelters here.' But Christ does not wish to tarry longer on the far-flung mountain heights, breathing the homely air of heaven. He has decided to descend into the degradation of human misery, to his great sacrifice. It is as if once again, the Tempter speaks through Peter, 'Stay up here, do not descend into your humiliation!' Time and again the Christ has to reaffirm his sacrificial decision. And thus the transfiguration is followed by the second annunciation of his suffering. No objection is voiced on this occasion. Only silent, uncomprehending sorrow settles over the souls of the disciples (17:22f).

The darkness that continues to work in Peter reappears once again during the passion. Out of his consciousness-darkening sleep at Gethsemane, he reaches for his sword to prevent the passion by outward force. And then he experiences his own three denials of Christ. The avower becomes the denier.

In the gospel, this denial is directly juxtaposed with another event which must inevitably remind us most forcefully of his avowal. As Peter sits by the fire in the courtyard, at almost exactly the same time as his denial, the high priest, with all the ceremonies of his office, questions the accused about being the Son of God. Rising from his seat, the high priest says, 'I charge you by the living God: tell us if you are the Christ, the Son of the living God' (Mt 26:63). These are the very words of Peter's avowal at Caesarea Philippi. Yet the one who had uttered them then succumbs to failure at this critical moment, when, in a sense, his avowal is at stake. He cannot follow through on what he had then discerned. He leaves Christ to answer for himself.

It lies in the very nature of this sublime and mysterious matter that Christ does not say this directly of himself, since what counts is for human beings to gain this insight by their own powers. It is up to them to perceive who stands in their midst. And thus his reply – 'You say it' – to the question urged upon him, has certain undertones that we must attend to. His answer is not simply, 'Yes, it is I,' but 'You say it.' This does not signify anything like a withdrawal, an offloading of responsibility. In the traditions of Judaism at the time, it was certainly an affirmative reply. But in this special context, something resonates through these words that Rudolf Steiner formulated as '*you* must say it'. It is for earthly humankind to discern the secret of the Son of God within Christ Jesus. The high priest of Jerusalem was certainly called upon by his office to greet the God who had appeared on earth, on behalf of all humanity. Instead of which he rends his garments because of the supposed blasphemy, and initiates the process leading to the death sentence.

In the darkened mind of Peter as he makes his denial, and still more in the betrayal by Judas, and altogether in the weakness of the disciples, the approach of the Adversary becomes palpable. At the end of his account of the temptation, Luke remarks that while the Tempter must withdraw for a while, this is only 'until a fitting moment' (Lk 4:13). This moment has now arrived: 'The Prince of this world is coming' (Jn 14:30). And now the gospel reader must recall that the twisted utterance from the devil during the earlier scene of temptation – 'If you are God's Son' – comes only twice, and is lacking from the third temptation concerning worldly power. One of the subtleties of the account by Matthew, in particular, is that he alone now reintroduces the third use of this same phrase, 'If you are God's Son,' and does so in a situation that corresponds precisely to the temptation of worldly power. Christ has *not* summoned the help of the 'twelve legions of angels'. He says to Peter, 'Sheathe your sword!' And in the consistent pursuit of his path of sacrifice, he then hangs defenceless upon the cross. This time, the Adversary makes his utterance through the mouths of a fanatical throng, 'If you are God's Son, save yourself and descend from the cross.' And the high priests, scribes and elders, inspired in their hatred by the devil, join in with this cry: 'Descend from the cross, and then we will believe in you' (27:40–42). Thus Matthew draws a clear line leading from the repudiation of the Tempter in the desert to Golgotha.

But he does not leave his readers with this devilishly distorted discordance. The hate-filled opponents of Christ are not the last in the gospel allowed to utter this phrase, the 'Son of God'. This Sonship of God is now fulfilled in its profoundest and fullest sense in Christ's passage through human death. This time, instead of the heavens, the earth with its rocks and graves is rent asunder. And from human mouths we now hear an echo of God's voice in tones of shocked awe and reverence rather than in the distortion of mockery. It is spoken by someone who is neither a prophet or initiate but who, as a completely ordinary person, stands with both feet fully on the solid ground of earthly existence. At this moment, witnessing the earth's quaking, he senses the invisible realm. This is the Roman guard whose illumination, if we heed the account by Matthew, also sparks the same in the legionaries participating in the crucifixion. 'But the captain, and those who guarded Jesus with him, when they saw the earthquake and what then occurred, were seized by great fear and said, "Truly, this was the Son of God".' (27:54).

5

THE SIGN OF THE SON OF MAN

> The sun will be darkened, the moon will no longer give its light, the stars will fall from heaven, and the powers of the heavens will be shaken. And then the sign of the Son of Man will appear in heaven. (Mt 24:29f)

Christian theology has hitherto strangely neglected the phrase 'the Son of Man'. This embarrassment, and sense of not knowing what to make of the expression, goes back to the earliest Christian times. The brief sentence devoted to the phrase in a Catholic publication – 'This designation no longer plays any role in primary Christian theology' – must surely strike us as astonishing.* The designation the Son of Man, which Christ so often expressly used of himself, was simply left to one side as Christian thought developed, unlike the phrase 'the Son of God' which has enduringly preoccupied Christian thinkers.

How can this have come about? It must no doubt be connected with the fact that humanity can only absorb from the gospels as much as corresponds to its current stage of consciousness. Christianity hitherto has lived with a degree of natural religious feeling for the sustaining Father-Ground of the World from which everything emerged; this religious feeling has sustained humanity since its first beginnings. Human beings regarded themselves as divinely created, not all that different from stone, plant and animal. But the distinctive secret of their human nature – their calling to move from being creatures to creators themselves – was something that had not yet fully dawned on them. Many biblical scholars have remarked that the mighty phrase of 'man made in the image of God' (Gn 1:26) stands alone in the Old Testament, an inspiration descending from sublime heights, but is

---

* Rahmer & Vorgrimmler, *Kleines theologisches Wörterbuch,* p. 239.

scarcely echoed anywhere in the further course of its books, excepting in Psalm 8. What could not as yet be grasped was that, while nature is 'finished', human beings, whose calling is freedom, are still immersed in the process of self-realisation. Humans cannot as yet be called 'human' in the same sense as a rose can be called a rose and a lion a lion, since they have not yet attained full humanity in the image of God. Thus, while nature has its focus in the past, human beings have their focus in the future. In terms of religion, therefore, we cannot only turn back towards the creation but, to a still greater degree, must turn forward to the Apocalypse, to eschatology, which is concerned with last things.

As a culture, we have fully absorbed what the Bible has to say about human imperfection and sinfulness, our need for grace. But less attention has been given to another thread that also exists in the Bible. Shortly before his arrest, Theodor Hauch, who was murdered by the Nazis in 1945, wrote this:

> The more I try to penetrate the hidden wisdom of the two Testaments, the more it strikes me that, in recent centuries, a key aspect of the divine message has been obscured: that the human being is not only fallen, sinful, small and pitiful, but also can partake of the divine to a degree that our lapsed age no longer comprehends at all.

But as we saw, it is not just in 'recent centuries' that 'a key aspect' of the divine message began to be overlooked. The twentieth century's excesses of inhumanity impress upon us today the now riper question of our intrinsic human nature. Human beings have become independent, grown-up, critical. We are now ready to ask about the meaning of our human existence and to seek longingly for what is 'truly human'. It is time to discover in the Bible the thread of human nature's real secret.

A view of the human being as open towards the future, specifically also in connection with Apocalypse and eschatology, arose at the beginning of the twentieth century in Rudolf Steiner's anthroposophy, and was offered for assimilation by modern consciousness: a *sophia* of the *anthropos,* a wisdom of the human being, which also concerned our future potential in indissoluble unity with the Christ and his seminal deed for humanity's future at Golgotha. This worldview makes possible a full confirmation that human beings can 'partake of the divine', and that this goal is the very essence of their being. In The Christian Community, founded in 1922, this view and vision has become nourishing ground for religious practice. This is already apparent in the name given to its central service, the Act of Consecration of Man – an appellation that was never previously used for celebrating the Eucharist. It tells us that we are still in the course of becoming human and await consecration to our true humanity, which we receive through Christ. Naturally, this new name should not be seen as being in opposition to 'divine service'. We serve God by allowing ourselves to become truly human through Christ. Our *humanity*, the *humane* nature for which our contemporaries call out of a painful sense of its lack, is ensured by the reality of Christ. The two names, anthroposophy and Act of Consecration of Man, accord fully with what the world is presently asking of humanity.

In its first pages, the Bible tells of a primordial time when only the World Creator was active. Day by day he reveals a new creative initiative, last of all creating the human being. This is followed by the Sabbath, which, unlike the preceding days, we are not told comes to an end. After creating man, God 'rested'. When Christ says, 'My Father has been working until now' (Jn 5:17), he is not contradicting the sacred text of Moses. But after the human being appeared, God, in a sense, changed the manner of his work, withdrawing it into higher realms of spirit: the world he created is henceforth no longer a field of his direct activity in the same way as it was during the days of creation. He cedes the created world to human beings for *their* initiatives. The literal translation of Psalm 115:16, is, 'The heavens of the heavens belong to the Lord but he gave the earth to the sons of men.' The original text does not say 'children' but the 'sons of men', and we can hear this as a prelude to the mystery of the Son of Man.

The sequence in which the human being appears and God 'rests' is as much as to say that God makes space for us. Perhaps this lofty mystery could be illustrated with a – no doubt inappropriate – comparison from the realm of ordinary human experience. A person who is in some way superior to others can easily exert a hindering, limiting effect on them. After Bismarck was dismissed from office, Kaiser Wilhelm II used a drastic metaphor: a mighty rock has been rolled away, but under it only worms are found. This outstanding man had burdened those around him and no independence was possible in his vicinity. We can see something similar even in the case of less famous figures. It can so easily happen that a skilled father takes a tool from the hands of his seemingly maladroit child – 'For heaven's sake, that's not the way to do it, give it to me!' If a more able fellow human being can smother or crush another, we can imagine what it would be like to have an omnipotent God looking over our shoulder.

At the death on Golgotha, the curtain in the temple is rent. Christ's death enables us to see into an otherwise hidden and most sacred sanctum. God reveals his being in sacrifice, for he is love. He can withhold his omnipotence. This omnipotence in fact would not be truly divine if the totality of possibilities at his disposal did not also include that of a freely chosen powerlessness. This relinquishment of power occurs when God cedes to the human being a field of action in a part of the universe. This renunciation does not result from weakness ('good but weak') but from strength, from a love for the freedom that human beings should develop.*

This self-imposed withholding of divine omnipotence, which becomes apparent at Golgotha, can already also be traced in the Old Testament, albeit in more concealed form. God's withdrawal into the Sabbath rest is soon followed by the story of the Fall. God allows the Tempter to approach Adam and Eve. And furthermore, God takes the fratricide Cain into his protection so that no one should kill him; clearly he sees in Cain, alongside something dangerous, a power that is intrinsically valuable and that – in God's far-seeing economy – should be preserved for the future. The Bible tells us that once the creation of the world has been accomplished, God only appears from his concealment and engages directly with humankind in exceptional situations. These manifestations become more infrequent during the course of human history. In this respect we can compare Abraham's experiences of God with those of subsequent patriarchs, and the accounts of the latter, in turn, with the time of David. Finally, after old powers of vision have faded, a new manifestation of God appears to a humanity, now fully 'arrived' in earthly consciousness during the era of the Roman Empire: not as fatherly ruler, but in fellowship as friend

---

* See Frieling, 'The mystery of the powerless God' in *The Essence of Christianity*.

and brother, and entirely relinquishing any tumultuous exercising of power. Precisely against the background of the Creator's 'authority', archetypally invested in him through his original 'authorship' of the world – which the Old Testament fully celebrates – it is all the more striking to see the reticence and renunciation of power with which human beings are invited into partnership with him.

That God allows things to happen should not be misunderstood as an indifferent laissez-faire, as a shoulder-shrugging permissiveness. All evil and harm are felt to their very depths of painfulness in the divine cosmic heart. The passion of the Crucified One is something like a focal point of universal divine suffering here becoming visible. In the light of the cross of Golgotha, we can gain an inkling of the divine love-sacrifice involved in 'giving space'.

The Son of God is eternally the true, original image of God. In the Letter to the Colossians, Paul calls him the 'image of the invisible God' (1:15). In Greek this word is *eikōn*, in Latin *imago*. Similarly in the Second Letter to the Corinthians (4:4), he is referred to as 'God's image'. He entered humanity to help raise us to the rank of sonship. 'He became as one of us' so that, in freely willed communion with him, we might come to resemble him as the Creator wished for us. In relation to this, his entry into human nature, Christ appears as the 'Son of Man'. Wilhelm Kelber's book about the Son of Man, *Der Menschensohn*, studies various aspects of this deeply mysterious phrase in detail. In what follows we shall confine ourselves to one particular aspect.

Starting with the period of the Babylonian captivity in the sixth century BC, the approaching Christ is perceived by prophetic seers in the form of the 'Son of Man'. But only through the deed at Golgotha is this finally and fully realised in him. Only through his chosen experience of an earthly human death does the Son of God immerse himself in the ultimate depths of human nature. Then, in rising from the grave, a new dimension has accrued to him. He brings his achieved unity with human nature as new influx into the heavenly world. It is as if he enters this world as a new God: bearing the stigmata, which hitherto could not have existed amongst the heavenly ones.

The phrase 'the Son of Man' can here be taken in its literal meaning. This 'new God' could only come into existence through earthly death and the subsequent resurrection; as such, he emerges from earthly human beings. The visionary John describes Christ's entry into heaven, after his passage through the earth, in the image of the Lamb with the death wound, which shakes all the heavens by his appearance in the higher world (Rv 5:6). The Letter to the Hebrews (9:24) represents the same occurrence as the entry of the high priest, Christ, into the holiest realms of heaven, bringing with him as offering his own sacrificial blood. He bears something into the higher world that could only come about upon earth, but which now renews and enriches the heavens. Thus in the New Testament we hear the phrase 'a new heaven' (Rv 21:1, 2Pt 3:13) which briefly shone forth in the Old Testament at the end of the Book of Isaiah (65:17, 66:22).

In so far failing to adopt the phrase the 'Son of Man', Christian theology has similarly made nothing of the expectation in the Bible not only of a 'new earth' but also of a 'new heaven'. Since the Fall, heaven and earth had become distant and separate. Each became quite alien to the other. There was a danger that above and below would part company altogether and be lost to each other. Through the mediating deed of Christ it became possible for the two worlds, in their different natures, to meet again in love and become fruitful for each other. The earth receives the renewing influx from above, but the mystery accomplished upon earth radiates back into divine heights and unfolds its efficacy in angelic realms.

Christ's Sermon on the Mount looks forward to a future state of perfection in which the Son of Man will 'sit upon the throne of his glory' (Mt 25:31). He will then raise his human brothers aloft with him to this throne, for he is the 'Son of Man' who passed through death and resurrection, and says to the seer on Patmos: 'To him who overcomes, I will give to him to sit with me upon my throne, as I also have overcome and sat with my Father on his throne' (Rv 3:21). Then the free human being, who has reached his goal in Christ, will achieve 'co-existence' with God omnipotent.

6

LORD OF THE ELEMENTS

MATTHEW 8:23-27; MARK 4:35-41; LUKE 8:22-25

In her novel *Jerusalem,* Selma Lagerlöf gives a magnificent portrayal of the elemental powers released during a tornado. She describes a community of country people who, sitting together under a protecting roof, fearfully witness a hurricane tearing through Swedish woods in a cold, ink-black spring night:

> From far away ... came a piercing sound; it was like a howling wind, but it could also have been a blast from a horn. Now and again a prolonged blare could be heard, then roaring and tramping and snorting.
>
> All at once the thing came dashing down from the mountain with an awful roar. They could tell when it had reached the foot of the slope; they could tell when it swept the skirt of the forest; and when it was directly above them. It was like the rolling of thunder across the face of the earth; it was as if the whole mountain had come tumbling into the valley. When it seemed to be almost upon them, every head went down. 'It will crush us,' they all thought. 'It will surely crush us.'
>
> But what they felt was not so much the fear of death, as terror lest it might be the prince of darkness himself coming, with all his demons. What frightened them most were the shrieks and moans that could be heard above the other noises. There were wails and groans, laughter and bellowings, whines and hisses. When that which they had supposed was

a big thunderstorm was right upon them, it seemed to be a mingling of groans and curses, of sobs and angry cries, of the blast of horns, of crackling fire, of the plaints of doomed spirits, of the mocking laughter of demons, of the flapping of huge wings.

They thought all the furies of the infernal regions had been let loose that night, and would overwhelm them. The ground trembled, and the hut swayed as if it were going to topple over. It was as if wild horses were prancing on the roof; as if howling ghosts rushed past the door, and as if owls and bats were beating their wings against the chimney.

At last the storm calms, but the people stay sitting there, shocked and silent as if spellbound. 'No one moved, no one spoke … Now and then through the stillness a deep sigh was heard.'

This is not only a poetic description of nature, in which natural forces are imaginatively personified or conjured through metaphor. Above and beyond the author's skill, it embodies an influx of eerie and uncanny reality, of spirit beings. It seems as if she here rekindles something of her soul inheritance from her Nordic forefathers, who experienced the natural world still with a very different kind of consciousness from our modern one.

Rudolf Steiner's science of the spirit once again enables us to understand the deep truth of the old myths and legends. People of past times possessed something like a primal clairvoyance in relation to nature, a vivid sense and feeling of it that allowed them to perceive the workings of spirit beings in the world. Understood in this sense, the gods were not imaginary, nor was the twilight of the gods. People felt the gradual fading of their ancient clairvoyance. The gods vanished from view. But besides disappearing from human vision, according to Rudolf Steiner they also really withdrew to some degree from the workings of nature, which they had formerly indwelt. But where the gods cede space, other spirits fill the vacuum. Thus, beings of lesser rank, and in some circumstances demonic powers, migrated into natural processes. If we allow ourselves to engage with this way of thinking, we find that it can shed light on many phenomena in the history of religion.

A wafting breath of air was originally truly experienced by the

Jews as the breath of Yahweh. Ancient Nordic seers perceived in the atmosphere the deeds of the sublime being Odin. As the twilight of the gods proceeded, Odin was very gradually and almost unnoticeably replaced by a less lofty figure. The 'wild hunter', the 'wild hunt', was an eerie experience people had of demonic elemental powers that could manifest in the air and winds. The description by Selma Lagerlöf is one example of this mode of vision, in which the natural world is pervaded by an influx of the uncanny and the demonic from invisible worlds.

The element of air has an intimate connection with the soul. It cannot be directly equated with it, but, in the same way that the principle of 'life' cannot be embodied on earth without the mediation of the fluid element, so soul can only manifest in earthly bodies where air offers its service. We can all observe how intimately the stirrings of the soul are imparted to our breath. The nirvana of Buddhism means 'wafting away' or 'blowing away' of all illusory impulses, as it were an expiry of all woes. On the other hand, we can speak of 'snorting with anger' or 'storms of passion'.

If we contemplate the possibility that actual demonic beings sometimes launch themselves upon the raging of unleashed elements, we find ourselves on the way to a new, realistic understanding of a biblical story as unique and striking as that of the stilling of the storm. Our demythologising contemporaries will regard it only as a product of ancient superstition when winds and waves threaten Christ and he soothes their raging with commanding words. They are certain that such a storm is merely a natural occurrence. But if we are to make progress in understanding the gospels, it is high time that we consider the possibility that supernatural phenomena can sometimes manifest within the natural world.

No doubt such special conditions existed when the highest divine being walked the earth in the incarnated form of Jesus Christ. It is scarcely surprising that in relation to such an event, the natural world now and then became a mediator of supernatural powers and their manifestation. It is scarcely surprising that at that time there occurred 'miracles' which did not involve a mere 'breaking' of natural laws (in the miraculous sense) but a 'breaking through' of higher modes of action and thus of a higher order.

6. LORD OF THE ELEMENTS

By pursuing these thoughts we can arrive at a 'biblical realism'. It becomes conceivable that demonic hosts, like a wild army, a wild hunt, launched themselves at that time upon a hurricane to capsize and destroy those sailing across the lake. Here we ought also to take account of the sequence of occurrences. What happens directly after the stilling of the storm? As they land on the East shore, the possessed man of Gerasa runs towards them from a distant burial place. He is driven in bedevilled, self-destructive fashion by the wild army of a whole throng of demons that calls itself 'Legion' (Mk 5:9). The storm demons over the lake appear here as a prelude to this Legion army that has settled upon a human being and casts him mercilessly hither and thither in a truly underworld existence. Christ, as the mighty, cosmic creator Word, opposes this uncanny throng of devils in strength and majesty. This occurrence is of such archetypal quality that it speaks directly to our souls. Goethe had a sense of the deep, symbolic power of this story of the stilling of the storm. It is worth reading the passage in his *Italian Journey* where he recounts a sea experience he had near Capri. His calm words helped prevent panic in his terrified fellow travellers.

> I lay down half dazed but with a certain feeling of contentment, due, perhaps to the Sea of Tiberias; for in my mind's eye I saw clearly before me the etching from the Merian Bible. It gave me proof that all impressions of a sensory-moral nature are strongest proven when a man is thrown completely on his own resources.*

Let us now turn to the story itself as found in the New Testament. We encounter it no less than three times: in Matthew (8:23–27), Mark (4:35–41) and Luke (8:22–-25), in other words in the three synoptic gospels as they are called. The story told in each is certainly not identical, but each evangelist adds something of their own to the account.

Common to all three is the basic pattern of events. The disciples are travelling over the lake with Christ towards the East shore when a

---

* May 14, 1787, p. 307.

storm suddenly breaks. In fear the disciples wake the sleeping Christ who commands the winds and waves, after which a great stillness sets in (*galēnē* in the Greek). The Lord chides the disciples for their lack of faith, and they turn to each other in wonder and ask, 'Who is this man, that winds and sea obey him?' After this comes the encounter with the possessed man on the further shore.

In Luke we can have a sense that he – a Greek – is telling the story as a member of a seafaring family. For him, it seems worth mentioning the experience that arises as they start their voyage: 'they pushed off from the shore', or literally, 'they were led upward'. The shore is left behind and before them stretches the broad back of the sea that they are sailing 'up'. In the same way, in describing the draft of fishes, Luke has the Lord say to Peter, 'Sail upward upon the heights' (5:4).* And in the account of the storm he writes: 'They were taken upward' – lifted up by the swelling tide. Then he dwells, at least for a moment, on observing the ship as it makes its initially undisturbed way over the water: 'and as they sailed onward …'. It seems connected with this that, as the ship sails calmly onward, Christ sleeps in the rhythmic rocking of the waves; the literal expression is 'sleeps away'. His soul releases itself from a body-bound state, and removes itself or 'sleeps away' into higher realms. (Nowhere else do we read anything about the 'sleep' of Christ.)

With his expertise in seafaring, Luke has the storm 'come down' upon the lake. Visitors to the Holy Land have often related how, on hot evenings, fierce storms suddenly 'descend' on the lake, which is surrounded by mountains. 'These blasts of wind occur because of the gorges that slope down from the north and the north-east' (W. Thompson).

> The wind has an enormous, instantaneously appearing power over the Sea of Galilee … The wind rushes across the surrounding high plain and, achieving unusual violence, rushes downward with incredible force as it reaches the edge of this huge declivity [200 m, 700 ft, below sea level]. You can more or less see the tornado falling upon the lake. (MacGregor)

---

* The mobility of Greek thought here uses a paradoxical expression: Sail out and upward upon the 'depths' *(bathos)* – for water is deepest on the 'heights' of the sea.

6. LORD OF THE ELEMENTS

Luke then uses a lovely ancient Greek word for the 'surging' waves that are calmed by Christ – *klydōn* – in which you can almost hear the blows and buffets of agitated waves.

Mark makes a significant connection between the calming of the storm and what immediately precedes it. For him, the occurrence is not only 'on one of those days', as in Luke, but at twilight of the remarkable day when Christ, speaking from the boat, has uttered the parables by the lake concerning the kingdom of heaven. Here, as so often, Mark introduces little tangible details that vividly conjure the scene before us. 'And leaving the throng behind, they take him with them, just as he was, in the boat. Other boats were with him, too.' Mark loves to leap into the lively present tense, so that we feel ourselves drawn into his narrative. 'A storm arises.' He describes in detail how Christ 'was sleeping, at the stern upon a pillow'. He preserves for us the words of Christ's command: '"Silence, be still!" And the wind calmed.' Mark, with his fondness for courage, also records the words of chiding, 'Why are you so faint-hearted?'

Matthew – as he commonly does – gives us the briefest account. But in the very few words of his sparing tale, he is able to invest the regal and noble figure of Christ with a certain iconic majesty. He says nothing about the suddenly rising storm, but only: 'And behold, a great tumult occurred in the sea.' (The word *seismos* is also used for the earthquake that shakes Jerusalem on Good Friday and Easter morning.) 'But he slept.' The cry for help from the disciples is given in brief intensity in the three calls, 'Lord! Help! We perish!' In Greek 'Lord' is *Kyrie*. In Mark, the word is 'teacher', in Luke *epistàtes,* which roughly signifies 'master', a word that was evidently also used for the leader of a circle of spiritual seekers. But Matthew has the disciples use the most reverent form of address of all, *Kyrie*. And at the end he speaks of them as the 'men' who cry out in wonder, 'What kind of one *(potapós)* is this?'

All three evangelists end with this question: Who is this to whom winds and waves are obedient? The disciples themselves are not yet mature enough in understanding to answer this. The reply comes from a quite different direction. In the subsequent tale of the possessed man and the wild army of the 'Legion', the demons give the answer. As supersensible beings they know more surely than human beings what hour has come. They express what then later sounds from a human mouth, 'You Son of God' (Mt 8:29), 'You Son of the Highest God' (Mk 5:7, Lk 8:28).

Selma Lagerlöf describes how, after the terrible night storm, the spell of the uncanny lingers for a long time. People who have witnessed it do not shake it off 'until the sun had risen behind the mountains'. It is a Sunday morning. This redeeming power of the clear day of the sun, which can drive away demons and ghosts, finds its highest manifestation in the sunlike Son of God, whose life on earth as Christ Jesus is recounted by the gospels.

7

THE GREAT 'TODAY' IN THE NEW TESTAMENT

The idea of experiencing time in three forms – past, present and future – is one that is familiar to us, but we are not always conscious of the fact that grasping the 'present' has its special difficulties. No sooner has something happened than it already belongs to the past, though until now it lay in the future. The present in time is like the point in space – it has no magnitude. If we can grasp it with 'presence' of mind before it has escaped us again, then something higher than the merely temporal is brought into play. Like lightning, eternity flashes in. Eternity is by no means just endlessly prolonged time, but belongs to a quite different and higher plane above and beyond the temporal.

Since there is such a special inbuilt possibility of glimpsing eternity in experiencing the present, words used for expressing present time, like 'now' and 'today', can be understood in a deeper religious sense. The mystic knows a *nunc eternam,* an eternal now. In the Bible, the word 'today' frequently has a very special overtone.

From our experience of Christmas there remains with us the sound of the angels' announcement, 'for to you is born this day a Saviour' (Lk 2:11). In connection with this Christmas gospel, profound Christian souls have always felt that, since Bethlehem, 'this day' lives on in Christendom. 'This day' was not only for the shepherds in the fields at that time, for it would long since have become yesterday and the day before yesterday; the mystery of the Saviour's birth wants to come about in every Christian soul anew. In the light of the Christian celebration of Christmas, 'this day' of long ago becomes something present, into which eternity shines straight from heaven.

Once the inner ear has opened for the special sound of the Christmas 'today', then you also hear it with new overtones and undertones in other places in the gospels. This is particularly the case with Luke, whose gospel includes the Christmas story.

If we turn the pages to the following chapter in his gospel, we find the baptism in the Jordan. If we go back to the original text of Luke still used by Clement of Alexandria and Origen, we find that he gives the words God speaks at the baptism somewhat differently from Matthew and Mark: 'You are my Son, today I have begotten you' (Lk 3:22). Superficially, this is a quotation from the Old Testament, from the Second Psalm (2:7). But how is it that the voice of God uses just these words? If we look it up, we see that in the psalm it is also God's voice that speaks. On both occasions it is the same voice sounding in heaven, which in Old Testament times came to the ears of the writer of the Second Psalm and which at the baptism was heard by Jesus and John the Baptist. Christ is, as our Creed says, 'the Son born in eternity'. His going forth from the Father is not an occurrence that lies in the past; as an eternal event it belongs to that higher plane that lies above the temporal. In an eternally procreative speaking the Father pronounces his Son, the 'Word'. The Second Psalm has caught something of this eternally happening event. It gives the Messiah the words: 'I will declare the decree: the Lord has said to me, You are my Son; this day have I begotten you.' The psalmist heard the same as was heard again later at the baptism in Jordan. With the baptism, the Son born in eternity finally descends into the earthly body of Jesus. The eternal 'Today' thereby shines into an earthly and temporal 'today'.

Soon after, in the fourth chapter, we are met by the third significant 'Today'. Luke records how, after the baptism and temptation, Jesus of Nazareth appears for the first time before men as the Christ. On the Sabbath he goes into the synagogue at Nazareth, with which he was well acquainted from his early life, and makes use of the right of adult members to take part in the reading of the scriptures. Luke gives us a clear picture of the preliminaries. 'And he stood up to read' (4:16). The scroll of the prophet Isaiah is handed to him. Providence is at work even in this minor event. He opens the scroll and 'finds' the Messianic passage, Isaiah 61: 'The Spirit of the Lord is upon me ...' This links up in a wonderful way with his experience at the baptism. He reads to the point: 'to proclaim the acceptable year of the Lord.' He ends the reading just at the point where Isaiah goes on to say, 'and the day of vengeance ...' There is a divine sovereignty in the way he breaks off at this point. 'He closed the book and gave it back to the attendant' (4:20). Then he sat down in order to add a word of his own to the reading, as a rabbi was permitted to do. The teaching was done sitting down, from the rabbinical chair, but what now comes is something quite different from the discourse of a rabbi. When Christ now speaks for the first time from his own inner being, it is the Word made flesh that begins to speak on earth. Luke's description captures the drama of this unique moment: 'and the eyes of all the synagogue were fixed on him.' What would his first saying be? 'And he began to say to them, "Today this scripture has been fulfilled in your hearing".' But those there are not equal to the historic moment. Full of wonder, they readily perceive the 'gracious' quality of his words, but they know no better than to say that this is 'Joseph's son'. They were not able to grasp the great 'Today' in which the angels' message and God's voice at the baptism still sounded, wanting to enter their small 'today'. Thus the tragedy of Golgotha already begins.

On a later occasion – after the healing of the paralytic in Capernaum – it seems as if a feeling for this 'Today' of the Christ-day that has dawned begins to stir in the people. They are seized with *ekstasis* in the face of the act of healing, which means to a certain extent freed from their everyday, body-bound consciousness, so that in 'awe', in holy amazement, they perceive the divine and cry out, 'We have seen strange things today!' (5:26). It is only Luke's account that so impressively concludes the whole story with the word 'today'.

The thirteenth chapter of Luke describes how Christ, on his way to his last Passover, receives warning of a possible attack by Herod. 'Behold, I cast out demons and perform cures today and tomorrow, and the third day I finish my course. Nevertheless, I must go on my way today and tomorrow and the day following; for it cannot be that a prophet should perish away from Jerusalem.' (13:32f). Christ is aware of his destiny: it is not yet, but soon; it will not be here in Galilee, but in Jerusalem. His allotted time on earth approaches its end. The God who has become man humbly accommodates himself to the pattern of events in time on earth. He feels how precious is the short span of fleeting time yet granted him, which he fills with everlasting deeds of love. The 'today' of time and space still applies to him; he knows that it can still continue into a 'tomorrow', but then will be the day for the final deed of fulfilment. He walks towards it. This 'today', overshadowed by the approaching passion, is a powerfully striking expression of Christ's feeling about the dwindling number of days allotted to him on earth.

In the story of the passion Luke, this time together with Mark, has the word 'today' in the pronouncement of Peter's denial, 'the cock will not crow this day' (22:34). It is the crowing of the cock that announces the dawning of the day of Golgotha. The word 'today' is spoken yet a second time on Good Friday, and again recorded only in Luke's account. Here on the last occasion it is once more the tremendous 'Today' into which the light of eternity streams in full brilliance. It is Christ's saying from the cross: 'Truly, I say to you, today you will be with me in Paradise' (23:43). The criminal on his cross experiences, in the last hour of his fast dwindling life on earth, how for him 'is born this day' the Saviour. The end and the beginning of the gospel are thus linked. Luke is therefore, in a special sense, the evangelist of 'Today'.

We must, however, draw on Matthew to supplement this in relation to the Lord's Prayer; for he alone (not Luke, if we keep to the original text) passes on the prayer that daily bread may 'this day' be given us. This speaks of the inner superiority over all anxiety about the future. But such a superiority can exist only if each day is experienced as belonging to God, if, that is, the great 'Today' of eternity shines into the temporal. (In the other place where Matthew uses the word 'today' its significance does not go beyond the usual use of the word and need not therefore be mentioned in our connection.)

'Today' once more plays a special role in the New Testament in the Letter to the Hebrews. The author, well-versed in the scriptures, quotes the Ninety-fifth Psalm. As with the Second Psalm, when we read it we notice the sound of divine inspiration. The soul of the psalmist is moved by what has gone before and is made receptive for listening to an inspiration from the highest realm. 'Today if you will hear his voice, do not harden your heart' (Ps 95:7f). He looks back to the fate of Israel, wandering in the wilderness, when the people fell into hardness and bitterness of heart and therefore could not find the way to rest in the Promised Land. The psalmist feels himself at a turning point in history when again – as in the time of Moses – God's voice calls to men. Again, as before, there arises a 'Today' pregnant with destiny. The New Testament Letter to the Hebrews goes back to this word and gives it current significance. It expresses the conviction that the full truth and decisive significance of this psalm which God spoke 'through David' (4:7) is manifest only after the Christ event. Only we Christians are fully able to understand it. Three times it is solemnly quoted: 'Today, when you hear his voice, do not harden your hearts' (3:7f, 3:15, 4:7).

Without prejudice to its historical reality, the fate of Israel – exodus from Egypt, journeying in the wilderness, entry into the Promised Land – appears as a prototypal event in which a yet greater one has already taken shape. After the loss of the old spirituality, the whole of humanity has entered the desert and is to find the Promised Land of the new covenant with God. So, for the Letter to the Hebrews, the full significance of what was recorded in the Old Testament was not exhausted with the events of those times. A new desert-wandering is in process on an enormous scale. God has called forth a new day of salvation with a new horizon, a new 'Today'. It concerns the hearing of the voice, the dawning of eternity in the consciousness of Christians so that the way can be found into the Promised Land. The Letter to the Hebrews seeks to bring about an apocalyptic awakening with this 'Today'.

We can make it our own in this present era. It has meanwhile again become 'much truer'. Even the soul experiences connected with the desert wandering, which the Letter to the Hebrews describes as a hardening of heart, we can see in a wholly modern light. 'Do not harden your hearts as in the rebellion' (3:15). Only the grasping of the presence of Christ in the present time, only the raising of the ordinary 'today' to the great 'Today' of the breaking in of eternity, can save us.

8

'COME TO ME, ALL YOU ...'

MATTHEW 11:28–30

It is because we are oriented to freedom that our redemption cannot be imposed upon us from without. If the divine will for salvation is to reach its goal in us, we also have to do something about it. At one point in the Book of Revelation it says, 'I will give to him to sit with me upon my throne, as I also have overcome and sat with my Father on his throne' (3:21). And so the advent, the coming of Christ to human beings, is complemented by our coming to Christ.

In the Gospel of Matthew we find a phrase that calls us with special, heartfelt insistence to take these steps towards Christ:

> Come to me, all you who are weary and burdened ...

We who live in the atomic age can feel ourselves no less directly addressed by these words than people of former periods: we too are weary and burdened. Most contemporaries in modern civilisation have felt that 'living' is more or less synonymous with 'struggling'. Existence becomes ever more complex. Despite all the technical equipment that supposedly makes life easier, life keeps getting harder.

This call from Christ reaches us precisely 'where we are' when he turns to us as weary and heavy laden ones. But now we need to set ourselves in motion, take steps towards Christ. If we instigate this movement, then through our conduct we enable him to move actively towards us. 'Come to me – and I will refresh you.' In the original language of the gospel, the I of the person speaking here is explicitly emphasised: 'I, I myself, will ...'

The 'I' in question must be a great and all-inclusive one if it turns to 'all' with such an invitation: an I of a higher order, indeed of the highest divine order, of immeasurably greater scope than an I of our kind is endowed with.

The I as we know it all too soon comes up against limits and barriers to its loving interest in fellow human beings. Connected with this is the general suffering from isolation and loneliness, precisely where millions of people gather in cities. Becoming a Christian leads to the discovery that a great, all-embracing, all-loving I exists that seeks to encompass every single individual and come to life in each one. To discover this, we must first turn our attention to something not apparent to our outward sight, but which lives as the invisible reality of being; and because it *is* a reality, this being has agency from which effects issue.

The word translated above as 'refresh' is *anapusein* in Greek. In this word we find our own word 'pause', and see that it is connected here with *ana,* which always expresses an 'upward' motion. The familiar expression, a 'creative pause', is a felicitous one, connecting something alive and creative with rest. This is deeply true. Creativity is not born from hurry and restlessness, but has its roots in tranquillity – not the silence of the grave but the peace of God. We might perhaps use the following words to encompass all this: 'Set yourself moving towards me – and then I, as the great, all-inclusive I, will grace you with creative rest. Like a refreshing breeze from divine worlds of peace, I will infuse this into the breath of your soul, bringing it relief.'

But there is more to say about this 'call of the Redeemer'. A further sentence follows. After the great I has given his promise of peace, he turns once again to human beings and shows them how to become inwardly active. The sequence here is significant. If a person has received something of that divine peace, this does not lead to inactivity but rather to greater work and activity.

Take my yoke upon you, and learn from me.

Many have observed here that merely doing nothing in no way accords with the desired repose. More healing, wholesome and nurturing than declining all activity is to surrender ourselves to great, inspiring goals. Not in inactivity, nor in distraction, which diffuses and disperses us, but in meaningful action we truly 'recover' and refresh ourselves. Thus, these words of Christ offer a transition from divine tranquillity to a new harnessing of our soul energies.

The image of 'harnessing' is appropriate here, and leads us to the image Christ uses, the 'yoke'. In fact there is a linguistic connection between 'yoke' and 'yoga'. When people in Indian culture speak of yoga, they mean the harnessing of inner powers. These powers should not be left to their own devices but grasped and set to work by intentional spiritual will. 'My yoke', the 'yoke of Christ', means harnessing these inner energies in the service of the great all-embracing I, the soul work to which the Christian feels called if he rightly understands his mission.

'And learn from me.' Once more, this is an appeal to activity. Learning in its strict sense is a specific human activity. It is wrong, really, to apply it to animals, for 'training' and 'dressage' are something very different. Similarly, merely 'filling' people with information, perhaps inculcation with the aid of technical devices, is not yet true learning since the latter depends on the activity of our I.

In the Gospel of John (6:45), Christ speaks of how we should 'hear from the Father and learn from him' in order also to find our way to the Son. Among other things, 'nature' is also assigned to the Father. If we allow the open secret of the changing seasons, the 'dying and becoming', to speak to our soul, we are 'learning' from the Father and thereby preparing ourselves to revere the most sublime expression of this primal mystery in the death and resurrection of Christ.

In the same way that we learn from the Father, so we should also learn from the Son. 'Learn from me.' The Christ appeared before our sight in tangible human form so that ever more reality would flow over from his great, all-embracing I into our own I if it opens itself in willingness to learn. Such learning is a deeply incisive, living process. What previously was external to us is drawn in to our own sphere of life and begins to pass over into flesh and blood. 'Learn from me.' We not only learn truths mediated to us by Christ but we should 'learn him'.

I would now like to characterise in more depth this Christ-I, given us for this living and life-enhancing 'learning'.

For I am meek and humble of heart.

Again we can see that the text moves back and forth between the divine and the human aspect. Having called upon humankind to harness powers and learn, it swings back the other way to where the great I reveals his being.

'Meek' – this recalls two other passages in the Gospel of Matthew: the Beatitudes, where the 'meek' are praised; and the entry of the 'meek' or 'gentle' king on Palm Sunday (21:5). The connection with 'inheriting the earth' and with the lofty nature of a king, clearly shows us that this word 'meek' does not indicate anything anaemic, any weakness or lack of inner 'iron'. In the sense of the gospels, to be meek means to be able to use the spirit to master and calm the powers of soul life.

And 'humble'? In Paul's Letter to the Philippians, the motif of Christ's humility appears in connection with his becoming man 'so far as to the death upon the cross' (2:8). It is, if you like, the divine social quality that the Christ invokes in his earthly descent. Out of love he makes himself a companion to earthly humankind, showing solidarity with us to the point of suffering our destiny of death. That he 'humbles himself' to do this does not mean any kind of self-disparagement. But the word suggests a vivid contrast to the 'haughtiness' of Lucifer, who seeks to 'lord it' and regards himself as too good to incline himself to what is of a lower order than himself.

An important epithet is added here to this word 'humble', which we ought not to overlook: 'humble of heart'. Let us be aware that we here meet something unique. Nowhere else in the whole of the New Testament do we hear any mention of the heart of Christ. Only here. The divine social quality with which Christ inclines, bends, lowers himself to humankind, and which ultimately leads him to Golgotha, is founded in his inmost being. This is truly a matter of the heart.

This, therefore, is the nature of the great, all-encompassing I that offers itself for humanity to learn from. Through willed, attentive focus upon him, harnessing our powers with willingness to learn, we gain once more a prospect of divine tranquillity that streams in like the breath of relief from above. The pendulum swings once again back to the human being.

You will find rest for your souls.

As human beings we must 'find' by our own powers, and only thereby truly make our own, what the Godhead seeks to gift us. 'Find' is a bright, fully awake experience of the I that illumines consciousness like lightning.

'I will refresh you – you will find rest.' In the Greek, 'refresh' and 'rest' are the same word on each occasion: first as verb *(anapauein)*, next as noun *(anapausis)*. If we use the word 'refresh' we should therefore also feel the creative repose within it; if we say 'rest' we must also hearken to the sense of refreshment and renewal, of inner relief and deeper breath.

'Find rest for your souls': more strongly still, no doubt, than in past eras, this can elicit in modern human beings an understanding and yearning response. The rest that is found in 'learning' the Christ-I is the peace that comes from the oceanic breath of divine life and its festive rhythms once a person has been reconfigured in his inmost core by the Redeemer. This peacefulness is the most effective of all means of healing the soul being of earthly humankind, overshadowed as it is by the Fall and rendered so deeply disordered and sick.

And once more the pendulum swings back to the aspect of Christ:

> For my yoke is easy and my burden is light.

For 'easy', the word in Greek is *chrēstos,* meaning 'gentle', 'mild', 'friendly', 'benevolent' (not to be confused with *Christos,* 'the anointed one'). Paul uses this word to speak of the benevolence of God, his amiability, which should awaken us to change our ways (Rom 2:4). The yoke of Christ is *chrēstos.* The hard, severe image of the yoke is warmly irradiated with benevolence and goodness.

But here we must avoid a dangerous misapprehension that can arise if we lose sight of the overall context. This concluding phrase, 'my yoke is easy and my burden is light' should certainly not be understood to mean that Christianity is a comfortable and undemanding affair that requires no determined efforts or sacrifice on our part. Elsewhere, precisely in the Gospel of Matthew, clear expression is given to God's expectancy of great dedication and heroic effort from Christians. 'Be perfect like your Father in the heavens' (5:48). Certainly what the gospel urges upon us as the very highest demands should not be diminished to an easily accomplished average. What is meant is this:

The 'yoke of Christ', and the harnessing of ourselves in service to him, is not imposed upon us externally as a law. The human deeds that God expects of us can only flow from love, and love is only present where there is also freedom. What Christ bears upon his shoulders was not a burden imposed by any taskmaster; he took it upon himself in freedom and love. The phrase, 'True, it is easy, but the easy is hard', can, in our context, be reversed: 'True, it is hard, but the hard becomes easy.' Daily life, after all, teaches us that something we would otherwise find hard to do is no longer burdensome at all if we do it out of love. For this reason the yoke of Christ is 'easy' and his burden 'light'.

The redemption of humankind cannot, after all, mean that we are freed of all need to carry a burden, that we can throw off every yoke. This would be a superficial and irresponsible view of the destiny of humanity. In the gospels, in various ways, we hear of weight-bearing shoulders: for instance, the Pharisees who tie up heavy burdens for other human beings and place them on their shoulders (Mt 23:4); or the shepherd who has at last found the lost sheep and joyfully bears it 'home on his shoulders'.

This does not mean that burdens and toil we have previously suffered in a 'worldly' context are to be exchanged, when we become Christians, for a possibly still more joyless and spiritual type of burden. Christians will not go about looking 'burdened'. To a much greater degree than Nietzsche proclaimed, with yearning and insight in his *Zarathustra,* the 'spirit of gravity' should be overcome if the human being, lovingly bearing the burden of Christ, is to follow his path with upright stance and light steps. With freedom and love, even the heavy grows light.

9

HE WROTE IN THE EARTH

JOHN 8:1–11

The story of Christ and the woman taken in adultery comes in the Gospel of John at the end of the Festival of Tabernacles. In Jewish tradition there are various autumn festival customs, not mentioned in the New Testament, that can shed light on the account of these days in this gospel, which take up a good deal of space (Jn 7:1–10:21). Among other things, we know that the Festival of Tabernacles concluded with a great illumination that lit up the whole of night-time Jerusalem. Around the great fire that burned in the temple grounds, a kind of popular festive mood would break out, sometimes intensifying into carnival-like exuberance. In this context, the events occurred that led the overseers to demand the punishment of stoning. They led the woman taken in adultery to appear before Christ – we hear nothing about her partner. The Scribes and Pharisees take the opportunity to set Christ a trap. 'Moses commanded that such ones be stoned. What do you say?' An answer in strict accordance with the law, they thought, would diminish Jesus' popularity, but if he declined to give it, he would be disputing Moses' authority, and thus throw himself open to criminal proceedings. Christ reacts in an unexpected way. He bends low and writes in the earth. When they continue to urge him to answer, he stands up again and says, 'Let he who is without sin amongst you cast the first stone.' Then he bends low again and continues writing.

In Old Testament times, people still possessed a kind of feeling knowledge that one person cannot pass judgment on another without further ado, since all human beings are subject to the Fall. They therefore sought a higher authority when making judgments. In the Old Testament, the judges were sometimes called 'gods' (Elohim).

9. HE WROTE IN THE EARTH

This was not tantamount to erasing the distinction between God and man, but it sought to express the following: when a council formed of several chosen people gathered in the right way, this made it possible for beings higher in rank than humankind to make use of such a community as their vessel, and to speak and judge through them. As humanity distanced itself ever further from an original experience of the supersensible, a designation like 'the gods' eventually became an empty phrase. Yet the sense had not completely vanished that ordinary people could not pass a sentence of death on another person without being elevated above the ordinary level so that they were no longer subject to the Fall. Here we should also note that on the same day Christ would say, 'Which of you can convict me of sin?' We read this in the same chapter (Jn 8:46). His accusers have a certain feeling for the reproach contained in Christ's question about the possibly sinless human being. They know that this stoning to death would be a riotous and unjust action. It would have had to be reported to the Romans as a spontaneous act of people's justice, for at that time, as the Jews expressed to Pilate, 'We are not allowed to kill anyone' except with the permission of the Roman authorities.

At Christ's words, the accusers fall silent, and steal away one after the other.

Christ remains alone with the woman 'standing in the middle'. In the meantime, Christ has continued to write in the earth. Now it has grown silent around him, he stands up a second time and turns to the woman. 'Has no one condemned you?' – 'No one, Lord.' – 'Then I also do not condemn you. Go, and henceforth sin no more.'

We can agree with the Protestant theologian Stauffer that Christ's conduct here is deeply humane and compassionate.* It reveals his generosity, his clear perception of the mendacity of the moral stance of the Pharisees, his chivalry towards the woman who is held to account while no interest is shown in her male partner in adultery. Doubtless this is also present in the story. But if this were all, a residue of dissatisfaction would remain. We would not find it hard to understand the ecclesiastical authorities who, in the early Christian era, removed this account from the New Testament. The story of the adulteress is missing from key manuscripts. For example, in the

---

* Staufer, *Jesus war ganz anders*, p. 123.

scholarly Nestle edition of the Greek text, the passage is printed in small font below the text proper.

Why did this specific story have such a hard time? Clearly, there were Church authorities concerned to uphold the strict community morality that had come down from early Christian times. One might gain a sense from the narrative that the adultery itself was not being taken seriously enough, that it 'wasn't that bad'; a certain laxity might be deduced, a relativising view that since all human beings are sinners, matters of immorality could be judged leniently.

In relation to these questions, which may have given anxious bishops some cause for concern, only a higher knowledge can help us, one capable of observing specific supersensible truths. Otherwise, the real depths of this story are not revealed.

The key to it is the striking language of the mute gesture – how Christ bends down and writes. This is the only place in the gospels where we hear of Christ Jesus writing anything.* It surely has significance that he himself, who was the Word, only communicated in living speech, face to face, in each instance speaking the right divine, creative word at the right moment. But nevertheless, on this one occasion, he wrote.

Whereas the spoken word is immediate, in writing we depart from this present immediacy. Writing is done with an eye to something coming later. The letter waits for its recipient, who will reawaken the words that have been written down; and someone's last written 'will' waits to be opened before it can be executed. Writing is therefore dependent on this future realisation and enactment, and does not occupy such a complete reality and possess such presence as the spoken word. It is always a kind of borrowing from the future.

When Christ writes in the earth in regard to the transgression presented to him, this means that he cannot for the time being encompass the full scope of the immediate situation. We can say that something is 'noted in advance' of later action.

The story takes place in the autumn of the last year before Golgotha, half a year before Christ fulfils his great sacrifice: before he dies and is resurrected, and so unites himself with the destiny of

---

* The motif of Christ writing reappear in a quite different context in Revelation, where it is the Resurrected One who writes (3:12).

humanity and the earth. He cannot undertake this union without 'taking the sins of the world' upon himself as the 'innocent Lamb of God'. He could have taken his further way over our heads in the heights of a divine world, for he was not subject to the Fall and did not need to taste death. His descent is grace, his death a different death from the one ordinary humanity experiences, and for this very reason it radiates a redeeming power. The self-sacrificing Christ takes upon himself the burden of everything that, following objectively from human misdeeds, becomes part of the body of the earth and integral to the world.

When we sin, we exceed our own capacities to make recompense. The harm we do to our own moral being can be repaired to a certain degree. For instance, we can be so shocked by what we have done that, in an extreme case, we become a saint. If conditions allow it, we can make amends still in this life for what we have done to others, or otherwise do so in a subsequent incarnation. But even for such redress, making good the harm both to the doer and to the victim still requires the inner help of Christ. But now there is a third possibility, faintly intimated by those who felt that the oriental or theosophically coloured form of the teaching of karmic compensation was somehow superficial. They sensed that this 'cannot be the whole story'. A misdeed unleashes something ruinous that exceeds the scope of the best desire to make redress. This is the consequence that becomes an integral part of the objective world, and human goodwill is powerless here. To deal with this, we need the merciful intervention of a being whose 'scope of action' extends further than our human possibility. This being is the Christ.

At the autumn festival in Jerusalem, half a year before Golgotha, we see Christ approach very close to this union with the earth. Twice, within this short account, we hear that Christ 'stoops down' (8:6, 8). And since he does not use a stick to write in the earth but, as expressly stated there, 'with his finger,' he must stoop right down. His writing tells us that the objective part of guilt, which has become world, belongs to the earth: to that very earth towards which he is making his way in order to unite with it, to 'dwell within the heart of the earth' as he states in another passage (Mt 12:40). There, in the Greek, we find the phrase 'heart *(kardia)* of the earth' expressly stated. This also means that he makes his own concern what lies at the heart of the earth and burdens it. It is striking that on the same day, the Christ yet again makes this gesture of stooping low to the earth when he heals the man born blind. This time he does not write in the earth but gives it some of his spittle, and thus his life force, to stir the mud that he then places upon the man's eyes (Jn 9:6). This almost alchemistic preparation of a mixture likewise requires him to bend down to the earth. On the same day he has spoken the words, 'I am from above' (Jn 8:23). This illumines the merciful, healing nature of his stooping to the earth. Half a year later he will give his blood to the earth. At that point, his 'writing in the earth' will take effect and become full reality.

Theological commentaries have never been able to make much of this writing in the earth. Goethe offers us a better aid to understanding (in the paralipomena or supplement to the *West East Divan*). The situation there is of course a quite different one. In the company of Marianne von Willemer in the Heidelberg Castle Gardens, he wrote her name in the ground in coded script with his stick. A playful act, but the symbolism of this action must have preoccupied him. In verses he finds words relating to the incident whose significance extends far beyond that moment in Heidelberg; and, if one were to take them in their full reality, they could be applied also to Christ's writing in the earth. Goethe sensed the earth in totality to be a great, organic, living unity. And he imagined that something that occurs on a tiny part of it does not remain confined to that part but can concern the whole earth. It can touch its heart if it is done with spiritual authority. In the poem he wrote about this coded script Goethe says:

> Inscribed in the moving dust, the wind
> wafts over it, but its power remains:
> impressed upon the ground, a spell that reaches
> as far as the centre of the earth.

But there is more. Christ embraces the earth, and, in the process, may have given the woman an intimating sense of the world significance of human culpability. Yet just as the words about 'bending down' occur twice in the text, so his standing upright also figures twice (8:7, 10).

The first time he rises from stooping is when he turns to the accusers surrounding him. This is the moment when he speaks the words, 'Let he who is without sin amongst you ...' If we picture the scene vividly, he must have turned his face to the accusers as he said this. That experience of Kundry – 'his gaze struck me' (in Richard Wagner's *Parsifal*) – is something we must here read between the lines of this brief text, and it belongs inseparably to the spoken words. When we hear that the accusers departed, 'moved to do so by their conscience,' this may no doubt be connected with the gaze of Christ which they encounter.

And as these accusers left one after another, Christ again stooped down and continued writing. When he rose again for the second time, the temple place was empty apart from the woman 'standing in the middle'. Again we can read between the lines here – 'his gaze struck me'. Without the context of deeply incisive experiences in the soul of the woman, the words now exchanged do not acquire their full weight. They, too, cannot be isolated from the situation and from what happens wordlessly.

And so, at last, Christ could speak these words of huge import to her, 'henceforth sin no more,' in this way summoning in her all possible powers of courage and trust for a new life.

From what has been described, it may be clear why anxious bishops once wished to remove this story from the gospel. Evidently, a deeper knowledge was no longer available at the time. In our century, Rudolf Steiner's insights have made it accessible to us once again. He gave special attention to this passage in the New Testament. Without this kind of deepening of our knowledge, it is possible that people could find this story lacking in a sufficiently serious attitude to guilt. As we have seen, this is not the case at all. Christ inscribes in the earth what he has determined to take upon himself through the approaching sacrifice upon Golgotha. He looks upon the woman with his divine gaze. And finally, in a phrase of full confidence, imbued with divine trust and the compelling obligation accompanying it, he raises her profoundly traumatised soul, showing that here God places his full trust in the human being and in the good that lies within us despite all sinfulness.

10

CHRIST AT THE FESTIVAL OF DEDICATION OF THE TEMPLE

CHRISTMAS THEMES IN THE GOSPEL OF JOHN

In the three years of Jesus Christ's earthly sojourn as recounted by the gospels, there is only one episode that occurs at the time of Christmas. This is to be found in John's Gospel (10:22–39).

It is preceded by the autumn Festival of Tabernacles or Succoth, which, with its significant Christ revelations, takes a whole three and a half chapters of the Gospel of John (7:1–10:21). The account relates to the autumn of the year 32, and is thus the last autumn festival before Golgotha. The evangelist leaves the intervening period unmentioned, so that his autumn section is immediately followed by the last Christmas before Golgotha.

The Festival of Dedication of the temple

'Then the Festival of Dedication was celebrated in Jerusalem. It was winter.' (Jn 10:22). The Greek word for 'Festival of Dedication' here is *enkainia* or 'renewal'. What does this 'renewal' signify? We can recall that the temple, built by Solomon in the tenth century BC, was destroyed by the Babylonians in 586 BC, then rebuilt between 520 and 516 after the return of the Jewish people from exile. In the year 168 BC, Antiochus Epiphanes gave this second temple over to the Hellenic rites. The 'true gods of Greece' were no longer being worshipped at that time. Antiochus of Syria gave himself the appellation of 'Epiphanes' – epiphany or divine manifestation, occupying with his cult of rulership the place that belonged to the approaching, true God-made-man. But as a result of this Hellenic episode, the date of the new birth of the sun each year – the point where, at its winter nadir, it begins to strengthen again for a new ascent – found its way into the Jewish calendar of feasts.

It came about like this: the Hellenists, in their sun worship, started their temple year at the winter solstice. After three years, the Maccabees recaptured the temple and rededicated it to the Jewish rites on the same date. This is described in the First Book of Maccabees (4:36–59). A new altar and new ritual items were procured. 'And they placed the incense upon the altar and lit the lights upon the candelabra'; and here it is expressly added 'and they let its shining *(ephainon)* appear in the temple'. This rededication was such a striking experience that each year subsequently it was celebrated again. The relighting of the candles was connected with the seasonal motif of sunlight reborn in the depths of winter. The Jewish author Josephus wrote near the end of the first Christian century that the rededication 'excited such great rejoicing that a law was made according to which, in future, the renewal of the temple would be celebrated for eight whole days. This festival we have celebrated since that time right up to today and we call it the Festival of Lights' (*Ant.* XII 7.7). Apart from the temple itself, synagogues and dwellings were lit up too. Still today, during this winter period, the eight Chanukah candles are lit. Chanukah means 'renewal', and is etymologically related to the name Enoch.

The Old Testament religion bears a strong element of moonlike spirituality. We might see it as a kind of providential gift that, before the Christ sun ever appeared within the body of the earth, the Christmas sun-birth was incorporated into the moon-related Jewish rites in this Festival of Lights, via an unlikely detour through the great adversary Antiochus Epiphanes.

When the Christ, incarnated in the body of Jesus, appeared at this Festival of Lights in Jerusalem, this marked a moment of profound fulfilment and, likewise, a prophetic event that casts its illumination far into the future. Christ's inhabiting of the temple of the human body signifies the true temple dedication, and at the same time the true renewal of light. 'And Jesus walked within the temple courts in Solomon's Portico' (Jn 10:23).

Solomon's Portico

This is the only time that the name of Solomon appears in John's Gospel. Solomon was responsible for building the original temple which, as we mentioned, was destroyed in 586 BC. But a small portion of the buildings survived the Babylonian fire: the pillared hall, which remained as a testimony to the time of Solomon and was therefore given the name Solomon's Portico. Josephus writes of it: 'The eastern hall was a colonnade running along the temple's exterior, beside a deep chasm ... the portico was made of very white blocks of stone; this was the work of King Solomon.' (*Ant.* XX 9.7). This hall had not only been spared the ravages of the Babylonians but also the luxurious, grandiose conversion that King Herod had ordered for the modest, second temple. The conversion works began in 20 BC, and by the time of the Christ events were more or less complete ('the building of the temple took 46 years,' Jn 2:20) but not entirely finished. The work continued until AD 63, thus until shortly before the temple was finally completely destroyed by the Romans in the year 70. Through the magnificent splendour of Herod's reign, the temple had become a world-famous landmark, but this outer pomp and wealth was matched by an inner impoverishment and the emptiness of rites of worship no longer apt for the time.

We might imagine that Christ felt this portico, which dated back to the time of Solomon, as a fitting place for him to be. This is also no doubt why the first Christian community used this colonnade as a place to gather (Ac 5:12) and why Peter gave an important address there.

'I and the father are one'

When, at Christmas time in the year 32, Jesus 'walked' in this portico, the Jews formed a circle around him. Hermann von Skerst expressed it as follows:

> Do the Jews experience him as the centre of a sphere of
> light that is not of this world? At all events, they feel the
> extraordinary nature of his appearance, otherwise they would

not have surrounded him in a throng and asked, 'For how
long will you keep our soul hovering?' They feel as if they have
been lifted out of the level of their daily existence.*

And it is now that Christ makes the inimitable statement, 'I and the Father are one.' From an earthly human body speaks an I that does not cover over the divine Father in self-involved fashion, but fully reveals him through his selfless I-hood. And by virtue of this, the temple of the human body experiences its full 'dedication'. This does not mean a dissolving of the self into the divine, but a mystic union of two beings in one. This is not to say, either, that Christ and the Father would be 'one and the same', but it is a harmony of the two in free, mutual devotion. The neutral word 'one' (in the neuter form) is, for John, not a denominator less than the person, a sub-personal something, but lies rather at a higher level. The 'I am' within the divine 'we' undergoes still further enhancement and elevation; and this will come to further unfolding in the High Priestly Prayer. Here, for the first time, the Johannine 'one' stands in the Christmas illumination of the Festival of Lights.

In tragic form we witness earthly humanity's alienation from the divine by the fact that this culmination of Christ's self-revelation is answered by the impulse to stone him to death. Is it accidental that the motif of stoning in the New Testament specifically appears in relation to the period of autumn and winter? (Autumn: Jn 8:5, 8:59, winter: 10:31. The stoning of Stephen, according to tradition, fell on December 26.) The cold, dead, hard stone is the expression of 'wintry' counterforces that seek to turn the human heart to stone. These are powers which, as the Edda sees it, are represented in blind Hodr who killed Baldur and so initiated the 'great winter'.

The evangelist John here shows how conscientiously his account deals with earthly circumstances. At the first attempt to stone Christ in the autumn, he wrote, 'They lifted up stones to cast them at him' (8:59). Since the conversion works of Herod's time had not been fully completed, there may have been stones lying around in the temple grounds which needed only to be picked up by those intent on stoning. But in Solomon's Portico, which was untouched by the

* 'Ein Weihnachstfest im Johannes-Evangelium' in *Die Christengemeinschaft*, 1950, p. 272.

conversion, there were no stones lying about, and they needed first to 'bring them' for that purpose (10:31).* That is how careful and precise the evangelist is.

The 'beautiful works'

Christ replies by speaking of the 'beautiful works' – the literal translation of *kala erga* – that he has done (10:32). The word *kalos*, 'beautiful' (usually translated as 'good') is found seven times in the John's Gospel. It is used for the good wine, 'kept back until now', at the marriage at Cana (2:10, twice). Then for the 'good shepherd' who, in the Greek, is called the 'beautiful' shepherd (10:11, twice, 10:14); and only here is it used for the 'good works' (10:32, 10:33). This is almost untranslatable. The Latin text makes do with the word *bonus* (good). But even if we use the word 'good' here, instead of 'beautiful', it is important to know that the original text refers here to divine 'beauty' in a sacred sense. We find something similar in Mark (7:37) after the healing of the deaf-mute, 'He has done all things beautifully.' In terms of the divine, the truly good is also truly beautiful. In the 'beautiful works', an element of divine artistry is revealed.

Christ 'shows' these beautiful works. 'Showing' was, in those days, a technical term in the language of the mysteries, and signified the turning of the gaze towards higher vision. Thus Philip asks, 'Show us the Father.' And, in the same way, Christ says that in his works he follows what the Father 'shows' (Jn 5:20). And now, for his part, he 'shows' human beings the 'beautiful works' which he performs before them 'out of the Father' (10:32).

'You are gods'

The Jews reply that they wish to stone him because 'you, as a man, make yourself into God'. In this back-and-forth, Christ now speaks again for the third time. Once again, he utters something singular

---

* Translations often do not differentiate between the two Greek different words, *airō* (picking up) and *bastazō* (bringing), to which Frieling is no doubt referring.

10. CHRIST AT THE FESTIVAL OF DEDICATION

and inimitable, from which a Christmas-like radiance issues: 'You are gods.'

This astonishing remark is initially introduced as a quotation from Psalm 82. There God holds the judges on earth to account for failing to live up to their high office. In ancient Israel, the judges who held power of life and death over their fellow human beings were called 'Elohim' or 'gods' (Ex 22:8). People had a deep sense that no one should sit in judgment over their fellow human beings as a private person. But when the council of appointed judges met together, it could become an organ of judgment and justice superior to human judgment. We still have the last vestiges of this sense in the special clothing worn by judges who make their verdict 'in the name' of a superior authority. In ancient times, human beings were more open to the higher world, and a higher nature could sometimes indwell them. Thus, it was not felt to contradict monotheism to give the name of 'gods' to judges inspired from above. People could be 'gods' by participating in the being of the one God. Christ uses here another unique expression, that 'to such people occurred *(egeneto)* the Word *(Logos)* of God'. Thus, the human being is fundamentally receptive to the divine. At certain moments the divine filled the elevated god-men of ancient times.

In the case of Christ, something greater is at work. He is not only a human being open to the divine, 'to whom the Logos occurs,' but he himself is this Logos. How much more, therefore, is he entitled to claim divinity and name himself the 'Son of God' since the Father has 'sanctified him and sent him into the world' (Jn 10:36). The Father has 'sent' him: here the door to a previous spirit existence in worlds of eternity opens to the retrospective gaze, looking back before his entry into earthly life. And still deeper in these eternal worlds lies the process, 'sanctified by the Father', that preceded Christ's mission. Nowhere else is this said in the same way. An intimation is awoken of a sublime occurrence within divine being, that preceded Christ's descent to earth as a prologue in heaven. Once again we hear the tone of Christmas.

In quoting Psalm 82, Christ at the same time appropriates the formulation found there: 'You are gods.' In doing so he takes up the primordial will of the Creator that the human being should be God's 'image and likeness'. When the serpent in Paradise insinuated into the still childlike human soul the promise that 'you will be as gods', this was not an original intuition but a kind of distortion of God's true aim, an abuse of man's unripe soul. Now Christ seeks to re-appropriate this 'being like God' from the Adversary and win it back for divine and truly human purposes.

It is clear from the whole context that this cannot signify a 'statement of fact' of what already holds true. The people who are surrounding him at this moment during the Festival of Lights have become so far distant from God that they respond to their encounter with God-become-man with the desire to stone him. The cosmic winter, with its spiritual darkness and soul coldness, has gained great ascendancy over the earth – winter without Christmas. Nevertheless, the phrase, 'You are gods,' resounds over wintry, frozen and hardened humanity like the promise of a future in which the deed of Golgotha (which, at this Festival of Dedication, has not yet occurred) will bear its fruit. In human beings lies the germ of higher life that can be long buried in the depths but is still there, awaiting its hour. The First Letter of John (3:9) speaks of the 'seed of God' in us. 'You are gods.' This stands as a bright Christmas star, full of promise, over the deep darkness of the human world.

Christ's address ends with an appeal to the power of light in the human being, to 'knowledge': 'so that you know, and know ever more, that the Father is within me and I in the Father' (Jn 10:38). The repetition of the word 'know' is unique here. To 'know, and know ever more' points to a process that is beginning. The soul warmth that in past times so naturally issued from the festival of Christmas is increasingly being lost nowadays. The warmth that saves us from the icy, deadly cold of winter will only be regained when people recognise that Christmas is truly a Festival of Lights. In all three Christmas Acts of Consecration we are, in a distinctive way, called upon to 'know'.

In the final sentence of Christ's Christmas-heralding address, truth is shown to be the focus and object of this 'knowing, and knowing ever more': 'The Father is in me and I am in the Father.' The Father in the I, and the I in the Father. What appears to be a contradiction in purely logical terms becomes true as soon as it is understood as a living process, as the rhythmic exchange of inbreath and outbreath. The phrase 'I and the Father are one' undergoes a further enlargement by encompassing life's movement.

Christmas not only signifies the birth of Jesus at Bethlehem. Behind it appears the birth, within the divine realm, of the eternal Son from the eternal Father. It signifies also, as we live into the future, the birth of Christ within the human soul, whereby we will one day be encompassed by the mysteries that play between Father and Son, by the illumining light and the warming love of the Holy Spirit. Without Christ, humanity would succumb to winter, winter without Christmas, signifying darkness, cold and death.

II

THREE PREDICTIONS OF THE PASSION

The deed of redemption on Golgotha includes not only the passion and death but also the resurrection. The death and resurrection of Christ are indivisibly bound together and form the Mystery of Golgotha. That is not all, however. More careful consideration reveals that yet a third element is involved. The full effect of the death and resurrection of Christ depends upon whether they are really taken to heart by humanity. To the death and resurrection there must be added the third element of their becoming manifest to humanity.

This can be brought about by the Holy Spirit, which can so illumine consciousness that the event of Golgotha permeates the thinking, feeling and will of Christians.

If we want to gain some idea of this illumination by the Holy Spirit, it can be helpful to look also at what is contained in the gospels as a sort of negative picture of it.

Matthew, Mark and Luke hand down to us what are called the predictions of the passion. There are certainly also isolated hints, but the three predictions of the passion have something like a religious solemnity in their foretelling of the event of Golgotha. They indicate how important it was for Christ that at least a small circle of people should be prepared for it with understanding and empathy when it happened. The predictions of the passion, which also already include the resurrection, are meant to serve that 'becoming manifest' mentioned above. But, tragically, they do not find the right response. The Holy Spirit is able to work directly for mankind only after Golgotha, from Pentecost on. Thus, each time a lack of understanding follows the predictions – the opposite of what should have been enlightenment.

11. THREE PREDICTIONS OF THE PASSION

The *first* prediction of the passion takes place in about the last summer of Christ's ministry. In time as well as place this is a long way from Golgotha. Christ is making a lonely journey with the disciples that has led them into the north, to the foothills of the snow-covered Mount Hermon in the region of Caesarea Philippi. After being absorbed in prayer on his own (Lk 9:18), Christ questions the disciples about who he is. Who do people say I am? What do *they* say? Peter is then inspired to say something, the import of which he himself is unable to see. 'You are the Christ, the Son of the living God' (Mt 16:16). Then, as if to say, 'now you shall also understand what you have said,' Christ proceeds to the first foretelling of his passion. Withdrawn from the world, in time and place still far from Golgotha, he reveals to the disciples the principle of the divine necessity of suffering. It is a 'must' of a higher kind: he 'must' go to Jerusalem and there 'suffer many things.' The authorities will reject and condemn him. He will be killed and rise again on the third day.

In answer to this on the part of the disciples there is only Peter's reaction. It is one of aversion. Though he has just been privileged to speak the glorious confession, he has now sunk back again into his still unchanged, all too human nature. He therefore protests: 'Lord, far be it for this to happen to you' (Mt 16:22).

A week later, Peter, together with two other disciples, is privileged to be a witness to the transfiguration. Soon after that – now in Galilee (Mt 17:22) – there follows the *second* prediction. It has a different character from the first. The remoteness of Mount Hermon has been left behind, and in Galilee we come closer to the arena of the forthcoming event. The second prediction is the shortest. It does not go into the kind of suffering, but includes the whole passion in the expression that the Son of Man 'is to be delivered into the hands of men'. In Luke's version this is, in fact, the only statement in this prediction (Lk 9:44). In the transfiguration, Christ Jesus had shone as the living monstrance, as the host irradiated by the sun. Now the second prediction of his passion introduces the picture of human hands reaching out for this host – though here are meant the hands of murderers. But if the sinful hands had not murderously seized the Saviour, there would not have been the possibility for human beings to receive into their hands the host, the bread as the body of

Christ, through the Eucharist – therein lies the paradox of the deed of Golgotha. It is this very picture of the Saviour 'delivered into the hands of men' that Christ wants to impress upon the feelings of his disciples.

Luke has a special sense for nuances of feeling, for mysteries of the soul. It is he who paints the picture of Mary, who preserves Christ's saying about hearing as a fructifying of the soul (8:10, 8:15, 11:28), and who records the saying, 'Take heed how you hear' (8:18). Thus there is a special ring to it when the Gospel of Luke introduces the second prediction of the passion with the words, 'Let these words sink into your ears.' Yet the expected empathetic understanding is lacking. 'But they did not understand this saying, and it was concealed from them, that they should not perceive it, and they were afraid to ask him about this saying' (9:45). The disciples could not 'perceive' this saying. Matthew supplements this. 'And they were greatly distressed' is the way he describes the disciples' reaction to this second prediction (17:23). Instead of the appropriate understanding that can boldly face the tragedy of the passion and death since it is able to rise to the super-earthly joy of the resurrection, instead of this strength of feeling to cope with the very depths and heights of feeling, there proceeds from their inadequate response only a dull and paralysing general misery.

The *third* prediction of the passion occurs very close in place and time to what has been foretold. Christ is going up to Jerusalem to his last Passover and is already in Judea, near Jericho.

It is always the case with foreseeing that the pictures become more detailed and precise the nearer the coming event approaches. The third prediction therefore already contains details of being delivered up to the Gentiles, that is to the Romans, the specific features of being mocked and spat upon, the scourging, and, for the first time (if we follow Matthew) also the manner of death in the form of crucifixion (20:19). 'Everything will be accomplished' (Lk 18:31). It is all characterised by an element of will. 'Behold, we are going up to Jerusalem.' Mark describes Christ's heroic walking ahead whilst his disciples follow with trepidation (Mk 10:32). This time, however, the disciples' powers of perception are even more clouded than before. This is expressed in a threefold way by Luke: 'But they understood none of these things; the matter was hidden from them, and they did not grasp what was said' (Lk 18:34). The lack of understanding never sounded so complete. The disciples 'understood' nothing – in Greek this suggests, 'they could not put it together'. They could not intellectually grasp it: they were unable to put death and resurrection together in one picture. They could not combine all this with the ideas of Christ they had formed until then. It remains 'hidden' from them. Finally, that unique and impressive word for 'grasp', *ginōskein*. But negative: 'they did not grasp ...'

From this negative counter-image it can become clear what we hope for from the Holy Spirit. It will make this understanding possible. Then nothing remains 'hidden', but the hidden mystery is able to become an open mystery; for it remains a mystery even when it is understood, indeed all the more so. Just as the better I know a person the more, not less, of a mystery they become to me. Then, too, enlightened by the Spirit, we are able to unite in our souls the apparently incompatible agony of death and glory of resurrection. Then paralysing sadness is replaced by Easter joy, the rejoicing in spirit, if the soul can immerse itself in the event of Golgotha and experience it as it is worthy of being experienced. Then, finally, the resistance to suffering is replaced by the joyful readiness to carry the cross as a follower of Christ, in order to participate in the agony of his passion and death and in his resurrection.

Through the Holy Spirit, the disciples' threefold failure over the predictions of the passion can gradually be made good and changed into its opposite. The event of Golgotha can only be fully effective if it is seen as comprising the trinity of Christ's passion, his resurrection and his becoming manifest.

12

SURRENDERING TO DESTINY

JOHN 12:20–36

John was the only one of the evangelists to recall the moment when Greeks from the throng of Passover pilgrims approached Christ in Jerusalem (12:20). That these travellers from afar ask for him, and 'wish to see him', signals his destiny to him: 'The hour is come when the Son of Man will be glorified.' As long as he walks the earth as Rabbi Jesus in the earthly body he assumed at the Jordan baptism, he is subject to the limitations of space and time that follow from a material body. Initially he has importance only for those whose destiny has led them to him in that land. But he descended from the divine world to be there for all people. Transformation of his existence is necessary: through resurrection and ascension he is endowed with the universality that enables him to come close to all human beings, and indeed to indwell them. But the price of this is death. God, who comes from a world of abundant life, far from death and alien to it, must seek out the death of earthly humankind. Only by virtue of this does he become entirely as we are, as the ultimate consequence of his assuming a physical body. The announcements of his suffering, which he has repeatedly expressed, have shown that he is consciously pursuing this death, and that he has come to Jerusalem at the Passover festival as if to this decisive Passover of death. Now the approach of the Greeks shows him that the 'hour is come'. He utters the law of 'dying and becoming' in the image of the grain of wheat that, remaining just a single seed if it does not fall into the earth and die, multiplies fruitfully if it does so (12:24).

But now, something wholly unexpected occurs. Seemingly involuntarily the phrase comes from his mouth, 'Now my soul is shaken, and what shall I say? Father, save me from this hour.' (12:27).

12. SURRENDERING TO DESTINY

How else can we understand this than as a flinching, a retreat, a trepidation before this hour that is arriving? What has happened in him? In speaking of the grain of wheat that falls into the earth he clearly has not been speaking only in terms of a general wisdom, as a guru might dispense it in relaxed composure. In this picture he suddenly has before him a direct experience of his own destiny, and it strikes him with all its force. Before him whose home is in light and life, the dark 'grave of the earth' opens wide. But isn't such flinching incomprehensible given that hitherto he has been consciously pursuing this same destiny?

At the age of 33, not long before he died, the poet Heinrich von Kleist wrote 'The Prince of Homburg'. The prince can truly be thought a saint. He has shown fearless courage on the battlefield. But now, condemned by a court of war, and expecting to be executed, he suddenly succumbs to a terrible fear of death: 'On the road ... I saw opening in the light of burning torches the grave that tomorrow was to receive my bones.' Incomprehensible? The poet shows the prince to be someone who possesses not only a hero's courage, but also a keen sensitivity of soul beyond the 'normal'. Heinrich von Kleist was very familiar with the realms of experience that, as opposed to everyday consciousness, can be called the 'night side of soul life'. This is apparent time and again in his works. What the prince succumbs to at the sight of the opened grave is not 'common fear' – which he, as a brave man, is superior to – but something like a primal chill that he could feel only because he possessed heightened sensitivity. This is the primordial terror of the soul that, originating in higher regions of light, finds itself in the moribund earthly body with which its experience is so closely bound up.

I have quoted this account by Kleist not because I think an easy comparison can be drawn here with Christ's experience. The Christ event unfolds at a unique and very much loftier level. Yet this poem can still direct our thoughts in a certain direction, and perhaps give us a distant inkling of what John describes. John is the evangelist who, with his spiritual eagle's eye, can see furthest up into the divine world, but who also, on the other hand, is capable of looking back down again to the physical, earthly plane and seeing it most clearly and exactly. We can see this in his Prologue, where he encompasses both above and below in the sentence, 'And the Word became flesh.' He is fully imbued with the conviction that God did not simply clothe and disguise himself temporarily in human appearance, but that in Jesus he truly 'entered as man into the earthly world,' as it says in the Creed of The Christian Community. It is part of this complete immersion in human nature that the God – far more intensively still than any other person, since he is aware of his heavenly being – feels this primordial horror of death as something completely other and alien to him.

The translation, 'Now is my soul troubled,' is too weak. The word in Greek points to an earthquake-like convulsion of Christ's soul. We hear the One who is the universal Word utter the words, 'And what shall I say?' It is as if the whole world suddenly stood still in divine perplexity at this moment. But now Christ regathers himself in prayer: 'Father, save me from this hour.' The content of this prayer is still trembling with the uncertainty of the question preceding it, 'What shall I say?' The word 'Father' is decisive. In not only speaking this petitioning prayer but also at the same time 'enacting' it, he turns to address the highest and ultimate reality. No doubt there have been pious people who found that, though their prayer for the prevention of approaching misfortune was not 'heard', nevertheless their turning to the divine in itself brought about an inner change, giving them a deep peace and a trusting willingness to embrace destiny. We see this here in the highest sense.

And now Christ says, *But on account of this I came to this hour.* What has happened here between the lines? The 'But' means nothing less than that Christ relinquishes his plea to be saved from his fate. In turning to the Father, the troubling cloud of primal horror that rose in the face of the opening abyss, and for a fearful moment hid his clear insight into necessity, has been swept away. By turning to the Father, Christ is led to his own source, the fount and origin of his Son nature. Once again he becomes fully aware of himself as the Son proceeding from the Father, and so finds harmonious accord again with his primal and eternal will, which has led him to 'this hour'. 'But on account of this I came to this hour.'

In our materialistic age, it is often thought that we are 'dealt a hand' of destiny without our knowledge or agreement. Sometimes people say things like, 'I never asked to live this life of mine.' To be 'dealt' a hand presupposes someone who deals it out to you, but few acknowledge this. Christ does not feel he has been 'dealt a hand' but

12. SURRENDERING TO DESTINY

knows that he was 'sent by the Father'. Nevertheless, this mission does not mean he has been dispatched without his will and is governed by motives not his own. He speaks equally of his 'having come' as well as 'being sent'. In the interrogation by Pilate, for instance, he says: 'I was born and came into the world to bear witness to the truth' (Jn 18:37). Being sent does not exclude the possibility of his 'coming' at the same time upon his own intrinsic mission. Here, being sent and coming, being given a mission and willing it himself, become one.

In taking hold of himself once again, he can transform his original plea to be saved and give his petitioning prayer a final form, *'Father, glorify your name'* (12:28). The 'name' we accord a being should sum up, encompass and encapsulate what we have come to know of this being. God, as the ultimate reality, cannot be consciously encompassed by any term and in this sense he is 'nameless'. But revelation continually issues from his archetypal being, giving ever greater clarity to his 'name'. The pre-Christian world's awareness of God now undergoes a decisive enlargement through the revelation in Christ Jesus, who, in the High Priestly Prayer, sums up his works in the words, 'I have manifested your name' (Jn 17:6). It is in this light that the Christ now sees his 'hour', and no longer seeks to be relieved of it. His prayer asks only that in passing through this hour the bright radiance of the divine name may become reality.

Let us look once more at this whole prayer's three brief sentences, between the lines of which such mighty things occur:

> Father, save me from this hour.
> But on account of this I came to this hour.
> Father, bring your name to still brighter radiance!

The spiritual reality of this prayer is so powerful that it calls down the answering voice from the heavenly world, 'I have revealed its [my name's] glory and will reveal its glory again' (12:28). The surrounding crowd senses the moment's import. Depending on their degree of sensitivity to supersensible impressions, some say 'it thundered' and others that 'an angel spoke to him' (12:29). Both are true. The event of this prayer caused something like an apocalyptic tempest, and an angelic being, as messenger, bore the divine word downward. But only the Christ grasps the highest level of what has occurred and hears the speech of the Father. At this point the word 'now' resounds again in the mouth of Christ. No longer, 'Now is my soul shaken,' but this 'now' of the arriving hour is like the flaming lightning of the apocalyptic storm: *'Now* the crisis comes upon the world. *Now* the prince of this world will be cast out' (12:31). With the sacrifice of Golgotha, a process is set in motion that will gradually push the Adversary – who has been able to become the wrongful 'prince of this world' through the failings of fallen man – out of the world again. Thus, the world misappropriated from the divine, creative powers can, by sacrifice, once again be returned to it.

The approach of the Greeks has turned Christ's gaze beyond his contemporaries in that land to the whole of humanity. Now, after the event of this prayer, the certainty stands before his soul that 'when I shall be lifted up from the earth, I will draw *all* people to myself' (12:32). This word 'draw' does not suggest compulsion but a decision of the heart which they can follow in freedom or also deny themselves.

This prayer-deed of Christ in the face of the hour that has come, can also shed light upon our own destiny. As we consider this archetypal moment in the gospel, we can also realise that however great the distance between our own I and the great I of Christ, we too are not 'cast' pointlessly into our hour of destiny. We too were in a higher world before this earthly existence, and were sent to earth from that existence. In this pre-earthly existence we also united ourselves with a divine mission in the sense that it was our decision to 'come' into this present incarnation. The complaint, 'Why am I here? Did anyone ask me if I wished to be here?' springs only from a superficial awareness. In the depths of our being we know about our pre-birth decision to embark upon this very life. Such deep knowledge, though, is repeatedly overlaid and deadened by everything that throngs about us here. When we study the gospel, what we have forgotten can be reawoken again. Whenever something hard or grave faces us, it should become possible for us to say, 'But on account of this I came to this hour.'

13

CHRIST JESUS' PRAYERS IN SECLUSION

As human beings we participate in two worlds at once, the visible and the invisible, and our task is to rightly combine both worlds. If we give our attention only to the realm of earthly visibility, we risk losing our soul to materiality. If we should seek to turn to the invisible realm alone, on the other hand, we would fail in our earthly task and become distant from the world.

The Christ truly became man in Jesus of Nazareth. He was there as helper for his fellow human beings and for their earthly plight. But he also needed to be alone, to withdraw inwardly to fill himself time and again with heavenly powers that flowed into his work on earth. What follows will explore this a little.

The experience of the Jordan baptism signified such a mighty influx into the consciousness and configuration of the being of Jesus of Nazareth that he needed some time to find his way into his new existence. He could not immediately begin his mission. For forty days he remained alone in the desert.

The evangelists here use expressions that can strike us as being almost at odds with the nature of Christ. According to Matthew (4:1), 'Jesus was led up by the spirit' from the Jordan basin into the mountains of Judea. According to Luke (4:1), he departed from the Jordan 'full of the Holy Spirit and was led by the spirit in the desert'. He 'was led' – the Greek imperfect indicates something longer-lasting, something that keeps recurring. We might say, 'He was driven hither and thither in the desert,' but this was not by the compulsions of restlessness or anxiety as we know them. What made Christ wander to and fro was the wealth, the abundant superfluity of the spirit pouring into him. He has not yet come to inner tranquillity: the spirit surging in him is at risk of bursting the narrow vessel of his human nature. The evangelist

Mark expresses this with a drastic violence: The spirit 'hurled him out into the desert' (1:12). Nowhere else do the gospels speak of Jesus in this way, of passively 'being led', even of being 'hurled'. We know him otherwise only as the sovereign master of his actions and his sufferings, in the tranquillity and majesty of his 'I am'.

Clearly this inner mastery must first be acquired after the Jordan baptism. The baptised one needs to withdraw for those forty days to come to terms fully with what has occurred. And it is precisely because the baptism experience is not yet fully integrated, and his inner state has not yet stabilised again, that he experiences the Adversary's temptations which, according to Matthew and Luke, extend throughout that time – until, finally, the three great temptations have been dismissed. Even the fact that Christ here cites ancient scripture – 'It is written that ...' – shows us that the fullness of the spirit is not yet fully encompassed by the I, and Christ does not yet speak in his full sovereignty.

But from then on, after the victory has been achieved, such 'passive' expressions no longer occur. Now 'Jesus went in the power of the spirit to Galilee' (Lk 4:14).

Flight on Sunday morning

We now see, in an especially striking way, Jesus walking and acting in the mastery of spiritual fullness. On the evening of that first, remarkable Sabbath at Capernaum, the 'whole city' (Mk 1:33) streams to the door of the house where he is staying – probably the house of Peter – with the sick and possessed, and 'he healed them all'.

Next, there occurs that singular moment the following morning, thus Sunday morning, when Christ 'arises' at a very early hour while all are still sleeping and deep darkness still holds sway. Mark uses the same word as for the resurrection: he 'arises', goes 'out' of the house and goes 'away' to a lonely spot where he prays. 'Out – away': it sounds like a flight. In keeping with that image, Mark uses the word 'pursued' in describing how Peter and the others seek him.

This remarkable and vividly described moment is a picture from that initial period when the equilibrium Jesus has achieved seems as yet fragile and volatile. This sudden withdrawal after the mighty expenditure of strength the day before possesses a quality of great urgency. Christ procures for himself the prayerful seclusion he needs, even if those around him do not understand this.

Luke, who describes the same occurrence in much less dramatic terms than Mark, gives in the following chapter an indication that, between his exertions, Christ repeatedly seeks periods to be alone and pray (5:16). Once again, the Greek imperfect tense points to something continually recurring.

The night of inspirations

Before Christ chooses the twelve disciples from the throng following him – the circle of apostles that is an earthly reflection of the zodiac encircling the sun – he passes the whole night in prayer upon the mountain. Simply 'the mountain' is referred to. The important thing here is the experience of elevation to a higher consciousness. He went 'out' to pray upon the mountain and 'passed the night in the worship of God' (Lk 6:12). Literally, he was 'night-imbued'. With the power of spiritual will he sustained this elevation to the divine for the whole period of the night. The 'worship of God' allowed heavenly powers to flow into him, which could replace the recuperation a night's sleep otherwise brings. 'When it was day, he called the disciples to him, and from them chose twelve to whom he gave the name apostles.'

Thus the creation of the circle of twelve has its prologue in heaven. From the star worlds of the Father, Christ draws in secluded prayer the inspiration of destiny that enables him to make the right choice the following morning.

The feeding of the five thousand

The twelve are sent out in twos. When they return, Christ says, 'Each of you go to a secluded place and rest a little' (Mk 6:31). 'For there was a coming and going of many, and they did not even find time to eat.' Thus they journey with Christ over the Sea of Galilee and seek a secluded place where they are 'entirely alone'. The Greek *kat' idian* means that they here come to 'their own', to what is 'intrinsic' to them.

They are initiated into inner practices. The uninterrupted demands from without would otherwise deplete and exhaust them. In the Greek word for 'rest', the word 'pause' is contained, here with the prefix *ana,* or 'upward'. They are to seek a truly 'creative pause', opening themselves upward.

Thus in John, too, we hear that, 'He ascended the mountain and there he was sitting with his disciples' (6:3). The outward ascent was at the same time an inner elevation, and their sitting down together something like a meditation. Christ is now far from being driven hither and thither by a superfluity of spirit: in this 'sitting down', which, for ancient people, always possessed a festive dignity, a sense of enthronement, the self-resting inwardness of the great I AM is expressed, in which the disciples are to participate. The closeness of the Festival of Passover gives a special context to this moment.

From this sitting together upon the mountain, Christ descends with the disciples for the feeding of the five thousand. Through the 'upward' communion, he is now able to call down the life forces of the stars upon the small quantity of earthly bread so that people can eat their fill 'through the giving of thanks to the Lord'.

Following the feeding, Christ returns to the same mountain, this time alone. 'He dismissed the crowd and ascended the mountain wholly by himself [fully entering into his own, coming to himself] to pray' (Mt 14:23). According to John, 'He withdrew once again to the mountain, he himself alone' (6:15).

This withdrawal, this resting in the centre of his I, is what enables him to walk upon the waters, during which Christ reveals his supersensible being – his I AM – to the disciples.

The key also to the later feeding of the four thousand lies in the reference to his preceding elevation upon the mountain: 'He went along the Sea of Galilee and having ascended the mountain, he was sitting there' (Mt 15:29).

The transfiguration

The gospel narrative now leads increasingly towards the passion. Christ has decided to initiate the disciples into what awaits him. He takes them with him on a long walk, high into the north, to the sources of the Jordan in the snow-clad Mount Hermon. Close to Caesarea Philippi he asks them what the people, and what they themselves, think of him. This question sets off a whole series of events: Peter's avowal, the first words about Christ's forthcoming suffering, the admonition to Peter, who dreads to think about this suffering, Christ's urging of them to follow him and bear his cross. We stand at a turning point in the three years between the Jordan baptism and Golgotha. Before initiating all that follows with his question, Christ withdraws for secluded prayer. 'And it happened that when he was praying alone, his disciples were together with him and he asked them, "Who do the people say that I am?"' (Lk 9:18). It sounds as if this withdrawal and seclusion lasted for a longer period, and was interrupted from time to time by his companionship with the disciples.

We can see an inner consistency in the fact that, a week later, in the 'octave' of this occurrence (Lk 9:28), he took the three chosen disciples with him when he ascended the mountain, where they witnessed his transfiguration. Once again he prays upon the mountain. This prayer is of such luminosity that the spirit not only irradiates the soul but streams on through the body and his garments. 'As he prayed' is the key for Luke (9:29). From his communion with the divine, Christ draws the strength to illumine his supersensible light form so strongly that it becomes visible to the disciples.

The Lord's Prayer

Not long after this, during the 'last walk to Jerusalem', Luke tells again of a withdrawal into secluded prayer (11:1). 'And it happened as he was praying, that he paused for a moment, and one of the disciples said to him, "Lord, teach us to pray".' The evangelist's brief reference to a 'pause' gives us insight into the actuality here. As Christ prays and communes for lengthy periods, there are moments when he pauses. In one of these, the request of a disciple who witnesses the praying causes Christ to give the Lord's Prayer to his followers.*

---

* To be accurate, we note here that in Luke this prayer is not yet given in its full, sevenfold form as we know it from the Sermon on the Mount at the beginning of Matthew's Gospel. In Luke, there are only five petitions, and in the address to the Father, 'our' is lacking, as is the reference to the worlds of heaven.

Luke has preserved the circumstances in which the diverse sayings of Christ were spoken. This is true also of the moment when the fundamental prayer of Christianity was revealed. Luke invites us to witness how this prayer, which later developed further into its full form as conveyed by Matthew, originates in Christ's experiences of deep contemplation.

Gethsemane

Christ's last withdrawal for secluded prayer bears the name of Gethsemane. Here again we find something that recalls the beginning, the inner wrestling in the desert after the baptism. The state of equilibrium required to be human on the earth, which the incarnating God had first to attain, is again in doubt during the night from Maundy Thursday to Good Friday. A light falls on the riddle of Gethsemane if we consider what Rudolf Steiner described out of his spirit vision: that the indwelling of a divine being in a sense burned and consumed the earthly body carrying it, and, by the time of the Passover festival in the year 33, had brought it close to death. At the Last Supper, Christ gave his life forces to the disciples; but they failed to find the right response to this surrender. Instead of closing the circle and, by staying with him, helping him to remain in his collapsing body, they succumbed to a dimming of awareness and left him abandoned. The ring of the twelve was broken; Judas went out into the night. Arriving in the garden, Christ had to dispense with a further eight disciples who, though they did not betray him, were in no way adequate to the challenge of the hour. The three trusted ones stay by him and, leaving the others behind, he goes with them deeper into the garden. Yet they too prove inadequate.

The evangelist Matthew describes most strikingly the stations of Christ's increasing loneliness. He presents us with three places which are at the same time places of the soul: first the place where the eight are left behind. 'Be seated here until I have departed and have prayed over there' (26:36); then the place of the three who continue with him. 'Stay here and watch with me.' In their prayerful accompaniment of him, they are to give him support for what he – distancing himself also now from the three as he goes deeper into the garden – must accomplish at the third place, which only he enters. But there he feels the lack of the prayers of these three flowing to him. And so he returns to them and seeks to awaken them. Again he prays alone in seclusion and again they fail him. Three times he goes back and forth in this way, the last time leaving the disciples asleep.

Luke, the physician, recounts this in a singular and distinctive way. He passes over the choosing of the three, as well as the three places in the garden. He speaks only of the group of disciples as a whole and of Christ separating from them (22:39–41). Yet, in describing Christ's passage into the depths of the garden, he uses an unusual expression. Rather than departing from them, Christ 'was dragged forth from them, a stone's throw away'. That he is 'dragged forth' from the disciples with such violence points to the death that is already prematurely beginning, that threatens to sunder him from his earthly human sheath. In this account it becomes apparent that what happens in Gethsemane is not a psychological crisis – terror of an earthly death – but the physiological crisis of a premature death and departure from the body. Christ is here battling not with a fear of death, but with death itself. His dying prematurely would prevent fulfilment of the divinely envisaged enactment of Good Friday, through to the death on the cross.

Luke knows of the angel who, in the place of the failing disciples, brings an influx of strength to the collapsing Christ. This strengthening by the angel enables Christ to pray still more fervently and to overcome the incipient agony which Luke, as a physician, understands (22:43f). In Gethsemane, therefore, we are truly concerned with the answering of a prayer.

The Letter to the Hebrews also speaks of a prayer answered: 'He was heard because of his surrender to destiny' (5:7).

The evangelist John keeps silence about these terrible things, but he describes Christ appearing from the darkness as conqueror and facing his captors with his 'I am he'. The words resound so mightily that they fall to the ground, overwhelmed by the self-founding power and authority that has been achieved in lonely prayer (18:6).

14

PETER'S DENIAL

One of the unforgettable incidents in the story of the passion is Peter's three denials of his master. It is astonishing how unreserved and open the gospels are in their account of the failure of a figure who enjoyed the very greatest respect among early Christians. But every serious reader of the gospels will realise from the outset that such failure gives us an unmistakable and archetypal picture of something that concerns us all and invites our self-examination – for 'that is you'. This immediate applicability of the story of the denial needs no further elaboration.

All four evangelists recount it. If we read each gospel in succession as they stand in the New Testament, then we read this story of the denial four times. And yet the impression this makes on us is more than that of mere repetition. Certainly, repetition is there, and, in view of the inexhaustible depths of the narrative, this can be felt as significant, a meaningful spiritual organism. But over and above this we become aware of how, in passing from one gospel to the next, new content accrues at each step, for each evangelist has his own perspective on the story.

The prediction

Christ said that Peter would deny him. According to Matthew, Mark and Luke, this happened as they were walking from the Last Supper to Gethsemane. Christ sees that the disciples' powers of consciousness are unable to contend with the 'atmospheric pressure' of the terrible approaching events. Peter resists such a thought. As on former occasions, he responds all too hastily, out of his depth and overrating himself: 'And if they all go astray from you, yet I will not.' Then comes the answer, 'Before the cock crows ...'. And Peter's rejoinder: 'Even if I should have to die with you ...' This is how the tale is told in Matthew (26:33–35) and Mark (14:29–31).

Luke adds a further, particular phrase addressed to Peter: that the Adversary has demanded him but that he, Christ, has prayed for him. Luke speaks more often than the other evangelists of Christ at prayer. Here again likewise. At the same time, Christ gazes beyond swiftly approaching events into the far future: he sees before him a Peter who has rediscovered himself and can now strengthen his brothers (22:31f).

John takes the prediction of the denial into the sacred sphere of the farewell addresses. Peter's presumption is kindled here in response to the motif of following. Peters hears only that he will *not* be able to follow Christ immediately on his path into the great mystery. In his eager impatience he fails to hear the words, 'You will follow me later' (13:36). Why not immediately? 'I will lay down my life for you,' Peter says. But the response from Christ are his words about the cock crowing: 'Before the cock crows, you will deny me three times' (13:38).

Here, in the context of the passion as told by John, we can sense that it is not a matter only of a disciple sharing his master's fate in true following. What is to happen at Golgotha is more than an ordinary death, however significant that might be. The disciple cannot penetrate into the 'spirit place' of this Golgotha Mystery. He cannot accompany Christ there now, but 'later' he will be able to bring it to life within him and then truly 'follow' his Lord.

The denial in Matthew and Mark

Already in Gethsemane it becomes apparent that, despite his fervent words, Peter, like the others, is overcome by the powers of this sinister night, which dim consciousness. 'Simon, are you asleep?' (Mk 14:37). But when Jesus is taken prisoner, we see him make an attempt at least to get a grip on himself. Misunderstanding his master, he draws his sword. Whereas the others have fled in disarray, he follows the crowd – though at a cautious distance – and arrives in the courtyard of the high priest's house. There he joins the guards who have arrested Jesus and who are waiting outside during the hearing of their captive. But he does not go unnoticed.

Matthew now describes the three denials, in swift succession and with increasing dramatic intensity. A maid says directly to his face that he 'was also with the Galilean, Jesus'. He denies it and withdraws into the darker part of the courtyard, near the portico building leading to the street. Questioned again, he reaffirms his denial a second time with an oath. Finally, when suspicion falls on him from those around him because of his Galilean speech, 'he began to swear and to curse: I do not know this man' (Mt 26:69–75).

'I do not know the man.' Twice, at the second and third denial, with gathering vehemence, Matthew clothes the denial in these specific words. Besides their self-evident meaning at that moment – the same as in Mark (14:71), when he has Peter avow, 'I do not know the man of whom you speak' – they surely also signify a far deeper dimension. In Matthew, this is underlined by the simple repetition of 'I do not know the man'. Whoever denies Christ, at the same time denies the 'human being'. And after all, the symbol assigned to the evangelist Matthew is that of the human being.

The account by Mark adds to this night-time scene an important pictorial element. He mentions the 'light' beside which Peter has sat down next to the guards to warm himself. If we only had Matthew's account, we would lack this Rembrandt-like aspect of the flickering light in the darkness.

Mark also reports a first warning cock-crow after the very first denial.

According to Luke

Luke expressly describes the kindling of the fire in the yard, in whose light the maid becomes aware of Peter. The third evangelist, who so often emphasises aspects of the story that speak to the soul, is the only one to preserve the moment when, as the cock crows, the Lord 'turned and looked upon Peter; then Peter remembered' (22:61). The words Richard Wagner has Kundry speak in *Parsifal* echo this: 'His gaze fell upon me.'

But surely Christ was inside the building, being interrogated? Was there a window? Luke suggests that, after the questioning was over, the prisoner was led out to the guards, who passed the time by mocking and maltreating him (22:63). There was, after all, an interval of time to occupy before the decisive official session of the full Sanhedrin could be held after dawn, as the regulations required (Mt 27:1, Mk 15:1, Lk 22:66). Christ's gaze may have fallen upon Peter during this interval.

In Luke, Peter's denial acquires a new form of words. Peter, in that context, expresses his second denial in the words 'I am not he' (22:58). In the Greek, 'he' is not there: *ouk eimi* means equally 'I am not he' and 'I am not' – or even just 'am not'. Naturally these words have their self-evident meaning in the context, but we can also hear the undertone of deeper meaning: 'am not'. With this motif of 'I am' we come close to the spiritual realm of the Gospel of John where the statement 'I am', and equally its opposite, finds very distinctive resonance.

According to John

In his account of the denial, John gives Peter nothing more at all to say than this 'am not', twice repeated (18:17, 25). By this means, he emphatically shifts the events into the I sphere. The I in its highest form is manifest in Christ. In Peter's denial, we perceive the weakness of the I as it is found in earthly human beings marked by the Fall.

A further distinctive aspect of the account by John is that he interrupts the story of the denial by interposing between these two 'am not' the preliminary hearing before Annas (which only figures in this gospel). The latter is the father-in-law of the current high priest Caiaphas, who succeeded him in this office. Christ is first led to him, the old high priest. John recounts how Christ replies in the full power of the I. In the Greek, the 'I' sounds emphatically three times and frames the whole hearing. '*I* have always spoken openly ... *I* have always taught ... these people know what *I* have said.'(18:20f) This contrasts with what precedes and follows it: the extinguished 'am not' of the denying Peter.

That the denials appear interrupted by the Annas hearing, in fact, does more justice to the actual historical course of events than the dramatic account given in Matthew, magnificent as it is in its own way. In reality, the different denials extended over a longer period of time. Already in Luke we notice an awareness of this, since he allows 'about an hour' to pass between the second and third denials. According to John, the longer pause intervened after the first denial.

It is to do with the distinctive nature of John that, on the one hand, as the 'eagle evangelist', he rises higher into the spiritual realm, but on the other also inclines downwards and encompasses the earthly plane with greater acuity than the other evangelists. In comparison with them, he is more precise in his details of space and time.

This penetration to the precise form of earthly, material processes, with their sequences and inner consistency, is also apparent at the beginning of the passage discussed here. John tells us more precisely how Peter gains entry to the courtyard of Caiaphas. An unnamed 'other disciple, who was known to the high priest' (18:15f) gained entry there for him. The 'maid' is more precisely named as Caiaphas' doorkeeper. After the hearing before old Annas, Christ is 'bound and sent to Caiaphas' (18:24). It seems probable that the former high priest and his son-in-law, the current high priest, resided in the same palace but perhaps in different wings of the same building, adjoining a common courtyard. Whereas the first three evangelists only report on the hearing before Caiaphas, John tells us of two hearings and the difference between them. However, he does not recount what happens at the Caiaphas hearing, only mentioning it in passing.

John also says that there was a 'coal fire' *(anthrakiá)* which the officers had lit. And he alone – and where else do we find a similar remark anywhere in the gospels? – expressly mentions the 'coldness' of this night (18:18). In Jerusalem's elevated position, there are very cold nights even in spring. But at the same time, this seemingly outward remark about the temperature becomes an expressive metaphor. We have Peter, shivering in his darkened I, coming forward to the flames and the glowing coals. It is as if he wants to gain the warmth from without as a substitute for what is not present within him. John has the phrase about the night's coldness and Peter's search for warmth follow directly after his first 'am not'. Then, passing on to the Annas hearing, he lets fall the thread of the Peter story for a moment, taking it up again afterwards with the phrase, 'Meanwhile Peter was still standing there warming himself' (18:25). This is followed immediately by the second denial, and the second 'am not'.

The third denial, finally, acquires still sharper focus, since John reports that the officer who is now pointedly questioning Peter, was a relative of the man whom Peter had wounded with his sword: 'Did I not see you in the garden with him?'

Easter sequel

Finally, it is again John, alone, who adds a third act to the prediction of the denial, and then the denial itself, which ends so tragically with Peter going out and 'weeping bitterly'. This carries the events into the bright realm of Easter where the painful dissonance finds the beginning of its resolution.

Only John tells us of an encounter that seven of the disciples had with the resurrected Christ at the Sea of Galilee. Christ stands on the shore in the early morning, as yet unrecognised. From there he has the disciples who are in the boat, pull in the great draft of fishes.*
They bring the full net to land and are invited to eat breakfast. Beside the Risen One burns a 'coal fire', with fish and bread. It has often been remarked that this coal fire repeats the scene in the courtyard of Caiaphas (and this phrase does not figure anywhere else in the New Testament). But now, after Easter, we are clearly concerned with experiences of a supersensible nature, albeit ones that nevertheless point equally to something 'real'. But they do not belong to material reality; they are seen in inner vision. We should carefully note the evangelist's mode of expression here. He does not simply say, 'there was a coal fire,' but 'they see a coal fire' (21:9). The early morning hour also seems reminiscent of that previous moment when the cock crew.

Three times Christ asks Peter whether he loves him. When he adds the first time, 'more than these', he is reminding him of his presumption ('And if they all go astray from you, nevertheless I will not'). Peter manages only a modest reply. He does not dare use the Greek word for sublime 'love' *(agapan)* but instead uses only the word *philein*. When Christ asks the question a third time, he also no longer

---

* See also Chapter 19 'The Miraculous Draft of Fishes'.

uses the word *agapan* but the more modest word, and in doing so casts doubt even on this level of Peter's love. 'Then Peter was downcast.' This is the unavoidable pain of self-knowledge: in the question Christ repeats three times, each time at a lower level, Peter has to experience the reproachful echo of his three denials. But at the same time he is mercifully received by Christ and receives his weighty mission. Now he can begin something that, at the Last Supper, was pushed away from him into the future with the words 'not yet'. 'Where I go, you cannot now follow me, but you will follow later' (Jn 13:36). Now he says, 'Follow me' (21:22). He is no longer to follow only an earthly teacher but the Risen One who has passed through Golgotha. And from the future shines in the possibility that Peter may one day be able to make true his great words, 'willing to go through imprisonment and death with you' (Lk 22:33). As an old man it will be granted to him to reveal or glorify God through his martyr's death (Jn 21:19).

Thus, the early morning hour by the lake during the Easter period leads on from that moment of the cockcrow on Good Friday. Where the crowing of the cock was a call to awaken to awareness of culpability, this awakening now continues towards the supersensible in the dawn light of Easter. Consciousness broadens into an encounter with the Risen One, who raises fallen man and calls upon him to follow and collaborate.

15

THE SEVEN WORDS FROM THE CROSS

Seven 'last words' from the dying Christ on the cross have been passed on to us. These seven are drawn from a survey of all four gospels. Luke and John each report three, while Matthew and Mark give us one that is common to them both.

If we wish to consider these seven words from the cross in their likely temporal sequence, we must no doubt begin with the plea in the Gospel of Luke (23:34) which directly follows the act of crucifixion: *'Father forgive them, for they know not what they do.'* Here Christ intervenes with active mercy in the fate of those who are inflicting this terrible suffering upon him. He is not only a passive victim, but also active in that he prays for them. When a criminal deed is perpetrated, the judgment made of it cannot only be based upon the actions of the miscreants. In regard to the further effect of the deed in a deeper, universal context, it is also very important to consider how the victim responds to what is done. We might in fact say that the one who suffers the wrong has a key role here: they can respond to the treatment received with a desire for revenge, or they can inwardly deprive the evil inflicted on them of its sharpness and poison – though to do so requires an inner connection with divine powers of love. Whether or not they can do so will mean a different karmic outcome from the whole matter, including for the perpetrators.

When those who perpetrated what occurred at Golgotha have died, they will, in the other world, have to look squarely at their guilt and perceive it with inescapable clarity. And then it will be of great importance that Christ has prayed for them. In doing so he has introduced, in freedom, a new, additional factor into the destined calculation, which alters the outcome. However, 'they know not what they do.' The more conscious the knowledge and will are that accompanied such actions, the less a will for forgiveness can intervene, for even in such circumstances, God respects human freedom. His will for love is limited by it. But, at the same time, there may be many intermediate stages between full knowledge and unknowingness.

While the plea for forgiveness works on into the future, the second word from the cross relates to something already present. Initially, after the crucifixion has been performed, the two thieves crucified on either side of Christ join in with the calumnies directed at him, as Matthew (27:44) and Mark (15:32) recount. It remains to the evangelist Luke to convey the change undergone by one of the two thieves. This may be because of the process of death that gradually takes hold of him. When the soul begins to release itself from the body, clairvoyant moments can arise. For this reason keen attention was paid in ancient times to the last words of the dying. The dying thief gains insight that 'this man has done no wrong' and that, despite all outward appearances, he is in truth a king. 'Think of me when you come into your kingdom.' To which Christ responds, *'Truly, I say to you, this day you will be with me in paradise'* (Lk 23:43).

This does not mean that the thief, after his death, will not have to look upon his past life on the earth in the light of eternal truth. But Christ will be with him: he will – 'today' – draw with him into the sun realm the higher I that has awoken at the very last moment of a misspent life; despite all culpability, he enables the thief to find his way to the pure, unspoiled spring of all human existence.

After the word for his enemies, after the word for the enemy who became a friend, Christ turns to those who were his friends previously, who have found the courage and strength to stand beneath the cross: *'Woman, behold your son ... Behold your mother'* (Jn 19:26). The dying one inaugurates a new, deepened companionship between the mother and the disciple whom he loves. Henceforth, John takes Mary 'to his own'. In the Greek, 'own' – *ta idia* – is a word we know from the Prologue of the Gospel of John. 'He came to his own *(ta idia)* and his own did not receive him' (Jn 1:11). This refers to a domain of the human I-being that has become aware of its intrinsic nature. In the farewell addresses, we hear these words: 'You will be dispersed, each one to his own, and me you will leave alone' (Jn 16:32). On Good Friday, the 'own' sounds for the third time, but now no longer indicating self-encapsulation, isolation, but that our intrinsic being, when permeated by Christ, can only now open itself to make true, deep community possible.

Mary, 'through whose soul the sword' of deepest suffering had passed (Lk 2:35), saw Christian spirit knowledge in a special relationship to divine wisdom, to the Sophia. At Jesus' conception she was illumined by the Holy Spirit, and at Pentecost, in the midst of the circle of apostles, she witnessed the descent of the Holy Spirit again. The pain she has suffered as Mater Dolorosa prepared her soul to be imbued with the 'wisdom that comes from above'. The realms of pain become the realms of radiance, to use the words of Goethe's Faust. Within the innermost self, Christ united Mary with the disciple who later wrote the Gospel of John with its profound wisdom.

The three first words from the cross that Christ addresses to humankind, and which are interwoven in such different ways into the Golgotha event, are uttered still in sunlight before an eerie darkness enshrouds the whole land. The four other words from the cross are spoken during this darkness and relate to Christ himself, to his great deed, in which he is now for a while alone.

'My God, My God, why have you forsaken me?' (Mt 27:46; Mk 15:34). We misunderstand this outcry if we imagine it to be a last cry of despair. These words, which Christ here reiterates and makes his own, have their precedent in the beginning of Psalm 22. It describes experiences of suffering that must be passed through on the way to an experience of divine glory. The sequence of experiences is inaugurated by a boundless sense of loneliness and abandonment. But ultimately a breakthrough is achieved to an enhanced consciousness in which the radiance of divine glory manifests.

From his knowledge of the Jewish milieu of those times, the Protestant theologian Ethelbert Stauffer has shown that Psalm 22 'plays a decisive role in the Messianic theology and Messianic expectations of the Hebrew people in those times.'* When, on his

---

* Ethelbert Stauffer, *Jesus: Gestalt und Geschichte,* p. 106.

own behalf and in reference to himself the crucified one speaks the words of this psalm, which embody the passage through suffering to glorification, we can see this as a sublime realisation of their Messianic claim.

Being completely alone and bereft in this way is an experience especially germane to earthly human beings, who experience themselves as isolated and encapsulated within the material body. Hitherto, Christ has expressed his inner sense of life in the words 'I am not alone, the Father is with me.' We read this three times in the Gospel of John (8:16 and 29; 16:32). Only as death – which does not exist in that form in higher worlds – approaches, does Christ have this full, earthly, human experience as ultimate consequence of his becoming flesh. If he sought truly to be in solidarity with us, if he wished to be as one of us, he had to take upon himself this passage through death. And, precisely by doing so, he was able to transform his hitherto purely heavenly being such that henceforth it could be comprehensible and communicable to earthly humankind.

Christ is not in himself by nature subject to the law that sin must be rewarded by death. As one standing outside sinfulness, he seeks earthly death out of a free decision made in love. But this also involves him having to receive into his divine soul the experience of being alone and bereft, of being cut off from the heavens, and, through doing so, to lay the ground for humankind in future to be able to overcome this abandonment at death. He had to pass through desolation to be able to convey to earthly humanity his inherent experience – 'I am not alone'. From now on, it has become possible for human beings to die 'in Christ', embraced by the encompassing higher I of Christ. In the words of the Lutheran hymn writer Paul Gerhardt, 'When I shall suffer death, then you will stand by me.' Christ could not stand by us in death's darkness if he had not himself passed through desolation and loneliness at Golgotha.

The same is true of the words *'I thirst'* (Jn 19:28). This certainly has its direct, tangible and terrible realism – the pangs of thirst of one being crucified. But we should not overlook the fact that this phrase appears in the Gospel of John, within which 'thirsting' plays a significant role. This gospel is such an inwardly coherent and integral spirit organism that we cannot assume that the word about thirst from the cross has no connection with the other statements it makes about thirst. Bodily thirst points metaphorically to a broad realm of soul life. In John, there are three significant prior references to thirst. In the conversation with the woman of Samaria, 'Whoever drinks of the water I give him will never ever thirst' (4:14). This began with physical thirst – 'give me to drink' – but then the conversation turned towards the supersensible. The second reference is in Christ's address at the Sea of Galilee: 'And whoever believes in me will never more thirst' (6:35). And the third time this word is used is at the autumn Festival of the Tabernacles: 'If anyone thirsts let him come to me and drink' (7:37).

Buddha, too, used 'thirsting' as a true figure of speech. He was speaking of the yearning that lives in the human soul, the desire for happiness, the hope of blissful fulfilment. Buddha taught that all this longing is illusory or delusional, a pointless desire, and that we should kill it off in the soul's deep roots. Christ's words about quenching thirst should be heard against the background of this – in its own way magnificent – relinquishment and resignation by Buddha. It is true that longing leads to illusion, in so far as a person often does not understand their own longing deeply enough and attaches it to superficial things. And this will make disappointment likely: *'That was not what I wanted after all,'* we might say to ourselves before the next, equally insubstantial mirage appears on the horizon. But if we understand the true depths of longing, a fulfilment can be found which Christ brings towards us.

If we have allowed these three references to thirst to speak to us, then we will not think it accidental that the same theme is taken up in the other writings of John, in the Book of Revelation. There likewise are three sayings about the divine stilling of human 'thirst' (7:16; 21:6; 22:17) with a relationship to the description of the heavenly Jerusalem.

Between these two sets of three sayings about thirst comes the word from the cross, figuring only in John as the fourth of a Johannine series of seven. By placing it in this overarching context it acquires special meaning. Clearly it is important for John that he who brings us the water of life, which stills our thirst for eternity, should be seen as the one who now thirsts; that the God becoming flesh in the full sense also involved him accepting the earthly human experience of 'thirsting' into his divine soul.

Christ's suffering, his 'passion', should not be seen as only passive in character. It was at the same time an active deed and, musically, possesses a major as well as a minor mood. This is apparent again especially in the third word from the cross that John recounts, *'It is finished'* (19:30). Christ remains master of the whole event to the end, he fulfils his death and consciously concludes it. The evangelist adds that he 'bowed his head' after saying this, and therefore the words were spoken with his head raised.

The death day of Christ is Friday, the sixth day of the week, and as such corresponds to the sixth day of creation. Genesis describes how man appears on the sixth day, as the image and likeness of his Creator. Christ has now brought to fresh light this image of God that was hidden by the Fall. On Good Friday the words *ecce homo* – 'behold the man' – resound. The Sabbath begins at sunset. Genesis tells us how God completes his creation at the transition to the seventh day: 'Thus the heavens and earth were finished with their whole array. And thus God finished his works upon the seventh day' (Gn 2:1f). Now God turns again to his divine inwardness – 'and on the seventh day he rested.' In the same way, Christ fulfils and finishes his earthly work and plants it as seed of the future in the divine Ground of the great Sabbath rest. When the Sabbath began at twilight on Good Friday, the burial had just been completed in the garden of Joseph of Arimathea. Easter Saturday began, the quiet eve of Sunday, in whose stillness the events that have happened fade away, in whose tranquillity the day of Easter begins to germinate: as the first day of the week this will inaugurate a new impetus in creation.

Between this fulfilment of his works and the occurrence of death, a prayer finds its place in the Gospel of Luke as the seventh and last word from the cross: *'Father, into your hands I commend my spirit'* (23:46). These are words from Psalm 31. Stauffer drew attention to the fact that this phrase was part of the Jewish evening prayer, and likewise of the death prayer.* 'In your hands are the souls of the living and the dead. Into your hands I offer my spirit.' In the mouth of Christ, this quote from the psalms becomes a new creation, giving the old prayer a new signature by prefacing it with the word 'Father',

---

* 'It is finished' can equally be translated 'It is fulfilled'. See here again Stauffer, *Jesus: Gestalt und Geschichte,* p. 107.

which acquires a unique resonance from him. The first word from the cross, the plea for forgiveness, began by addressing the Father, and now it comes again at the end, as Christ gives the deed he has accomplished and fulfilled to the powers of destiny who have their ground of being in the Father. The dying Christ directs his spirit towards the Father.

This has a mysterious affinity with a 'last will'. Each night, as we fall asleep, as the soul releases itself from conscious life in the body and enters a different world, much depends upon how this departure is accomplished: whether it is preoccupied to the last moment only with more trivial things until sleep fetches it, or whether it 'commends itself to God'. Depending on this, the last stirrings of fading day consciousness direct the soul into that other world in different ways, just as we can push off from the banks of a river in a boat in a particular direction. If we fall asleep with unspiritual contents of soul, we cannot reach higher regions 'on the other side' by the virtue of the power of attraction which, in the world of spirit, draws together things that bear affinity to each other. The incomprehension that materialism has spread over ancient, intimate experiences of soul life, mean that the significance of the evening prayer has largely fallen into oblivion. Rediscoveries are needed here.

The same is true of the much more radical and greater departure from the earth at death. Far-reaching consequences follow from the direction in which the soul embarks upon its steps into the other world. It was of great significance that the thief on the cross was able to direct his soul towards Christ at the last moment. Such moments acquire special value at the hour of death, and their influence on destiny can compensate for whole decades of previous life.

In the highest sense we see Christ enact this mystery of the last will as he commends his spirit into the hands of the Father.

16

'CENTRE' IN THE GOSPEL OF JOHN

It is surely no accident that the Gospel of John, which repeatedly points to the inner centre of the 'I am', has a special relationship to the 'centre'. However, this only becomes apparent if we are willing to attend to certain intimate aspects of this Johannine text. Then we discover that the passages that refer to the 'centre' resonate with one another throughout the whole gospel. Let us take a look at these passages.

At the Jordan

From the mouth of John the Baptist we first hear a reference to the centre: 'In your midst stands one you do not know' (1:26). We could translate *mesos,* 'midst' as 'at your centre'. These words of the Baptist are only given in the Gospel of John

Initially, certainly, the outward meaning applies: that someone is standing there in the throng who will one day come to great prominence. But in the Gospel of John we can hear an undertone of something else: 'In your midst' or 'at your centre' also suggests the inner core of each person's being. In his book *Theosophy,* when he was seeking to give his readers an idea of the nature of the I, Rudolf Steiner used a phrase by Jean Paul from the latter's autobiography, where he recounts how he first became aware of his own I as a child. He calls this childhood experience something that occurred 'only in the hidden, most sacred shrine' within him. Referring to this, Rudolf Steiner speaks of the I as the 'centre' of soul life. The experience that 'I am an I' does not come to us from without but dawns in the inner core of our being. Does this special mode of perceiving awareness only hold true for an experience of our own I, or would it be possible that something else, something still higher, might perhaps be waiting to dawn upon us within our hidden, inmost shrine? Here we touch on the secret of our relationship with Christ. As long as he remains 'someone else' for us, standing outside us and regarded by us from without, he cannot yet manifest his full, redeeming power. He wishes to dawn in our inmost core; he wishes to become manifest as the higher, superordinate I at the same inner place where we become aware of our personal I.

Why is there so much mention in the Gospel of John of the 'I' and the 'I am'? Certainly not because it describes someone who wished only to 'speak of himself' in the mundane sense, but rather because it seeks to point to the locus of experience, that concealed shrine within, where not only our own I but also the I of Christ opens to our vision.

'In your midst stands one you do not know.' In the inmost realm of the soul stands, as it were, a still veiled figure, the 'unknown God' who awaits his hour. Paul puts it like this in his Letter to the Galatians (1:15f): It 'pleased God ... to *unveil* his son within me' (*apokalypsai* in the Greek).

The whole of the rest of the content of the Gospel of John seeks to help our ignorant unknowing of the God in our midst, at our centre, become a knowing, a knowledge – a knowledge that is not intellectual in nature, but that encompasses and pervades the whole of us from that centre.

'The middle of the festival'

We next encounter the theme of the centre in John in Chapter 7, which describes the Festival of Tabernacles. This was celebrated in autumn, over the period of a whole week. Through this festive week, the souls of the celebrants gained an intimation of the principles and order of greater, divinely ordained spans of time. Not only the creation itself, but also our human development is subject to the sway of seven, of a great week as it were. During the first three days of the week of the tabernacles, Christ is no doubt 'present' but hidden, *in occulto,* as the Latin text puts it. Not until the fourth day does he emerge from this concealment and enter the temple to teach. Greater, overarching spans of development are reflected in this. Through the preceding world days of humanity's evolution, Christ was surely present as divine, creative spirit, but he had to wait with his intrinsic gift and mission until the 'time was fulfilled'. Only then can he appear in the 'temple' of his earthly body, revealed as the one he is. For this moment of his manifestation the evangelist uses the phrase, 'now at the middle of the feast' (7:14). The quality of the centre is here palpable in the temporal realm.

'And placed her in the midst'

In the next chapter comes the story of the woman taken in adultery, whose punishment is to be stoned to death. The scribes and the Pharisees lead the woman to Jesus and place her 'in the midst' (as it says literally in 8:3). Here again, this 'centre' has its obvious outward meaning in the narrative. It is the centre of the circle of people around her. But once again, outer, spatial dimensions become transparent. The woman who has been drawn forth from the darkness of her 'wayward' actions into the light of scrutiny, stands in the middle before Christ, whose gaze she now encounters. The sinful human soul meets the great, central I AM who inscribes her guilt in the earth, adding it to everything else that the Lamb of God is about to take upon himself as the 'sin of the world'.

And once again: 'the woman in the middle'

Under the sway of the words spoken by Christ, the would-be assailants and supposed guardians of virtue have silently left the scene. The temple is empty, and only Christ (soon to speak the words 'I AM the light of the world') and the woman remain there. Once again, the evangelist stresses the words 'in the centre'. In a literal translation it would be, 'being in the centre' (8:9).

The woman has narrowly escaped death and now she faces Christ, who has raised himself again from writing in the earth and is looking at her. She is now truly 'in the centre' and hears the divine words of encouragement, 'from now on sin no more'.

At Golgotha

After this we only meet the theme of the centre again in the passion story. It is worth heeding Rudolf Steiner's remark here, that every word in the Gospel of John should be 'placed on golden scales'. All four evangelists tell us there were three crosses on Golgotha, and that two criminals were executed along with Christ. The first three evangelists speak in the same terms of the two who were crucified with him: 'one on his right, one on his left'. Though it is implicit that Christ is in the middle, only John actually says this directly. He expressly writes, 'and Jesus in the centre' (19:18).

We might easily overlook this difference in the account if we had not by now come to hearken attentively to the special resonance of the word 'middle' or 'centre' in John. This 'in the midst', or 'in the centre' as John conveys it, can speak volumes to us.

The evening of Easter Sunday

When the disciples are gathered on the evening of Easter Sunday in the inner room, with the doors shut, the Risen One comes and stands 'in the midst' (20:19). Luke too, in his account of that evening, also speaks of the 'middle' (24:36). But in John, the word resonates immediately with the meanings that have accrued around it in his gospel, and thus it acquires a different quality.

In the preceding gospels we have clearly heard of the circle of disciples who surrounded Christ. But it only becomes apparent at Easter what is signified by this circle having Christ at its centre. We already find an echo of this in Luke's account of the Last Supper: 'I am in your midst as the one who serves' (22:27). But the full experience of this 'central position' only comes into its own at Easter. After the body of Jesus had been laid in the grave, this 'rising' into the upright, by the power of the resurrection, is now the true revelation of the central I AM.

The first Sunday after Easter

John is the only evangelist to recount the appearance of Christ a week after Easter. It was Sunday once more, and the disciples experienced for the first time how on the Christian Sunday – an 'octave' to the Easter event – Christ reveals himself with special power. On that first Sunday after the resurrection, he shines so brightly that doubting Thomas can no longer conceal this reality from himself. And once again, John uses the expression, 'He stood in the midst' (20:26). Thus this comes twice in quick succession in the Johannine account of Easter, and the repetition, which has a liturgical feeling, gains emphasis and significance in consequence.

This is the last time – the seventh! It leads us back to the beginning, to the first reference to the centre: 'In your midst stands one whom you do not know.' Now, on this first Sunday after Easter, the unknown God, who hitherto stood veiled at the centre of the human being, becomes the God perceived and recognised. The one who has suffered doubt is the very one who may profess Christ-knowledge in the highest terms: 'My Lord and my God.' What descended, as if from heavenly choirs in the Prologue to the Gospel of John ('and God was the Word'), now surfaces again from the mouth of Thomas, the one healed of doubt: 'Lord and God'. But we should also attend to the word 'my', which accompanies these two lofty words. It would not accord with the spirit of the Gospel of John to understand this word 'my' as some kind of egoistic gesture of possession. The 'my' that sounds here must always be seen in connection with the secret of the I. The I lighting up in the hidden, most sacred shrine within, at the centre of our being, becomes the organ of perception and the devoted bearer of the divine I AM that comes to us in Christ, dawning within us. Thus, Thomas's profession points to the Lord and God who embodies the secret of the centre and manifests in the inner place of the human I.

17

THE SEVEN EASTER STORIES IN THE GOSPELS

It strikes us again and again how Providence, rather than chance, has brought the four gospels together. We do not, for example, find the seven words from the cross complete in any one gospel, but together the four give us this precious legacy. It is the same with the description of events after the resurrection.

How many appearances of the Risen One are actually recorded – not just mentioned, but fully described? First, there is the experience of the women, particularly Mary Magdalene, in the early morning at the grave. In the afternoon, the journey to Emmaus. In the evening, the appearance to the disciples behind locked doors. One week later, the appearance for Thomas in particular. There are two further appearances in Galilee, not precisely dated, one on the mountain, one by the lake. Finally, the last appearance to the disciples is linked with the ascension. Exactly seven. It is apparent that these were not the only ones. Paul mentions appearances to Peter (also mentioned by Luke), to James, to 'five thousand brethren'. But only the seven are actually described and given in detail.

Can this be accidental? If we try to perceive the special character, the particular mood of each of these seven stories, we can come to the feeling that the same 'seven' is involved as in the seven planets spoken of by ancient wisdom. This tradition has been corroborated by Rudolf Steiner's spiritual research, where it is presented in a new way. It concerns the working of cosmic forces in seven different ways, known of old to be connected with Moon, Venus, Mercury, Sun, Mars, Jupiter and Saturn – those of Venus and Mercury being to some extent interchangeable. Notwithstanding modern astronomy, these observations are correct.

The women at the grave

The women are the first in whom there awoke a clairvoyant perception of the Risen One. The *Moon,* understood not merely as a heavenly body but as a special field of forces, has a special connection with the feminine. As the moon sickle can appear as a bowl of silver, so may the feminine in human beings become a vessel to receive the sunlight of Christ. For Mary Magdalene, whose deep sorrow becomes the eye whereby she sees the Risen One who completely fulfills her devoted soul, this is a revelation of the noblest possibilities of the lunar quality of the soul.

On the way to Emmaus

There is a different mood in the story of the two disciples who walk to Emmaus. They are also very sad, though their sadness is not so much the personal, heartfelt pain of Mary Magdalene – it is rather caused by mental suffering. As they talk, they struggle to comprehend the incomprehensible, of which they were witnesses on Good Friday. Their sincere search for the truth makes it possible for the third one to join them. While walking with them (while in movement) he illumines their understanding. He teaches them to grasp the secret meaning of scripture. 'Was it not necessary that Christ should suffer?' This 'was it not necessary?' makes a divine demand upon the human power of understanding. The death and resurrection of Christ are not an incomprehensible miracle that one blindly accepts. 'Was it not necessary?' opens the way to seeing what, in a higher sense, is 'to be seen'.

Here we feel something of the quality of *Mercury,* of Hermes. The Greeks regarded him as the messenger of the gods with winged shoes, moving between gods and humans to help bring understanding between them. The art of interpretation or exposition, which makes clear 'what is meant', is called 'hermeneutics', The corresponding verb, *hermēneuō,* actually occurs in the original Greek text. He 'interpreted to them in all the scriptures,' reads: *di'ermēneusen* (Lk 24:27). The Christ walking with the two is like a more sublime Mercury-Hermes figure.

Easter evening

The Easter evening story, especially as it is described by John (20:19–23), seems as if imbued with the element of spiritual love. (The parallel accounts in Mark 16:14–18 and Luke 24:36–43 rather give a summary of the whole forty days leading up to the ascension.) On this occasion 'Peace be with you' is said for the first time after the resurrection. The disciples respond with joy. The Risen One shows them the marks of the wounds of his great deed of love. He breathes on them and so lets them share for the first time in the Holy Spirit so that they can heal the sickness of sin. *Venus,* once the star of Lucifer, is Christianised. Venus Urania, the heavenly love, is here at work between Christ and his disciples.

In the sense of the above-mentioned interchangeability, one can also feel in this 'healing of the sickness of sin' a Mercurial element, because Mercury is also the inspirer of the work of healing. On the other hand, the Emmaus story (like Luke's story of the nativity) shows the most beautiful New Testament description of the love-bearing beauty of a spirit-pervaded Venus element.

The appearance to Thomas

The Easter evening has its continuation on the evening of the following Sunday, the first 'octave' of Easter. This time, however, the appearance is meant especially for Thomas, whose doubts melt like snow in the sun. He immediately recognises the reality and divine sovereignty of the Risen One. The confession of Thomas, 'My Lord and my God' (Jn 20:28) shines sunlike amidst the Easter stories. Here we are in the region of the *Sun*. As modern research in the history of religion has shown, the expression 'Lord and God' was applied in particular to the sun god. The Caesars impiously claimed the title for themselves. Domitian had himself called *Dominus ac Deus noster,* 'our Lord and God.'

Mary Magdalene's very personal cry from the soul, 'Rabboni – Master,' is complemented by Thomas's words a week later in the sunlike realm of the spirit. To the 'Master', to the glorified human Jesus, is added the recognition of the 'Lord' *(Kyrios)* in his sun-glory. Behind and at the same time above that, is the 'God' – the eternal

Logos of whom the Prologue of John's Gospel says he 'was God'. These words of Thomas signify that the disciples are fully conscious of the rising of the Easter sun.

The mountain in Galilee

The appearances on the mountain and by the lake in the 'cosmic' Galilean landscape, from whose whole nature we may assume to belong to the later part of the forty days, now indicate an even greater dimension. On the mountain in Galilee, Christ reveals himself as one to whom 'all authority in heaven and on earth' is given (Mt 28:18). He turns the attention of the disciples to the whole of humanity. 'Go, therefore, and make disciples of all nations ...' A human race baptised into the mystery of the Holy Trinity is to arise in place of nations held together by ties of blood and waging wars with each other. The little band of disciples was sent out to undertake the greatest conquest the world ever saw. Immeasurable encouragement and enthusiasm for action flow from the words, 'I am with you always.' The forces and energies of *Mars* are here raised to Christian powers.

The Sea of Galilee

The meal of bread and fish by the lake after the miraculous draft of fishes (Jn 21) is wholly *Jupiter*. The planet of wise priesthood shines upon the sacramental mystery of this meal. Jupiter is also the planet of plenitude, which is so impressively expressed in the superabundant gift of the catch of fish. (Traditionally, Jupiter stands in a particularly close relationship to the sign of Pisces, the Fishes.) So, too, the different commissions of Peter and John given afterwards, which settled the question of leadership, bear the signature of the priestly sphere of Jupiter.

Ascension

The last appearance finally passes over into the ascension. The Risen One now completely merges with the profound and sublime forces of the Father. He does not really go away – the 'I am with you always' still holds good. Rather, he now outgrows and surpasses the disciples' power of vision, and in that sense goes 'out of their sight'.

Saturn was always known as the stern guardian of the entrance to the world of the Father. He is the guide up to the realm of the fixed stars and stands guard before the gate of eternity. Saturnian gravity pervades the story of the ascension. The Christ refers to the ultimate and sublime mysteries of world destiny hidden in the Father when he answers the disciples' question about the time of restoring the kingdom to Israel. 'It is not for you to know the times or seasons which the Father has fixed by his own authority.' But he promises to send the Holy Spirit, and the angels who appear speak of a renewed seeing of the Christ in the future when he returns in the clouds of heaven. As with the Galilean appearances where we hear of 'the close of the age' (Mt 28:20) and of John's remaining 'until I come' (Jn 21:22), the sphere of the initially more personal experience here, too, broadens to encompass great and universal concerns.

The place of the ascension, the Mount of Olives, also has something of the threshold-guarding gravity of Saturn. It was on the Mount of Olives, in Gethsemane, that Christ struggled for strength to fulfil the will of the Father right to the end. It is as if the Mount of Olives were always associated with the gravity of facing the final and ultimate. From the Mount of Olives, the disciples see the Lord enter into the eternal will of the Father.

Through higher inspiration, the gospels 'selected' precisely these seven Easter stories that so clearly bear the character of the seven planetary stages. We can thus feel that ascension at the end of forty days is no abrupt and unexpected event, but that it is organically prepared. The Risen One 'grows' within the forty days, the powers of ever fresh supersensible realms stream towards him, he bears the resurrection body deeper and deeper into being, makes it from day to day more 'existent' and more substantial, until, in the ascension, he is ready for union with the Father in Heaven. Thus, at the beginning of this process, the goal is already anticipated when, on Easter morning, the Risen One says to Mary Magdalene, 'I am ascending to my Father and your Father, to my God and your God' (Jn 20:17).

18

WALKING WITH THE RISEN ONE: THE WAY TO EMMAUS

Luke's narrative about the disciples on the way to Emmaus speaks directly to the heart. It places the content of archetypal human experience before our souls: the shared way of those bearing sorrow, the conversation on the journey, entering the house, the meal. But the most profound mystery of our earth existence accompanies and plays into these ordinary events of human life: the resurrection.

The Risen One walks with the two disciples

The resurrection of humanity on the Last Day is the long-range objective presaged from afar for the earthly human being. But it has its everyday image each morning when we get up from lying down and stand upright. We do this with unthinking matter-of-factness, until perhaps sometimes an illness provides us with a little consciousness of what it means to be able to get up. Whenever we raise ourselves into the vertical, we carry out in brief what we had to learn with great effort as children. The upright stance is a manifestation of the truly human, as is our walking on two feet a consequence of it. Walking is not only a biological function serving essential locomotion as with any animal. We would not apply the phrase 'way of life' to the existence of an animal. Human movement in walking takes into itself something higher. We speak of the 'way of life', whereby 'wayfaring' is open both to 'going on the way' and to 'changing our way'. The Old Testament speaks mysteriously of Enoch who lived in distant antiquity and 'walked with God' and was taken up into the invisible (Gn 5:24).

Human movement is wonderfully composed into the rhythm of the cosmos. If a wanderer could march forwards uninterruptedly in a reflective tempo, they would come round the earth in 365 days, corresponding to the sun year. Is it a coincidence that this same number of the sun year appears in connection with Enoch who walked with God, in that the age of 365 years is ascribed to him?

On Easter morning, Christ, anticipating the Last Day, wrested his earthly human body from the powers of death and let it resurrect. As the Risen One he is now involved in an advancing movement of a higher kind. In the realm of spirits there is also progress, advance. In the Apocalypse, Christ promises his disciples in Sardis that they will 'walk with him' (Rv 3:4).

The Risen One walks spiritually with the two disciples who are on their way to Emmaus on Easter afternoon. Together, they search for the meaning of what they have just experienced, something incomprehensible that weighs heavily on their souls. That walking together can be conducive to a common searching for the truth is a well-known phenomenon. Plato lets his conversationalists in his last dialogue, *The Laws,* develop their thoughts on a walk that takes them from Knossos to a temple of Zeus. The peripatetic school of philosophy takes its name from 'moving along': *peripatein.* (This word also occurs in the Emmaus story, Lk 24:17.) Through the seriousness of their common striving after knowledge (*syn-zētein,* 'to look for in common'), the two Emmaus disciples create the precondition for the Risen One, stepping forward unnoticed out of the Easter landscape towards evening, to associate himself with them and to bring his step into harmony with their walking pace. 'He approached them.' The two are so absorbed in their conversation that the approach and addition of the third one is hardly noticed. So he walks with them, listening, silent.

He speaks with them

This silent accompanying must have lasted a considerable time. (The Greek uses the imperfect here, 24:15, to express what is lasting.) But then he breaks the spell of his silence. He speaks.

In so doing, he opens up a second realm of the truly human in addition to walking upright. A new impetus plays into the events. 'They stood still, downcast' (Lk 24:17). They stood still – their walking was interrupted. This little detail from Luke's account can be seen in a greater context. Luke has a special relationship to the 'way' or 'path'. For instance the events from 9:51 to 19:29 are all part of the journey to Jerusalem, describing the stations on the way. The raising of the widow's son at Nain took place as Jesus was on his way to Nain. In the Acts of the Apostles, Luke describes Paul's Damascus experience as being 'on the way', which ultimately led to the great journeys of Paul. That makes the moments when the movement is interrupted all the more striking. At the raising of the young man of Nain, when Jesus and the disciples going to Nain met the funeral procession coming from the town, Christ touched the open coffin, 'and the bearers stood still' (Lk 7:14). At Damascus, 'the men travelling with him stood speechless' (Ac 9:7). In the Emmaus story, the moment when Christ speaks leads to a break in the walking of the three: 'They stood still.' (It is clear from what follows that they must have resumed walking.)

Attempts to seek the origin of human speech in animal sounds only reveal a blindness to the spiritual impact from above with which we are concerned in the human word. Human speech cannot be understood from below. It has descended from higher worlds 'which are penetrated by the pure living way of God's word' as Goethe said in his *West East Divan*. Christ is indeed himself God's word, the Logos. And as he entered into the rhythm of the disciples' walking, so he now also weaves his speaking into theirs.

Christ's first words are a question. 'What kind of words are these which you are exchanging with one another as you walk?' Why does Christ ask? Has he not noticed that they are really talking the whole time of nothing else but the events of the past days, of him? They cannot comprehend his question so they respond with one of their own: 'Are you the only one in Jerusalem who does not know about these events?' And again, a question comes from Christ, 'Which events?'

How are we to understand this questioning? Is it only meant pedagogically, rather like teacher eliciting a piece of knowledge from a pupil that they themselves already know? Or are we to think of a quite original 'genuine' questioning? Could it be that the Risen One, coming from experiences that lie completely outside the consciousness of the disciples, had to bridge over something like an abyss of a growing alienation? Did he not first have to live again into the soul condition of those who, during his passage through death, despite the shock to their souls, nevertheless continued their former existence? Through their words he was confronted by how his destiny appeared from outside. Perhaps it was significant for him to have this view brought to him from earthly human beings. So he listens to what his own followers say about Jesus of Nazareth.

They express what he meant to them in a kind of declaration of faith: 'Jesus of Nazareth ... a prophet, powerful in deed and word ... they condemned and crucified him ... we had hoped he would save Israel.' This avowal goes so far as to recognise the great prophet, but it stops short exactly where the actual mystery starts. The grave may have been empty on this morning, the women may have seen something, but of the disciples who then went to the grave it is only said (mirroring the resignation of 'we had hoped'), 'but they did not see him.' Here their Christology ends. The light shining from the prophetic figure is extinguished with the death on the cross and leaves them in an even deeper darkness.

Christ sees that he must give them some support in their understanding. He takes a third step towards them. He enters into their thinking, which is so very much in need of illumination.

He thinks with them

Modern science wrestles more keenly than ever with the problem of the origin of the human being. In this, three basic questions are constantly raised. How did humans come to their upright walk? How did they learn to speak? How did they develop into thinking beings? One tries in vain to understand all this in terms of an evolution out of the animal world. Rudolf Steiner demonstrated a long time ago a quite different way to the solution of these three questions. He often showed from his spiritual vision how these three faculties, which only develop after birth, are brought into being in the first years of the child with the help of the highest spiritual powers.

We might have expected our technical age to be able to see these faculties, which earlier ages had taken for granted, in quite a new light. At a time when our means of transport are so overdeveloped we could rediscover the miracle of our own ability to walk. In the age of radio and sound recording, we could feel all the more deeply the mystery that lives in the directly spoken word. In the age of the electronic computer, a new possibility opens up to grasp how it differs from truly creative thinking.

Walk – word – thought. This triad also determines the sequence of the Emmaus story.

Taking into consideration the picture that the disciples had gained of him and of his destiny, Christ now uses human thought forms in order to try and get his divine knowledge across to them. This cannot be done without a feeling of divine pain, 'O foolish men, and slow of heart.' For a being of a higher order that can comprehend the most diverse span of factors in split-second intuitions, the brain-bound thinking of earthly beings must appear obtuse and sluggish, and it must be painful to have to adapt to this kind of thinking. 'Foolish men'; in the original text *anóētoi,* those standing outside *nous,* the perceptive spirit reason. 'And slow of heart,' earthly man has certainly become adept in the use of his intellect, but the heart organ, without whose participation knowledge of a higher kind is not possible, has lost much of its sensitivity and become sluggish.

But Christ did not stop at this painful feeling of alienation. He sought in love, despite the inability of men to understand, to prepare the way for his great mystery to enter the thought world of earthly man. Since both disciples are pious Jews, he links on to what already lies prepared in their souls about Moses and the prophets. He lets the images, which had darkened with age, become transparent, as when the sun's rays lighten up the colourful windows of a cathedral. Luke here uses the word *di-hermēneuein* in which is contained the name of the messenger of the god Hermes (Mercury), who is the genius of all mediation. Shedding light in this way on the Old Testament leads them to an ever greater grasp of the fact that provides the entry into the whole of his teaching: 'Did Christ not have to suffer all this to enter into his glory?'

It is the truth of suffering that is expressed here, albeit in another form to the one preached half a millennium earlier by Buddha. All earthly human existence, so Buddha had taught, is unavoidably pervaded by suffering. This suffering is, for him, in itself a valid objection to human existence. If we want to be liberated from pain, our will to live must be completely eradicated. Then all earthly incarnation and existence will come to an end. According to this view, the whole development until now of the personality in an earthly body appears as a wrong path of evolution which has to be put right. Thus Buddha. Rudolf Steiner, however, has described how Christ amended Buddhism, not theoretically or doctrinally, but practically, since through his act of salvation he created an altered world situation within which the consequence of negation need not be drawn any more. New possibilities appear: out of all the bad all the greater good can come into being. In the light of the change brought about through the deed of Christ, suffering can appear in a totally new context. For only through taking suffering upon himself could Christ attain to that revelation of glory through which also the stigmata are transfigured.

For Buddha, his deep insights were not the abstract opinion of a scholar but the result of a path, an inner way, which he had travelled. His teaching was gained in walking this way. The teaching on suffering that the Risen One gives to the disciples is a truth 'on the way' in a still higher sense. Luke's account is significant even in its apparently unimportant details. We see how after Christ's first question the disciples stop walking. Surprised and sadly bewildered they 'stood still' (24:17). But then, reading between the lines, we gather that his words of teaching brought them into movement again, for 'they drew near to the village to which they were going' (24:28).

Entering

The way leads to the goal. Both disciples see the house before them which is to receive them. But Christ appeared to be walking further. (24:28). It is not a matter of course that their being in company with Christ should continue into the house. The disciples have come into contact with a being of the higher world on their way. This contact has its own momentum. If it is to continue into the quite different setting of the house, the disciples have to do something out of their own initiative to retain the presence of the Lord with them. They have to 'invite' him.

In the house the experience of the disciples finds its last enhancement and also its end. The Risen One sits with them at table. He has a meal with them, linking on to the meals that he had celebrated with his own until the Last Supper on Maundy Thursday. It is absolutely a matter of course for the evangelist to give his account here in just that ritual stylisation that we know from the great feedings and from the Last Supper, that he spoke the blessing, that he 'took' bread and 'broke' it and 'gave' it to his own. The one who offers the meal is not only teacher, he is also dispenser of substance. He himself is the bread of life, which is experienced in the communion as a creative, constructive force right into the bodily nature. In this act, the bodily nature is affirmed.

Buddha strove to eliminate the deeply rooted will to live and to make the reconstruction of the earthly body impossible in order to effect a final escape from suffering. This goal of his is represented by him in a highly suggestive metaphor: 'House-builder [the power that builds up the house of the body], you are discovered! Never again will you build the home. Your beams are broken up and the roof of your house fallen in.'* This metaphor is directed against the carpenter whose work is to come to nothing. But Jesus *was* a carpenter. His profession *was* the building of the house with beams and roof. Christ speaks of it when he said he would 'raise up in three days' the demolished temple, the 'temple of his body' (Jn 2:19–21). What Buddha negates is here divinely affirmed. Christ built the resurrection body as his eternal 'home'. Through the communion, he now wishes to build the eternal home of a resurrection body for human beings, which is to be completed on the Last Day. Then they may be permitted to live in this body, fashioned out of immortality – when the day of outer world existence will have declined and evening will have descended on all outer life.

---

* See also Rudolf Frieling. *Christianity and Reincarnation*, p.59.

19

THE MIRACULOUS DRAFT OF FISHES

One of the Easter stories in the gospels is that of the miraculous draft of fishes described in the last chapter of John's Gospel. It is worth noting that there is a parallel to it – also a similar story about a draft of fishes, but one that takes place not after the resurrection but much earlier, right at the beginning of Christ's ministry. It is described by Luke (5:1-11).

Faced with two such closely related accounts, modern criticism hastily concludes that we are dealing with the same story: that it is quite obviously a case of one and the same 'legend', which John places in connection with the resurrection appearances, while Luke thinks it belongs to the earlier time.

Such a superficial way of looking at it cannot do the gospel justice. One really has to take time to look at both accounts in order to see that there are characteristic and significant differences.

The fifth chapter of Luke takes us into the 'Galilean spring' of Christ's work. Christ is staying by the Sea of Galilee. He gets into Simon Peter's fishing boat and asks him 'to put out a little from the land'. Thus he speaks from the boat to the multitude thronging on the shore. Then he says to Peter: 'Put out into the deep ...' (literally, according to the Greek), that is, the middle of the lake furthest from the shore where the water is deepest. There they are to cast their nets. Peter says: 'Master, we toiled all night and took nothing! But at your word I will let down the nets.' As a result they make the miraculous catch. He brings them such abundance that the nets break. The other boat has to help save the catch, and the boats themselves threaten to sink. Peter falls down before Christ and says, 'Go away from me, for I am a sinful man, O Lord.'

At the time of this catch the baptism in the Jordan does not lie so far behind. At the baptism, the Christ entered into the body of Jesus of Nazareth, but he first has to take full hold of it and penetrate it. He is still too much a heavenly being to be fully at home in the earthly world. The great transformation of his divine, cosmic powers into the human and terrestrial has only begun; it will only be completed in the earthly death on Golgotha. So far the earthly element is strange to him.

It is not accidental that of the four elements (nowadays one speaks of physical states) one bears the name 'earth'. It is as if our planet, Earth, were really only itself within the range of solid elements – as if the other elements, although also found on earth, do not in the same sense belong to it. In fact, the water on earth is not so thoroughly earthly. It is like the intrusion of a more rarefied kind of existence which is fluid, more versatile and permeating. The liquid element is able to serve on earth as the vehicle for super-earthly life-forces; it is like a visible earthly representation of them.

Christ frequently stays by the lake. As a non-earthly being he feels, as it were, at home and familiar with the element of the sea. It is as if the lake made it easier for him to use his higher powers. When he allows himself to be taken 'a little from the land' by Peter for his sermon, it need not be only a practical measure in order to be able to speak to the multitude from a more favourable position. We can imagine that something of the pressure of physical existence was thereby removed. And now this goes even further: 'Put out into the deep ...' Again we can imagine that with every stroke of the oars away from the shore something of the oppression of being physically incarnated falls from him. Out there, where the influence of the solid earth is least felt, he can become more aware of his innate divine, cosmic being, and unfold its powers. On 'the deep' he reveals to the disciples the hidden richness of the sea.

What the disciples experience there with him is that he is truly a heavenly being who, out of inexhaustible abundance, is able to offer the gifts of a supersensible world. The great haul of fish – whether it happened physically, which is perfectly conceivable, or was a vision of the disciples in a certain state of excarnation – becomes a pictorial expression of this experience. The disciples have caught nothing during the whole of the previous night. Their nets have remained empty. This

19. THE MIRACULOUS DRAFT OF FISHES

becomes a symbol of how man is no longer able to gain anything for his daily existence from the nocturnal immersion of his soul in the sea of supersensible life. He no longer brings from the higher worlds any inspiration for the following day. Christ helped the disciples towards a new and fruitful connection with the supersensible.

Out on the deep water the disciples perceived something of the supra-earthly, heavenly quality of Christ's being, which became perceptible to them as quite different from their dark, burdened, earthly nature, something strange, frightening, judicial. This comes out in Peter's words: 'Go away from me, for I am a sinful man, O Lord.' Such a profound upheaval of the soul could certainly not have been caused by an outer event alone, by an unexpectedly successful catch of fish.

The disciples, however, are but imperfectly prepared for the great moment wherein, as if by a lighting up of the cosmic mystery of the Christ, the hidden riches are revealed to them. They can salvage only a part of the catch – 'their nets were breaking'. We have perhaps experienced on waking that melting-away losing of a significant dream, of which we can perhaps rescue only a few scraps into waking consciousness. It is an experience that gives an indication of how we can understand this 'breaking of the nets'.

The other draft of fishes after the resurrection mysteriously mirrors this catch at the time of the beginning in Galilee. An experience that the disciples were privileged to have at the beginning of their discipleship returns. Now, however, it is significantly transformed.

It is also the case with the event described in the last chapter of John that the disciples have cast their nets in vain the night before. They have remained empty. Again Christ helps them to an abundant catch. But this time he is not with them in the boat. This time he is standing on the shore. They see him there as the boat nears the shore in the grey light of dawn. He gives them the advice to cast their nets 'to the right'. As a result they make the great catch. This time – the evangelist emphasises it – the net does not break. Peter draws it ashore intact. There, Christ has the early morning meal with them.

This time the catching of fish is connected with an appearance of the Risen One during the forty days between Easter and Ascension. He appears standing on the shore. From there, from the land, he works the miracle of the opening of the sea. We see in this the great change that has come about since the event of Golgotha. Christ as God of heaven stood first of all outside the fate of death; he did not by nature, as it were, know death. Now he has taken it into the sphere of his divine experience, and thereby established kinship with human beings on earth, which is necessary if he is to be truly able to communicate with them. Only now, after he has been through death, which is peculiar to humans on earth, has he become like one of us and can really call his own, 'brothers' (Jn 20:17). The great transformation is complete: heaven has set foot on earth. It is from the earth that he now transmits his great power to the disciples. It is from the earth that he now makes the supersensible world fruitful for his own so that it yields nourishing food for the tender spiritual seed in man. It is to this that Christ appeals in the disciples when he asks them: 'Children, have you anything to eat?' (Jn.21:5).

It is not by chance that John's account repeats the word *gē* (earth or land) three times. The disciples were 'not far from the land' (21:8); they 'disembarked onto the land' (21:9); Peter 'drew the net to the land' (21:11).

There is also a connection between this Earth-Mystery of Golgotha and the Risen One giving advice to cast the net 'to the right'. On the right side we are more consciously oriented towards earthly things. The right hand is normally the skilful one, which has the task of taking hold of the substance of the earth and actively transforming it. When those of ancient times wanted to make contact with the supersensible world, they gave themselves up more to the dark, dreamlike forces of their soul. At that time this was justified. At one time the Lord gave to his own in sleep without their doing anything. Then the net was cast, as it were, on the left side. Meanwhile, human beings learnt more and more about dealing with the material world and thereby developed and exercised altogether new powers of alertness and self-awareness. These powers should not remain outside the sphere of the religious and spiritual. As they continue developing in our era, human beings on earth have to learn to transform their alertness, which all too often serves quite unholy, egotistical interests, into something holy. If they do not manage reverently to offer the clear consciousness and presence of mind they have gained to a higher world, its gifts are less and less able to reach them. The self-awareness that has arisen in the earthly world can be changed into 'selfless selfhood', and this selfless selfhood is the means of becoming aware of Christ. The powers of the 'right side' are also to be conquered for dealing with the spiritual. It is on these powers that the Risen One calls when he says, 'Cast the net on the right side.'

Moreover, this is connected with the fact that this time the whole catch can be brought ashore. By emphasising that despite the multitude of large fish 'the net was not torn' (Jn 21:11), the evangelist clearly wishes to bring out the difference from that other draft of fishes. This time the proceedings are not characterised by failure to cope properly or by danger (the nets breaking, the ship being in danger of sinking). The full, undamaged net is brought in.

The increasing of their awareness is also noticeable in the way the disciples gradually come to full recognition of the reality of Christ's presence. At first, everything is more like a dream; they do not know who the figure on the shore is (21:4). Then John's words of recognition come like a flash: 'It is the Lord' (21:7).* His recognition that they actually have the Risen One before them first spreads to Peter and then to the other disciples as well, although for them it is still at first a strange dreamlike mixture of knowing and not knowing (21:12). But then the Risen One 'comes' (21:13) and takes the meal with them. He 'comes', he reveals still more forcibly that he is absolutely real; he as it were exists still more for the disciples. And that happens in connection with the sacramental event of the breakfast. In bread and fish the gifts of the earth and sea are linked. Through Christ the earthly, like the heavenly, contributes to the building of the being of man. In the blessed presence of the Risen One, Peter, although guilty of his recent denial, no longer speaks as before, 'Go away from me.' By means of Golgotha and Easter, Christ has given sinful men the possibility of transformation. Instead of the tragic 'Go away from me' there comes the holy meal, the Communion.

---

* Friedrich Rittelmeyer once pointed out how this sentence resounds three times in the account (21:7 twice, and 21:12), and how the Greek words *ho Kyrios estin* could at the same time be understood as 'The Lord is'.

20

STAGES OF RESURRECTION

'Let the dead bury their dead' – a frighteningly harsh saying (Mt 8:22), yet one that can give us deep insight into Christ's feeling for life. Clearly he felt the people surrounding him, with all their busyness and bustle, to be like living corpses who had only borrowed a merely outward appearance of life. Compared to the divine fullness of life continually springing up and streaming within him, they inevitably appeared dead to him.

The single word 'awakening' could express what Christ Jesus sought to bring about in the people who encountered him. Whether he comforts or heals, teaches or admonishes, always he is concerned to awaken the consciousness of higher, divine life that lies, as if in deathly sleep, within each person. 'Your mind is closed, your heart is dead', Goethe wrote in *Faust*. If our mind opens to Christ, then our heart also begins to stir. In the Gospel of John, those who thus open themselves to the workings of Christ are said to 'have crossed over from death into life' (Jn 5:24). This figure of speech is drawn from the physical reality of crossing a border. The Christian's experience, in leaving behind the zone of death and entering the new territory of higher life, can be as vivid, real and tangible as crossing into a quite different country. John the evangelist has so deeply encompassed this thought that he identifies wholly with it in his epistle: 'We know that we have passed over from death into life; for we love the brethren. Whoever does not love, remains in death' (1Jn 3:14).

To experience this awakening, at least in a preliminary way, would be a first step on the path that leads us towards the Easter mystery. We can well understand that many people today gain no relationship to the Easter message of the bodily resurrection from the grave. Here it is worth recognising that it cannot at all be a matter of immediately adopting a stance on whether this is believable or unbelievable, whether we accept it or reject it. If we were to bring our mundane consciousness with us 'off the street' to form a view about this, in the sense of a simple 'yes' or 'no', we would not get very far. Ultimately, we have to consider that each of the four gospels arrives last of all at the fact of Easter. This forms the 'last chapter', in the face of which we stand, leading at last to this crowning moment. But an albeit very preliminary experience of inner heart awakening through Christ's impression upon us, need not be beyond our reach. We can first allow ourselves to dwell upon the bodily resurrection on Easter Sunday, or we can regard it as a profound symbol, a rune of deep meaning. Our place of departure, at least, can be a very inward experience of awakening. In each person this may look very different – brought about in some cases by a very incisive occurrence of destiny, or in others by slow, almost unnoticeable inner processes of maturation.

If our heart has been touched and awoken by a higher, divine life, this has a further significant consequence that becomes apparent as death approaches. Christians too must die like everyone else. And yet not like everyone else. Death is not at all a great leveller. One death is not the same as another. Since St Stephen – who saw the heavens open before him – 'death in Christ' possesses an unmistakable, distinctive tone of joyous, blissful sublimity. 'Whoever believes in me will live, even if he dies' (Jn 11:25).

Even if the particular circumstances do not allow death to appear conscious or blissful, it is nevertheless true that the life after death now beginning has a different signature for the Christian. This is an original and intimate experience of Christianity, and is also confirmed by the spiritual research of Rudolf Steiner. Not only is one death not the same as another, but the same holds true also for 'being dead'. From those who have died can come blessing and help to those left behind, but also sometimes troubling and disconcerting qualities. The reverence which was soon felt towards 'saints' in Christianity can be traced back to experiences that people had in relation to those who had 'died in Christ'. The Revelation to John speaks of how the Christ, as the Lamb of Golgotha, leads souls in the other world to the eternal springs of life (7:17).

The dawning of the light of immortality in dying people, in the disembodied soul, the 'life in death', described a second stage on the Easter path. Through the centuries, Christian people have had an intimation of this secret.

Above and beyond this, a further prospect can open for us. Through blissful death in Christ, death loses a great portion of its ancient power, but it is not yet finally vanquished. It is overcome for the soul but not yet for the body.

Bodily death means that the soul and spirit can no longer keep within the body. They must vacate it and relinquish it to perish. And yet the body was given to us at the creation, belongs to us as a God-willed aspect of our being. During our lifetime it receives the deep imprint of spirit and soul into the finest imponderables of its form.

This body that has so intimately belonged to us is lost at death. In this respect, dying marks a defeat of the spirit-soul principle, which is here compelled to retreat, even if the eternal has victoriously shone forth in the soul. The power of eternity may have been able to spiritualise the body to a certain degree, but is not strong enough to transform it wholly into spiritual form and fetch it finally from the perishable realm into eternity.

May we say, not *yet* strong enough? For Christian hope, the gaze opens here upon a conquest of death that might one day become possible in this ultimate way too. The 'raising at the Last Day' for which Christians hope means, after all, that at the end and goal of all human evolution, the human being will stand there in his God-willed wholeness as spirit-soul-body. Of course this cannot be a material corporeality. 'Flesh and blood cannot inherit the kingdom of God' (1Cor 15:50). We have to work our way towards the idea that corporeality must not necessarily be bound up with the coarse materiality in which it is plunged today. Whenever we seek to envisage a body in its 'form' and 'expression' but without the material substance that fills it, we are embarking on a path to this higher knowledge and perception of the body. Thus the resurrection body hoped for at the Last Day can be conceived as one that has passed through complete transformation. Only in this way can we at last take it with us into eternity as sum and yield of our earthly experiences, as expressive form and active organ of our eternal I-being.

Then, indeed, the victory will be complete when 'the last enemy to be destroyed is death' (1Cor 15:26). This would be a fulfilment of the promise that looks even beyond the 'life within death'. 'And whoever lives and believes in me, will never die' (Jn 11:26). Christ adds this to the preceding sentence, which runs: 'Whoever believes in me lives, even if he dies.' In the phrase 'nevermore die', the final conquest of death is contained.

Modern Protestant theologians pit the resurrection of the body against the immortality of the disembodied soul, as if this were an either/or. By contrast, we have seen that the soul-spiritual immortality dawning in death is the precondition for the hope that the body will ultimately attain eternity. And this dawning in death, in turn, is predicated on us taking an inner step, here already in daily earth life, 'from death into life' through the heart's inner awakening.

Having considered these stages of resurrection, let us look once again at Christ Jesus as he is shown in the gospels. Can we find there something of the 'three stations' of the Easter path?

The first would be an inner awakening here and now in earthly life. This awakening did not have to happen first in Christ Jesus, but existed already. From the Jordan baptism onwards we see him in the full wakefulness of God-consciousness. His loneliness and desolation on the cross is in truth the abandonment of God by earthly human beings who have become separated and distant from him – an isolation and loneliness that he takes up wholly into himself. This is part of his work of redemption. But of himself he could say that he always 'is in heaven' (Jn 3:13), even during his sojourn and travails on earth. From the beginning, there shines forth from him a consciousness that 'has passed over from death into life'. Within him, death has in principle already been overcome, and the Easter candle has been lit. This is why, though incarnated in an earthly body, he can still say, 'I AM the resurrection and the life' (Jn 11:25).

The second follows from this with inner consistency. As he is dying, he can promise the thief crucified with him, 'This day you will be with me in Paradise' (Lk 23:43). So that when his body lies in the grave, as a discarnate being of soul and spirit he will 'stand by the souls of the dead'. As such, he brings a shining light into the soul world of the departed, and makes real the thought of 'life in death'.

This sunrise of immortality in the soul world, albeit so mighty, is not the last and ultimate thing. The third and ultimate stage, which we saw hitherto only as a dim and far-off goal, now arrives as the hope of the Last Day. This final overcoming of death as the 'last enemy' at the end of earth now also happens in the realm of the body. Christ accomplished it as historic 'prefiguring' in his deed of Easter Sunday, as something that now, already in our age, heralds what for ourselves is still only a far-off hope on the distant horizon: a portion of the Last Day, so to speak, a portion of the furthest future, planted as seed into our human world on earth. On Easter day, Christ not only reveals the immortality of his spirit-soul – for he did so already as he walked through the realm of the dead as one who had himself died – but, for the first time, he appears victorious on the field of battle upon which otherwise the spirit and soul must always retreat when death seizes the body. The resurrection body of Easter has been wrested from the grave. Materiality has, as it were, been consumed, and a wholly spiritualised body has arisen.

But now it is important that earthly human beings gain a connection with this future that impinges on our present existence. Christian worship has the mission of bringing about this 'awakening' to the extent that we come to feel and grasp the 'life in death'. Its culmination in the Communion also reaches our body and integrates into it – as we receive the body and blood of Christ – the first foundations of what is ultimately to become our own, and intrinsic to us, at the Last Day.

21

THE ASCENSION OF CHRIST

Luke told the story of Christ's ascension twice: at the end of his gospel and at the beginning of the Acts of the Apostles. The One, the Unique One and the Lonely One stands at the centre in the twenty-four chapters of his gospel. He dies and transforms himself into the Risen One. He experiences a further transformation through the ascension: He grows into the widths of space and cosmic greatness. He again attains the divine, heavenly dimensions for human nature, which he had taken into himself and transfigured. He achieves that limitless mode of being by virtue of which he can encompass and span the whole of humanity and all the earth. What emerges in this way as the crowning end of the gospel, at the same time forms the precondition of the Acts of the Apostles, which gives an account of the many who became Christians.

As Luke begins his Acts of the Apostles, he first looks back at his gospel as the 'first book' that he has 'made'. There, he has taken the narrative 'until the day when [Christ] was taken up'. He further added the important supplement that the appearance of the Risen One lasted forty days. Next, he immediately draws the reader into the situation of the last discourse, which the Risen One had held with his followers on the Mount of Olives. The last words run: 'and you shall be my witnesses in Jerusalem and in all Judea and Samaria and to the ends of the earth' (Ac 1:8). The growth into the widths of space lies in this sequence: Jerusalem, Judea, Samaria, the ends of the earth. In Jerusalem, Christ went through the most terrible contraction of his heavenly being in the experience of earthly, human death. 'I have a baptism to be baptised with; and how I am constrained until it is accomplished' (Lk 12:50). With these words, he has expressed his feeling for life at the approach of death. 'How I am constrained' – literally: 'How I am pressed together'.

The new spreading and becoming expansive started with the resurrection and ascension and became 'omnipresence' over the whole earth. This process of spreading out first makes the diffusion of Christianity comprehensible. Christianity does not expand through the world in the footsteps of the Apostles, but Christians follow the footsteps of the Lord with their missionary activity.

It is not what is today called propaganda, in which you make other people believe something that would otherwise have been quite alien to them. The wandering Apostles were in truth 'drawn along' by the Christ being, which poured itself out into the widths of space. On earth they only try to follow after his ubiquity, which is founded on the ascension. Basically, they only try to make people everywhere conscious of a reality that came into being through Christ's deed, and of which everyone must have knowledge if they wish to become a true human being. Something of this reality lives in the divining depths of the soul; otherwise the mission would not meet with the strength of 'faith'.

From Jerusalem to the 'ends of the earth'. 'Earth' is the last word of the disappearing Risen One. His gaze and his will are directed to the whole earth. The saying of Archimedes has been passed down, 'Give me a place to stand, and I shall move the earth.' He referred to the law of the lever, which dawned on him. To be able to lift the earth with all its weight, he would need a point of application outside the earth. In a similar way, Christ, through his elevation to heavenly being, had to find the point of application from which he was able to get near to transfiguring and transforming the earthly. He is, to speak in the language of our ritual, raised to heavenly being *for* earthly being.

After Christ had spoken his last words about the 'ends of the earth,' the actual ascension event starts. 'As they were looking on, he was lifted up' (Ac 1:9). It is not a question of a process within crass material substance, which would have been visible to everyone, but a question of something that took place before the opened souls of the disciples.

Here the narrative of the Acts of the Apostles is significantly supplemented by the otherwise scanty account of the ascension at the close of Luke's Gospel: the Risen One 'lifted up his hands and blessed them' (Lk 24:50). So this ascension is not like the departure of someone who takes his leave and turns round to start on his journey, at the same time turning his back on those staying behind. Christ remains fully

21. THE ASCENSION OF CHRIST

turned towards his followers. Indeed, he is turned towards them as fully as he can be: he spreads his arms over them, he blesses them – that means, he lets his being stream towards them, he is there wholly for them. But does it say 'he parted from them'? (Lk 24:51). The Greek word is from the same stem as the word 'distance'. A distance grew between the blessing Christ and the disciples, an increasing, intermediate space. The blessing empathy towards them does not stop, but doubtless the process of perception by the disciples does stop.

The Risen One transfigures himself to a still more elevated, a still more spiritualised, mode of being. In relation to this, the disciples' power of perception comes to its limit. They can no longer keep up, their consciousness does not keep step with the tremendous thing that is happening here. He 'outgrows' their supersensory power of perception. And just this is represented in the image – the ascending One disappears from their view.

This process of being 'carried up', of which the end of Luke's Gospel speaks, has its parallel in the process of being 'lifted up' in the account of the Acts of the Apostles, to which we will now turn. The Greek word for 'lifted' contains a reference to the element of air. So we can say one 'airs' something through lifting it up. The powers of 'lightness' act in relation to weight as they hold sway in air and light.

Our earthly expressions never measure up to supersensory events. Each word image always contains a one-sidedness, just as each appropriate simile always has shortcomings. Therefore, to arrive approximately at the process which is meant, we must bring the various expressions used together. He was 'carried up' (Lk 24:51), and he was 'lifted up' (Ac 1:9). The first time the carrying forces of the Father are experienced, the second time more the powers of lightness and of the light which lift the Risen One up into still higher glory.

Yet a third word is used: Christ was 'taken up' (Ac 1:2, 11). Heaven 'takes' him up. It is something like taking communion of the highest kind. Human nature, which Christ had taken upon himself and transformed through his death and resurrection, is received by the higher worlds. Humanity, consecrated through Christ, is a new, enriching element for the heavens, and is not only spiritualised and ensouled, but also 'embodied'. In this sense, noted earlier in his gospel, Luke summarised the whole Mystery of Golgotha, from death through resurrection till ascension in the words 'taking up'. 'When the days drew near for him to be taken up, he set his face to go to Jerusalem' (Lk 9:51).

In these three cases, it is expressed passively. He is carried, he is lifted, he is taken (or received). Something happens to him. This can also be said actively. The Risen One 'went' into heaven (Ac 1:10). In the original text, we read the same word that is used for the going of Jesus from Galilee up to Jerusalem, and similarly for when the Risen One walked with the two disciples to Emmaus. The meaning indicated by earthly 'going', to be in active movement towards a goal, takes its continuation also in the supersensible. In the realm of souls and spirits, too, ways are walked. So ascension is both something that happens to Christ, as well as something that is his very own doing. The truth we are looking for here lies at the point where these two – on an earthly plane, contradictory – assertions coincide.

Similarly, a contradiction exists between the two descriptions: the receding, blessing figure, and the One 'going into heaven'. One aspect of the event is taken up in each of these descriptions. Both pictures, each in itself bringing an experience to expression, together yield an impression of what happened at that time.

The further 'going' of the Raised One was veiled by a cloud. The form is lost to the disciples' view. However, the supersensible experience has not yet come to an end with all this. They have not fallen back into everyday consciousness. 'And while they were gazing intently up into heaven as he was going, behold, two men stood by them in dressed in white' (Ac 1:10). Just as at the empty grave early on Easter morning, so here, two angels appear beside the emptied field of vision. The disciples not only see them, they also apprehend the angels' words in their spiritual hearing. Just as the angels at the tomb ask Mary Magdalene why she was weeping, so here a question stands at the beginning: 'Men of Galilee, why do you stand looking into heaven?' (Ac 1:11).

It could appear as if such questions, directed from higher beings to earthly humans, were meant 'educationally' from the superiority of the wiser. This might well play a part under certain circumstances. But couldn't these questions be genuine and seriously meant? Beings meet who belong to quite different worlds. No wonder that the earthly partner usually has to overcome a deep fright if the 'completely different' confronts him. But couldn't it happen the other way round, that the materially bound human being evokes deep consternation in the other world? On Easter morning, jubilation held sway in the realm of the angels.

How strange it must appear to the angels that human souls yield to their desperate grief, human souls who, since the Easter event, had only perceived the negative picture of the empty tomb. So at ascension might the angels also be surprised about the strange mortals, who stare painfully at that place where only a moment ago there was something, and where there is now nothing more for their failing spiritual gaze. The Greek word that is rendered in English as 'gaze' signifies a seeing with an intention or will, which would like to apprehend something definite visually. But this intense looking now goes into the void, its object has withdrawn from it. The angels must perhaps first get used to the soul-disposition of these mortals and to become aware as to what possibilities they do or do not have in this higher kind of seeing. But then they can bestow on them their angelic comfort. 'This Jesus, who was taken up from you into heaven, will come in the same way as you saw him go into heaven' (Ac 1:11).

With that, the bridge to the future is forged. The gaze falls prophetically on the return of Christ, which, according to the promise of the gospel, will become apparent 'on the clouds of heaven'. On the same Mount of Olives on which the ascension was experienced, Christ spoke on the Tuesday of Holy Week of this return. The sphere of the clouds is that part of the earthly realm where the earth, in its atmospheric and in its fine etheric material forms of water and air, stands open to heaven's interweaving. From the clouds of heaven, which in their continual lively forming and transforming activity animate and arouse the soul's power of observation, Christ will show himself anew to human beings when he 'comes', when he makes a movement of his own accord towards the consciousness of human beings.

In the rendering of this angel promise, Luke introduces another word to do with vision: Christ will return in the same way as they saw him go into the heavenly worlds. Here is a new, solemn kind of seeing. When the hour of return is here, the gap that has arisen in the consciousness of mankind will close.

The new vision will again join on to where it was broken off at that time on the fortieth day after Easter, when the Risen One outgrew his people's faculty of perception.

22

THE COMING OF THE SON OF MAN

THE MOUNT OF OLIVES PROPHECY

Advent not only reminds us of the coming of Christ in an earthly body at the turning point of time. Christ's coming then initiated the possibility of him coming increasingly and continually, living ever more as the Risen One into all humanity. The one who came then still stands before us.

Christ Jesus spoke of this, his further coming, in what is called the Mount of Olives prophecy or the eschatological discourse (Mt 24, Mk 13, Lk 21). This was in Holy Week, on the evening of the Tuesday, as he left the temple and climbed the Mount of Olives with four chosen disciples.

This scenery can affect us strongly. The Mount of Olives rises at the eastern side of the Kidron Valley, opposite the Temple Mount to the west. As Christ looks over from the Mount of Olives to the temple, he is gazing into the flaming-red evening sky. Full of wonder, the disciples have pointed to the imposing edifice of the temple, grandly restored by Herod. 'Master, what great blocks of stone!' The building stands there as if for eternity. But Christ now speaks the sobering words, 'No stone will remain upon another.'

History recounts one of its darkest episodes in the catastrophe which shook Jerusalem and the temple in AD 70 with the Roman conquest. There is no reason to doubt that Christ had prophetic knowledge of these dire events. When entering the city, he had wept at the sight of it; and it is clear that he saw the future clouds that threatened it. On other occasions he had imparted his prophetic vision to mankind.

22. THE COMING OF THE SON OF MAN

But here, in the vision on the Mount of Olives, something greater is involved. What will happen in the year 70 is only the foreground to a landscape of destiny that extends far beyond it into the depths of the future. Here, the 'temple' is not only the tangible building as it could be seen in the year 33, but also a true image of global significance. It signifies everything that has ever been a 'temple' on earth.

The temples of the ancient world were never randomly designed. In its proportions, in its coherence between interior and exterior, the temple embodied heavenly orders within the realm of earth. It made the saying 'as it is in heaven, so also on the earth' into something visible and tangible. It was a pledge of the connection and the cohesion between the earth of human beings and the higher world of origins. Whatever fearful chaos broke out beyond its sanctified precincts, the temple itself was respected. Its continuing existence offered the solace of a connection with the higher world that was not ruptured. This is why people were so horrified when the temple was eventually violated. The sight of a burning, collapsing temple filled people with a mood of apocalyptic horror.

'No stone will remain standing upon another.' Perhaps it is only today that the full scope of this saying is starting to dawn on us. Today we are witnessing how the old orders, unquestioned and unquestionable for former generations, are losing their cohesion and stability. So much is starting to totter. 'No stone ... upon another.' This appears to be heading for literal fulfilment.

Christ's prophetic gaze perceived this sundering of humanity from ancient, sustaining orders. He saw what this would lead to: wars, diseases, hunger – chaos of all kinds. He also foresaw how the human gaze would no longer look up to the heavens. An earlier humanity looked up to the sun, moon and stars with unquestioned reverence. In instinctive clairvoyance human beings perceived divine, spiritual beings whose outward aspect faces us in the lights of heaven. This slowly ceased. 'The sun will be darkened, and the moon will not give light and the stars will fall from heaven' (Mt 24:29). What once deeply inscribed itself in souls in the golden rays of the sun and the silver rays of moonlight, faded from human consciousness so that nowadays we attend only to the outer, material aspect of cosmic phenomena. In Christ's saying that 'the stars will fall from heaven,' modern people in a myth-dismissing era see only an impossible, outmoded and outdated, childish worldview. But we need only learn to read the hieroglyphs of this pictorial language in the right way. In Mark (13:25) it says literally: the stars 'will be falling'. This is not to be conceived as a one-off event but something enduring. We could put it like this: since Newton saw the course of the planets and stars as a great celestial mechanism, as the gravitational play of material masses, the stars have been 'falling from the heavens' for people over the past few centuries. Subject to gravity, they 'fall' in human observation from the higher contexts of life and spirit within which people once saw them. Imponderable realities withdrew from human perception, leaving behind only the ponderable matter of 'falling' stars.

But Christ sees that the catastrophic developments will have another aspect too. He gives them a hopeful name, calling them 'birth pangs'. Something new is coming to birth. No longer as in ancient times sustained and supported, 'delivered' human beings are now self-reliant to a more radical degree than ever before. History urges them to become attentive to their own human secret. They have the opportunity to discover hitherto unrealised possibilities of 'upward' self-development, in alliance with Christ. Christ, as the God become man who passed through death, and as the Risen One, the only heavenly being who bears the wounds of his earthly passion, can now be seen in a quite new way in his unique connection with the mystery of humanity. The divine or celestial nature, which in ancient times sustained earthly existence from the cosmos, was a divine realm standing outside humanity. By becoming human in Jesus, a new divine nature has come to birth, a human-divine nature. The Son of Man replaces the heavenly gods of ancient times.

In his version of the Mount of Olives prophecy, Matthew especially retains the sentence, 'Then will appear the sign of the Son of Man in the heavens' (24:30). Before the Son of Man himself is perceived, his 'sign' appears in the heavens that have now become empty. Compared to real being itself, the 'sign' is still something abstract, rune-like, something conceptual. When we perceive and recognise material objects, this starts with sense perceptions that are then augmented by the dawning thoughts that join them to their full reality. Perception of supersensible realities occurs in the reverse way. First we have a thought, more or less pale, but nevertheless an initial connection; and then, as we gradually enliven and deepen such thoughts,

22. THE COMING OF THE SON OF MAN

perception – though not now sensory but supersensible – can develop and render our connection to the being in question, a spiritually tangible and fully valid one. Thus a 'sign' first heralds the Son of Man in his reality, as his initially abstract representation in human consciousness. Something of this sign, this 'signature' of the Son of Man, already exists today in abstract terms in many vague sentiments and demands about 'humanity', 'human dignity', 'humane qualities' and so on.

But then he himself comes to our vision. Yet before this occurs something else must happen in the way of preparing and opening human souls. In Matthew (24:30) we read, 'and then all the peoples of the earth will mourn'. What is there given as 'mourn' literally means 'beat themselves'. In the Greek this even has a striking rhyme, *kopsontai kai opsontai* – 'they will beat themselves and they will behold.' This 'self-beating' is also present in Luke's account of the passion. There he relates that many of those watching the crucifixion went home afterwards from this 'spectacle' *(theoria)* deeply downcast, and beating their breasts (23:48). We might interpret this as also 'slapping their foreheads'. To strike our own forehead and chest is a gesture of trying to wake up, of the desire for self-knowledge. We want to wake up fully from a dull dreamlike awareness to a clarity that is just starting to dawn – we appeal to our own head and heart to attain this clarity, which announces itself as a painful and shattering experience. Thus Christ's words on the Mount of Olives convey that something like a great, painful, shattering awakening will come upon humankind. In the same way that Parsifal attains the painful insight that 'It is I, I am the one who created this calamity,' human beings will at last become aware of the destruction they have wrought in their alienation from God, not only upon their fellow human beings and the earth, but also on themselves. The pain of a radical and complete self-knowledge that ploughs up the depths of the soul is necessary to draw forth the power to perceive Christ.

They will perceive him in the clouds of the heavens. The realm of the clouds stands for the part of the earthly world that has not yet suffered compression into solidity but remains pliable and changeable. Depending on whose the sculptor's hands are, everything as yet unformed can assume the shape either of a monster or an angel. This is the field of potential that encompasses our earth. It is in this realm that the Son of Man appears, now as fully real person of spirit, with vigour and the light of revelation.

The gospels give a further special characterisation of such vision: it will be like lightning – 'For as the lightning that comes from the east and shines as far as the west, so will be the coming of the Son of Man.' (Mt 24:27) The whole horizon of consciousness rips open. The striking brilliance of Christ perception concerns all humanity, from the east to the west. The lightning power of this vision brings direct certainty with it, and provides indubitable 'evidence'.

These Advent occurrences will call upon human beings in their true, intrinsic being, in their God-willed freedom and dignity. Hitherto, our human dignity has been realised only in our bodily form. Our erect stance, our head raised towards the heavens, is already a bodily prefiguring of our human sanctity, and is, as it were, 'cast ahead' of the inner, soul-spiritual fulfilment that corresponds to such a form and figure. The body prefigures what still approaches – and 'reproaches' us – from the future. We must feel this noble bodily form to be a reproach to us as long as our inner life does not match it, is not commensurate with it. What comes to expression in this form still awaits realisation. And this happens when we, as human beings, awaken to the coming Son of Man and allow him to consecrate us into our true humanity. It is surely not accidental that, in Luke's account, the Mount of Olives prophecy culminates in the lineaments of human dignity apparent in the God-created bodily form. When these things begin to take place, those witnessing it should 'raise yourselves up' (Lk 21:28). This self-raising is joined by the prompting to 'lift up your heads'. And, as concluding truth, there comes the picture of 'standing before the Son of Man'.

II

HEALINGS

23

DEEDS OF POWER – SIGNS – WORKS

CHRIST'S MIRACLES AS DESCRIBED IN THE WORDS OF THE GOSPELS

Bible-readers often have difficulties with the miracles performed by Christ as recounted in the gospels. It can be a help for our understanding if we simply consider the actual words the evangelists use to describe these occurrences. We find various expressions that can show us the miracles of Christ from various angles.

The Acts of the Apostles contains a passage in which three different terms come together. In his Pentecost address, Peter names Christ Jesus as 'a man shown to you by God by deeds of power, wonders and signs' (2:22).

Let us first consider the word translated here as 'wonders'.

Wonders

If we are faced by something that does not initially fit with our habitual view of the world, then we 'wonder' about it, we are surprised. Our perception is not yet illumined in the usual way by our thinking, which we now feel the urge to apply to resolve the conundrum. This is why the ancient Greeks said that all philosophy starts from wonder. In Greek mythology, the rainbow is embodied as the goddess Iris, a daughter of Thaumas, whose name contains the word wonderment, and wonder. The appearance of a rainbow invoked in the Greeks a primal experience of wonder and surprise.

But this word *thauma,* which corresponds to our word 'wonder', is not the one used by the evangelists. They do sometimes employ the verb 'to wonder' *(thaumazein);* as, for instance, Matthew does when he describes the impression made on the disciples when Christ calms the storm (8:27). In this passage from the Acts of the Apostles, Luke uses *teras* for the word translated as 'wonder'. *Teras* is not as soft and docile as 'wonder'. It bears a certain nuance of shock and fear. Though it points, as does 'wonder', to an occurrence that does not fit with our habitual expectations, it also conveys a powerful inner wrench.

This word is also used in a disparaging sense in the gospels. Christ refuses to prove himself by giving 'signs and wonders'. Those who demand such self-legitimation from him are not letting the 'shock' of wonder inscribe itself deeply enough in their souls. That other world from which this shock comes, which is so far removed from mundane life, is so alien to them that they cannot truly awaken to it. Instead they feel only a certain titillation when they behold doubt cast on the all-too ordinary world by something inexplicable, when the world otherwise unshakeable for them is suddenly, gently lifted. Yet this is all they experience – a superficial sensation that scurries across their skin but goes no deeper.

Christ absolutely refused to meet this desire for miracles. Faced with the lust for sensation of the tetrarch Herod, he could only fall silent (Lk 23:8f).

Teras is used affirmatively only once in the New Testament: in Peter's Pentecost address in relation to Christ's miracles. When the 'blow' of something unusual acts rightly, it becomes the impetus for inner movement. It loosens the weft of human nature that, in daily consciousness, is too tightly bound up with the body, and can – perhaps only initially – enlarge the scope of awareness into the supersensible realm.

We often meet expressions which describe the reactions elicited in those who witness the wonders, the shock of *teras.* Translations of the Bible give this as 'alarmed' or 'terrified'. In the original, we find a verb for this whose corresponding noun form is familiar to us all nowadays – 'ecstasy'. In an event such as the raising of the daughter of Jairus, Mark uses this word in both its verbal and noun form. This cannot really be translated, but roughly speaking it is: 'They (the parents of the awoken girl) ecstasied with a great ecstasy' (5:42).

Here we must closely examine the picture evoked by the genius of language in the formulation of such expressions. Daily awareness in 'normal' life requires the subtler supersensible sheaths or bodies of the human being to be suitably interwoven with our visible, material corporeality. But states of loosening can occur. Ancient wisdom gave us the metaphor of the shoot emerging from its husk, or the sword drawn from its sheath. The clairvoyant eye observed how, in supersensible experience, the human being 'within' emerged from a tight connection with the bodily fabric and appeared like a second person alongside the outward one. This 'standing outside' is the fundamental experience invested in the word 'ecstasy'. Dying was beheld similarly as an *exitus:* a final and complete 'going out' from the body in the truest sense.

We have similar expressions in English. We talk about getting 'out of ourselves', or of 'out of body' experiences. Such insights, which have found their way into everyday speech, can be taken as accurate and literal expressions of reality.

Mark says on one occasion, paradoxically, in relation to Christ walking on the water, that 'They (the disciples) were exceedingly in ecstasy within themselves' (6:51). Logically, this is a contradiction: they were *out of* themselves yet *in* themselves. But a form of expression like this, which defies mundane logic, can give us an inkling of the very different nature of supersensible experience. The disciples experienced something 'out of themselves', outside the body, but this 'outsideness' is not a spatial state: it is at the same time a form of deeper awareness and interiority in someone who grasps themselves in their intrinsic, supersensible nature.

Alongside 'ecstasy', the evangelists use a further, still more powerful term that expresses such experience in radical form: *ekplēssein;* which literally means 'struck forcefully out of oneself'. This happened, for instance, to those who hear the Sermon on the Mount (Mt 7:28). Mark uses the word after the healing of the deaf and mute man (7:37). Luke chooses this strong term to describe the effect of the twelve-year-old Jesus upon his parents when they rediscover him in the temple and find him so greatly changed (2:48); and again he uses it after the healing of the possessed boy at the foot of the mountain of the transfiguration (9:43).

These few citations must suffice here. It must be apparent by now what all these passages that speak of amazement and astonishment are trying to express; how they relate to that aspect of the 'wonder' or 'miracle' that is expressed in the word *teras*.

Deeds of power

When the awakening impetus of wonder leads to an enlargement of awareness, then we can also enter the realm wherein dwells the mysterious something that we call 'power' or 'strength'.

Is strength not an enigmatic matter? In an ordinary healthy state, in our naive assurance about life, we hardly notice it. It is simply unquestionably available to us. But when we fall ill and lack it, then we become aware of it. It is there, it is not there, no one has ever seen it with their eyes. All that we can see, or measure, are effects. But do we know strength itself?

The Greek word is *dynamis*. It is quite often used in the gospels in relation to the miracles. Sometimes translated into English as 'mighty deeds', the New Revised Standard version frequently uses the word 'deeds of power' for this. For instance, 'the cities where most of his deeds of power had been done' (Mt 11:20). And, 'The disciples began praising God joyfully with a loud voice for all the deeds of power they had seen.' (Lk 19:37). For 'deeds of power' the original text has the plural form, *dynameis*. The translation is not quite accurate. A 'deed' always encompasses the person of the doer, but this is not the case with *dynamis*. Nothing is contained in this word about the bearer of the strength, but only about the power or strength itself. In these passages the evangelists draw our attention initially only to the *dynamis* manifesting in the miracles or wonders.

By using the word *dynamis* for Christ's miracles, the gospels offer us an important pointer to understanding. In all discussions about the question of the miracles from the Enlightenment onwards, people have given too little heed to this aspect. Citing the impossibility of violating the laws of nature, they have declared the miracles to be a fantasy.

We would beg our readers' indulgence for a moment if we reach here for a seemingly over-simple example. Think of a stone lying on the ground. The laws of nature state that it cannot fly through the air, and is subject to gravity. Yet sometimes we see it fly – when someone throws it. The law of gravity holds true, and yet it is possible for a different power to encroach and, at least for moments, to 'dispel' gravity. Or think of this: we all know how hard it is to carry someone incapable of movement. Where is this burdensome weight in a healthy person? Here a higher power plays easily with such weight, allowing us to walk, dance, leap. Thus we can never entirely exclude the possibility that a power hitherto unknown could in principle come into play. We can never determine in advance what may or may not exist in the world and what kind of powers could stream into a unique being such as Christ Jesus was during his years on earth.

Signs

Besides *teras* and *dynamis,* Peter uses a third word when describing Christ's miracles: *semeion,* 'sign'.

It is combined with *teras* on several occasions, but in a derogatory sense: 'signs and wonders'. Christ dismisses signs and wonders in so far as they are sought for their sensation value, or are required as outward 'proofs' instead of the heart's affirmation. But he does affirm his miraculous deeds as divine 'signs' for those who do not seek such outward evidence, but instead find in his acts a 'proof' of his being, which they have already inwardly embraced. During the feeding of the five thousand he reproaches those who adhere to their experience of being fed without seeing it as 'sign' (Jn 6:26). The right way to interpret the sign of this miracle of feeding appears soon afterwards in the words, 'I AM the bread of life.' In a similar way, the saying, 'I AM the light of the world,' belongs intrinsically to the healing of the man born blind, and 'I AM the resurrection and the life' to the raising of Lazarus. The miracles are deprived of none of their tangible reality, of their actual occurrence, in consequence. They are not intellectual allegories. Yet in all their reality they also point beyond themselves. They become runes, letters, that are asking to be 'read' and not only to be amazed at. Then they reveal a world that extends far beyond what any literal description could offer.

It becomes apparent that the *dynamis* of Christ's miracles is no blind power. Over the already supersensible realm of 'powers' shines a meaning-bearing and meaning-endowing higher world of spirit, which Plato called the world of ideas.

It is characteristic of the sublimely spiritual Gospel of John that it illumines the miracles of Christ with the light of the word 'signs'. It expressly states that the deed of Cana marks the 'beginning of the signs' (2:11). It describes the healing of the feverish boy as the 'second sign' (4:54) and in this way – without pedantically continuing these enumerations – it guides the reader to attend to the seven 'signs' of which John tells.

Works

Finally, we should consider another word, a fourth aspect in addition to the three named by Peter. In the same way that 'sign', referring to the influx of higher meaning, especially belongs to Johannine thinking, so does this word *ergon*, or 'work'.

The Greek word *ergon* appears in Matthew only once in relation to Christ's miracles. John the Baptist, in prison, hears of the 'works' of Christ' (Mt 11:2). And in Luke we find the word used by the disciples at Emmaus when they say that Jesus had been mighty *(dynatos)* in work and word (Lk 24:19).

The word *ergon* plays an incomparably greater role in the Gospel of John. Like 'sign', it becomes there a distinctive formulation and designation. A wealth of passages could be cited.

Above we rejected the translation 'deed' for *dynamis* because the former points to a doer, to an act necessarily invested in a person. An animal cannot do a 'deed'. This focus on the doer only comes to full emphasis in the Johannine use of the word *ergon*, work, for work requires a conscious actor. Here we come to the highest level in the gospels, where our gaze reaches beyond the realm of powers and of ideas, to penetrate to the highest personal, tangible spirit being.

'Work' as such does not tell us in more detail about its inherent content. The work of the carpenter is tables and chairs; the work of Christ is the healing and awakening of the human being. The term 'work' for such astonishing deeds as the healing of the blind man or the awakening of Lazarus almost sounds like understatement – the choosing of a humble word that falls far short of grander sounding expressions (which are, nevertheless, still inadequate for what is being described). In the word 'work' lies a certain self-evident naturalness. It lies in the nature of a spirit being that it seeks to be active beyond itself. This holds true through all the ranks and orders, right to the summit of the hierarchies. 'My Father is working until now, and I am working' (Jn 5:17). Sounding self-evident, this is a natural action in accord with the being of a true self.

The Father 'shows' the Son the works to be done, and will show him still greater works (5:20). He 'gives' the Son the works, and leaves them to him to 'finish' or 'fulfil' (5:36). The 'beautiful works from the Father' that the Son has 'shown' to human beings testify to his divine nature (10:32).

Just as it is natural for the sun to shine and warm, so Christ's fulfilment of his deeds is a natural and self-evident expression of his being. The miracle experience is derived from the deeds as such, and directed towards the great 'I AM', whose works are an expression of this. This 'I AM' as eternal, divine person-being, which in Jesus took humanity into itself, is the true theme of the Gospel of John. This 'I AM' of Christ is, ultimately, *the* miracle per se.

24

THE HEALING UNDER THE OPENED ROOF

MARK 2:1–12

Among the accounts of healings there is one that is particularly impressive in the picture it puts before us. It is that of the paralytic whom his bearers let down to the Saviour through the opened roof because the crowd prevented them from reaching him in any other way.

'Jesus saw their faith.' He saw that it was the deep commitment of their hearts to the divine that made them inventive and prompted this original idea. By this strange action they presented a symbolic picture of a significant fact.

In young children, the top of the skull still has a weak spot; the fontanel at the top of the head is not yet closed. Parallel with this is the fact that children are not yet cut off from the world of their heavenly origin. Their souls are not yet fully drawn into their bodies; they still keep open their connection with heaven, even if only when sleeping and dreaming. The hardening of the skull is the visible expression of what then gradually comes about: the door above is closed and the soul wakes into sense-awareness of the earthly world.

In the paralytic whom the four men bring to Christ, there lives a soul that has forgotten its eternal origin, being too much under the spell of earthly existence. It has become entangled in grievous sin and has fallen too far from the world in which it once had the angels for its companions. Nevertheless, the sick man has an instinctive feeling that in Christ Jesus someone has appeared through whom all can be made well again. Through him can again be established what apparently lies so unattainably remote: the still uninjured, divine freshness and purity of the child on its way from heaven and only just parting company with the angels. This belief is shared by those who carry him. And so they embark on their extraordinary deed; they take the roof off so that the meeting comes about, with the blue sky looking into the closed chamber and the breath of the divine worlds blowing in unhindered.

Christ knew what was in this man. He sees directly into this man and his destiny, his estrangement from heaven and his painful homesickness for the good and holy. Before he deals with the bodily ailment, he heals the soul. His comforting pronouncement begins with an unusual salutation. How does he address this man? 'Child.'

Nowhere else in the gospels is there a similar form of address. Where Christ addresses an individual grown man he calls him by his name, or even calls him 'man', or in the case of a woman, 'woman' or 'my daughter'.

In rare cases, Christ addresses the disciples all together as 'children', even 'little children'. This is far from being sentimental or 'preachy', but has very real meaning. It is chosen because in a higher sense it is factually correct when he addresses what is only just beginning to grow in the disciples, what is hidden behind their apparent maturity – the undeveloped future human. As the apostles see the rich young man turn away, the man who could not bring himself to leave the past behind him, who, burdened by wealth, sinned against his future – then Christ addresses them as 'children' (Mk 10:24). After the washing of the feet, Christ calls the disciples 'little children' as he proceeds to set before them the 'new commandment' of love (Jn 13:33). The Risen One asks the disciples in the boat: 'Little children, have you nothing to eat?' (Jn 21:5). By means of the wonderful draft of fishes he gives them the holy breakfast, which nourishes the future human being in them, the 'little child'.

But that he says 'my child' to an individual happens only with the paralytic when the sky is visible through the opened roof. It is precisely to *him* that he says it, the one who has so alienated himself from his child nature and become a sinner. Christ may indeed say it, for he is able to take upon himself the 'sins' that darken the child in this man, and deal with them as a god.

The scribes are not essentially in the wrong when they object: 'Who can forgive sins but God alone?' They know that when man sins he always 'puts himself in debt'. Indeed, he does something beyond all human possibility of reparation to a higher world, ultimately to God himself. And that can only be put right by a deed on the part of the one to whom it has been done, by a revelation of the very Godhead of what he is, which creates a new state of affairs through the power of sacrifice. Only God can take away sin – but, as the scribes know, God is in heaven. Yet here, Jesus of Nazareth is standing as an earthly man and says, 'Child, your sins are forgiven.' How can he usurp God's prerogative? The scribes do not see that something greater than a man stands before them. In him, heaven has come to earth. The power of healing sin has been brought down into the human realm by God's having become man.

Therefore, Christ can say that 'the Son of *Man* has authority on *earth* to forgive sins.' This is what is new. And he proves this power in public by adding to the healing of the soul quite logically the healing of the body. He tells the paralysed man to stand up and walk.

25

THE HEALING OF THE DEAF AND MUTE MAN

MARK 7:32–37

Human dignity comes to expression among other things in our capacity of speech, a unique endowment among earthly creatures. Speech cannot be understood as coming 'from below', as a further development of animal calls. It is a gift from higher worlds. In human speaking, something appears that is active in the world as a divine principle of creation that, according to the Gospel of John, arose through the Word, the Logos. The Creator Word, which 'in the beginning was with God' (Jn 1:2), lives anew in human beings. We could put it like this: 'The human being now takes up the Word.'

But do we really? We can repeatedly feel that quite other powers increasingly 'take up the word' in the world of human beings – powers that are alien and hostile to what is intrinsically human. They threaten our human capacity for the Word in two directions at once, both in hearing and speech. Under attack on all sides from insistent material stimuli, the soul is in danger of losing its subtler capacity of hearing, of becoming soul-spiritually hard of hearing and finally deaf. At the same time it is at risk of losing the truly creative Word, and of having 'nothing more to say' of any essential significance.

The Gospel of Mark recounts the healing of a man who is deaf and mute. The characteristics of this deed strike us forcibly. If we see Christ's miracles as 'signs', they point beyond themselves to the great truth that Christ has come not only to help particular needy people at that time in Palestine but, in the further effects of his deed of sacrifice, to heal humankind as a whole of its impairments, and fully establish its God-willed dignity.

'And they bring him a man who is deaf and mute and ask him to lay his hands upon him' (7:32).

The plea makes clear that people had already gained an impression of Christ's healing power. If they expected something helpful from the touch of his hands, this was not out of some kind of superstition. Through the hand, which is more than a mere sensitive bodily apparatus, powers of a higher kind can flow that are not visible to material observation but whose effects can be detected. It is a fact, for example, that certain people have good hands for the care and cultivation of plants. Through the hands of Christ stream a very different order of active powers.

Christ first takes the man away from the throng of people, to 'come to himself' as the Greek might be translated literally. He detaches him for a while from his daily circumstances and then 'places his fingers in his ears'. He also touches his tongue with his spittle. There is nothing superstitious or magical about this but a transfer of powers is at work. As an intimate bodily fluid, spittle can serve as the bearer of finer life forces. It also plays a part in Christ's healing of the blind. By touching him in this way, Christ gives the deaf and mute man something of his own life.

Now, in this case of the healing of the deaf and mute man, something very distinctive occurs.

'Having looked up to heaven, he sighed deeply and spoke to him' (7:34).

We hear of Christ looking up to heaven in other accounts in the gospels. The visible sky was, for Christ, the outer aspect of a higher world, which he knew he was uniquely connected with – as witnessed, for instance, in the feeding of the five thousand, and the high priestly prayer. But in all the healings, this gaze up to the heavens figures only here, in the healing of the deaf and mute man. Is this accidental? 'From above' Christ asks for the power of the Logos, which descends from heaven, from higher worlds.

Before it arrives fully in the earthly realm, it passes through something like an intermediate stage. In Mark we find that curious reference to the 'sigh' of Christ. When people approached him urging him to give them a sign, he also 'sighed' (Mk 8:12). Here the sighing clearly has the obvious meaning of bringing to expression an inner pain. But is this ordinary understanding enough to explain his sigh in relation to the deaf and mute man? How should we understand this?

We can compare this moment with other deeds of power enacted by Christ when, similarly, certain bodily expressions of his are observed whose inner cause cannot be regarded in the simple and ordinary way. In the chapter about Lazarus, for instance, John relates that Christ 'wept' and was 'troubled' and 'groaning' before his deed of raising and awakening. But can this be the ordinary kind of weeping and groaning? The usual interpretation of weeping – lamenting for the dead – is in fact based on a misunderstanding. The weeping has another cause. Something occurs within the being of Christ as he readies himself to awaken the dead, and this works through into his body, manifesting as symptoms ordinarily caused by pain. The same is true of the *embrimaomai,* literally 'to be moved with anger', often translated as 'groaning'. Many exegetists have vainly sought reasons for such an outburst or upsurge of feelings at this point in the narrative. Within Christ there is a surging and seething: spiritual powers and soul energies are stirring and moving in him, gathering themselves for the extraordinary deed he is about to do. Under the 'atmospheric pressure' of such a harnessing of forces, bodily symptoms appear that would otherwise only manifest in expressions of indignation. Friedrich Rittelmeyer translates this passage very aptly as 'He flared up in spirit.'

The 'sigh' he makes when healing the deaf and mute man clearly has the same unusual cause, different from our ordinary awareness of it as the expression of a troubled soul.

In the Edda, where Odin's initiation into the runes is described, there is an important parallel to this sigh by a divine being. The insights of anthroposophy enable us to acknowledge real higher beings in the heathen figures of the gods, whom clairvoyant perception of past times clothed in images. In Odin, the Nordic peoples – who retained their clairvoyant powers for longer than Mediterranean peoples – revered a being who was especially at work in primordial times when human beings required help in developing their capacity of speech. People experienced Odin in the blowing of the wind, in his special connection with the element of air, which, after all, is needed to carry the resonant word.

As a supersensible being of a higher order, Odin intrinsically belongs to a level of existence where there is nothing as 'coarse' and dense as our air. But, in order to affect earthly human beings' capacity for speech, this high spirit being has to undertake the sacrifice of descending to a lower level of existence to be active in the realm of air. This descent cannot be compared with the grandeur and nobility of the Golgotha sacrifice, where the most sublime being descends into the depths of death. Christ comes from a higher place than Odin, and descends more deeply. Yet the sacrifice of Odin goes in the same direction. It is not possible for Odin to incarnate as a mortal, earthly human being, but his power of sacrifice allows him nevertheless to live his way down into the element of air. The Edda expresses this in the image of the God who 'hangs on the windy tree' for nine days and nine nights, 'pierced through by a spear dedicated to Odin, myself to mine own self given' (Hávamál 137).

Through this sacrifice, Odin attains his dwelling in the realm of earthly human speech. He is, as it were, 'initiated' into the secrets of speech sounds, he learns the runes, he 'takes them up', and does so 'groaning' and 'sighing'. Here, therefore, we meet the motif of sighing in connection with the fact that a God seeks to bring humankind the gift of the spoken word. In Odin's sighing there is surely not only an experience of pain, albeit intrinsic to a higher being's immersion in a comparatively denser and coarser sphere. But here as well, in connection with the secret of speech, the 'sighing' strikes us as something characteristic, as a preliminary stage to human speech. When we sigh as earthly human beings, the stream of breath narrows, and what we have felt inwardly presses itself into audibility. Thus a sigh is on the way to becoming an audible word. And the reverse appears too when a dying person's extinguishing speech fades away as a last sigh.

In the New Testament, Paul speaks significantly of sighing or groaning. His now proverbial formulation concerns the 'groaning of creation' which awaits realisation of its true, higher being. The groans or sighs of creation, audible first in the calls of animals, still lie below the level of words. Human beings, too, participate in these sighs in

25. THE HEALING OF THE DEAF AND MUTE MAN

so far as they still live unredeemed at a level lower than would accord with their inherent nature (Rom 8:22). In the same chapter, Paul then speaks of groaning or sighing in another sense. The human being is still immersed in unredeemed creaturehood, but at the place where we should unfold our higher nature, the Holy Spirit streams full of promise into our soul as a breath of future perfection. Paul sees the Holy Spirit, in as much as it can already achieve efficacy in us through humankind's relationship to Christ, as 'interceding' for us to herald future things. 'We do not know what to pray for as we ought, but the Spirit himself makes intercession for us with groanings that cannot be uttered.' (Rom 8:26). Whereas the sighs or groans of creatures lie lower than the level of human speech, the 'groanings' of the Holy Spirit exist 'above' that of words, in the realm of our as yet not fully developed higher humanity. From above, the wind of spirit enters us, which is still in the process of realising itself in the breath-borne, earthly, human word, and will in the end do so.

On one occasion, Paul relates his supersensible experiences to the Corinthians. He was lifted into the third heaven, into Paradise, and there heard 'inexpressible words which no one is permitted to speak' (2Cor 12:4). Thus he penetrated into the realm of heavenly germinal powers, in which future worlds of spiritual speech are being prepared. These are, as yet, withheld from the human being since, at the present cosmic hour, we are not ripe enough for them. From this sacred future of things still inexpressible, of what remains as yet unspeakable, an influx enters us from above. We become dimly prescient of it as the 'inexpressible groanings' or 'sighs' of the spirit that occupy, and substitute for, the place where the fully awoken higher human being will one day 'know what he should pray for' – will know how, as spirit in a world of spirit, we should speak the Word.

After this seemingly roundabout route, let us return to Mark, finding now perhaps that the 'sighing' or 'groaning' of Christ as he gives back the gift of speech to someone, stirs greater resonance in our soul. We see the Christ raise his gaze and thus his whole soul to the high, broad sphere of the heavens, as if to draw the Word down from there. Out of the sublime world of the unspeakable, inexpressible, the wind of it descends and first becomes audible in sighs that are initially wordless. It is as if the whole journey of divine creation leading to the Word-endowed human being is reiterated here in intense brevity. And then it breaks through and can be heard as mighty word of spirit – *Ephphatha*. The evangelist left this word in the original Aramaic, adding, for the Greek reader, the translation 'be opened'. And immediately Mark brings the fulfilment: 'And his ears were opened.' Hearing is first returned to him, and then, after deafness, muteness is overcome. The band of his tongue is loosened, and 'he began to speak plainly'.

There is no propaganda intention here. The Christ impresses silence upon the people who witness this. What has happened in the body must ripen upward to the spirit in the protective enclave of silence. It was, after all, a 'sign' for things to come of still further and deeper import, for the overall regeneration of the Logos gift and capacity in humanity. This protective mantle of silence is not honoured, however. The people cannot keep such an unusual occurrence to themselves. And yet something pleasing also results from this failure to keep things to themselves. As if in spontaneous communal inspiration, they strike up a hymn-like song of praise: 'Everything he has done is good and beautiful;* he makes the deaf hear, and the mute speak.' (7:37). This conclusion to the account can give us the impression that the Logos power activated here by Christ 'overflows', and encompasses in its stream all who stand there. The gathering of people becomes the communal vessel for a Logos inspiration. The divine beauty *(kalós)* of the deed of Christ, as the people feel it so immediately, finds its comprehending echo in a beautiful patterning of words. The beautiful, the good, the true and the godly all resound together harmoniously: 'Everything he has done is good and beautiful; he makes the deaf hear, and the mute speak.'

---

* The Greek word *kalós* signifies good as well as beautiful.

26

THE WILL TO BE HEALED

JOHN 5

'Do you want to be healed?' This was what Christ asked the sick man at the Pool of Bethesda. One might think it a very strange question for it is surely obvious that the sick man wants to be well. On the other hand one would not like to suppose that the Gospel of John lets Christ ascertain something unimportant and obvious.

Let us look at the setting. There is the Pool of Bethesda with its healing waters welling up from time to time. At the pool are the five porticoes with 'a multitude of invalids' who await the favourable moment – 'blind, lame, paralysed' – all the miseries of humanity are portrayed in this wretched crowd.

If you read the story in Greek, you note with surprise that in the course of academic editing the impressive passage about the angel who 'troubles' the water has been relegated to a footnote, as the text is not considered authoritative. It is actually missing in some important manuscripts. This could be explained by the fact that in the times when Christianity was beginning to be channelled into ecclesiastical orthodoxy, so naive an expression as that about the angel 'troubling' the water may have been felt as a possible encouragement of 'heathen' nature worship. But does not the Apocalypse, the Revelation to the same John, tell of an angel who is specially in command of the waters? (Rv 16:5).

It is the very movement of the water bubbling up from time to time (the original text here uses the word *kairos*) that gives the opportunity for an invisible, spiritual being to take shape, as it were, in – or rather 'on' – it. One would not actually want to use the word 'embody'. It is a case of an angel, very fleetingly, taking bodily form by means of a suitable physical phenomenon. Water was always regarded by the ancients as such a phenomenon – especially when it was not stagnant, dead water, but was alive with movement, springing up, rippling and splashing.

They experienced angels as moving up and down. Jacob the patriarch saw this in his nocturnal vision of the heavenly ladder. Christ also speaks of this to his disciples at the beginning of his ministry (Jn 1:51). When they 'ascend', they carry up to higher worlds what is ripe for heaven. When they 'descend', they permeate what is receptive on earth with the blessing that comes from above. So when the moment of grace, the *kairos,* is given, the angel of the Pool of Bethesda carries down healing forces from a higher realm and momentarily makes the bubbling water the medium of etheric activity.

Water plays a special part in the imagery of the myths and tales that arose from ancient clairvoyance, which is even reflected in the popular legend about the stork picking up babies from the pool. Human beings on earth, estranged from their heavenly origin, fallen into sickness and frailty – are they not in this sense really 'left high and dry'? But the Pool of Bethesda (House of Grace in Hebrew) with the mystery of its angel, still somehow links them with their original condition at the time of creation.

Nevertheless, with a significant diminution. Only the one who steps in first finds restoration to the original state of God-given health. 'Whoever stepped in first' (Jn 5:4). This is no more a popular superstition to be excused by the modern reader than the descending angel. It rather quite realistically indicates a field of experience fraught with problems.

We can find a key to it if, for example, we consider the following. Suppose a city-dweller in need of recuperation makes an excursion into the neighbouring countryside, let us say on Monday. Everywhere there are the unpleasant traces of the thousands who swarmed there the previous weekend. It is not only that the disfigurement of nature by the scattered remains offends the eye; even if all the trippers have gone away leaving everything tidy, the impression still remains that something destructive must have passed over the landscape. Meadows and trees look almost like lifeless pasteboard scenery, the lovely green world seems to have had its vital forces sucked out. In the course of the week, if it is left to itself, it slowly regains something of them,

26. THE WILL TO BE HEALED

until the next sucking out. Therefore whoever can, seeks recuperation in an undisturbed part of the countryside, in which something of the divine quality of nature can still be felt. Not everyone is in this position, however. Let him for whom it *is* possible be thankful, but not without giving the matter some thought. He can gain strength from the undisturbed divine forces of nature for the very reason that 'the others' are not there. The moment those others, his fellow humans, were to come, if only in hundreds – to say nothing of the hundreds of thousands and millions – the healing power would be done for. It can, then, always be comparatively few who are restored to health at this fountain of youth. It goes relentlessly according to the rule: 'Who comes first is healed – the others are the losers.'

The sick man of the Pool of Bethesda had belonged for many long years to those at a disadvantage in the race. He waited habitually, though having almost given up hope that it would one day be his privilege to come first. And now comes Christ and takes a quite different approach. What is decisively new about his miracle? The sick man, stuck fast in his thoughts, can only say: 'I have no one to put me into the pool when the water is troubled, and while I am going another steps down before me.'

This is the only way he knows how to answer the question, 'Do you want to be healed?' But Christ does not go into that; he does not provide for someone to carry the sick man to the water in time. Instead, he calls upon his innermost being. This call to the will sleeping in the depths of his being, first of all receives only the man's hopelessly resigned answer. The mood of weariness that has become chronic in the course of years of disappointment still runs on almost automatically. But one could imagine that while this continued on the surface of consciousness, Christ's words, 'Do you want to be healed?' had already stirred a positive reaction in the depths of the soul. The sick man would not otherwise have been able to respond to Christ's next words, 'Rise, take up your pallet and walk,' by actually shaking off his disability. Without recourse to the Pool of Bethesda, he found health and uprightness through what had taken place between his innermost being and Christ.

This opens up a wide perspective for the future. It will become more and more evident that the healing needed by human beings can no longer be adequately supplied by physical means. It will be more and more important what sort of relationship they establish towards Christ. This is where the *will* for being healthy comes in.

There are two possibilities of dealing wrongly with this will. On the one hand there is the danger that it is weakened from within. Being ill can very easily become disastrously associated with egoism. Thus some people become totally absorbed in their illness, developing a self-centred interest and expect everyone they meet to share it. Being ill, with the associated privileged treatment, accustoms many patients to enjoy a kind of special position. In this way, the sincere will for normal health, entailing once more the prosaic daily tasks that no one notices, is greatly weakened. On the other hand, some people actually flee from difficult situations into being ill. This begins comparatively harmlessly with schoolchildren who long for a bit of illness when faced with an important test or exam. It can later grow into a real deserter attitude in the face of the difficulties of life.

Therefore, the question, 'Do you want to be healed?' in no way implies something that is a matter of course.

The will for good health that Christ inspires in men is also always the will for fulfilling life's duties. It is not for nothing that Christ commands the man who has been healed to carry away the pallet on which he lay. There is something deeply symbolical in this. The man is no longer someone who is a burden in need of being carried, but who should now get used to taking up and carrying burdens himself.

On the other hand though the will to be healthy can be quite sincere, egoism can still creep in to adulterate it; it becomes a self-centred striving simply for physical strength and is only out for what one could call an animal state of health. In Christ's sense, bodily restoration is to be only incidental to an inner healing, an inner rising from the fall into sin. The story of the sick man at the Pool of Bethesda has a sequel. Christ 'finds' the man afterwards in the temple. He knows how to find him, he knows how to meet him again at the right moment in order to confirm and complete what has gone before. It is a meeting in the privacy of the holy place. The man is made aware: 'See, you have been made whole!' From this awareness is to be born a new will. The will that was first called upon for the restoration of the body is raised into the sphere of higher aims, and now appears in its true and profoundest form. The 'Do you want to be healed?' changes in Christ's third utterance into 'Sin no more'. Overcome the sickness of sin with your will.

The actual time of the event at Bethesda can also tell us something. It was then a feast of the Jews that, according to the usage of the time, probably meant the autumn Festival of Tabernacles following the great Day of Atonement. It therefore happened in the autumn – we would say in a Michaelic atmosphere. In autumn, we are more particularly concerned with our inner life, and so it is at Michaelmas time that we experience the question, 'Do you want to be healed?' in all its seriousness. We take pains to answer it sincerely with 'Yes' so that Christ can approach us with his healing will and restore in us the image of man willed by God.

27

THE HEALINGS OF THE BLIND IN THE GOSPELS

Alfred Heidenreich published an essay about Christ's healings of the blind, showing characteristic differences between them.* In what follows I will take up his fundamental observations and elaborate on them a little by offering specific details from the gospel accounts.

It becomes apparent that the Christ addressed different strata of human nature depending on the particular person who stood before him, initiating healing from whichever level was necessary – the body, soul or spirit.

Rudolf Steiner's anthroposophy has given modern confirmation of the old tripartite division of body, soul and spirit. The soul is not only engaged with the body, but is also able to extend its feelers upward, towards the spirit.

We will begin with a group of healings in which the powers of the *soul* are addressed especially. Matthew gives an account of two blind people who, with loud cries for help, turn to Jesus as he passes (9:27–31). They have heard about him and feel trust in him. They run behind him for a little way, crying 'Have mercy on us, Son of David!' They even push their way into the house where the wanderer is staying for the night. Christ asks them if they have faith in his healing power. 'Yes, Lord.' At this he touches their eyes and says, 'Let it be done to you according to your faith!' And they regain their sight.

A second such healing later on, also with two blind people, in Jericho, takes a similar course (Mt 20:29–34). They sit begging by the roadside and likewise call loudly upon Jesus' mercy. Matthew expressly

* 'The Healing of the Blind' in *Healings in the Gospels* (originally in the journal *The Christian Community,* 1954, p. 110).

says that Jesus was seized by profound pity, and, in this mood, touched their eyes so that they saw again.

In this group of healings, strong soul energies are at play: from the blind people in the form of urgent demands to be healed and active trust, and from Christ, who responds with a powerful sense of pity. In those days, when the intellect was not such a presiding force, strong motions of the soul could work through into the life organisation of the body in a much more direct way than nowadays, and in this way bring about wondrous things. The pity of Christ works together with the power of faith of the blind people so that touching their eyes is enough to restore their sight.

The initially strange aspect of the first account in Matthew, where Christ, after healing the blind people, warned them and sternly urged them to silence, can also be understood from this 'soul' perspective. Translated literally, the word used is not 'warn sternly' but 'flare up in anger'. Christ responds to the souls of the healed men with a strong expression in order to curb their excessive upsurge of emotion and prevent them speaking to all and sundry without restraint – which they nevertheless do.

The healing of a blind man in Bethsaida, of which we read only in Mark (8:22–26), is a very different matter. From the outset this blind man gives the impression of being a more 'passive' kind of person. He makes no effort on his own behalf but is brought to Christ by other people. He himself seems not to set any particular soul forces in motion but lets things happen to him. Accordingly, there is no mention anywhere in the account of the blind man's 'faith'. He does not run after Christ. But Christ takes him by the hand and leads him out of the village. By giving him his hand he already imparts to him something of his own forces. From the orbit of the village, where people live cheek by jowl, Christ leads the blind man out into the open. There, where the great breath of God wafts over the fields, it is easier to address *life forces*. This time a laying on of hands is not enough. Instead, Christ uses a special substance, his spittle, an intimate body fluid which is pervaded by the healer's life forces – or etheric forces as anthroposophy calls them. This causes life to stream through eyes that were previously dead.

Only now does Christ speak. But as we have seen, he does not ask the man to express his trust and faith but asks, with almost clinical objectivity, 'Can you see anything?' The blind man 'looks up' and says 'I see people walking about like trees.'

It appears, therefore, that the healing has not yet been thorough at the first attempt, and that the man's eyes, as yet, give only hazy images. A second intervention is required.

But why a comparison with 'trees'?

The Edda, with its ancient Nordic vision, relates how the three creating Aesir gods discover the as yet incomplete human being on the seashore: a man and woman named Ask and Embla. These are tree names – ash and elm. The human being is still at the plant stage, and as yet lacks red blood and soul stirrings. Ancient clairvoyance was able to perceive the living etheric nature of the human body in pictures that were drawn from the plant kingdom. In those days it was still possible to discern a person's 'tree of life'.

When the man at Bethsaida first sees other people as 'trees', he is rapidly passing through the whole evolution of vision. In ancient times the eye was still strongly imbued with etheric forces, enabling supersensible visions to mingle with outward sight. In the course of time, the eyes grew 'prosaic' enough to have sense perceptions only of the naked material world, without any clairvoyant influx. The clarity of sight was no longer to be impinged upon and hindered by visionary perceptions. Christ wishes to give the blind man the visual capacity normal in our era for people awake to the earthly world.

Christ therefore touches his eyes a second time, this time not using spittle. We might imagine that the first laying on of hands, with the transfer of spittle, served to bring etheric life back to dead eyes, but that this life was too vigorous. From such excess of life forces comes the visionary perception that can clairvoyantly perceive people's 'life trees', but disturbs clear outward vision. The second time Christ touches the man's eyes would then not supply them with further etheric life but might 'take away' some of the superfluity. The eyes, first dead, then for a while too full of life, are reduced to the degree normal for a living organ, and then the man 'sees rightly'.

The three different prepositions used by the evangelist in succession in the original text, to qualify the verb 'look', are extraordinarily expressive: first the man looks *up* after the spittle touches his previously dead eyes. Here they open wide for the first time. This upward look still extends into the supersensible, and, above and beyond what is physically visible, shows people's etheric life trees. After the second, reducing touch, the man 'sees through' *(dia* in Greek). Now his sight is 'corrected'. The gaze is no longer caught up in an influx of visionary perception but, with a selfless objectivity appropriate to the sense of sight, it reaches *through* to the surrounding objects. 'And he saw everything clearly.' Here, at the end, an *in* appears with the word 'look': he 'looked into' everything clearly. The objective gaze arrives 'in' the objects it perceives.

As far as 'clear' seeing is concerned, there are two aspects of this in the original text. One of them would mean roughly 'revealed through the eye-beam', while the other suggests the gaze 'streaming into the distance'. The gaze overcomes spatial distance and sits 'far off' within its object of vision. That is how precise and accurate the evangelist is in his expressions!

Here we should also mention that Mark uses the poetic word *omma* for 'eye' when he speaks of the first 'upward' look of the healed man; then, after his sight is 'corrected', he reverts to the more ordinary word *ophthalmos* – a subtlety that can scarcely be conveyed in translation.

After healing him, Christ gives the man a last instruction: he should go home and not mingle with the rest of the village. Again, this is wholly in keeping with the picture we, as readers, form of the blind man. Given his evidently frail and passive nature, he first needs the 'protection' of his four walls so that the cure can anchor and consolidate itself properly in his body. He must withdraw for a while from all 'friction' with his surroundings such as might easily occur in a close-knit village community. How different from the faithful and trusting blind men in Jericho, who after being healed followed Christ on his last journey to Jerusalem.

And how different again in turn is the healing of the 'man born blind' (see the following chapter), whose cure takes up the whole of Chapter 9 of John's Gospel. The chapter gains its drama precisely from the fact that, in this case, Christ not only does not protect the healed man from 'friction' with his surroundings, but actually encourages him to engage with it. He leaves him quite alone for a while, and exposes him to collisions with, in this case, a hostile environment, in divine trust that the healed man will stand his ground, will survive these conflicts, and thus develop certain powers until he discovers how to 'find' him at the right moment. Now Christ can reveal himself to him, and thus truly fulfil and complete the healing of his blindness at a still higher level. It accords with the Gospel of John's distinctive spirituality that we here witness the drama of a person with a strong I who stands firm against hindrances, and at last can achieve a reverent knowledge of the higher Christ-I.

The active collaboration of the man born blind is called upon already during his healing. Christ sets him the task of going to the Pool of Siloam and washing off the clay mixed with spittle that he, Christ, has made for him by a mysterious alchemy, and placed upon his eyes. When he gains his sight by this washing, he finds himself alone, and must now fight his corner until that second encounter, which opens his eyes in still deeper fashion. It is no accident that this healed man is the only one, apart from the Christ himself, whom the evangelist allows to speak the phrase 'I am' (Jn 9:9). The human I here enters the light realm of the divine I AM, prefigured already in the saying 'I AM the light of the world', which precedes this whole tale (Jn 8:12).

The more carefully we study the various accounts of the healing of the blind in the gospels, the more Alfred Heidenreich's insight is confirmed: that Christ acts at different levels upon the nature of those he heals. In the case of the blind men who awaken his pity, he can engage with their strong emotional stirrings. In the case of the passive blind man of Bethsaida, he helps the latter's bodily life organisation directly with his own life forces, without particularly addressing the soul. Finally, the man born blind in the Gospel of John experiences at the spiritual level of the I AM, a healing that at the same time extends downward to the alchemy of the earth element – which is in fact the resisting foundation of human I experience.

Modern theologians have spoken disparagingly of the 'miracle tales' in the New Testament. But if we make the effort to study these stories in more detail, we can increasingly feel astonishment at the, in the best sense, appropriate and objective nature of the evangelists' accounts.

28

THE HEALING OF THE MAN BORN BLIND

A DRAMA OF LIGHT AND DARKNESS IN THE GOSPEL OF JOHN

'I AM the light of the world.' These words were spoken in the autumn, as the Festival of the Tabernacles ended. The days are growing shorter and darkness is gathering its power. Christ speaks these words of light into the growing darkness of the world. 'Whoever follows me will no longer walk in darkness but he will have the light of the world' (Jn 8:12).

The man blind from birth is healed on the same day. This story of healing vividly shows us the unique quality of the Gospel of John. The other evangelists also recount healings of the blind, but they restrict themselves to each healing itself, then continue their account with other episodes. John is different. In his gospel, the healing as such is only the beginning from which a dramatic sequence of events unfolds. His account extends far beyond the 'narrative unity' common in the other gospels, and takes up no fewer than 65 verses, from 9:1 to 10:21.*
The whole account can be divided into seven scenes.

1. The healing (9:1–7)

The healing of the man blind from birth has an important connection with what precedes it. The whole of Chapter 8, dominated as it is by

---

* The chapter divisions that only came about in the thirteenth century are not always organic. We should not let the beginning of Chapter 10 rupture the thread of this narrative.

the saying 'the light of the world', speaks repeatedly and strikingly of 'seeing', 'discerning' and 'knowing'. In the gathering world darkness, an inner light is to be kindled for human beings. The end of the chapter describes a tragic occurrence: those unreceptive to the Christ light wish to stone the one who stands before them as the light of the world. Though they are 'Abraham's seed', it becomes horribly apparent that these antecedents do not preserve them from a spiritual blindness. In earlier times it could be the case that someone who was 'well-born' or even 'high-born' at the same time acquired certain clairvoyant capacities from the cradle. But this now belonged to the past and was no longer possible. Despite descending from Abraham, the people in the temple cannot perceive the light of the world that reveals itself before them in human form. Heredity is no longer a factor in encompassing the divine spirit. The human being is no longer 'clairvoyant from birth' but 'blind from birth'.

There is, therefore, dramatic significance and signalling in the fact that at this moment, where 'being blind from birth' comes to such horrific expression in the picking up of stones, a 'man born blind' appears. Though this man, blind from birth, sitting outside the temple entrance as a beggar, is certainly not an 'allegorical' figure, a mere metaphor, in his human reality he is nevertheless at the same time a 'sign'.

In healing him, Christ returns again to the theme of 'the light of the world'. 'As long as I am in the world, I am the light of the world' (9:5). By, as it were, citing himself, he once again invokes this secret of his own light nature: it is because he himself is light that he can give sight to eyes. Goethe said that 'the eye was formed through the light and for the light'. First the quintessential cosmic light exists, and then it creates an organ in the human eye whereby it can encounter itself. It has invested something of its own nature in the eye, without which the power of sight, the deed of vision, could never arise.

John has the healing begin with Christ 'seeing' the man blind from birth as he departs from the temple (9:1) following the evaded threat of stoning. He does not simply see him in the ordinary way but at the same time perceives the man's destiny and the creative significance of the moment. He 'sees' him as one in need of healing. Whereas the disciples deliberate on the question of guilt that might have led to his blindness, the Christ sees that, in this case, no past culpability exists, but that 'the works of God are to be revealed in him' for the future. The original text has a double meaning: on the one hand the works of God should be made manifest in him; but we can also understand it to refer to the works 'of God within him' – that is, the divine nature germinal in him but as yet concealed, the higher I that still awaits unfolding. This aspect is reinforced in the statement that soon follows, 'You are gods' (10:34).

It is a singular aspect of this story of healing that Christ also gives a task to the man who is to be healed: he is to go to the sacred waters of the Pool of Siloam and there wash off the clay and spittle that Christ has placed on his eyes. He does so, and when he returns he has gained the power of sight.

If the healing was only an outward one, the curtain could fall on the story at this point. But for John, the story is not yet at an end.

The fact that the blind man was sent to the Pool of Siloam means that he gained his sight without Christ being present. Christ himself has not yet seen the man's now seeing eyes. Only when this also happens will the healing be completed in a deeper sense. Then the creative ray of light from Christ's eye is reflected back to him: Christ's 'sight' of the man is augmented by vision in a reverse direction, from man to God. Ultimately, all knowledge and perception depends upon the original light that has streamed into us, being carried back again to God in human vision: 'knowing as I am known'. To begin with, Christ *saw* the blind man; at the end, the healed man will *see* Christ.

But before then, various things must happen. Thus we are led on to the following scenes.

2. The neighbours (9:8–12)

Returning from the Pool of Siloam, now with the power to see, the man stirs doubt in his acquaintances. They know him only in his former condition, and cannot believe that it is really he. They doubt his identity, and this is precisely what allows the doubted man to speak words that otherwise, in the whole of the rest of the Gospel of John, are reserved only for Christ: 'I am'. The neighbours ask themselves, whether it is he or not. 'But he spoke, "I am [he]".' (9:9). In the Greek, we do not have this 'he'. The phrase is the same – *egō eimi* – as in the divine I AM words of the Christ.

This does not mean to suggest that the healed man was not simply telling his neighbours that they could believe him, that he really was the one they had known before. But if we have become attentive to the way the evangelist handles words, we will not regard it as mere chance that here – and only here – the sacred formulation appears, albeit initially veiled in its more outward meaning.

His neighbours now want to know how he came to be cured. From the account he offers them, it becomes clear that as yet he knows his healer only by hearsay – 'the man whom they call Jesus' (9:11). To their further question as to where this Jesus is now, he can only answer, 'I do not know.' In the Greek, the words 'see' and 'know' have a similar sound. The fact that he says, 'I do not know,' means that the true eye-opening has not yet reached its conclusion. More is still needed.

The healing arose from the 'I AM the light of the world'. I and light, light and I, belong together. What occurs within the healed man is on the one hand a growing gift of light, a continuing opening of the eyes, increasing perception and knowledge, and on the other a growth of inner I strength, which is destined to become the true Christ organ; yet this does not develop in a simple, linear fashion, but only in the course of resistance, suffering and struggle. Growing light – growing I – growing by pushing against resistance. What follows stands under this sign.

3. The Pharisees (9:13–17)

With his neighbours and acquaintances, the healed man had only to overcome their doubts about his identity. He encounters far more hindrance from the Pharisees, who ought by rights to be his spiritual protectors, his guiding shepherds. He must give them, too, an account of what has happened, but it is significant that, in this case, his tale is far poorer in words than the detailed one to his neighbours. If we compare 9:11 and 9:15, we can glean indirectly, reading between the lines, how something hostile emanates from the Pharisees, and therefore the words seem to come only haltingly and unwillingly from the man's lips.

The Pharisees take offence at the breaking of the Sabbath, which in their view Jesus has committed already by mixing the 'dough' of clay and spittle. They vehemently declare that 'this man is not of God', although some of them do seem to express themselves more cautiously (9:16). Finally, the healed man is called on to give his opinion: 'What do you say of him?' And now progress becomes apparent in his perception, a growing light. Against their resistance an insight awakens in him that the one whom, to begin with, he could only vaguely say was called Jesus, must be a 'prophet' (9:17).

4. The parents (9:18–23)

The parents of the healed man are now fetched, since there is still doubt about his identity. In their comments, the words concerning 'knowing' and 'not knowing' are again striking. 'We know that this is our son, and that he was born blind. But how it is that he can now see, we do not know. And likewise we do not know who has opened his eyes.'

The parents can no longer support their son but have to allow him his self-reliance. This release from hitherto sustaining protection is also part of the developmental trajectory of the 'growing I'.

The parents are obliged to refer now to their son's own intrinsic being, independent of them: 'Ask him yourselves. He is of age. He should speak of himself!' (9:21).

5. The Pharisees once more (9:24–34)

Now assigned to his own self-reliance, the healed man is brought before the Pharisees a second time. Their opposition has by now hardened – the more obdurate elements among them have prevailed. They greet him with words whose lofty emphasis lays claim to a 'knowing' that they do not actually possess. 'We know that this man (Jesus) is a sinner.' With this loud assertion, and the laudatory invocation 'Give glory to God,' they seek to undermine his self-reliance. His answer is, 'One thing I know: I was blind and now I see.' Once again they demand to hear his account of how the healing occurred – clearly, in their view, in a suspicious manner. 'I said to you already, and you would not hear. Why do you wish to hear it a second time? Do you wish perhaps also to become his followers?' (9:27). Here, a tone is introduced that we otherwise scarcely hear in the New Testament. Driven into a corner by the 'authorities', the healed man must preserve his integrity. Here, again, we have before us a stage in the evolution of the I: a critical, dangerous phase has arrived. Facing the need to defend his skin, the healed man is close to hardening himself and growing bitter. Cutting sarcasm speaks from his words. Mockery lies in the words, 'Do you wish perhaps also to become his followers?'

No wonder, therefore, that the latent hostility of the Pharisees now comes to open expression. They revile him, and stress their 'knowledge' once more. At this the healed man speaks again, opposing their 'knowing' with his own, 'We know that God does not listen to sinners.' He knows that this Jesus cannot be a sinner, that he must be devout, and indeed that he has 'come from God' (9:31–33).

At this he is expelled from the synagogue. 'They cast him out.' His parents had already been fearful of this conclusion. And just as they, his physical progenitors, had released him into self-reliance, so now he is expelled from the mothering lap of his religious community.

The development of the growing I, and of the growing light, has led him into loneliness.

6. Christ reappears in the story (9:35–39)

At this critical moment, Christ appears a second time. He had arranged the healing in such a way that the man who gained his sight had first to pursue his own path alone, without the healer's presence. This reflects something of the pedagogy of God, who leaves human beings their freedom and the self-reliance necessary for the development of their I. But then this independence must in turn find its right connection with the divine rather than losing itself in loneliness. This can only happen when the Godhead mercifully comes towards us.

Four scenes (2 to 5) have unfolded in the story in the absence of Christ. Now the time has come. 'He heard that they had cast him out, and found him' (9:35). He found him – he knew to find him, and, after all that has occurred, he meets him a second time, just at the right moment. The healed man stands before his healer, seeing him for the first time with opened physical eyes. But his eye of spirit is not yet fully opened. Christ asks him, 'Do you believe in the Son of Man?' He replies: 'And who is he, Lord, in whom I shall believe?'

Once again the evangelist can hint between the lines at inner realities. How differently the healed man responds now compared to his words to the Pharisees. How naturally the reverent address, *Kyrie* (Lord), falls from his lips: he is open and devoted. And therefore he can partake in Christ's self-revelation: 'You have seen him – he who speaks with you – this is he.' The man passes through the stage of sight and hearing to arrive at the flash of insight and intuitive realisation: 'This is he.'

The healed man had to pass through his loneliness, which brought him to the very edge of hardness and bitterness, and now he meets redemptive uplifting. What hardened in the defensive battle against opposition can be released. What had frozen into sarcasm and mockery can melt. From the depths of the soul the strength for worshipping devotion can rise up. 'He spoke, "I believe, Lord," and worshipped him' (9:38). The gradual opening of his eyes has been completed, and, at this juncture, perceptive sight becomes one with heartfelt belief – the highest insight uniting with the deepest reverence.

7. Christ's concluding words (9:40–10:21)

After Scene 6 has unfolded in the intimacy of these two figures together, the evangelist allows his account to shift almost imperceptibly to the broad, public domain. All of a sudden, we see the Pharisees, surrounding Christ, who disputes with them in concluding words. He rejects their claim to knowledge and reveals their spiritual blindness. By contrast to the loveless manner they demonstrated towards the man blind from birth, Christ reveals himself as the true soul guide, who becomes the 'door' and the 'good shepherd' for I-endowed human beings. This final scene extends beyond the end of the chapter to 10:21, where, once again, in summary, the 'eye-opening' theme appears. If we review the whole story, it becomes apparent that the four scenes without Christ's presence (2 to 5) are balanced by three scenes in which he figures (1, 6 and 7).

The motif of perception and knowledge resonates mightily once again in this concluding scene. 'I AM the good shepherd and I know my own, and they know me.' The ray of light with which God creatively apprehends the human being is reversed within us and becomes human vision of the divine. Friedrich Rittelmeyer often pointed to the 'just as' phrases in the Gospel of John, which place heaven and earth in a sacred relationship. Such a 'just as' comes here too. The mutuality of perception and recognition that occurs between the Christ and the human being is an image of the sublime mutual recognition between the Christ and the Father. 'I know my own, and they know me, just as the Father knows me and I know the Father.'

29

THE RAISING OF LAZARUS

AS PERCEIVED BY RUDOLF STEINER

Christianity has always regarded John's account (Jn 11) of the raising of Lazarus on the fourth day after his death – Christ's mightiest deed prior to the event of Golgotha – as something singular and distinctive. It has impressed itself deeply upon Christian soul life and sensibility, from the catacomb pictures through to Dostoevsky's character Raskolnikov. Curiously at odds with this is the fact that modern theology, under the influence of today's prevailing materialism, cannot make anything much of this narrative. After all, it is found only in the Gospel of John which, because it is thought to have been written later than the other gospels, is regarded as being historically unreliable. The account is seen as a fantastical exaggeration of the awakening of the dead recounted by the first three, the synoptic, gospels: those performed on the very recently deceased daughter of Jairus, and on the young man of Nain, who was no doubt buried on the same day that he died. But the *fourth* day after death? It seems evident that it must be a miracle legend that can only be taken as a 'symbol' of the power over life ascribed to Christ Jesus. Characteristically, there is no mention at all of it in the book *On Being a Christian* by the progressive Catholic theologian Hans Küng, whose aim there is to describe Jesus' historical reality.

In what follows I want to try to show, in relation to the specific example of the raising of Lazarus, how Rudolf Steiner's anthroposophy can contribute to a new understanding of the gospels.

As early as 1902, in his book *Christianity as Mystical Fact,* Rudolf Steiner devoted an entire chapter to the Lazarus miracle. He placed it in the context of the initiation ceremonies that existed in the ancient mysteries. His interpretation of the raising of Lazarus later underwent further elaboration through the development of anthroposophic insights into the human being, as described in the books *Theosophy* and *Esoteric Science,* as well as numerous lectures. Here I will briefly outline Steiner's view.

To a form of perception that can penetrate the supersensible realm with scientific deliberation, it becomes apparent that we can only fully grasp the nature of the human being in terms of the 'sheaths' or levels that constitute us. Our earthly body is bound up throughout life with a supersensible organism of forces, the etheric body, that sustains it. The soul belongs to a higher supersensible level. Finally, a further step in knowledge and perception is required in order to discern the 'I', which, in self-awareness, raises itself above all soul consciousness and belongs to the realm of spirits. These four levels interpenetrate in us in waking life.

In sleep, a certain separation occurs, as the soul and spirit more or less loosen themselves from their inherence in our living body. When asleep, we do not hear the ticking of the clock because our spirit-soul is not present 'in the ear', having slipped out as we fell asleep. But this separation is not a complete one: the spirit-soul is, as it were, still in close proximity, 'within call' of stronger sense impressions that draw it back in again. Consciousness, but certainly not life, has departed from the sleeping body that remains in bed. The life-sustaining etheric body can therefore pervade the body all the more fully, restoring and healing it without interference from consuming and possibly destructive influences of consciousness. The spirit-soul that is 'outside' us – though of course these spatial terms cannot adequately describe what happens – dwells during sleep in the supersensible world. Rudolf Steiner explains the fact that, apart from vague dreams, it loses consciousness by saying that it is still, after all, tied to the body, though now more externally, and that the body 'pervades it with torpidity'.

Like sleep, death too is attributable to a change in the mutual configuration of the sheaths, though this separation is now much more radical. The spirit-soul departs permanently, and also releases the etheric body from its previous lifelong connection with the earthly body, taking it with it into the supersensible realm. The body left behind becomes a corpse. The soul-spirit has now sundered itself from all earthly connection. No longer 'pervaded by torpidity' from the earth, it can slowly and increasingly awaken to the higher world.

However, there can be certain intermediate states, a kind of apparent death, from which the departed human soul and spirit, along with the etheric body they have taken with them, returns. In this case, the lifelong bond between the earthly body and the life organism has not been finally ruptured. For a while, as it were from without, the two have still cohered. Such a state can only last for a while.

The mystery centres of ancient times employed this possibility in their initiation practices, understanding how to induce it artificially. In earlier eras, the human constitution was capable of some things that are no longer possible in modern civilisation, and are only occasionally seen in exceptional cases. The ancient mysteries were able to cause 'reversible' death for a limited period of three or four days. Once this period had elapsed, and the critical moment had passed, then death became irrevocable. Not everyone could be subjected to such a process. The person had to fulfil certain prior requirements and pass through rigorous schooling in order to consolidate his soul and spirit more strongly and inwardly. Once he reached this point, the initiated spirit guide – the hierophant – and his helpers, placed the candidate through powerful concentration into that reversible state of death, calling him back again at the right moment as one who was now initiated. As such, he could turn back at the last moment from the 'country from whose bourn no traveller returns'. He had looked behind the great veil and now possessed deeper insight and stronger spiritual powers than before.

In its further evolution, humanity would pass through certain changes, learning to take possession of the earth through the bright light of the intellect. The individual would work through to an ever freer and more independent I-consciousness. This happened at the cost of ancient spiritual capacities of perception, which had to be lost in their earlier form. In the same way, the possibility of a reversible 'initiation death' also faded. In the symbolic coffin of Freemasonry ritual we find a last echo of this.

In the Lazarus account, Rudolf Steiner recognised the characteristic features of an *initiation drama:* the reversing of death after a certain period of time, recalling the person from the realm beyond through a powerful spiritual invocation. But, at the same time, he also observed the significant difference between mystery initiation of the old kind, and the Lazarus event. It occurs in an age when humanity had acquired sufficient selfhood to mean that it would no longer be right to affect someone's destiny by a magical intervention. There is no group of hierophants at work here, whose magical, hypnotic actions might have placed Lazarus into the state of reversible death. In this case destiny causes it. Experiencing the love of the Lord that revealed itself to him and encompassed him, he also had to learn at first hand the truth of the old saying, 'To see God is to die.' He experiences a developmental crisis: he must shed what is incompatible in him with higher existence. He must offer up his 'old Adam' to death. He falls ill. There are illnesses that appear at a critical point of development in someone's life, and have the function of clearing away certain hindrances to make new possibilities available.

Lazarus' illness, as Christ says, 'will not end in death', although a death ensues. It serves a greater revelation within Lazarus of God and thus of Christ as the Son (11:4). The Greek word for 'glory' signifies a bright and radiant revelation. This illness of destiny gives rise to reversible death, from which Christ recalls Lazarus at the right moment, after three days have elapsed. In his lecture cycle on the Gospel of St John, Steiner says, 'The old form of initiation must end, but a transition had to be made from the old to the new age.'* The ancient form of initiation, possible only for specially chosen persons, was, after the event of Golgotha, to be replaced by every single human being's upward gaze to the Christ who passes through death and resurrection. This deathlike sleep lasting three-and-a-half days is now replaced by the power emanating from Christ, if we allow this power to work upon us sufficiently.

If we can be open-minded enough to allow ourselves to entertain this interpretation of the Lazarus story, we soon see how fruitful it turns out to be as a working hypothesis. Certain hitherto enigmatic traits of this apparently so important narrative cease to seem objectionable.

There *are* objectionable aspects to it. For example, Rilke gave expression to the feeling that Jesus had clearly been traduced here, albeit reluctantly, into using his extraordinary higher powers 'preparing to do what is not done to that green silent place where life and death

---

* *The Gospel of St John,* lecture of May 22, 1908, p. 64.

are one.'* The poet describes the macabre scene, how 'the enormous cocoon of the corpse began to stir' and stood there 'squinting at the light'. There is something terrible in this unnaturalness. If we see only the earthly side of what happens, without the supersensible reality, the mere reanimation of someone who has been dead for days, who takes up his interrupted life and continues it, seems to possess a dubious quality – unless we consider Rudolf Steiner's interpretation. And then we do not stand any longer before a miracle contrary to nature, but before a spiritual deed in the realm of the supersensible.

It is clear from Christ's conversation with Martha that we cannot think of this in terms merely of reversing death and embarking again on a previous existence. The different natures of Martha and Mary, the two sisters of Lazarus, are described here in the same way as in the Gospel of Luke (10:39–42). Mary, we hear there, hearkens in stillness and devotion to the words of the Master. Martha, on the other hand, misses the grace of the moment through misplaced activity and busyness. In the chapter on Lazarus, Martha also displays an insufficient inwardness, a superficial, external activity.

The message of the sisters to the absent Jesus had been informed by a fine, heartfelt tact: 'Lord, behold, the one you love is sick' (Jn 11:3). Not a word more than necessary. It is left entirely up to Christ to respond as he will. No plea is expressed. Now the Lord comes on the fourth day – seemingly too late. Martha has rushed to meet him at the entrance to the village, 'Lord, if you had been here, my brother would not be dead' (11:21). A little later we will hear the same words from the lips of Mary, but in her case, as she lays herself in full humility at the Lord's feet (11:32), they have a different resonance, implying 'Where you are, there death has no place.'

Both sisters say the same, but to a careful reading the original text divulges small yet characteristic differences. A sensitive and subtle theologian of the second half of the nineteenth century, Frédéric Louis Godet, drew attention to this. What Martha says is a touch more crass: 'He would not be *dead.*' Mary's words are: 'He would not *have died.*' It is as if she is still experiencing the painful moment in which death occurred. And the unusual word positions in the sentence spoken by Mary lend the 'my' in 'my brother' a

---

* Rainer Maria Rilke, 'The Raising of Lazarus' from a notebook fragment written in Spain in 1913 (tr. Franz Wright).

stronger accent, and convey more tenderness and inwardness. Godet comments: 'It is as though a part of herself were gone.'* Her literal words are: 'My brother would not have died *from me.*' Martha's slightly crasser soul quality becomes fully apparent when she adds, 'And I know that whatever you will ask from God, he will give you' (11:22). We can hear the hint of a reproach here – 'Why did you not come sooner?' Yet she believes she must impress upon him a very extraordinary possibility to make amends for his lateness, to salvage it. At his request, God will grant something unheard of – the return of Lazarus to his previous life.

It is this view, that of Martha, that has been the common and prevalent one of the Lazarus miracle. And Christ corrects it. He replies: 'Your brother will *rise again*' (11:23). If the unheard of thing that Martha asks for is to happen, this will not mean the mere reviving of an earthly life, but something higher. Called back into life, he will be a 'risen one' – not yet in the final, all-comprehending sense of Christ's resurrection at Easter, his transformation of his earthly body, but Lazarus will have risen again in the spirit. Once again, Martha fails to understand the depths and immediacy of this. She hears in it only a comforting phrase about the Last Judgment, the Last Day, which is, after all, still so far off. But it is precisely this more superficial mentality of Martha that enables Christ to speak mighty words that stand like a radiant star over the Lazarus narrative: 'I AM the resurrection and the life' (11:25). In the reality of Easter, the Last Day is already prefigured in this world era of ours. Surely we should be grateful to Martha's more superficial nature that she solicited this extraordinary statement from Christ about himself.

These events were not long before Easter Sunday. If we assume Easter occurred on April 5 in AD 33, and if we recall the tradition that the raising of Lazarus took place on February 23, then a span of forty days intervenes, a period that has much significance in the Bible. The great I AM words that Christ speaks here in the course of the conversation with Martha are a spiritual engendering, a lightning intuition, a coming to full awareness of himself. It is not as if he is simply dispensing some previously known teaching. Something happens that is not without significance, even for Christ himself. He

---

* Godet, *Commentary on the Gospel of John*, Vol. 3, p. 18.

becomes fully aware now of the power of resurrection that indwells the depths of his being.

This perspective also illumines an otherwise enigmatic, 'objectionable' aspect of the Lazarus account: Christ's becoming 'enraged'. (The King James version uses the word 'groaning'.) When he saw Mary and the other mourners weeping, he 'raged in the spirit and convulsed himself' (11:33). The Greek word that is usually translated as 'troubled' actually signifies a severe shock or convulsion. And then again we hear that, 'angry within himself he came to the grave' (11:38). Interpreters have sought in vain to explain any illuminating reason for this 'anger'. At all events it is not directed at anyone in particular, albeit elicited by Mary's weeping: it stands alone without any otherwise usual object. We must not think of this as anger in the usual sense. Rather, it refers in general to a 'vehement motion of the soul'. Friedrich Rittelmeyer saw this clearly when he translated the words as 'he flared up in the spirit'. Something very powerful transpires in the spirit part of Christ's being (11:33), in his profoundly intrinsic self (11:38). The Easter power is stirring within him. The words that say he 'convulsed himself' surely mean that he was *not* overwhelmed, that he did not passively succumb, did not lose his sovereign inner mastery despite this flaring of tumult within. His weeping (11:35) was no doubt connected with what was occurring within him. Ultimately, this whole, enormous spiritual energy pours forth in the words he calls out in 'a loud (or great) voice': 'Lazarus, come forth!' (11:43). We can tell from this 'great' voice that it reaches into another world, that it is also heard in the 'other realm' and is able to draw Lazarus back into earthly existence.

'The one who had been dead came forth, his hands and feet bound with graveclothes, his face enwrapped in a cloth.' 'Unbind him!' (11:44). This truly is the 'delivery' of a newborn. Already in the Prologue to the gospel we heard the words 'born from God' (1:13). The one whose hands and feet are bound is released, unbound. He must now learn to 'walk' and to 'act' in the new, higher life that has been woken in him.

Still more 'objectionable' in the narrative than the seemingly incomprehensible anger or enragement, is the fact that Christ allows two days to pass after the message reaches him from Lazarus' sisters, despite knowing by his own insight that he has already died. Does he wish, by delaying, by raising someone who has been dead for days already, to present a still more striking proof of his powers? The message reached him by the Jordan, and he waited another two days. 'Thereafter, after this', he tells the disciples that they should now set off for Judea. The expression 'Thereafter, after this' (11:7) gives us a sense of how this enigmatic, passive waiting period must have troubled the disciples, although they are in turn also alarmed that they are to return to the dangerous land of Judea. Without any further message, Christ knows clairvoyantly that Lazarus has died (11:14). This must have been on the day the message reached him from the sisters. Jesus arrives in Bethany on the fourth day. The journey there by foot from the Jordan took at least a day-and-a-half. This period, together with the two days of waiting, makes four days. Christ has therefore arranged things so that he arrives at the grave after three-and-a-half days.

The 'objectionable' nature is cancelled if we understand this moment as the critical one, the right moment before the last thread connecting the soul to the body would finally rupture; the last moment when, in a higher, 'technical' sense, he could be called back to life. Allowing time to pass until the fourth day arrived, was intrinsically necessary to the whole occurrence.

Christ's 'gladness' at the increased 'belief' that will be awakened in the disciples (11:15) and in the throng (11:42), is not a matter of the propaganda value that might be expected from a colossal miracle, but of the historical need for mysteries that were formerly strictly concealed to now become public knowledge. What once had been enacted in the strictest secrecy with only a few, specially selected candidates, is now to appear before all the world, and be understood by all who are of goodwill. Above, we cited Rudolf Steiner's words about the event of Golgotha, the death and resurrection of Christ, 'replacing' past initiation processes. This great revelation and manifestation at the Mystery of Golgotha is preceded forty days earlier by its prefiguring prelude in the raising of Lazarus, which ends the ancient mystery era and introduces the new epoch.

Throughout Christianity, receptive people have had a sense of the inexpressible quality intrinsic to the Gospel of John. If we have once felt something of this Johannine 'breath' then we will not find it so hard to affirm a further comment by Rudolf Steiner: that the figure of Lazarus conceals none other than the author of the Gospel of John himself. It seems illuminating that this unique, unmistakable Johannine spirituality should have its origin in such a convulsive and deeply incisive occurrence. In his gospel, the evangelist never mentions himself by name, but he does point to himself when he speaks of the disciple 'whom the Lord loved'.

This phrase appears first after the Lazarus event (13:23; 19:26; 20:2; 21:7), but it is prefigured already at the beginning of the Lazarus account in the words 'he whom you love' (11:3 and 11:5). Over and above human sympathies, this points to a master-pupil relationship of a special kind. The face of the one who came forth from the grave was covered with a cloth (11:44). If this cloth falls, the face becomes visible of the one graced with recognising the Lord most profoundly – the face of the evangelist John.

III

PARABLES

30

THE HUMAN SOUL AND THE GOOD EARTH

LUKE 8:4–15

Luke, the Marian evangelist

Luke, to whom we owe the Christmas story, is at the same time also the evangelist of Mary. We meet her in the two opening childhood chapters as the soul of this Advent and Christmas world. It begins with the angel of the Annunciation appearing to the Virgin in Nazareth. As the 'handmaid of the Lord' she willingly and devotedly accepts her part in the forthcoming sacred events. The angelic greeting is soon followed by Elizabeth's words about Mary being 'blessed among women', to which Mary replies with the Magnificat hymn – 'My soul glorifies the Lord.' At Bethlehem, she lays the child in the manger and recalls the angel's words in her heart. At the presentation in the temple, we hear the passion bell sound from afar – 'through your soul a sword will pierce'. And as she stands before the enigma of the twelve-year-old in the temple, the pain already begins for her, yet she takes the strange words of the boy deep into her soul.

In Luke's holy and tender narrative of Mary, people have always found something archetypal. Irrespective of its historical accuracy, the structure of events and vivid images possess a quality that allows certain secrets of the human soul to become perceptible: 'You must be like Mary and bring a God to birth in you.' The human soul itself intuits its highest capacities in the figure of Mary.

It is intrinsic to the soul to be receptive, open, able to conceive. What it experiences and dwells upon finds in the soul's depths a mothering soil in which it can develop further and fruitfully ripen. And when the soul opens receptively, in purity, to the highest reality, then it becomes the Virgin Mary, who, overshadowed by the Holy Spirit, gives birth to the Christ child.

If we read on through the Gospel of Luke, we notice that this theme of the soul's Marian secret does not end with the two childhood chapters. It continues to be present, albeit in a quiet and unintrusive way. We feel it, for instance, in the not infrequent passages where a woman plays an important role. I will not cite these places in detail now, but instead focus upon a text that Luke has in common with Matthew and Mark, though in the Luke version, despite all seeming correspondence, the Marian theme is clearly discernible. This is the well-known parable of the sower and the different terrains.

The parable of the good earth

It would be a superficial appraisal to think that the same story is told three times in the New Testament. Attentive study shows that what appears the same, in fact stands in a different context with each evangelist and is differently illumined. In Matthew, the parable is the first of the seven parables by the lake, which together form a particular configuration. In Mark, it is the first of a group of three. In Luke it stands alone and has a dominant place in the whole context.

Matthew, Mark and Luke – who, because of a certain equivalence between their accounts, are seen together as the synoptics – all follow the tale with explanatory words with which Christ translates his pictorial words into the form of thoughts. Here the Luke version is alone in starting this interpretation with the classical formula 'The seed is the Word (Logos) of God' (8:11). The seed is the Word – the Word is the seed, and hearing is therefore a fertilisation. In the parable of the sower, the earth is the mother. The interpretation tells us that the same process occurs again at another level when the soul in devoted hearing receives (conceives) the Logos seed, protects it and nurtures it carefully and at last brings its fruit to light. We read this in all three evangelists. But there is stronger emphasis in Luke on the soul's connection and relatedness to the soil. Let us compare the text of the three synoptic gospels:

Matthew 13:23	*Mark 4:20*	*Luke 8:15*
The seed sown on the good earth is he who hears and understands the Word and then bears fruit, some yielding a hundredfold, some sixty or thirty.	And those [seeds] that are sown on the good earth, hear the Word and receive it, and bear fruit, one thirtyfold, one sixty and one a hundred.	And what fell upon the good earth are those who, in a good and beautiful heart, hear the Word and hold it fast, and bring forth fruit in patience.

Each of the three has a different emphasis. In ancient Greece, the world of Plato, the two words 'beautiful' and 'good' had been brought together in one phrase *(kalós k'agathós)*. Luke, the Greek, adds this fruit of high Greek culture to his gospel in the words 'a good and beautiful heart'.

On listening

Is it accidental that hearing acquires special importance in Luke particularly? Christ follows his explanation of the parable with an admonition. This is absent in Matthew; in Mark it runs: 'Attend to *what* you hear.' In Luke there is a slight but telling difference: 'Attend to *how* you hear' (8:18). This may remind us of Goethe, 'Consider what, but more consider how.'

The parable of the sower in all three gospels is given close in time to a scene in which the mother of Jesus appears. Mother, brothers and sisters have come from Nazareth full of anxiety to fetch him back to the family. Since the Jordan baptism they have not yet been able to come to terms with his altered nature – and will only be able to do so after the resurrection. The Christ is surrounded by a great throng of listeners. Matthew and Mark give a dramatic description of Christ asking, 'Who is my mother? And who are my brothers?' As he says this he extends his hand over the throng, looks around the circle of them and then says: 'See, my mother and my brothers.' This should not be misunderstood as a cold repudiation of his blood relatives, his 'own', but as a way of clearing the ground for a still higher commonality and community founded on the soul and spirit. 'Whoever does the will of my Father in the heavens, he is my brother and sister and mother.' With this reference to doing the divine will, Matthew and Mark both lead on directly into the parable of the sower.

Luke has this scene *follow* the parable. And once again, we can discern a subtle difference in his concluding words, *'My mother and my brothers are they who hear and do the Word (Logos) of God'* (8:21). Here the accent is on 'Word' and 'hearing' rather than on the will. The mother is not merely one of the relatives here, but a distinction is made in which 'hearing' is assigned to the mother, and 'doing' to the brothers: 'Whoever hears the Word of God is my mother.'

Again, let us compare the three versions:

Matthew 12:49f	*Mark 3:34f*	*Luke 8:21*
And he stretched out his hand over his disciples and said, 'See, my mother and my brothers. For whoever does the will of my Father in the heavens, he is my brother and sister and mother.'	And looking around at those sitting in a circle around him, he says, 'See, my mother and my brothers. Whoever does the will of God, he is my brother and sister and mother.'	He answered and said to them: 'My mother and my brothers – they are those who hear and do the Word of God (the Logos).'

As we read on, we soon come to the account of Christ's visit to the sisters Mary and Martha – this too is found only in Luke. Martha is wholly taken up with managing the household, while Mary 'sat at the feet of the Lord and listened to his words' (10:39). Commentators have said that this is Mary Magdalene, and it may be so. Luke first names Mary with the epithet 'Magdalene' (which means, the one from Magdala) directly before the parable of the sower.

At the beginning of Chapter 8, he mentions the serving women who accompanied Christ on his wanderings. Referring here to a Johanna and a Susanna, but above all 'Mary Magdalene, from whom the seven demons had departed' (8:2). The seven demons are also mentioned in Mark 16:9. Rudolf Steiner taught us to attend to the quiet, yet significant, 'compositional' language of the gospels: how one thing follows another and thus various things are hinted at or suggested between the lines. We can become aware, therefore, that this mention of Mary Magdalene is directly preceded – again only in Luke – by the account of the sinful woman (7:36–50). The sinful woman, who has hitherto misspent her devotional power in the wrong way, is freed of the demons by Christ, is healed and transformed so that the 'eternal feminine' can manifest within her. In 'hearing' the divine Word, and taking it up with full, loving devotion of the soul, she truly becomes a 'Mary'.

Thus contexts of meaning run like golden threads through the gospel. The one we have been tracing comes to a conclusion in an occurrence which only Luke recounts, in Chapter 11. Moved by Christ's address, a woman in the throng raises her voice and praises the mother of such a son as 'blessed' (11:27). Is this merely the somewhat predictable, stereotypical reaction of a woman – to hear Christ and think immediately of the woman who is his mother? Christ has a deeper understanding. Behind this acclaim of his physical mother he discerns the hidden, subliminal longing of the human soul for Maryhood. Thus he intensifies the woman's cry with a further beatification: 'Blessed are they who hear the Word of God and keep it safe' (11:28). Basically he is saying, 'You too can be my mother, you too, as Mary, can give birth in your soul to Christ.'

The counter-image: 'Think of Lot's wife'

The soul's high calling to be the mother of God becomes still more clearly discernible when we consider our potential lapse from this ideal. In the case of this 'great sinner', the demons of passion sought to prevent her turning to the divine. But there is also another way to err. In Christianity, hitherto, people have largely been aware of the adversarial powers who threaten the soul with passions. But alongside this 'hot war', a 'cold war' is waged too, one that in our era is becoming ever more dangerous. It can happen that the soul is seized by such weariness, resignation, indifference or hopelessness, that it sacrifices its living qualities to cold, mechanistic, robotic drives, succumbing to rigidity and hardness.

All three synoptic evangelists convey Christ's prophetic words about his Second Coming, and the catastrophes that will precede it, in what is known as the Mount of Olives Prophecy or the Olivet Discourse.

Luke introduces some of this content already at an earlier point in the narrative, while Christ is still on his last journey towards Jerusalem (17:22-18:8). He speaks of the 'day on which the Son of Man will be revealed' – *apokalyptetai* in the original text. *Apokalyptein* literally means disclose, reveal, unveil, remove a covering. In regard to this future new manifestation of Christ, admonishing images of catastrophe at the same time surface from ancient times – the Flood, the destruction by fire of Sodom and Gomorrah – from which, on each occasion, the germ of a future humanity is saved. The apocryphal Wisdom of Solomon has wonderful words for this saving: 'And at the beginning, when the proud giants perished, the hope of the world governed by your hand took refuge in the ark, and left to the cycle of ages the seed of a new creation' (Ws 14:6). Like Noah saved from the floodwaters, so Lot is saved from the fire of Sodom. In these long-distant catastrophes the future apocalypse is prefigured and reflected. For this reason, in this prophetic address about his Second Coming, Christ recalls ancient terrors. And in doing so – though only in Luke – says the words *'Remember Lot's wife'* (17:32).

Did Lot's wife not change to a pillar of salt because she turned back again to the terrible things that were happening behind her? When the angels snatched Lot and his family from destruction and led them out and away into the open, they said to him: 'Save your soul! Do not look back! Do not remain in the plain! Take flight to the mountain so that you do not perish!' (Gn 19:17). The people who, as the 'hope of the world', were to make the transition that would allow new evolution to begin, have to decide to turn to the divine that is coming towards them from the future, from above. 'No one who lays their hand upon the plough and looks back is fit for the kingdome of God' (Lk 9:62).

Such wrongful looking back can be to the supposedly 'good old days' whose time is past. But it can take other forms too. It occurs also if people allow themselves to be fascinated by what takes root out of anti-spirit and God-alienation, but which contains the seeds of destruction; if we succumb to the hypnotic suggestion of what is rushing towards the abyss instead of 'leaving it behind us'.

Lot's wife does not persist in moving onwards and upwards. She stops, turns round, looks back to the fire and smoke of Sodom, and petrifies into a pillar of salt. Spellbound by the destruction she sees, she loses her vitality and is 'mineralised' by the powers of death: she 'dies the death of matter'. And, in doing so, she loses her future potential to become the mother of God.

If we learn to read the picture language of the Bible once again, then we begin to sense the meaning of this brief sentence from Christ's prophetic address: 'Remember Lot's wife!' Such a warning becomes ever more topical with every passing year. If, in the mood of Advent, we look and strive upwards towards the future, then we are on the way to hearkening to the prompting of the saving angels: 'Save your soul!'

31

THREE PARABLES OF LOSING AND FINDING

LUKE 15

Losing and rediscovering is one of the fundamental themes of human life, and Chapter 15 of the Gospel of Luke is devoted to it. Christ relates three parables here: the shepherd who seeks the lost sheep, the woman who seeks the lost coin, and the father who greets his returning son.

In these three parables, losing and finding is recounted from the divine perspective. Rather than man's search for God, they relate to God's search for man.

Man's search for God is tinged with a memory that once we possessed an intimate connection with a higher world. This shone into the human world in former eras of humanity, as it still does into each person's childhood – 'I once possessed this.' It faded away in a twilight of the gods, which allowed us to forget the divine and to encompass instead the material earth in bright, waking consciousness. But there are still echoes remaining of this as yearning, as hope that we will one day rediscover the connection to primal, creative powers. Such longing alone could not lead us to the goal if the divine itself did not come to meet us from the other side, as 'love from above'. In the three parables, Christ indicates that the divine world, for its part, painfully experiences the loss of the lapsed human being, and that it is hoping to find the lost one again.

The shepherd and the lost sheep

As Christ begins to speak of this divine movement towards the human being, he draws on common human feelings. 'Who among you would not do the same?' This refers to the shepherd who leaves his 99 sheep in a lonely arid region and goes to seek the lost sheep. When he finds it at last he takes the exhausted animal upon his shoulders, not reluctant at this burden, but 'joyfully'.

However short and simple this story is, we have here a fabric of words that are not accidentally configured but in reciprocal relationship. Three times we hear the word 'lose' (Lk 15:4, 4, 6), three times 'find' (15:4, 5, 6) and three times 'joy' (15:5, 6, 7).

The end of the parable is radiant with joy. The shepherd who bears the rediscovered sheep 'joyfully' home, invites neighbours and friends to 'rejoice with him'. The story ends with words about 'joy in heaven'. Outwardly, there seems little cause for such a special celebration. The shepherd has his hundred sheep back again in the end, as before. But things are not simply as they were. Naturally assumed possession has received new impetus. The experience of loss gives rise to a new awareness of what is valuable. The joy of rediscovery brings a sense of heightening that contrasts with 'what once was'.

Christ seems like a loving observer as he describes the shepherds of the Holy Land with their ability to celebrate joyful feasts despite impoverished circumstances, and to share selflessly in the joys of others. In this happy commonality, Christ sees the earthly reflection of something higher. 'So will the joy in heaven be at one sinner who repents.' In the parable itself, the lost one, here a sheep, plays a passive role. The shepherd sought it and bore it home. But at the end, Christ does not hesitate to go beyond the terms of the story's metaphor and augment it by referring to the necessary participation of human beings in the sense of their 'repentance'. We cannot fail to discern the hint of irony attaching to the phrase concerning the '99 righteous ones who have no need to repent'.

The woman and the lost coin

The parable of the shepherd is immediately followed by a second parable, that of the lost coin, a drachma. This is a silver coin that we can think of perhaps as a day's wages, ten of which clearly constitute the whole of the woman's fortune.

It might seem as if the same thing is being said again as in the parable of the shepherd. But looking more closely, the art of the narrator becomes apparent in the way that he introduces new perspectives into the repetition, varying the images. We cannot help noticing that 'one in a hundred' is something different from 'one in ten'. Another characteristic difference is that the shepherd searches far and wide in a broad landscape, whereas the woman is concerned with the 'small world' of her domesticity, the household she lovingly tends. She 'seeks with care' after lighting the lamp, and sweeps and cleans the 'inner room'. Here the word 'seek' first appears, which so far did not figure as such. As in the shepherd parable, 'finding' sounds a triad (15:8, 9, 9), and here again a celebration is held, once more with the participating joy of the neighbours and friends who are invited – a transparent image of the joy in higher worlds 'before God's angels'.

The Greek text, if we read it in one possible variation, offers us an intimate subtlety. Like the shepherd, the woman also 'calls together' the neighbours to the feast. But here the word 'call together' does not appear in its active form, but in the 'medium' case that Greek has as a third possibility alongside 'active' and 'passive', which introduces into an action a particular, personal and soulful nuance. Roughly we can say: 'within herself' she calls her neighbours together.

The father and the lost son

The chapter with the three parables is now crowned by the great tale of the prodigal son. This time he is 'one of two', and everything unfolds between human beings. Generously, the father gives the departing son some capital *(ousia)* and subsistence *(bios)*. He lets him gather experience abroad, until the lost one 'goes into himself' and readies himself to return home. The father receives him with overwhelming love and celebrates a great and joyful feast with the whole house. In a repetition that sounds liturgical, he twice uses the celebratory formula by which losing and finding again is linked to the archetypal secret of death and resurrection. The lost one 'was dead and now is alive. He was lost and is found' (15:24, 32).

The triad of the three parables

An overview of all three parables confirms that by no means is 'the same thing said three times' in these three pictorial narratives.

The chief figure of the first parable is the shepherd. This is like a prelude to the Johannine saying of Christ, 'I AM the good shepherd.' In the catacomb paintings, in reference to this parable, the Saviour was often depicted as a young shepherd bearing the sheep upon his shoulders.

The second parable, about the woman, is only found in Luke. Here it resonates with other passages – this gospel has several – that emphasise women, beginning with Elisabeth and Mary in the tale of Jesus' childhood. Seen in this larger context, the image of the woman who lights her lamp to search, gains special significance.

The figure of Mary, as related by Luke, is like an archetype of the soul, which, overshadowed by the Holy Spirit, is to bear the Son of God. Like the soul of the Pentecost occurrence, Mary reappears amongst the disciples at the beginning of the Acts of the Apostles, also written by Luke, when the Spirit pours out upon them. As the soul devoted and surrendered to the Holy Spirit's illumination, she becomes a manifestation of Sophia, of higher wisdom. The woman in our parable, with that very simple and natural gesture of lighting the lamp, is surrounded by a delicate luminescence from the Sophia mystery.

She has nine drachmas lying on the table. The tenth has fallen into a dark corner. Christian wisdom has always known of the nine orders of angels, the hierarchies that indwell the higher worlds of heaven. As *angeloi* – that is, as 'messengers' – they are God-revealing and God-serving beings. Man is to be permitted to join this order and realm of spirits once we overcome sin, which makes us a being whom the divine ray does not permeate, who conceals rather than reveals God. If we allow ourselves to be redeemed by Christ, we may join the choir of angelic worlds as the tenth hierarchy. Is it merely accidental that precisely in this parable the last words change from 'joy in the heavens' to 'joy before the angels of God'?

The third parable speaks of the understanding goodness of a loving father. The word 'father' figures twelve times in the tale. It is true, however, that nowadays many people – whose own father experience may not have been comfortable – find this word difficult in the religious context. Whoever becomes the father of a child, takes upon himself the responsibility for not sullying the father image as a window through which the divine can be perceived.

Apart from distortion of this image through human failings, the word 'father' is often linked nowadays to the idea of a freedom-quashing, suppressive authority figure. By contrast, it cannot be sufficiently stressed that in our parable the Christ created a completely different image of the father. Here the father does not impose his prohibiting authority on the son, who wishes to travel away from home. He gives him his portion and leaves him free to take his own way, to experience the world for himself. This is not through indifference – the way in which the father receives him when he returns clearly shows how he loves him. He has kept a lookout for his return, and, seeing him coming from afar, runs to meet him and embraces him, without a care for his fatherly dignity and authority. Likewise, he stands up from the celebratory feast and goes out to speak with the older son, who, refusing to come in, stands outside in bitterness. Clearly the father is not afraid to relinquish his dominant position by showing understanding and speaking lovingly to him, even comforting him with the words, 'All that is mine is yours.'

Jesus' listeners, familiar as they were with the patriarchs of the Old Testament, may have found this conduct of a father surprising or objectionable. 'No one knows the father apart from the son, and they to whom the son desires to reveal him.' (Lk 10:22)

In these three parables, therefore, with their different nuances, the Trinity is illumined: In the youthful shepherd who goes out to look for the lost sheep, we have the Son as Saviour. In the figure of the woman who lights her lamp, we have the Sophia, and through her the Holy Spirit. And finally, in the figure of an earthly father, we have the all-loving Father God himself.

32

THE PARABLE OF THE WEDDING BANQUET

MATTHEW 22:1–14

It is clear that humanity has come to a critical point in its history. The evolution of our intellect and technology means that we have awoken fully to the earthly world. We have come of age, are grown up. As never before we largely hold our own destiny, and that of the whole globe, in our hands. But are we really equal to this new-won independence?

We are so only if, from this place of self-reliance, we can also forge a new connection with the now almost forgotten divine realm – a connection that fully accords with this adulthood. To put this differently, it means discovering Christianity anew. The time has now come to recognise that Christ is the form of God's manifestation appropriate to a humanity that has come of age. It is time to see in a new light what is meant in the New Testament by the secret of his Sonhood.

Christ – the 'Son' of God. Over time this has become an incomprehensible dogma. We need to regain the deeper meaning of the old dogmas. The 'son' is more than the 'child'. He asserts his independence in relation to the father. The archetype of all sonhood is the Christ in his particular relationship to the Father God, as the 'Son born in eternity'. He descends and enters into humanity so as to raise human beings also to the dignity of this sonhood if they wish to accept him in freedom into their own being. Then, as the intrinsically human God, he can lead us anew to the Father in insight and freedom.

The gospel reading in The Christian Community that comes at the beginning of each Michaelmas period must be seen in this light: the parable of the wedding banquet (Mt 22:1–14). It contains the secret of sonhood in a distinctive form, with all the serious responsibility this asks of human beings.

The parable begins powerfully, telling of a king who was preparing a wedding feast for his son. In this image we can find something that gives meaning to all human development: that it should serve to glorify the 'Son'. When Christ, the divine Son, unites with the single soul, unites with humanity, then the great wedding is celebrated.

But the parable has knowledge also of the adversarial powers that have taken root in an ever more independent humankind, and that now, rising from a sullied and distorted human nature, seek to sabotage the divine plan of the great wedding. This becomes apparent at the moment when the king dispatches his messengers to call the invited guests – literally the 'called ones' – to the wedding. They have been called upon from the beginning and, until now, this calling has slumbered in their souls. But the great moment has arrived when God's messengers are to awaken the called ones to an awareness of this vocation. These servants of the Godhead can approach humankind in various forms, in different kinds of destiny.

It is at this moment, however, that the Fall asserts its effects. Those called upon to attend to the highest calling wish to know nothing of it at the critical moment. In the terse expressiveness of the parable, 'they did not wish to come'.

The Godhead is patient. The king sends other servants who are to speak more clearly and with greater insistence: 'Tell the called ones: behold, I have prepared the best for them.' The Greek word means both 'meal' or 'feast' and 'best'. Those called upon are to realise all that has been done and sacrificed for them already. The king, who has generously prepared a truly princely feast, becomes in the parable an image of the Godhead that gives and sacrifices its best. 'All is ready. Come to the wedding!' In Richard Wagner's *Parsifal* we hear the words, 'Do you hear the call? So thank God you have been called to hear it!'

And once again, the fated refusal to come. Those called upon do not concern themselves with the invitation. According to the Greek text, this is not so much out of 'disdain' but a disinclination to see any importance in it, an indifference. In other words, other things seem more important to them. They 'depart' as if nothing had happened.

'One goes to his fields.' We should not overlook the addition to the original text here of the word *idios* – his 'own' fields. The possession of land is especially inclined to develop a sense of self-reliance and independence, which, in itself, is fully justified. In the great context of the evolution of humanity, this is an inevitable stage. But if property and settled comfort become an aim in themselves, preventing our souls from hearing the voice of a higher calling, this 'going to the fields' will lead us astray. The same is true of the other possibility in which other kinds of people are continually 'on the road' in pursuit of business and profit, which again becomes an end in itself and drowns out the higher calling.

The profound inner insight apparent in the parable describes other responses to the invitation besides indifference: there are some people who seize, mock and kill the king's messengers. Under the surface of uninterested and refusing indifference, in deeper strata of the soul, inspired by the adversary powers, there lies a deep hostility to the divine. Wherever religion has been attacked, more is present under the surface than an honest desire to 'enlighten' people and 'liberate' them from superstition. Nor is it only an – often very understandable – protest against the inadequacies of 'religious representatives'. Undertones always accompany these purported reasons, arising from this hostility to the divine and a secret desire for destructiveness. Those who 'do not wish to come', who have refused the divine, do not want to be bothered with it. They react to the messengers, through whom after all the higher world only reminds them of a non-binding invitation, with violence and enmity. The powers of mockery and derision are also invoked: these are always present when a materialistic intellectualism seeks to keep at arm's length the disturbing feeling that 'there are more things in heaven and earth than are dreamt of in your philosophy,' as Hamlet says to Horatio. 'And finally this drives some even to kill the messengers.

The parable sustains its metaphorical picture in describing the king's reaction to such outrages: 'He grew angry.' Humanity wishes to take no notice of the divine. But it can continue to do so only for a while, even if in universal terms a historical 'while' might seem a very long period to us. But in the end, the fundamental laws of human existence, oriented as it is to the divine, cannot be disregarded without repercussions. The divine asserts itself again, but since its intrinsically loving nature is not accepted in love, those standing outside its love see this as 'anger', in the same way as the blissful fire of love in Faust's ascension causes pain to the devils. The consequences of their crimes follow inevitably for the 'murderers' in the parable. Now blow follows blow: 'He sent out his armies, destroyed those murderers, and set fire to their city.'

Since the Second World War, we read such a sentence – 'and set fire to their city' – differently. The 'city' is a second world, which humankind has erected over the God-given natural world, a world that is entirely its own in a sense. It contains nothing that has not passed through the human brain and through the work of our hands. But this second world, added to the first, can only be of higher value if human creation is penetrated also by the creation of the divine Son. Then a God culture, or civilisation, can join God nature. But if we build 'our' world without connection to the higher world, we find, paradoxically, that what we have built evades our possession in a deeper sense: it becomes something alien to human values, that even has a subhuman quality. The Revelation of John sees in the heavenly Jerusalem the possibility of a God culture above and beyond God nature. In the picture of Babylon consumed, on the other hand, it sees the other, fateful possibility. There too the city is in flames, conveyed with a terrible magnificence all the more striking for not trying to directly describe it. Instead, it hints vividly at something unspeakably awful through the cries of woe of those who 'stand far off', and gaze upon the sea of flames (Rv 18:10, 15, 17).

Memories of such fires have been preserved in human history, and people have more or less unconsciously felt them to prefigure the future apocalypse. Troy, Jerusalem, Rome. A chronicler of the Thirty Years War reported the destruction of Magdeburg as an 'eternally unforgettable sight' when, as a prisoner, he watched the town completely consumed in flames. Many witnessed similar things in the last world war.

The king in the parable announces his judgment: 'The wedding feast is ready, but those called were not worthy of it.' And, for the third time, he sends out his servants. They are to invite 'whomever they find'. The Godhead seeks those who hearken. The messengers are sent to places where roads end, and branch off. People who are 'on their travels' are invited: those who have reached the end of their ways and means, and stand at a crossroads. In such situations, the messengers can find them.

Both 'good and bad' hearken to the invitation. The time is apocalyptical. With the city's burning, an age of catastrophe has begun, and, as a consequence, human destinies have come into flux again. In the ancient, destroyed world, there was an acknowledged division of people into 'good and bad'. Destiny ran on its appointed, fixed course. But now everything comes into motion. Entirely new possibilities dawn and destinies can take a new direction: everywhere there is change and new departure. Enormous, undreamt of things can break through or forth from people who might formerly have been labelled useless, devoid of all prospects. And those who formerly bore the stamp of 'good' now find that they can no longer simply rely on their goodness, while 'bad' people can bring unexpectedly good things to light. Destinies can be convulsed and turned upside down. This is the sign of a Michaelic age.

The second part of the parable begins with the entry of the new crowd of guests into the wedding hall. The first part described people who did not hearken to the call, and wished to remain 'outside'. They did not want to enter the interior space of the wedding hall and, instead, united their whole being with an outward and ephemeral world – they thus became wedded to destruction.

The second part of the parable speaks of how the new-found people do enter this inner world, but how this 'entry' can have its own particular opportunities for erring. The king goes in and 'regards' his guests. In the Greek text, the festive word 'to look closely' stands here. This is vision of a supersensible kind. Many readers of the Bible have asked themselves why the king reproached a guest, who has just been fetched in off the street, for 'not wearing wedding clothes'. Here it helps to know the customs of the time: on festive occasions, the host would himself provide his guests with festive clothing, which they received and put on upon entering the house. Just as today there are events where those arriving are given a flower or badge for their lapel to show they belong to the proceedings, so in the ancient world every well-off household had a number of festive clothes to lend people so that they could wear the 'garment of the house'.

In a fine sense it is as if the guests of a great host, a king even, feel unable to adorn themselves appropriately. They take the invitation to enter as a gift of grace from their host. Whether or not we hearken to a call is completely up to us, and no one else can make the decision for us. But that is not yet the whole story. Grace, love from on high, must be present as well, and clothe us from above in the soul garments that allow us to be seen there. The Book of Revelation relates how martyrs will be given a white dress in the other world (6:11).

The culpability of the unworthy guest in the parable lies in the fact that he enters with the attitude that he is 'fine as he is'. He does not think it necessary to let himself be clothed in the garments of grace. Though he does not remain 'outside' like the materialists, the way in which he enters cannot please the divine world either. This is the type of person who does possess an interest in spiritual things, in inward life and the supersensible, but does not feel that a great change is required of him if the higher world is to tolerate him in its realm. He lacks reverence for this other realm into which he penetrates in his soul's everyday clothes. He must therefore experience the corresponding rebuttal by divine laws of life. When interrogated by the king, he 'is silent'. But this is not a holy silence, for which the Greek possesses a different word. Rather it is the powerlessness of the speechless. In that higher world, spoken words possess the character of a deed to be done out of one's whole being. But to do this requires something of the dull guest that he does not possess. Corresponding to the way he sought to enter in impure, headstrong capriciousness, he now receives a rebuttal in the form of a loss of freedom: he is bound hands and feet and cast into outer darkness. This relapse into the darkness is the answer to an impure striving for the light that is devoid of reverence. In the world of unholiness, 'wailing and gnashing of teeth' prevails. The nature of the soul, which can come to such deeply human expression in weeping, is distorted into uncontrolled, wild and emotional 'wailing'. The will, which can clench the teeth, degenerates into a cramped and 'biting' misery.

'For many are called, but few are chosen.' This concluding word of the parable does not infer a doctrine of predestination, a prior fate for salvation or damnation. The sentence becomes clearer if we translate it literally: 'few are chosen ones.' This expresses the tragic reality that, although the will to heal and redeem issues from God, many do not engage with this call in the right way. Therefore, though they are 'called upon', this does not proceed, and cannot be transformed into, the next and higher condition of 'being chosen'. God's omnipotence has limited itself by stopping short of human will, out of love for our freedom. In this lies our human dignity but also at the same time, our danger and responsibility.

33

THE PARABLE OF THE GREAT BANQUET

LUKE 14:16–24

The attentive reader of the New Testament will not fail to notice that there is a parable in the Gospel of Luke – the parable of the great banquet – which is strikingly similar to the wedding banquet in Matthew. Here, too, an invitation is issued which is regarded disdainfully by those to whom it is first given, and which instead later benefits very different 'unexpecting' guests. Such an evident affinity between the two could easily lead us to think they were 'doubles', two identical stories that have assumed different forms by passing down through different traditions.

It is surely permissible to consider, though, that in the three years of his ministry, Christ surely was free to use a particular theme and imagery in different ways on different occasions, depending on his audience and on the time and place. The best point of departure is always to take the gospels as they stand, and allow them and their circumstances to speak for themselves. Then the fact that the Michaelic parable in Matthew acquires its particular significance by being spoken on Tuesday of Holy Week, three days before Golgotha, can be illuminating. This gives it an ultimate, apocalyptic and decisive gravity, which makes it so akin to the being of Michael.

The banquet parable in Luke occurs at a very different time, in the context of the last journey to Jerusalem.

Chapter 14 of Luke, where the parable comes, begins immediately with the theme of 'the meal'. Luke clearly has a special connection with this motif. The old Church regarded Luke's account of the Last Supper on Maundy Thursday as the 'real' one. In Luke's Easter narratives, eating and drinking is strongly connected with the Risen One. The sacramental shimmer that emanates from these holy meal experiences also invests the other Luke texts in which eating and drinking figure with a special radiance.

This is also true of Chapter 14. Christ has been invited by a Pharisee to 'eat bread' with him. In ancient times, when people still regarded the God-given natural foundations of existence with a self-evident piety, a shared meal was never only a profane matter, especially not if, as here, it was a festive Sabbath meal. Luke first recounts various words that Christ speaks at this meal. We hear about the social ranking of those present. The discoveries at Qumran have shown once again the importance of such table rankings. Christ admonishes the people present at the meal to be humble and modest, and goes on to say that in giving a meal one should invite 'beggars and cripples, the lame and blind'. For him every meal – in which the goodness of the Creator is granted to us – can only ever be a meal of love. Its true nature is distorted when ambition intrudes with a desire for the place of honour. Or else when social exclusivity prevails, so that people wish to sit only with others of the 'propertied classes'. For Christ Jesus, every time food was eaten it was, at the same time, an experience of divine love. Therefore, an appropriate soul-spiritual atmosphere should hold away amongst those united at a meal.

Luke has preserved an expressive instance of how sitting at table with Christ can affect a receptive sensibility. One of the guests calls out spontaneously, 'Blessed is he who eats bread in the kingdom of God' (14:15). He feels as if raised up into a higher world, and an intimation of the sublime mysteries of nourishment pass through his soul. This hymn-like invocation, so fully in accord with the spirit of the Gospel of Luke, is what directly elicits the parable of the great banquet. We should not overlook this seemingly minor detail – that Christ speaks his parable not to a 'general audience', but to the receptive ear of a particular person who uttered this intimating beatitude: 'But he [Christ] spoke to him.'

Now follows the parable. 'A man prepared a great banquet and invited many people, and sent out his servant at the hour of the evening banquet to say to the guests, "Come, all is ready".'

'At the hour of the evening banquet.' If we have the whole of the gospel in mind as a spiritual organism, then this strikes us already as a foreshadowing of what is expressly mentioned later at the Last Supper on Maundy Thursday: 'And when the hour had come, he sat at table and the apostles with him' (Lk 22:14). The Last Supper has its hour. Humanity had to pass through many eras and diverse, preparatory destinies, before Christ could reveal the mystery of the great banquet of love on earth that he himself had 'longed inwardly' to celebrate. As he gathered with the disciples for the Last Supper in the chamber at evening, this cosmic hour was striking.

It is because such a great prefiguring glory lies upon this parable that Christ speaks of a 'great' banquet prepared by the host. Here, already, we can discern a different quality from that of the Matthew parable. Surely the meal described there could have been described – with more right – as a 'great' one, since a 'royal wedding' was to be celebrated, the exaltation of the king's son. The Luke parable is far removed from such grandeur: it takes place in modest, unassuming circumstances. The host owns a house, but it does not seem that he is particularly wealthy. On each occasion he sends only 'his servant' – so does he perhaps only have one? This contrasts with the vassals and servants and armies that the king has at his disposal. The host in the Luke parable, whom we can picture as a man of average assets living amongst farmers of a small, rural town, is likewise a humane and caring person. When he sends word that 'all is ready' we can be sure that much self-sacrificing labour has gone into the preparations. Without doubt it has cost him something to invite a larger circle of acquaintances to a festive meal. While it does not take place in surroundings fit for a royal wedding, the man's loving attention and warm-heartedness make it a 'great' banquet, and thus a worthy parable for the infinitely sublime.

The host receives the same disregard as the king does in the Matthew parable. Those invited to the royal wedding 'did not want to come'. The whole depravity of the soul that has grown alien and hostile to God, becomes starkly apparent in mockery, maltreatment and murder. Evil is illumined in its crassness, and in the global consequences of a catastrophe that strikes us as apocalyptic. There is something of the meting out of divine fury in those mighty sentences in Matthew that tell of the king's anger as he sends out his armies, kills the murderers and sets their city on fire. By contrast, the Luke parable keeps to a smaller scale. Everything unfolds in quieter, milder form.

33. THE PARABLE OF THE GREAT BANQUET

Here too the host grows angry, but his response to the neighbours' refusal consists only in the tragic realisation that none of the guests will taste his repast. He leaves them to the self-excommunication that they have brought upon themselves.

In Luke, too, the disinclination of the guests to come is not as brutal as in Matthew, where we seem to see into the very pit of evil. At least the invited guests make excuses. In this picture of 'excuses' we might well see that outlook that still hears the fading echo of a vanishing experience of God – to the extent that it has a bad conscience at least when it now gives itself up entirely to only material interests. There is a feeling at play here of 'Really I ought to ...' like the feelings some may have occasionally on a Sunday morning when they concern themselves with entirely mundane matters, and the far-off ringing of a church bell reminds them that quite different things of importance may exist. This feeling, though, is not enough to motivate them since they are too much in thrall to transient things.

Three of these excuses are given verbatim. Let us pause here for a moment and look at how these three excuses, one after another in succession, are an example of narrative mastery. Seemingly the same thing is reiterated three times, not, in fact, identically but with subtle differences each time.

The first man has just bought a field. Of all of them he still clearly thinks he ought to attend the banquet, but he is unable to put this above his material interests. 'Really I ought to ...' He feels this strongly, and therefore soothes his bad conscience by stressing the really very urgent nature of what detains him. He says he 'absolutely has to' go and take a look at the field. And politely he adds, 'Pray, let me be excused,' after explaining that, unfortunately, there is no other option.

The second guest, who has purchased five oxen and has to go to inspect them, doesn't have quite such a bad conscience. For him it is already self-evident that this matter takes precedence. He sees no need even to specially highlight the 'necessity' that detains him, which would be to ask for the host's kind understanding. But he too says, 'Pray, let me be excused.'

Even this is omitted from the third person's excuse. He says only, rather gruffly and abruptly, 'I have just married a wife, so I cannot come.'

The text is shaped in such compositional detail. In the same way that the degree of politeness declines through the three excuses, so, albeit differently, there is a similar sequence of the field as the plant-sustaining earth, then the animal realm, represented by the cattle, and, finally, the human world embodied in the marriage.

At this, in the Luke parable, the host issues a completely new invitation. In Matthew, where 'good and bad' are fetched from the crossroads, we see the fate and drama of a Michaelic age at work, in which people depart from their accustomed tracks, questioning everything and allowing undreamt of possibilities to emerge. In Luke, on the other hand, it is not a matter of 'good and bad', but simply of pity and mercy. Some have remarked upon the particularly 'social' outlook of the Gospel of Luke. This gospel has indeed most strikingly embodied the truth that, in Christ, God's infinite mercy approaches humankind, an unconditional love that bears a human countenance.

The host has 'poor and cripples, the blind and lame' fetched from the great thoroughfares and the small alleyways of the town. Clearly these are people in pitiable conditions. Ultimately, in their misery, they are all at a far remove from their true home as earthly human beings, dwelling in the darkness of the Fall. But not all of them recognise this. Often such 'misery' is hidden behind outward prosperity, or also superficially self-satisfied 'rectitude'. Receptivity to divine mercy is often greater in those who can no longer doubt their misery. Wealthy people find it harder to acknowledge the truth that Luther so vividly expressed before he died: 'We are beggars, that is true.' The outward appearance of being a cripple brings to figurative expression the fact that we cannot embody the full God-willed 'form' of human nature in its harmonious beauty; that in contrast to our archetypal being we are 'crippled'. And, intrinsically, blindness means that our inner power of vision can no longer penetrate to the divine. Lameness, likewise, is figurative of the paralysis that can seize hold of our deeper soul energies and prevent us 'journeying' onward and changing. Beggars, cripples, the blind, the lame: humanity in all its distress. But to all comes the invitation of divine mercy. All should be allowed to taste the 'great banquet'.

As there is still room at the banquet, once again the host sends his servant 'so that my house shall be full'. Before, he sent him to the streets and alleys, now it is to the footpaths and hedgerows: clearly yet another step downward to those who stand outside society at the margins of humanity. They, too, bear a human countenance and are invited to the feast.

'Compel them to enter' – a phrase that at some points in ecclesiastical history has been terribly misunderstood and misused, as if it contained a justification for compelling people to accept Christianity, or a particular denomination, as part of the machinery of state. When the host, as he sends the servant for the last time, says he should 'compel' them to come in, he is thinking of their marginalised lives. It might happen that the invitation is so unforeseen and unexpected, is so far outside their usual sphere, that they cannot summon themselves to accept it. They may be unable to get beyond their despair and bitterness. They do not require compulsion, but they do need very active love, which approaches them with warmth of heart, declines to accept their refusal, and is able to emancipate them from their 'inhibitions' through dedicated commitment. Here the parable reaches its culmination.

It is clearly apparent that this tale of the great banquet, despite all similarity to the parable of the wedding banquet, stands on its own and has a quite different orientation and emphasis. The Michaelic parable of the wedding banquet reveals the seriousness, scope and grandeur of human responsibility. If we repeatedly allow ourselves to dwell upon this seriousness, we also prepare ourselves in the right way to take up into our souls, as a breath of higher life, the truth of Christ's utterly human mercy.

34

THE WORKERS IN THE VINEYARD AND THEIR PAYMENT

MATTHEW 20:1–16

At various times between early morning and late evening, the owner of a vineyard goes to hire labourers. In the evening, he gives them all precisely the same payment, without account of the different lengths of time they have worked. Each one receives their coin, the last who came to work no less than the first. Surely this is unjust. The objection we can feel at this can become an occasion to concern ourselves more closely with the parable. What is its biblical context?

What precedes it?

Beforehand, we hear the story of the rich disciple who could not resolve to make the great sacrifice of relinquishing his wealth. Peter cries out, by contrast: 'Behold, we have relinquished everything and have followed you' (Mt 19:27). Christ acknowledges this and makes a promise to the disciples, which ends with the words: 'And everyone who has left houses or brothers or sisters or father or mother or children or lands for the sake of my name, will receive a hundredfold and will inherit eternal life.' What seems missing in the parable, therefore, comes into its own: each one will receive their reward according to their deserts, according to the law 'What a man sows, that will he reap' (Gal 6:7). What those willing to make a sacrifice have given will be returned to them a hundredfold.

The house: poorer city-dwellers of today, living in insecure rental accommodation and often moving, feel themselves in a perilous position. They still have an inkling, though, of the protection and homeliness once represented by a house that belonged to the same family for generations. Modern hand-to-mouth existence is becoming ever more 'unhomely'.

The family: this figures here in full: siblings, parents, children. Once again it is a value that is disappearing. People often speak of the loss of a sense of love and security, and of the grave consequences of this loss.

Lands: people in rural communities always felt that their connection to the soil, to mother earth, gave them a whole context of meaning and purpose. This was before they became increasingly isolated and deracinated amidst the tarmac of big cities.

House – family – lands. These once sustaining values are in Christ's thoughts as he beholds the future of the disciples. They will have to relinquish these things, but they are to find them again in a new way. With this renunciation the disciples voluntarily take upon themselves a sacrifice that will one day fall to all humanity. Today we can clearly see what is afoot, and we are aware primarily of the loss of sustaining ways of life. But it is important that the disciples should not only experience the 'negative' aspect of this, the void created by this loss. It should be far outshone by the new, future-sustaining value that has dawned for them as the life-sun of the 'name of Christ'. In a new, spirit-born community of love, they will receive the human warmth that formerly could be found only in the narrow circle of blood relationship. They do not feel themselves to be 'unhoused' for, in the great family of the spirit, they may feel themselves 'at home' everywhere. They can endure having no permanent city, for they know they are on their way to the city of God. At its heart, the humanity founded in Christ nurtures the secret of transformation. This is why he establishes a context of meaning connected with the earth: 'You are the salt of the earth' (Mt 5:13). This is true even if they possess no land.

If we take a closer look at this promise of 'reimbursement', we notice that it does not lie at the same level as the loss. Those who wish to partake of it, must raise themselves into a higher realm 'in the name of Christ'. It certainly does not mean that someone who has lost his house can expect to be given a hundred houses to replace it. This refunding is no longer a matter of owning real estate. A transformation lies between.

We cannot help hearing a false tone when Peter, with a sideward glance at another's failure, stresses his own service and asks, 'What then will there be for us?' (Mt 19:27). Clearly he has not yet understood the nature of the transformation required, an inner dimension of experience that is implied in the 'name of Christ'. And it is this false tone that elicits the parable, which now, with a radical one-sidedness, tackles the sense of acquisition that is wrongly introduced into the spiritual realm.

The parable

The vineyard owner goes out and hires labourers in the early morning, thus around 6 am. Then again at 9 am (the 'third hour'), midday, 3 pm and, finally, one hour before the working day ends, thus around 5 pm. The day passes with its various phases: the fresh morning, the bright forenoon, the afternoon hours with their burning heat, the coolness of evening.

The tale, with quiet artistry, keeps repeating this hiring of workers with subtle changes each time. A proper agreement is concluded with the labourers who are hired first. The employer agrees (*symphonein* in the Greek) one denarius as their payment, a silver coin. He does not negotiate in the same way with the workers he takes on later in the day, merely issuing the promise that 'what is right will be given you' (20:4). They rely on this and go to work with faithful goodwill. It is different again with the hands who are hired latest of all, an hour before the end of the day. The vineyard owner expresses his dismay that these men are still standing around idly without work. When they reply that no one has yet summoned them to work, he says only, 'You too, go to the vineyard' (20:7). The sentence repeated in some translations, 'what is right will be given you,' does *not* actually belong to the authentic text on this second occasion. The fact that it is missing here in the Greek can tell us that the last-called, when they go to the work that has finally become available, do so without any corresponding promise of remuneration.

In the evening, the owner has the hired men paid their wages, each one receiving their coin. Here a festive-sounding designation is used, 'the lord of the vineyard' (20:8). It is as if, in the twilight, the world of daily, mundane reality is starting to become transparent for higher meaning. The 'lord' (*kyrios* in Greek) appears as if illumined by a hidden world.

But first things continue in a very earthly fashion. The first-called, who have been working all day since early morning, demur. If the employer wishes to be generous, surely they have earned a bonus payment? But the employer turns to one of them – the narrative here conjures for us the face of an intelligent spokesman – and says, 'Friend, I do you no wrong.' 'Friend' – in the original Greek, the ordinary word for this, *philos,* is not used, but *hetairos,* comrade or companion. In those days, this could point to someone who belonged to a more intimate group of like-minded people, or a spiritual community, in the same way that Freemasons speak of 'brothers'. This distinctive form of address is one we encounter in two other places in Matthew: in the parable of the wedding banquet, the king employs it when speaking to the guest who fails to wear festive clothing (22:12), as if he wished to say, 'I find you here as one of those who belong in this smaller circle'. And in Gethsemane, Christ addresses the betrayer in the same terms, as one who is nevertheless deeply connected to him (26:50). If we look at these significant passages, it shows that we should not overlook this form of address in the parable in question. It should not be thought that it is a patronising or even ironical condescension to a man of lower rank. For the lord of the vineyard, this labourer is a true *hetairos,* a participant in a common task.

The parable becomes transparent

In the final words of the 'lord' which end the tale, the underlying meaning becomes fully apparent. If we can translate it into our abstract language, it would be: 'Whoever works in this vineyard, collaborates with God on the great "human enterprise".' The Lord gives each a share in what the vineyard owner calls 'mine'. 'Or do I not have the right to do as I will with what is mine?' (20:15). We have learned to attend to the special resonance that always accompanies

Christ's words 'I' or 'I am'. This is never a trivial matter in the gospels. The great, divine mystery of the I underlies it. Similarly, this is true when the 'mine' which belongs to the 'I' is uttered. 'Mine' points to the original, intrinsic I-substance of God, from which he draws to endow each human being with his own I. This is embodied here in the image of the denarius. (We should not think of a penny but of a silver coin.) The denarius, a silver Roman coin bearing the image and name of Caesar, also plays a role in the question of the 'temple tax'. The round coin – as it were, the great world in miniature – can stand as a figure for the self-enclosed human I. In Latin, the word *denarius* means 'containing ten'. This is a number of concern to the human being in so far as we are to join the ranks of the angels eventually as a tenth hierarchy.

'So take what is yours' (20:14). God sunders from himself what hitherto was 'mine' for him. It becomes a 'yours' through the power of divine will. This 'right to do as I will with what is mine' should not be mistaken for despotic caprice. Rather, it points to the potential for the highest sacrifice by the Creator. 'Right' and 'will' are joined here, significantly, by the motif of 'goodness'. 'Or is your eye evil because I am good?' (20:15). It is as if we heard from higher worlds a divine I AM infuse what the lord of the vineyard says, and resonate with it: 'I am good.' Being good makes it possible to give away something of what is intrinsically our own and leave it entirely to another being. Thus the I originating from God henceforth belongs to human beings. This appropriation is of such an order that another can never say 'I' for us. And it is *this* that the human being takes with him in the course of the divine enterprise as truly 'his own'. In the imagery of the parable, 'each one receives their own'. No less. No more.

Receives no *more*? We return here to our initial question. It has become apparent that the higher accomplishments and merits of this I, lead us above and beyond the bounds of possession. With their just consequences they are, like Bruckner's *Ninth Symphony,* dedicated 'to the beloved God'. Early Christianity knew of the 'community of the saints'. Later theology formulated the somewhat intellectual doctrine of the 'superfluous' good works of the saints, which benefit others thanks to this mysterious context. If we strip away the legalistic thought forms of this theology, we can put it like this: in a deeper sense every good work is truly 'super-fluous', that is, it flows over: it brims to the very top of the vessel of the personal self and pours over into the divine and human world. The law of 'reaping what you sow' remains valid. But properly understood, it cannot be confined to the idea of wages commensurate with work. In the very focus on 'wages' and, as here, on begrudging others, the good deed would cease to be good. It would render itself ugly, and even make those who came first into the last-called. In the sense of eternal justice, the great sacrifice of the disciples has its due consequences, but these belong to a higher level of existence, in whose pure air all ownership and self-benefit – 'What then will there be for us?' – can no longer survive. Our I should become our own possession. But this acquisition is only wholesome when the I grows beyond itself in selfless love.

35

THE PARABLE OF
THE WICKED TENANTS

BEING HUMAN – AN END IN ITSELF?

At Michaelmas the gospel reading in The Christian Community is the parable of the wedding banquet (Mt 22). In grave apocalyptic images, this tells of the responsibility of those who receive the call of the spirit. It was spoken a few days before the event of Golgotha. Directly preceding it is the parable of the wicked tenants (Mt 21:33–46), which is to be found also in Mark (12:1–12) and Luke (20:9–19), in the same context. In the cycle of the year, Michaelmas stands opposite to the beginning of Holy Week. It offers a special possibility of reflecting on this great mystery in all autumn clarity, and becoming aware that, as well as a gift of God, it is at the same time a task and mission for the human being. The deeper content of Michaelmas – we might say its intrinsic fact of salvation – is the Christian human being who grows more self-aware.

The parable of the wicked tenants which can, in this Michaelic sense, serve our self-reflection in relation to the deed of Christ, unfolds over several acts.

I

First we hear, in loving detail, how a landowner establishes his vineyard. He fences it off, digs down into the ground to set up the winepress, and then also builds a watch tower (Mt 21:33).

In biblical language, wine has a connection with what we develop as personal qualities of the I. When Christ turns the water into wine, he is affirming the step from the impersonal to our full-blooded personal nature. But at the end of his sojourn on earth, he transforms the wine again into his blood. The personal nature of the human being, which makes us say 'I', is in danger of succumbing to egoism. But through the Christ it can be redeemed into higher, selfless I-hood.

In our earthly existence, as we 'cultivate' our cultural life, we are preoccupied with unfolding forces of personality. We 'labour in the vineyard'. God calls us to do so. God began the great 'human enterprise' and established the vineyard.

Seen from this perspective, even small details of the parable show us their pictorial importance. The vineyard is surrounded by a fence. No personal existence is possible without self-delimitation; no I-consciousness can develop without the experience of 'this is mine'. I take what is mine, I 'take myself out' of general world existence and delimit myself from the 'not I'. I erect my fence. And here, as already suggested, the danger of egoism rears its head. But it also has to be acknowledged that we cannot lovingly give away something if we ourselves have nothing, indeed, if we ourselves are nothing. We can only give away by first possessing.

In setting up the winepress, the landlord digs into the depths. Something like grape-pressing occurs continually in the depths of the soul. During the course of life, we feel ever more clearly how things we experience are processed in the depths of the soul below the level of waking consciousness. All the many things we experience slowly sink into forgetfulness and lose their form. But they are not lost. They live on in transmuted ways, like a pressed juice, an 'inner essence', that contains the aroma, the 'bouquet' of what we have passed through.

Just as the winepress set into the ground points to the depths of the soul, so the high tower points to spirit heights. If we climb a tower, our horizon widens: we gain a prospect of things from a higher standpoint.

Thus the parable's pictures illustrate the human being's divine beginnings: our spiritual potential, our soul depths, our separate self as most vividly experienced through our own, self-contained and self-enclosed body, by virtue of which, likewise, the self-contained personality develops.

Everything that belongs to the human being was laid down in the best possible way by the Godhead. The parable says that the vineyard owner then 'gave out' or 'let' the vineyard to the tenants and moved away. The labourers in the vineyard were left to themselves. The divine entrepreneur of the 'human enterprise' was certainly able to establish and set up everything, but he could not complete the human being as an individual destined for freedom. The human being had to be ceded the necessary space to labour and collaborate upon his own evolution. His own activity would not have come properly 'into its own' if he had not, to a degree, been left to his own devices by God: to himself, to his own actions and to his experience of their consequences. The doubting question so often voiced – 'If God exists, how can he allow such things to happen?' – is answered ultimately by the love of God who seeks to let us grow into our own freedom and dignity.

The vineyard owner 'let' the vineyard to the tenants and moved away. In Luke come the added words, 'for a sufficient time' (20:9). His absence does not last for ever. A certain period is envisaged by the cosmic plan for the human being to grow independent – lasting as long as divine wisdom deems 'sufficient'. The original text even states literally, 'sufficient periods' thus using the plural of 'time' *(chronos)*. Centuries, millennia. But within the great unfolding of the cosmos only a transient episode.

Thus the fruits gradually ripen which the entrepreneur was concerned to cultivate. Since the existence of human beings is not, unlike that of the angels, close to the bright presence of God in heaven, an independence can develop for which God had, as it were, to first invent the earth. It could not have arisen in the same way in heaven alone. But then this separation must at last be overcome again, so that heaven and earth find each other once more in a kind of fertilisation.

The brief phrase in the parable, 'he moved away,' contains everything that human beings experienced long ago as the tragedy of the twilight of the gods: the gradual fading of the divine from the human field of consciousness.

II

The 'sufficient times' will eventually come to an end. 'The time of fruits was approaching' (Mt 21:34) – though, here, the word used for time is not *chronos* but *kairos,* which means a decisive point in time, an incisive moment.

The vineyard owner sends his messengers to ask for the now ripened yield, or, in the Mark version, for at least a fair portion of it. In other words, humanity is expected to be capable of sacrifice, of offering something up. The messengers appear. The higher world slowly announces itself again, begins to ask to be remembered. It makes its claim felt. It 'wishes to have something' from the fact that earthly human beings have been able to evolve in their independence. But things go badly for the messengers. The tenant labourers in the vineyard have become so used to being left alone that it does not occur to them that another, higher authority should have any say in their lives. They have come to feel that they need only concern themselves with themselves. They have completely lost sight of the fact that their work on earth has been planned to feed in to a higher context beyond the horizon of their awareness, as awaited outcome and yield. They, and their work, have become an end in themselves.

Earthly humanity as an end in itself. This thought gives us an opportunity to consider a highly topical problem of our age from a somewhat unusual perspective. On the one hand, there is something extraordinarily important and great in the thought that the human being living on earth could be an end in himself. It took a long while, and cost much sacrifice, to reach the point where, at least for a portion of humanity, this self-purpose of the individual could be acknowledged. The individual must not be a means to an end. And yet this acknowledgement still stands on very shaky ground.

It lies in the imperatives of our era that we must work towards greater, expanding, global and superordinate contexts. But at the same time, the temptation can arise in various ways to overlook single human beings and their claims as something subordinate. Is it not rather small-minded for the legally protected individual to insist upon the right to secrecy in their communications by letter or telephone? One can even have the impression, that many people who are in a position to enjoy such rights no longer value them properly. The more that world-encompassing, communal interests come to the fore, the more we can expect to see doubt cast on human self-determination.

And yet if this were lost, then everything would be lost. It is actually nonsensical to think that you yourself are nothing, that your superordinate community is all – add as many noughts together as you like, and you will still produce only zero. The individual's self-purpose and self-determination must come to full self-awareness of its dignity. If we look at how human existence today is so often squandered upon inessential trivialities, this dignity could all too easily start to seem questionable.

The secret is this: we can ripen into the insight that, irrespective of our self-determination, we are also part of the divine plan. Through our human existence, something should arise that God can build in to new, higher creations. In the Book of Revelation it says that they who overcome may become a pillar in the divine temple, which can be built upon their sustaining strength (Rv 3:12). The pillar, in its royally upright state, is not there only for itself, but may bear the roof of the temple. Everything depends upon the human being acknowledging this secret. The free I, the self-determining and self-purposing individuality, is endowed by God, but this highest gift will only serve us well if we mature to the degree that we can surrender ourselves freely and gratefully to the higher realm. If we learn to offer ourselves up in this way, then we make our self-determination within the earthly realm into something fully justified in cosmic existence. It might be objected that, by doing so, we again become a means to an end, directed for a purpose not intrinsic to us. But in relation to the divine, the expression 'purpose' as we usually employ it is not accurate unless, like the poet, we speak of 'higher purposes', meaning something that lies in worlds higher than all other ends. On our journey upwards, we grow beyond our narrower self into a higher I that approaches us in the Christ.

But, returning to the parable, the mission entrusted to the messengers comes to naught. They encounter the most extreme unwillingness to make any sacrifice. More than being turned away and sent home with empty hands, they are treated with appalling violence. This aspect of the parable shines a light deep into the abyss of soul life. Within the human being who has shed all feeling for the divine, lives more than mere indifference to this divine realm. Under such apparent indifference, something like hatred often glimmers. Certainly, it does not come from the intrinsic depths of the soul that originally proceeded from God. But in the periods of our sundering from the divine, adversarial powers saw their opportunity and grasped it; they were able to take root in the soul. And so from this soul there sometimes springs a direct hostility and destructive rage towards everything that might remind it of the divine.

III

'At last he sent his son to them, and said: they will feel respect for him' (Mt 21:37). In Mark's version, the distinctive nature of *this* emissary is emphasised still more strongly: 'He had still one, a beloved son. He sent him as the last' (*eschaton,* Mk 12:6). In the version according to Luke, we become witnesses to a monologue in which the vineyard owner considers the best course of action at a moment of perplexity, when everything seems to grind to a halt and there appears to be no way forward. 'What should I do?' Then, as if after a breathless moment, he takes the great decision, 'I will send my beloved son.' Perhaps they will feel respect for him' (Lk 20:13). The voice of God from the Jordan baptism resounds clearly in the 'beloved son'. By comparison to the messengers sent hitherto, he is the incomparable 'one', the 'last', his dispatch therefore an ultimate and extreme measure. In the monologue of 'What shall I do?' is reflected, in the form of the parable, the divine resolve preceding the surrendering of the Son, who was, after all, called the Messenger of the Great Resolve by early Christians.

The tenants observe the son approaching, and in the vineyard they too make a resolve. They spoke (literally) 'within themselves' (Mt 21:38): 'This one is the heir. Let us kill him and take his inheritance for ourselves.'

'You are the heir' (or 'kinsman-redeemer'); these words were once spoken by the grain-gleaner Ruth to Boaz, the wealthy landowner, as she approached him humbly during the night (Ru 3.9). This was an unconsciously clairvoyant phrase, for behind Boaz appears his descendant David, and behind David, the crowning of this lineage with the Messiah. Intuitively, Ruth linked herself to the chain of life formed by the foremothers of the Redeemer. The 'heir' – in the New Testament, this word is applied to Christ in the Letter to the Hebrews (1:2). It is he to whom the true yield of the great enterprise of humanity is ultimately to accrue, by virtue of him taking up humanity into his own sonship and there glorifying it. In his *Book of Hours,* Rainer Maria Rilke celebrated this motif of the divine heir of humanity, to whom ultimately all true human achievements belong, speaking there not especially of Christ but of God in general. Rilke could sense that all real values arising from humankind exist for the sake of a higher context of meaning, which will encompass and preserve them at the end of time:

> And every song that deeply rang will shine
> Upon you then as if a precious stone.

It will not adorn the poet for their own glorification, but 'you', God. In the same sense, Christ was able to say that good deeds for others 'you did to me' (Mt 25.40). Similarly, in the parable, he sees himself in the image of the 'heir'. 'Here is the heir.' And yet these words sound very differently in the mouth of the wicked tenants. Here, too, there is a certain clairvoyance in the words, as once there were in those of the maid Ruth, pointing far beyond the superficial meaning. In the tenants, too, there is a kind of inspiration at work, but in this case it comes from the Adversary. It is he, after all, who desires to profit from the increasingly apparent sundering of humanity from its divine origins. The Adversary can no longer alter the fact that God was the 'first' and stood at the beginning of everything. But he does believe he can contest with God for the rank of the 'last' who will stand there, finally, at the end of creation. He wishes God-alienated humanity to culminate in his own kingdom, thus seizing for himself the yield of the great enterprise. It is the Adversary who acts within the wicked tenants and utters through their mouths the phrase: 'This one is the heir. Let us kill him and take his inheritance for ourselves.' Ourselves? Deceived human beings, in their short-sightedness, wish to believe this. They do not know that in truth they are doing the devil's business and are being harnessed to goals that are actually alien and hostile to intrinsic human nature.

A single sentence in the parable then points to the tragedy of Golgotha. 'And they seized him and threw him out of the vineyard and killed him.'

What follows now steps out of the flow of the narrative in so far as Christ turns directly to his listeners: 'Therefore, when the lord of the vineyard comes, what will he do to those tenants?' The audience, spellbound by the story, answer, 'The bad ones he will destroy, and will give the vineyard to other labourers, who deliver him its fruits at the due time' (Mt 21:41). This has been interpreted as the tragedy of the chosen people who did not recognise the Messiah, so that

Christianity passed to other peoples. That may be there, but there is more to it. A parable has multiple meanings, not merely one. Basically, this is not just about one race of people contrasted with others. We could also say that humanity, as a whole, is something like a 'chosen people' amongst the various ranks of the hierarchies, by virtue of the fact that the divine Son entered into an incomparably intimate and close relationship of destiny with it, becoming a human being. What is to happen if humanity founders and does not make the right use of its freedom? Might it come to the point where God calls upon other spirits in the place of humanity to fulfil the great plan, and thus earthly evolution must be given up for lost?

Luke adds another important aspect: 'Having heard this they said, "May this never come about".' (Lk 20:16). It is like a counterpart to the affirmative and endorsing Amen – 'Yea, so be it.' In the parable, humanity is given a glimpse of the abyss at whose edge it teeters. It is to wake up to the full, dire seriousness of its situation, and in wholesome terror form a decisive resolve: 'May this *never* happen.' At this, 'Jesus looked at them'. Literally, he 'looked into them,' looked into their inward being as if to fathom the depth of their outcry, 'May this *never* happen.' Then he follows this with words of comfort and redress, whereas the parable so far has been unremittingly bleak: 'Is it not written, the stone that the builders rejected has become the keystone?' The abysmal meaning of the event at Golgotha is illumined. The tragedy of God's murder had to be fulfilled. But the free deed of sacrifice of the one murdered brings about the great change. The event of Golgotha does not consist only in Good Friday. It culminates in Easter Sunday. The rejection of the Son is precisely what, through his divine self-sacrifice, inaugurates the resurrection. In this, the keystone for a resurrected humanity and earthly world is laid, for the 'heavenly Jerusalem'. But since humanity cannot be redeemed and led to its goal without its collaborative will, it is necessary for it to awaken in profound and terrible inner self-knowledge through the tragedy of the murder of God, and turn again to the one who died and was resurrected for its sake.

36

THE RICH MAN AND DEATH

LUKE 12:16–21

The story of the rich man and poor Lazarus is well known. Perhaps less well known is another parable that also deals with the death of a rich man and also occurs in Luke's Gospel. It is very concise, a really short story, but the few sentences are momentous and worthy of detailed study.

It begins, 'The ground of a rich man brought forth abundantly.' Before this particularly fortunate harvest the owner was therefore well-off. Now he becomes richer than before. And just as the poor have their troubles, so do the well-to-do. The enormous yield comes as an embarrassment to him. Where shall he put it all?

'He was reasoning within himself, "What shall I do, for I have nowhere to store my crops?"' Then the idea comes to him: 'And he said, "I will do this: I will tear down my barns, and build larger ones; and there I will store all my grain and goods".'

What does it say in the soliloquy? My crops – my barns – my grain. My – my – my. 'My barns' – that may pass. But 'my crops', 'my grain'? He apparently does not consider that with all his wealth he cannot produce a single blade of grass. What grows and ripens is a gift of grace from the divine creative powers.

The soliloquy, however, is not yet finished. After the rich landowner has thought of his plan of action, he anticipates with self-satisfaction the agreeable state of his own soul in the future. 'And I will say to my soul, Soul, you have ample goods laid up for many years; take your ease, eat, drink, be merry.' – Again the possessive 'my': 'my soul'. It is true that in the same gospel, Mary says in her song of praise, the Magnificat, 'My soul magnifies the Lord,' but when two people say the same thing, it is not the same.

'Rest, eat and drink, be merry.' The gospel would not object to these things in themselves. Indeed they are honoured throughout the gospels.

'Rest.' Anyone who is able to draw breath again in peace after the pressure of hard work can have a direct experience of something 'heavenly'. For the hardworking person such tranquil drawing of breath can become a religious experience that allows them to sense something of the peacefully breathing life of the divine. The same verb, *(anapauein),* occurs in the passionate cry of the Saviour that goes forth to 'all who toil and are burdened': I will give you rest, I will give you this heavenly rest (Mt 11:28). With the rich man in the parable, however, this resting, taking his ease, acquires quite a different character. In his programme, it signifies quite simply the final dismissal of every desire to work, the letting go of every readiness to exert himself, the intention to live only for himself. The experience of rest is thus denuded of its heavenly connotations and degenerates into simply 'doing nothing'.

'Eat and drink.' It is the same here. In a healthy, natural working life eating and drinking, preceded by hunger and thirst, can also be a religious experience. It can become symbolic for satisfaction on a higher level. 'Taste and see that the Lord is good!' says Psalm 34:8. When grace is said, eating and drinking are consciously raised to the level of religious devotion. In the sacrament it undergoes its highest transformation. At the opposite pole stands the 'eat and drink' of the rich man who has settled down to take his ease. For him, eating and drinking is an end in itself, an important part of his programme for enjoying life. Thus it falls away from its higher potential and is lost in the purely material.

'Be merry.' Again, one could not advance arguments from the gospels against being happy and cheerful. This is shown particularly well by the three parables in Luke's Gospel about losing and finding (Lk 15). The same Greek word in that context is translated as 'Rejoice!' The shepherd who has found his sheep again, the woman who has found her silver coin – both call their friends and neighbours together, 'Rejoice with me.' These are small events in the lives of simple people. But Christ had a loving eye for how often it was just the simple person involved in the struggle for existence who preserved a special capacity for cheerfulness. The finding of the sheep and the silver coin, in themselves no world-shaking events, become the occasion for great rejoicing, whereby despite their poor and modest circumstances people are glad of heart. Higher things can be revealed through them. 'I tell you that in the same way there will be joy in heaven ... In the same way, I tell you, there is joy in the presence of the angels of God.'

Christ Jesus felt for the poor, but he could regard with equal warmth a man who was rich in worldly goods. It is not the fact of possession itself that is reprehensible. However, it is pointed out again and again in the gospels, often very radically, that there is a danger of the soul being enslaved by ownership if it does not watch out. It is the state of mind dominated by possessions that is warned against. This is epitomised in the rich man in our parable. In contrast, a sympathetically drawn rich man is found in the parable of the prodigal son. There the father is described as a landowner who has a great fortune at his disposal, who has numerous hired servants in his service who all 'have bread enough and to spare'. In this man, Christ lets us see the fatherly kindness of God in an earthly model. Here, too, is the great feast of rejoicing, with singing and dancing. 'It was fitting to make merry and rejoice, for this your brother was dead, and is alive; he was lost, and is found' (Lk 15:32).

Again, in the case of the rich man in our parable, being merry, just like resting and eating and drinking, has degenerated into an end in itself. The same idea of making merry, that sounds so differently on the lips of the lazy landowner and the father of the prodigal son, also occurs in the story of poor Lazarus, where the rich man 'was clothed in purple and fine linen and ... feasted sumptuously every day.' But in this kind of pleasure taking there is not a single gleam of heavenly joy, and, after his death, the man who lived every day so pleasurably finds himself in the purifying flames of burning desire, since in his enjoyment anything resembling the life of the spirit was blotted out.

'Rest, eat, drink, enjoy yourself!' So much for the rich man's soliloquy. And now begins the parable's other part. 'But God said to him'. In no other parable are the words of God himself introduced so directly, so undisguised. In other parables the lord of the vineyard perhaps speaks the decisive word, or the master of the house, the bridegroom, the king, and we sense the higher being they represent. Here, however, it says with astonishing directness: 'But God said to him'.

36. THE RICH MAN AND DEATH

But how is one to think of this speaking of God to the rich man? He was quite evidently no mystic, no pious religious man who listens with devotion to divine revelations and is blessed with inspiration. God speaks to him through destiny. He makes him die a sudden death.

A man can fall into a singular mood before his 'unexpected' death, a death which is in no way to be foreseen. Perhaps he is suddenly overcome by an unusual sadness, an inexplicable feeling of farewell, or by a strange agitation; perhaps he makes a strange remark. All quite unmotivated, as one thinks. In fact, however, such occurrences furnish intrinsic evidence of the fact that the 'unexpected' death was not so unexpected after all. Something in the man already knew. It is only that this knowledge, already there in the bottom of the soul, could not yet rise up into the light of full consciousness. So it made itself felt in a different way in the soul.

Thus in the day before the tragic event the rich man also heard in the deeper levels of his soul God's pronouncement of his fate.

And the content of this divine utterance? First: 'Fool!' The Greek word denotes someone who is without reason, without sense. This word resounding towards him from the divine world contains the judgment of the life he has lived until now, and which now faces its end. This existence, envied and considered happy by many people, is scathingly judged by a higher court.

Secondly, there follows the announcement of the catastrophe. 'This night your soul is required of you.' Nothing is described in detail in this austere parable. We do not discover in what form the catastrophe will occur. All the more sinister are the words 'this night'. There is divine mastery in the telling of this story which, in a few words, conjures up a whole world of experience. This night: elsewhere the gospel also speaks of the blessing of night, which is dark only to keep away the glaring brightness of day and make the soul receptive for a different kind of light. But here, only the darkness of night is left. It is the lightless night that is no one's friend. 'This night your soul is required of you.' Who will take his life remains unknown, which makes it all the more terrible and full of foreboding. One could think of a murderer. 'Your soul is required' is ambiguous. It may imply murder, but at the same time it also leaves open another meaning. The murder can in the end only kill the body. The disembodied soul goes into the hands of higher powers who demand back through the fatal event the soul they once sent down to earth.

Your soul. However short the parable, there is yet room for literary counterpoint. We are reminded of the self-satisfied words, 'I will say to my soul'. Now there comes like an echo from the divine world, 'This soul of yours' which you looked upon as a private possession, which will now be demanded back by its true owner.

The divine message contains a third element: 'and the things you have prepared, whose will they be?' What was hoarded in order to guarantee a life of enjoyment 'for many years' must be left behind. If his earthly possessions were everything to this man, then it must be terrible for him to hear the question: 'To whom will they now belong?'

The coming of death is announced in a threefold way: the existence that has come to an end is assessed and judged by a higher court; the soul is demanded back by the divine powers; the earthly goods pass on elsewhere.

There the curtain falls. We are not, however, dismissed simply with the shock of the sudden disaster. Being shocked makes us receptive for the saying that takes up the strain of the story that has just ended: 'So is he who lays up treasure for himself, and is not rich towards God.'

There arises the ideal of striving for *that* treasure. 'Be rich in God.' Then death loses its terror.

37

THREE PARABLES ABOUT CHRIST'S FUTURE COMING

MATTHEW 25

In Christ's discourse on the Mount of Olives, we hear the great Advent gospel of the future coming of the Son of Man in the etheric light and the clouds of heaven. Matthew's Gospel has preserved for us three parables that form the conclusion of this apocalyptic discourse and at the same time answer the question how we should behave in relation to this coming. They are the pictures of the ten maidens, the talents and the Last Judgment.

1. The wise and foolish maidens

The character of this parable already reveals itself in its title, and depends on the two words 'wise' and 'foolish'. The wise maidens have thought about fuel for their lamps with which they are to meet the bridegroom. The foolish let their lamps go out since they had not bothered about oil.

It is the contrast of spiritually alert and spiritually dull, the one responsible, the other irresponsible towards the light.

The picture of the bridegroom who comes only at midnight still reflected for people of those days something of the mysteries. The bridegroom is the one to whom the soul should be completely devoted. He is the sun that shines at midnight. Essentially he is light, but pure inner light that shines brightest when the glare of outer light has faded and the soul's deeper faculties emerge 'at midnight'.

The maidens go to meet this bringer of divine light, and it is important that they go to meet him with lighted lamps. Light wants to be welcomed with light. The outer physical light can illumine what is dark and so make it bright. The inner light, however, does not simply light superficially. It seeks to *en*lighten; but to do so it must be able to be inwardly welcomed. This is only possible when its like is already there. In Goethe's tale of the Green Snake the old man with the lamp pronounces the law that only like recognises like with the words: 'You know that I may not light up what is dark.'

When the one who is entitled to call himself the light of the world is coming, it is therefore not enough to wait passively for him. We should go to meet him, we should bestir ourselves, we should carry the light to meet him, the light already given us, which is there for our use – if we take care of it and do not let it fail.

The human soul's power of pure thinking has something virginal about it. The ancient Greeks revered the virgin goddess, Pallas Athene, who sprang forth from the head of Zeus. This power of inner brightness and clarity of perception has also been recognised in early Christian tradition as the holy Sophia. The virgin in the gospel who meets the bringer of light with lighted lamp can be seen as an image of this Sophia.

2. The talents

Quite a different kind of imagery dominates the second parable. There are no maidens here, but men, servants of their master, used to hard work. Their lord has entrusted them with his property, giving to each a number of talents. The very word 'talent' suggests the possibility for action: man may put his talents to work.

The master's property is handed over in individually proportioned amounts; one gets more, the other less, but the chief thing is that no one goes without; everyone gets something. Every man is given something of what is God's own. One is able to do more, another less, but no one is quite incapable; everyone can do something. It all depends on the one who can do only a little in all modesty working with even this little. This is much more important than looking askance at another who can do more and, at the sight of his advantage, getting an inferiority complex which often, as paradoxical as it sounds, springs from unconscious vanity. It is really a lack of modesty if one does not quite objectively accept the little one has, in order to work all the more diligently with it. So the two sayings, 'Do what you can,' and 'What you can do, get on and do,' are both valid in this respect.

Just as a person is responsible that the light given them does not go out, so they should increase the talent given to them by their hard work. They are not only to meet the divine with the perceptive power of their thinking, they are also to offer it their ability to work, their energy.

The religious life must again acquire something of the seriousness and the method of real 'work'. It cannot be an unprofessional pursuit of an occasional Sunday religious mood; it needs the sustained will, the energy of hard work. How splendid and accurate is the old-fashioned expression, 'religious practice'.

The two servants who have increased what was entrusted to them 'enter into the joy of your lord'. The third, however, puts what was entrusted to him in the earth – the picture of a man who invests all his energy in the transitoriness of earthly things or, better expressed, 'buries it'. Thereby, he robs himself of the great experience of joy shared by those who have really worked spiritually.

3. The Last Judgment

The first two parables address themselves to human thinking and to human will. They say: You owe your thinking and your working ability to the divine. Take care of the light that is given you and work according to your abilities, and then you prepare yourself worthily for the midnight coming of the bridegroom, for returning an account to the Lord when he requires it. The third picture, the account of the Last Judgment, adds something more of the greatest importance.

It begins straight away with the motif of the coming of the Son of Man in revealing light: 'When the Son of Man comes in his glory, and all the angels with him, then he will sit on his glorious throne.' Once enthroned, he is called 'the King' (Mt 25:34). He judges people according to whether they have shown mercy or not. '... as you did it to one of the least of these my brethren, you did it to me.'

Here it is not a case of particular types of humanity (maiden, servant), of man and woman, but of the purely human itself. This time the emphasis lies not upon the alertness of the spirit (although the deeds of mercy will be done 'with understanding'), nor on the energetic will to work (although the deeds of mercy have to be wrested from inertia). The opposites this time are not wise and foolish, not hardworking and lazy, but merciful and unmerciful. It is a matter of the truly human feeling of the heart that experiences others as the brothers of Christ.

The series of three pictures therefore speaks of thinking, will and feeling. It indicates that the future coming of Christ can only be our salvation if it can find some inner connection with us, if it meets what we have prepared for it in the way of pure, spiritually orientated thinking, active will, and heartfelt love.

Overview

The differences between the three parables stand out more sharply if, for a moment, we look at the 'negative' pictures. Each parable contains its negative: we are told of the unfortunate fate of the foolish maidens, the lazy servant, and the unmerciful.

Each time a different punishment comes into force. Closer observation, however, shows that they are not exactly punishments imposed from without. It is unmistakable how in each case those concerned bring about their own fate, how each time, therefore, the punishment with intrinsic logic suits the offence.

What happens to the *foolish virgins?* They stand in front of the closed door which will not be opened again for them. The bridegroom answers their knocking with: 'I do not know you.'

The closed door indicates something significant. A door is a wall that can cease to be a wall, a wall that can allow the view to open into a space not previously perceptible. Whoever lets their light of perception fail finally runs against the wall of the boundaries of knowledge built up by the merely earthly, intellectual consciousness. They then notice that only behind this wall lies the real thing, but no door will open. The impotence of perception in the face of what is finally recognised as the meaning and value of existence, the supersensible, is painfully experienced as their own guilt, since they have negligently allowed their light to go out.

In the spirit, all knowledge is at the same time a 'being known'. Anyone who never strives to know the divine does not shine in the world above as a spiritual form. They do not perceive, and are therefore not perceived. 'I do not perceive you' or 'I do not know you' (as it says in Mt 25:12).

The *lazy servant* is cast out into the 'darkness where there will be weeping and gnashing of teeth'. He who buries his will in transitory, worldly things, is left to the misfortune of a merely physical existence, which from a spiritual point of view is darkness. The soul weeps in uncontrolled pain since, in its desolate egoism, it is a burden and a pain to itself, while the I, 'gnashing its teeth,' grows harder and more cramped in the death of matter.

The *unmerciful,* however, are consigned to the fire. The fire of hell is not here described in the gruesome way so unfortunately common in a crude and very dubious form of Christianity. Here, in the gospel's austere parable about hell-fire, we are able to look at the original image, free of preconceptions. Again, it is not 'punishment' imposed from without by a vengeful judge, but a self-induced consequence. At the end of Goethe's *Faust* we see the Devil and his crew take to flight before the divine fire of love. The very element that is bliss to the good inflicts pain on the evil. It is one and the same fire. As far as God is concerned, it is only love. The Godhead cannot be other than itself; it subsists in the fire of love. They who place themselves outside this love feel it as a tormenting reproach when they meet it. They suffer in the fire that burns to the torment of the Devil and his angels. Those who have stifled the voice of their hearts bring this torment upon themselves. For the merciful, however, the return of the 'king', before whose throne man is finally judged by his worthiness or unworthiness, opens the way to 'eternal life'.

38

THE WORKS OF CHARITY

MATTHEW 25:31–46

In the account of Matthew, Christ concludes his prophetic, eschatological words on the Mount of Olives on the Tuesday evening of Holy Week, with a powerful apocalyptic image. The whole of humanity, with all its peoples, is gathered before the countenance of Christ. He himself appears in the revelation light of divine glory, surrounded by the hosts of the angels who serve him. The evangelist Matthew has a special attunement to the royal and majestic nature of the figure of Christ, and this comes to expression here too. He, the one who has come again, is called 'the king', and 'sitting upon the throne of his glory' he speaks his judgment upon humanity. This judgment is decisive for the further path of human beings, who are divided into two groups on his right and his left. The judgment is determined by people's actual, practical conduct towards their fellow human beings, their compassion or lack of it. The king in all his majesty is at the same time the Son of Man who calls the least human being on earth his brother. 'What you have done to one of the least of my brothers, that you have done to me' (25:40). He does not mean 'as if' – I will judge your actions 'as if you had done them to me'. The direct and literal truth here is that 'you have done (these things) *to me*'. All who bear a human countenance have, since Golgotha, been implanted with the seed-like Christ potential. Thus, all service to fellow human beings is at the same time service also to this still hidden Christ seed.

Giving to eat and to drink

The six good deeds listed, impressed all the more strongly upon us by their four repetitions, can be divided into three pairs. The initial hunger and thirst clearly belong together – *'You gave me to eat ... you gave me to drink.'* It surely would not be right if, in seeking a deeper understanding of the gospels, we were to think that this is meant only in a 'metaphorical sense'. In war and in imprisonment, many of us have had an opportunity to learn what a piece of bread can signify, and what it means for one person to give it to another. It is certainly meant literally here, although, from this realistic point of departure, prospects inevitably open upon further conditions of life right through to super-earthly ones. Such profound realities of our bodily existence as eating and drinking are archetypal and reach into sublime spiritual realms. We do not live from material bread alone, and hunger, therefore, cannot be only for material bread. We can sense, for instance, how a merely outward, dead knowledge gives us 'stones instead of bread', whereas we hunger for living knowledge. We can hunger for human kindness. In the sense of the Sermon on the Mount we can 'hunger and thirst' for justice.

In hungering we have more of a need for something solidly substantial that nutritiously fills the emptiness we feel. Thirsting arises from the feeling of inner dryness, which hampers or inhibits the flow of living fluids. We want to imbibe something that is dynamic, that stimulates lively motion in us, a springing, pulsing and even streaming and rushing flow. Whether we feel we lack something more as a hungering or thirsting has a different nuance. Eating and drinking start from our primary bodily experience, but can ultimately reach up as far as the realm of the sacramental.

Taking in strangers and clothing the naked

'I was a stranger and *you took me in.*' Literally: 'you took me along with you'. This, too, has its initially very tangible and practical meaning, though at the same time there is a clear transition into a realm essentially of the soul. Millions have experienced in our era what it means to be a stranger: immigrants, refugees, displaced persons

– all have tasted the bitterness of not belonging. Even in modern, prosperous societies, the thousands of immigrant workers pose a significant human challenge. But over and above such immediate neediness, the idea of 'being foreign' or 'alien' has a still more wide-ranging meaning. We feel it, or may even be made to feel it, in every human context where we are 'different' in some way from the status quo. Many school children have the devastating experience of being excluded from a particular group, with all the unwitting or naive cruelty this involves. Similar experiences can arise in all possible situations in life, so that people feel forsaken or marginalised. 'And you took me along with you' – you relieved me of the feeling of being alien, you allowed me to feel 'at home' with you.

This giving of welcome is directly connected with 'I was naked *and you clothed me.*' If we read the text superficially, we might think that this motif of clothing the naked should belong more with feeding and giving of drink, since it is seemingly at the same level of primary bodily need. The word 'stranger' has, in the meantime, led us further into the soul realm. But specifically because the 'soul tone' has been struck so audibly there, the words about clothing acquire a more inward resonance. Once again, we can start from tangible reality: at times when war-torn refugees have been forced to suffer the cold, giving clothing has its very practical and often life-saving meaning. But again this goes beyond such immediacy of need, and also has something to say to those who live in relative prosperity. The shift from strangerhood to nakedness is entirely consistent. If we do not feel we belong, and must 'stand outside' a community, we also feel cold. The old picture of the 'cloak of neighbourly Christian love' may be rather well-worn, but it still holds true.

Clothing also has another meaning apart from warmth, and being naked is not only about being cold. The story of the Fall relates how Adam and Eve became aware of their nakedness. An ancient and wise tradition still spoke of them being clothed in garments of light before this occurred. In other words, originally people still beheld themselves dressed in fine, supersensible raiment. Only after the Fall did this original clairvoyance fade, so that human perception became limited increasingly to coarser materiality. The 'shame of nakedness' (Rv 3:18) is, basically, an ignominy we no longer feel at all today: that of regarding the material body as the whole human being. In the same way, in the death camps in the Second World War, the human being was regarded as nothing more than a certain weight of destructible living matter.

In the rites of The Christian Community, the priest's garb also serves to offer to our eyes something that is not physically visible but belongs to the human being, rooting it anew in our living feeling. The wedding garment referred to in the gospels thus becomes very tangible again.

In his book *Die Botschaft Jesu,* the Protestant theologian Ethelbert Stauffer, speaks of the 'festiveness' which Jesus wished to introduce into human life. This is beautifully and accurately put. But we must ask further what all true 'festiveness' ultimately depends upon. Is it not true that Sunday worshippers sense, in a certain mood of elevation, their eternal, heavenly nature? When the festive mood is genuine, something shines in from the supersensible. Then festive clothes are not illusion and outward show, but the revelation of a deeper truth about the human being.

The 'shame of nakedness' is increasingly widespread today – the outlook that considers only material existence and regards it as the sole reality. Ultimately, this renders all existence arid and meaningless. Thus 'clothing nakedness' opens up a wide field of work and endeavour.

All of earthly humanity is waiting to be ensouled and spiritualised again by the transformative power that proceeds from Christ, so that it can once again appear arrayed in the aura of the divine mystery. Clothing the naked does not only mean giving warmth to our fellow human beings, but also relieving them of a comfortless, merely outward existence and giving them something of the festive, elevated awareness of their true human dignity.

Visiting the sick and imprisoned

As the fifth and sixth deed of human kindness Christ cites *visiting the sick and the imprisoned*. Once more, these two acts form a pair. Common to both of them is that rather than responding to a direct and immediate need, we must first form a resolve of will, set ourselves in motion, to seek out suffering that occurs away from our sight: in the seclusion of the sickroom and the prison cell. Both require effort on our part.

Christ does not speak of healing the sick, which few of us can do. He speaks of something that all could manage: that we 'look to the sick' (*episkeptomai* in Greek). It is connected with our spiritual aspect that we can feel a selfless interest in a life that does not directly concern us. Then we step outside our own, narrow circumstances, seek out those we do not know, and inwardly engage with them. For the patient it is also a 'spiritual' gratification if the other – even if they cannot help us directly – shows interest in our fate and 'asks after us'.

Visiting prisoners is similar. If we initially take this literally, we may soon come to the limits of what is possible today. In ancient 'heathen' Athens, the followers of Socrates were able to visit him in prison when he was condemned to death, and discuss philosophy with him all day long until the evening sun sank behind the mountains. The incarcerated martyrs in Caesar's Rome were allowed visits from their comrades in faith. Since then, such things have become more difficult. In respect of this work of human kindness, we may emphasise all the more that all of us can do it in an extended sense.

Living together with other people is so difficult because we have to deal with more than just each other's true being and nature. All of us also possesses something like a dark double in so far as we bear egoism within us in one form or another. Our true being is more or less a prisoner of our lower self. In this sense, every person is to some degree self-imprisoned, even if they can do what they like in outward life. Such inner constraints, the things that hamper and hinder us, can express themselves in myriad ways, even in the intellectual or spiritual domain if a thinker becomes the prisoner of their own ideology.

In relation to the sick, Christ's words were, 'you looked to me'. In the case of the prisoners, 'you came to me'. There is a subtle difference here, though they seem to be saying almost the same thing. In 'coming to me' lies a stronger activity and resolve, a self-activation required to find the other in the place where they are, by putting oneself in their place. If we go out towards our fellow human beings, we can help them to gradually release their higher I from the prison of their lower self. In doing so, we can serve the Christ potential hidden in the depths of their being.

Thus, these three times two instances – from the direct giving of bread to the 'you came to me' – encompass the realm of human kindness in its relation to body, soul and spirit.

IV

WITNESSES OF THE APOSTLES

39

PETER'S PENTECOST ADDRESS

ACTS OF THE APOSTLES 2:14–36

For the span of forty days, the apostles held discourse with the Risen One. But during this whole period, and also during the ten subsequent days following Ascension, they were unable to speak to other people about the events of Easter. They could only do so when, on the fiftieth day, at Pentecost, the Holy Spirit opened their lips. The Acts of the Apostles of Luke conveys to us Peter's address to the gathered crowd, which was the very first occasion of Christian preaching.

I

His first words already point to the theme of knowledge: 'Let this be known to you.' In the Greek, 'be known to you' is *gnoston,* from the same root as *gnosis*. Peter wishes to bring about a 'knowing' in his listeners.

First, he wants them to understand that the enthusiasm of the disciples filled with the spirit is not 'drunkenness'. He quotes a passage from the prophet Joel, 'I will pour out my spirit upon all flesh.' This forms the first part of the Pentecost address (2:14–21).

Joel is one of the twelve so-called minor prophets, his book comprising only three chapters. In what context do his words there speak of a future outpouring of the spirit? The Holy Land had been terribly plagued by a swarm of locusts. The seething, endless hosts of locusts, consuming everything in their path and leaving destruction behind them, appeared to the people of those days like a visible embodiment of demonic powers of destruction. The sight of them elicited visions of apocalypse: people felt themselves filled with terrible intimations of future downfall. We also find the locusts in the visions of the Revelation to John. Joel was something like a Hebrew prophet of apocalypse. As such, he speaks of the 'signs' of disaster in the heavens and below on the earth. The sun grows dark, the moon acquires a blood-red hue. And on earth there is blood, fire, and seething clouds of smoke.

It would be wrong to see in the Revelation of John only images of horror, for it also has another side. Contrasting with the destruction of earthly existence is an awakening to the eternal. This positive, light-filled aspect of apocalyptic writing is also to be found in Joel, in his great message of a future outpouring of the spirit that will come to 'all flesh', to all human beings living on earth and not only the few 'chosen ones'. The all-embracing, human nature of this address is also apparent in the fact that distinctions between young and old, man and woman, master and servant, which had formerly prevailed so decisively even in cultural life, no longer play a role. 'Your sons and daughters will prophesy, your old men will dream dreams, your young men will see visions.' Even 'manservants and maidservants' are to receive the spirit (Joel 2:28f). The spirit sent forth by God will work in a universally human and all-encompassing way, it will allow heightened states of consciousness to awaken, through which the supersensible shines into souls.

Thus, despite all darkness and devastation in the transient realm, the 'great day of the Lord' is to come, at the same time bringing *epiphanes,* epiphany, the manifestation of God.

Peter cites the whole apocalyptic context from the second chapter of Joel, including the words of comfort, 'And it shall happen that whoever calls upon the name of the Lord will be saved.' Whoever raises themselves to the I AM that speaks in Christ, whoever clings to this inwardly, may hope that they will be torn from world destruction and saved for eternal life.

II

The prophet Joel, in ancient times, was able to look ahead into the far spiritual future – a future that Peter is certain begins on the day of Pentecost. Joel's prophetic vision, however, is lacking precisely what can give humanity hope of this spiritual future: the sacrificial deed of Christ. In the second part of his address (2:22–28), Peter now comes to speak of this, of the death and resurrection enacted at Golgotha. In direct, temporal proximity to this event, he presents his listeners with the picture of Jesus of Nazareth who only a few weeks previously walked visibly amongst them. He calls Jesus the Nazarene a 'man accredited by God to you by deeds of power, wonders and signs' (2:22).

This is a remarkably differentiated characterisation of Christ's miracles, here uttered from direct testimony. The deeds of Christ are *dynameis,* dynamic workings of power. That is the divine will aspect of the matter. 'Wonders', as these deeds are called secondly, express how the human soul is shaken by their unusual nature. This unusual quality does not mean here an arbitrary overturning of the natural order established by God, but the influx of higher laws, higher orders, through which the earthly order is rightly revoked. In wonder the human soul is raised above the daily, mundane level to an intimation of such higher orders. The third aspect is 'signs'. The Gospel of John especially uses this term for Christ's miracles. Here the focus primarily is on the significance, for the perceiving spirit, of the capacity to read the revelatory runes of the spirit. 'Thus did God through him in your midst, as you yourselves know' (2:22). Peter is therefore expressly appealing to his listeners' own experience, to what they themselves can know if only they reflect properly upon this knowledge of theirs. 'This man' they have delivered up to death – although this, at the same time, was God's plan that became reality.

And now follows the great Easter message, here for the first time proclaimed in the power of the Pentecost spirit: 'But God raised him again, having loosed the birth pains of death' (2:24). The resurrection is shown here in the light of the spirit as a higher birth from the womb of death, and thus discerned in its deepest meaning. Rather than simply expressing the fact itself, insight into this fact is simultaneously offered. 'Since it was not possible for death to keep its hold on him.' Hitherto, commentators have been surprisingly silent about what Peter says here. If, in relation to some unusual occurrence, I were to say something like 'It could not have happened any differently,' then I presume a certain insight into the occurrence, albeit perhaps a very modest one. I do not stand wholly outside it, simply remarking on it, but I have a certain knowledge of it too.

The resurrection of Christ, as a unique event, certainly surpasses all understanding. But it makes a great difference whether it is presented to me as an intrinsically incomprehensible miracle that I must accept on authority, or whether I can be shown the first steps on a path towards understanding it, which, even if I cannot fathom it entirely, allows me to intuit a perspective through which I might eventually come to fully understand it. If, in my inner life, I have experienced the 'savour of resurrection', then I gain access to the hope that the Easter power may, in a far future, one day also thoroughly transform the human body. Then the 'resurrection on the Last Day' is no longer only a dogma for me.

Peter expresses his inner access to the resurrection in the little word 'for', with which he now weaves in to his address a citation from the Old Testament, from Psalm 16:8: 'For David says of him, I have set the Lord always before me.' The evangelist Luke hints at what the Risen One spoke of with the disciples during the forty days. He spoke of what is written in Moses, in the prophets and in the psalms about him. He 'opened their spirit understanding *(nous)* for the scriptures' (Lk 24:44f). Besides the books of the prophets, the psalms are also expressly mentioned here.

When we see Peter, on the day of Pentecost, reach into the Old Testament with such assurance, and quote from it texts from the prophets and psalms, it may surely not be too far-fetched to think this may reflect those teachings during the forty days. Peter thus affirms his astonishing statement that 'it was not possible' any other way, with a passage from Psalm 16, which points to a path of mystic experience. The passage begins with 'having the Lord before me always', and leads on from this to a prospect of the soul surviving through death: 'You will not leave my soul to the world of shadows'; and finally, even, the keen hope is expressed of a bodily resurrection: 'You will not allow your holy one to see corruption.' All of this is overlit by the phrase: 'You have made known to me the paths of life.' For Peter, it is certain that a millennium previously, David composed this psalm in a state of inspiration, and that he was speaking 'in the person of the Christ who was to come'. Only on the day of Easter was this psalm fulfilled completely. This does not however negate the fact – in fact, it affirms it – that the psalm is speaking of the 'paths of life' as granted to ancient mystical experience. Even if only small steps were taken upon these paths at that time, they lead to intimating, prefiguring experiences of the resurrection.

III

In the third and last part of his address (2:29–36), Peter again returns to the overcoming of bodily death and makes it clear that David himself could not have been speaking of his own person. 'For he [David] has already died and was buried, and his grave is with us to this day.' The grave where David's body had rested for a millennium is on Mount Zion in western Jerusalem, in the same building that also houses the Cenacle, the room of the Last Supper, which we may also regard as the place where the Pentecost event occurred. David did not rise again, but, 'foreseeing this, he spoke of the resurrection of Christ' (2:31). Once again, Peter proclaims the great message that 'this Jesus God has raised up, whereof we are all witnesses'. In the second part of his address, he leads on from the resurrection to the ascension through which the Son will be connected once again to the Father, at whose right hand he sits.

Peter impresses upon his listeners this ascension mystery of 'sitting on the right hand of the Father' by quoting a third time from the Old Testament, this time from Psalm 110. This important psalm, which refers to the priest king Melchizedek, who is otherwise mentioned in only one other place in the whole of the Old Testament (in Genesis 14), was previously used by Christ as a Messianic text on the Tuesday of Holy Week. It is invoked also in the profession that Christ makes before the high priests that he is the Son of God (Mt 26:64).

Peter's address passes, with an inner, organic naturalness, from the outpouring of the *Spirit* to its precondition in the death and resurrection of the *Son* and from there to the ascension that reunites the Son with the *Father*. The Trinity is emphasised in the three citations: from the Prophet Joel, from Psalm 16 – which speaks of the paths of life – and from Psalm 110, 'The Lord spoke to my Lord, Sit at my right hand.' Peter addresses his listeners directly three times also, at the beginning of each of the three parts of his speech: 'Men of Judea and all inhabitants of Jerusalem' (2:14), 'Men of Israel' (2:22), 'Men, brothers' (2:29), marking a development that broadens ever more into the universally human.

Towards the end of his address, after Peter has led his talk to the Father God, he returns once more to the beginning, to the pouring out of the Spirit: 'From the Father he has poured out what you now see and hear.'

Through all three parts resounds the word indicating knowledge: 'Let this be known to you *(gnoston)*'; 'You have given me to know the paths of life'; and at the end of the address, 'Therefore let all the house of Israel know assuredly' (2:36). The Holy Spirit, who seeks to illumine humankind, thus impressed its threefold seal of 'knowledge' upon this first Christian sermon.

40

PETER'S EASTER NIGHT IN THE YEAR 44

ACTS OF THE APOSTLES 12:1–17

The Easter event stands within our world as incomparable and unique in all human history. Only when the Christian gaze turns hopefully to the furthest future horizon, does something that corresponds to it become very distantly apparent – the 'resurrection on the Last Day'. Then the final spiritualisation of a bodily nature redeemed from death, which was accomplished on Easter day as the mystery of the God become man, will at last be a reality for a multiplicity of Christ-permeated human beings. What occurred uniquely in Jerusalem at the turning point of time, initially seems to fade away and disappear into the flux of history. But it flows on in hidden depths to reappear again at the end of time, now encompassing all humanity.

Before the mystery of Easter Sunday begins its long, silent passage through humanity's further destiny, we see its vivid afterglow in certain experiences of the first Christian community. The mighty event was as yet so close to those 'first witnesses' that its echoes and resonance gave rise to unusual occurrences, as we find these in the Acts of the Apostles composed by Luke. This afterglow of what had so recently occurred is, on the other hand, also a prefiguring, a pre-illumining of future spirit potency working through into the world of substance. Of this kind is the freeing of Peter from the dungeon, as related in Chapter 12 of Acts.

In the period before Easter in the year 44, the young community of Christians felt the rough hand of King Herod Agrippa.* He seized James, son of Zebedee, from the group of apostles, and had him decapitated. Seeing that this brought him favour in certain circles, he also had Peter arrested. A show trial against him was planned, intended to lead to his execution. However, this trial was postponed to await the end of the holy Passover festival that had already begun. Thus the date for it fell on the first day of the week after Passover, on Sunday, the Christian Easter day. What Luke reports as an unexpected intervention by higher powers occurred the preceding night, the eve of Easter Sunday.

During this night Peter was asleep in prison, chained to two sleeping soldiers beside him. Acts gives a vivid picture of the scene. Herod, who clearly assigned special importance to this inmate as the leader of the Christian community, had entrusted four groups of four soldiers each to guard him, each group probably taking one of the four night watches. Peter was chained to two soldiers while two others stood guard at the entrance (12:6).

Suddenly a wondrous brilliance filled the chamber.

Before we turn to what this sudden influx of light led to, it would be good to dwell upon a sentence with which Luke prefaced his account, which is far more than a passing note: 'But the community was making earnest prayer to God for him' (Ac 12:5). Luke repeatedly shows himself to be the evangelist of prayer. Both at the Jordan baptism and the transfiguration, he sees the supersensible events developing from the praying of Jesus. The words of the dying Redeemer on the cross as he preserved them also have a prayerful character. In Acts, in place of this great Christ figure of prayer, he now places the praying community of Christians. The concentrated prayer 'in the upper room' after Christ's ascension by those gathered there for ten days, prepared the Pentecost outpouring of the spirit. Now the gathered power of prayer of the first Christians, as 'one heart and one soul' (Ac 4:32) works like an elemental force: 'And having prayed,

---

* This was the grandson of the Herod who had ordered the murder of the young children. Herod Agrippa, albeit under Roman jurisdiction, was able to gather all of Judea, Galilee, and the land beyond the Jordan River under his rule in the years between 41 and 44.

40. PETER'S EASTER NIGHT IN THE YEAR 44

the place where they were gathered was shaken' (4:31). This power also becomes active in this night before Easter. Even the prayer of a single Christian was a powerful experience back then. In the Letter of James, it says, 'The prayer of a righteous person has great power when it is earnestly undertaken' (literally, 'carried by energy', 5:16). Where a deeply connected community gathers, the separate energies of prayer are multiplied, or potentised even.

Such a substantial and essential plea gives the angels something that enables them to intervene more strongly than usual in earthly circumstances. Such a plea does not act in a directly horizontal way upon the person to whom it is directed, but takes its way upwards to the powers at work above them, according the angels something which, coming from the earth, can serve them in their helping succour. Thus those 'gathered in the house of Mary, the mother of John also called Mark' (12:12) are intensively united in prayer, and into their plea also streams the special grace of an Easter eve. Outwardly, the two scenes – the house of Mary and the prison – are spatially separate from each other, but in terms of 'inner space' they must be perceived as one.

'And see, an angel of the Lord stood before Peter and a light shone forth in the cell.' (12:7). Luke uses expressions familiar to us from the Christmas nativity story to clothe this supersensible light experience in human words. The angel 'stood' before Peter. In the Greek, the word for 'stand' is prefixed with the word *epi*, which indicates, or hints, that the angel does not simply stand there neutrally in outward space. Its standing is a spiritual act; the angel turns entirely to Peter with all the intensity of its angelic being, which streams upon the apostle as if from above. It is hardly surprising that the sturdy soldiers do not experience this supersensible occurrence at all. But Peter, too, cannot shake off the dullness of sleep so quickly, and so the angel has to intensify its influence. Peter experiences this as a 'blow to his side'. Now he can hear the angel's awakening call: 'Rise up in haste!' The word for rise up in Greek is *anásta*. To get up, and to rise (in the sense of resurrection) are the same word. The spiritual power of the Easter event calls this mighty *anásta* into the chamber, and at this the chains fall from Peter's hands. The Easter power can burst fetters. In Faust's ascension, Pater Profundis speaks of the spirit imprisoned and tormented in the 'bonds of the dull senses, in the pain of fetters tightly bound'. Unfettering is an archetype of Easter. That Peter must hurry, must 'rise up in haste,' points no doubt to the suddenness of this experience, unfolding within ordinary time like a flash of lightning, with the rapidity of thought.

Peter hears the angel speak a second time after his hands are free and he rises: 'Gird yourself and put on your sandals!' In sleep, the soul lives outside the body. As it awakens it returns to its bodily dwelling. But this does not always happen so smoothly and naturally. There can be intermediate states between sleeping and waking, when the soul has not yet fully engaged with the body and so is still open to supersensible impressions. The angel has to help Peter into his body. 'Girding' himself makes him more aware of his bodily form, and putting on his sandals makes feet readier to step upon the hard ground. Following the angel's command to put on belt and sandals, Luke writes, like an echo, 'And he did so'. Peter follows the angel's directions as if still plunged in a dream. The angel now addresses him for the third and last time, 'Wrap your cloak about you and follow me!' It is as if the whole earthly human being were built up once again anew before our eyes, with his upright stance, his free hands, with his form girded between above and below, with his feet that tread the earthly ground. Now, beside all this, comes the cloak also, which envelops him and wafts around him beyond the solid form of his body.

Apart from appreciating the imagery of this account, we can also admire the realistic way in which Luke describes its earthly scenery. The way the prisoner has loosened his belt for sleep and taken off his sandals is conveyed in a very real, down-to-earth way. Lying on the ground, he has used his cloak as covering. All this stands vividly before us. Let us return now to the third command of the angel, 'Wrap your cloak around you and follow me!' Again, there is an echo to this command in the sentence, 'And having gone out, he followed him' (12:9). Raphael has depicted this moment in the Vatican's Room of Heliodorus. If one looks at Peter's face in this painting, we see how wonderfully Raphael conveys a sleepwalking quality in the way he walks behind the angel. As he leaves the cell, Peter is not yet fully in possession of his waking consciousness. 'He did not know that what was happening through the angel was real, and thought he saw a vision' (12:9) – a spiritual vision, but not one rooted in earthly reality.

Luke precisely describes the stages of this semi-sleepwalking: following the angel, Peter went out of the cell, the two figures 'passed the first and the second guards' unchallenged, then they 'came to the iron gate leading into the city', and then once more they 'go out' but now into the open, to freedom. Anyone who has ever had the experience of imprisonment may remember that as they were released, as the gate opened before them, it had something of a dreamlike, unreal quality. Psalm 126 says, 'When the Lord released the captivity of Zion, we were like those who dream.'

Part of the wonders of this Easter night is that the chains fall off the prisoner and the iron gate of the prison building open by itself before the walkers. Perhaps it was an earthquake that caused this, like the bursting of the prison doors in Philippi which, as Luke describes it, released Paul and Silas (Ac 16:26). The historian Josephus relates in the *Jewish War* (VI 5.3) how, before the outbreak of the war, during Passover, the 'eastern gate of the inner courtyard, despite being made of bronze and enormously heavy ... opened suddenly by itself at midnight.' Whatever may have happened in the case of Peter, the opening prison doors are at the same time something archetypal. The picture of closed doors opening is important in the New Testament.

What is a gate or a door? We might reply, a part of a wall that can cease to be a firm partition and, by opening, can make visible and accessible a realm that previously was concealed from view.

A notable variant of the text follows the 'going out' through the iron gateway with the sentence, 'They descended seven steps.' These steps can be seen in Raphael's painting. Descending by stages, by steps, at the same time conveys the transition in consciousness from being caught up in a higher sphere to finally awakening to the earthly world. Peter's sleepwalking gradually becomes our ordinary walking upon the ground. Yet the other world does not so quickly fade from his awareness. For a while, as 'they went along one street' (12:10), he still sees the angel accompanying him. Then 'suddenly' the angel is no longer there. The Greek word means literally, 'he stood away from'. A critical scholar of the Bible once expressed his dismay that the angel, after all that had occurred, should simply vanish without a word. But we can feel that Luke describes what happened with great faithfulness to its reality. We can understand it by recalling certain dreams we may have had on awakening, of talking to a dead acquaintance who was vividly present to us, who, as we awoke, was suddenly far off and all at once had vanished.

Peter finds himself alone again, and from now on must again take responsibility for himself as an independent human being on earth. Luke describes this moment very accurately: 'And having come to himself'. He had taken hold of himself fully once more. And now, for the first time in this story, Peter himself speaks. Hitherto he has been silent but now has regained his power of speech. He says to himself, as he considers what has occurred, and so begins to make sense of it, 'Now I know in truth that the Lord has sent his angel and has delivered me from the hand of Herod.'

He has taken hold of himself again and regained his speech, and finally this new-won earthly waking consciousness and self-direction extends to his bodily senses. He incarnates as it were into his visual sense. Luke coined a phrase for this that is hard to translate. English translations often say, 'And when he had considered (or realised) this'. In the Greek there is a verb that literally means 'seeing together'. In waking life, we combine all the impressions that enter through our eyes into a unified, interconnected picture of our surroundings – we 'see them together' into a whole. With this earthly orientation that he himself must bring about, and with new-found clarity about the situation, Peter now walks on purposefully through the sleeping city, brightly lit by the moon – bright because this was the time of Passover full moon. And, finally, he stands before the house of Mary. Luke reminds us again that the Christians were 'gathered there together to pray' (12:12). We should not forget that they had continued to pray during the night, throughout the time the events in the prison had transpired.

Peter stands outside the door and knocks. The danger of persecution hovers over those gathered there. A knocking in the night could mean soldiers and arrest, and so they do not open immediately. The doorkeeper stays listening within for a while until Peter speaks as well as knocking. The house of Mary must have been a fairly large building to accommodate the community gathered there. It had a gateway as it says in the text. Like the entrance to the palace of the high priest, a maid takes care of door-keeping duties.

The doorkeeper in the house of Mary is a Christian. As she

recognises the voice of Peter she is so overwhelmed by a flood of joy that she acts without thinking. Instead of opening the door she 'runs' to the assembled people inside and tells them the incredible news. 'For joy' she did not open the gate, says Luke (12:14). We can often observe in him a fine sensitivity to the stirrings of the human soul. He knows that it is not only 'from sorrow', but also 'from joy' (Lk 22:45, 24:41) that our ordinary consciousness can be disrupted. Luke, the evangelist of Mary, also repeatedly shows a special understanding for the nature and importance of women. This doorkeeper maid now also becomes one of his female figures. A servant and member of the Jerusalem community, of little apparent importance, she steps into the narrative's bright illumination for a moment and then disappears again from view. Luke has preserved her name – it is Rhoda, which means 'rose'. Her elemental outbreak of joy gives us a sense of the powerful transport of feelings of which those early Christians were capable.

As Rhoda calls into the assembled community that Peter is standing outside the door, they do not initially believe her. Then they suspect that it is 'perhaps his angel'. Something that today we might seek to recognise anew was at that time still self-evident: that angels are a reality, and that each person is specially assigned one. No doubt they meant by this that the angel's appearance here indicated Peter's death. But, finally, the door is opened to Peter, who is still knocking, and he himself enters the gathering. At this sight those assembled there are 'astonished'. But, with a gesture of his hand, he brings the joyful tumult to stillness and relates what has happened. However, he cannot stay any longer. He must flee into the night, going underground to find safe refuge until the danger of pursuit passes. Yet as he embarks upon his further destiny, he takes with him the ineradicable experience of the resurrection power that burst his dungeon open on the eve of Easter day.

41

THE MARTYR STEPHEN – THE DAY AFTER CHRISTMAS

ACTS OF THE APOSTLES 6:5–7:60

Traditionally, December 26, the second day of Christmas, bears the name of Stephen. He was the first Christian martyr, dying by stoning at the hand of his fanatical opponents in Jerusalem. This picture of stoning may strike us as having nothing in common with Christmas. Is it therefore a mere historical accident that this bloody murder is thought to have taken place on this very day, or is there perhaps a deeper meaning in the fact that this first known martyr of Christian history, the first to 'die in Christ', stands within the radiance of Christmas?

Stephen the Hellenist

The Acts of the Apostles, written in Greek by Luke, relates certain tensions in the original Christian community in Jerusalem between Hebrews and Hellenists. The latter, like the Hebrews, were also Jews in origin and religion. But outside Judea and Galilee, in the Diaspora, they had come into contact with Greek culture, had adopted the Greek language and read their holy scripture in Greek translation. From the group of these Hellenists, seven deacons were appointed to support the apostles. All seven bear Greek names. Their relationship to the Sophia, to thought-illumined religious knowledge, also played a part in choosing them (Ac 6:3). In pride of place among the seven, Stephen is named as one 'filled with faith and the Holy Spirit' (6:5).

He soon proved successful in his mission, skilful in contesting and disputing with those who thought differently, and showing himself superior to his opponents in 'wisdom and spirit'. Since no one could vanquish him in this realm, they chose other means to do so. He was prosecuted for blasphemy, accused of the same thing that was cited in the trial against Jesus. Stephen, it was said, had invoked the Nazarene's pronouncement that he wished to demolish the temple and rebuild it anew (6:14).

In Christ's words of demolishing and rebuilding, his opponents at the time had wrongly imputed that he wished to destroy the temple. They could not understand that the temple in Jerusalem, which for centuries had been an exemplar of the 'body' which the approaching God would assume when he took on flesh, had now lost its meaning. It had become superfluous. In AD 70, the guiding hand of history employed Roman military might to eradicate this temple – an important, incisive event also in the history of developing Christian consciousness. The entirely new element, encompassing all humanity, the global impulse of the future embodied in the consequences of the Christ event, emancipated itself from the shell of Old Testament religion, which had now fulfilled its mission of preparing it.

In the days of Stephen – we are probably at the end of the Golgotha year here, AD 33 – the temple was still intact. The Hebrews of the Jerusalem community were as yet scarcely aware that, as Christians, they already belonged now to a quite different world. They continued unquestioningly to participate in the temple rituals. The Hellenists on the other hand, as people who had journeyed further afield, outside the narrow limits of Judea, were more able to intuit the universal character of the Christ event. This is clearly apparent in Stephen. In the reproach made against him that he was preaching an alternative to Mosaic customs, and the destruction of the temple by Jesus, we see a distorted version of the truth that Stephen was able to see the radically new element in Christianity that would lead people beyond Moses and the temple of Solomon.

The speech of Stephen

Commanded to appear before the Sanhedrin, Stephen gives a broad survey of the history of the Israelites, starting with Abraham. He shows how, in this sacred history, resistance and hostility repeatedly arise towards the 'coming of the Righteous One', which culminates in the killing of the Messiah. The 'coming' of the Righteous One is *eleusis* in Greek. In the mouth of a Hellenist, in the scripture of the Hellenist Luke, this word – which after all was also that of an important Greek mystery site – has special resonance. *Eleusis* is *adventus* in Latin.* We must also not overlook the fact that, in Stephen's speech, the motif of the Sophia appears, when he speaks of Joseph in Egypt (7:10) and of Moses, who 'was instructed in all the wisdom of the Egyptians' (7:22). It is sometimes asked where this last passage is to be found in the Old Testament. It is not to be found there. It is in the speech of Stephen, who thus shows that he knew of other traditions not contained within the Old Testament.

This is apparent also in the way that he speaks of the 'angels'. It was Yahweh who revealed himself to Moses in the burning thorn bush but this revelation was mediated through an angel being (7:30, 35). In the same way the Ten Commandments given on Sinai were mediated by angels as 'living words' *(logia zōnta)* (7:38 and 7:53). We find also in Paul (Gal 3:19) and in the Letter to the Hebrews (2:2) a knowledge of these angelic workings not mentioned in the Old Testament.

The countenance of an angel

Stephen shows himself not only to be one possessing knowledge derived from Sophia of the angelic world, but he is also the only figure in the New Testament whose face is described as appearing 'like the countenance of an angel' (6:15). This happens when he stands before the Sanhedrin facing death.

In our modern times we have come to see the human being one-sidedly, as related only to animals. There is no doubt about

---

* There are two other places where the word *eleusis* appears (in the Codex D variant): spoken by the disciples (Lk 21:7) and by the thief crucified beside Christ (Lk 23:42). On both occasions this word figures in the gospel of Luke, the Hellenist.

this connection and affinity, but it is a false conclusion to derive human origins as such from the animal kingdom. In the human being, the upward movement of an evolving and self-perfecting bodily evolution encounters an opposite movement, descending from above, of a spirit being who incarnates in an earthly body, and makes us human in the true sense. In a downward direction we come up against animal nature, while in an upward one we reach towards the angels. We overlook an intrinsically human quality if we regard ourselves only as the highest mammal. We belong to a realm of spirit rising in stages and degrees above us, of angels and archangels through to Cherubim and Seraphim. The human level is the germ of a new 'hierarchy', which is to supplement the nine ranks of the angels – of whom Christianity has always had knowledge – with a tenth.

The ascending orders of angels are not something that hide our view of God, as certain theological theories claim. To speak of 'spirit beings who hinder and conceal our view of God' would be to refer accurately, instead, to the entities that have always been regarded as devils, as adversarial powers. The word 'angel' – in Greek *angelos* – means 'messenger'. When has a true messenger ever hindered a view of the one sending the message? The angelic beings were experienced as God's instrument, as the organs through which he carries his revelation to humankind.

The nine ranks or orders of angels, the hierarchies, are the realms of God-revealing beings. As long as we have not been permeated by Christ, we conceal God more than we reveal him. Darkened by egoism, we do not allow the divine rays to shine through us, and so we are, as yet, far from being 'God's representative on earth'. We will become this to the degree that we take up Christ into ourselves. In so far as Christ comes to life within us, we can join in the hierarchies' God-manifesting hymn of praise.

Christmas, especially, stands within this mystery pervaded by hope. The ever-increasing superficiality, the commercialisation and kitsch of thoughts about Christmas, has also ruined many contemporaries' view of angels, though these of course belong to the Christmas festival. It is high time that people in Christian circles reflected on the realities of a supersensible world and learned to take angels seriously again. What would the Christmas gospel be without the influx of these beings of light who came to the attention of open-minded and open-hearted human beings in the period around the birth of Jesus? The angelic world belongs intrinsically to the child in Bethlehem.

Above and beyond the birth of Jesus, Christmas is the festival of the birth of Christ, in the sense of the words of the mystic *'You must become Mary'*. The birth of Christ in the human soul becomes historically visible for the first time in Stephen. Man's affinity with the angels appears in him, to the extent of an outward visibility that even his adversaries perceive.

The birth of Christ in the soul

The shining countenance calls forth the adversarial powers. The accusers 'gnashed their teeth' (7:54). They are as if possessed by the forces that would entirely petrify the human being within the earthly realm, delivering him up to the 'death of matter'. The time of winter – winter *without* Christmas – manifests these powers of death that threaten humankind in icy cold and frosty torpor. But Stephen responds without hate to the hate that snarls at him. He dies – the first such death since Golgotha – an archetypally Christian death.

Many have observed that the three things said by the dying Stephen in the Acts of the Apostles are reminiscent of the three of Christ's seven last words from the cross recounted by Luke. People comment that Luke may have used his talent as a writer to shape Stephen's words into conformity with Christ's words. But an outward view of this kind does not reach to the depths of what occurs. Stephen has absorbed the nature of Christ so deeply that these three words from the cross, which he no doubt learned from the oral tradition of the first Christian community (no gospels had as yet been written) sprang again in his soul as if original and new.

Before the stoning had even begun, Stephen 'full of the Holy Spirit looked up intently into heaven and saw the glory of God, and Jesus standing at the right hand of God' (7:55). This intense gaze upward to the visible heavens opens his eye of spirit also for the supersensible world, which, unfolding in ever more glorious ascending levels, shines forth as 'the heavens'. From such vision his first dying words are born: 'Behold, I see the heavens opened and the Son of Man standing at the right hand of God' (7:56).

41. THE MARTYR STEPHEN

This is the only time that the Acts of the Apostles uses the phrase the Son of Man. It is therefore characteristic of Stephen's visionary experience. Christ on the cross similarly opened the higher world to the dying thief beside him: 'This day will you be with me in Paradise' (Lk 23:43). Stephen, close to death, gazes through sensory appearance and is vouchsafed a Christmas vision of the glory of God revealed in heavenly heights; but this *Gloria in excelsis* is now indivisibly united with the vision of the Son of Man who incorporates the human element into the heavenly world.

As the stoning begins, Stephen calls to Christ, 'Lord Jesus, receive my spirit' (7:59). When Christ on the cross felt death approaching, he spoke the death prayer of Psalm 31, 'Into your hands I commend my spirit,' prefacing these words with 'Father' (Lk 23:46). To commend one's spirit expresses the human power to give inner life a specific direction. It lies very much within our own will where we wish to direct our inner interest, either upward or downward. In earlier times people knew this better, and should seek to recognise it anew today. Such knowledge has its consequences, already for the manner in which we direct the soul before falling asleep with a nightly prayer. This determines whether our supersensible aspect, as it releases itself from its connection with the body, reaches higher or less high regions of the other world. Much depends on our 'last will', both as we end each day, and still far more as we close our whole lifetime. Stephen dies in Christ. He gives his intrinsic being to eternity, and directs his spirit towards Christ.

Falling to his knees under the blows of the stones, he prays last of all: 'Lord, do not hold this sin against them' (7:60). Literally, 'Let this sin not stand against them.' The crucified Christ had said, 'Father forgive them, for they know not what they do' (Lk 23:34). For the further destiny of a murderer, the attitude towards him of the murdered person has far-reaching consequences. The grave consequences the murderer incurs can be assuaged by the plea of his victim. Indeed, this can become the foundation for future transformations. It is not for nothing that the account of the stoning of Stephen names Saul (7:58). What Saul, one of these persecutors, here experiences, will work on in the depths of his soul and contribute to the event at Damascus, turning him from Saul into Paul.

With its saints, Christianity saw the prophetic dawning of higher human capacities following the deed of Christ. Stephen marks, as if archetypally, the beginning of these ranks of the saints. With angelic, transfigured countenance he stands in intimate proximity to Christmas, participating in the light that shines there amidst the darkness. Thinking of him one can recall the words of Novalis: 'A sign of comfort in the darkness – a higher humanity's joyful beginning.'

42

THE POWER OF TRANSFORMATION: INSIGHTS OF ST PAUL

Paul's life and work follow the motif of transformation. The persecutor of Christ becomes a disciple of Christ, Saul becomes Paul. It is out of this background of destiny that the words should be read which Paul wrote in his letters on the theme of transformation; not as 'armchair-theology', but as something drawn from concrete experience. It is as if Paul tries to pin down what is difficult to express by making use of different words offered by the Greek language. In what follows, three such different statements will be considered alongside one another.

1. Transformation

In order to make clear the difference between the Old and the New Covenant, Paul refers (2Cor 3:7) to the Old Testament story of the shining face of Moses (Ex 34:29–35). For forty days and forty nights Moses had remained in the holy sphere of Mount Sinai and the Lord had spoken to him 'face to face, as one speaks to a friend' (Ex 33:11). Through this, Moses' face had become radiant as a reflection of this divine encounter. The Israelites were not strong enough to bear this other-worldly radiance when Moses returned to them, and so he covered his shining face with a veil.

As a further development of this motif, Paul sees as in a picture how a humanity that has not yet been touched by Christ also wears a veil before its face. This restriction of vision stems from the heart which, too, is covered by a veil. If someone finds Christ, then this veil is removed. In becoming a Christian they receive 'enlightenment', because Christ works together with the Holy Spirit, who brings insight and understanding. 'The Lord is the Spirit' (2Cor 3:17). The view is cleared for seeing the divine. Paul describes the process with the words:

> For God, who said, 'Let light shine out of darkness,' has given a bright light in our hearts for the enlightenment [*phōtismos*] of knowledge [*gnōsis*] of the revealing glory [*doxa*] of God in the face of Jesus Christ. (2Cor 4:6)

For Paul, this process is of equal rank with 'Let there be light' on the first day of creation.

In this connection, Paul formulates the sentence about the transformation of a Christian:

> We all, with unveiled faces reflecting the revealing glory of the Lord, are being transformed into the same image from glory to glory as from the Lord of the Spirit. (2Cor 3:18)

This concentrated saying is heavily laden with meaning. It is necessary to take the time to consider it word for word. The sentence begins exultantly with the Pentecost-like 'We all'. What was reserved for Moses alone in the Old Testament shall now become possible for all Christians. The original text does not say 'is reflected in us' but *we* reflect: it is our activity. The picture of a mirror is not meant in a negative sense here, glassy, cold, distorting and indistinct; it is meant positively, as when a stormy and wildly lashing sea comes to rest and the heavenly stars can be seen in its smooth surface. We reflect the glory of the Lord when our active inner effort stills the storms of the soul, and we hold up this calm sea to the divine revelation in devoted expectation.

In so doing we 'expose' ourselves to the divine image and give it the opportunity to create in us. In the kingdoms of nature the divine images work by a kind of compulsion. The rose is not asked whether it wants to become a rose; it is shaped and developed by its archetypal image as a matter of course. With human begins it is different. We can hide from the radiance of our archetypal divine image, or on the other hand expose ourselves in freedom to this radiance. 'Where the Spirit of the Lord is, there is freedom' (2Cor 3:17). Through brightness of heart, we can devote our beholding with unveiled face to Christ, who is the archetypal image above all others. As the Son born in eternity he is the likeness of the Father. 'He is the image of the invisible God' (Col.1:15). According to the intention of the divine Creator, human beings are to become the likeness of God (Gn 1:26).

A likeness makes like: whoever devotes their soul to the influence of an image receives a transforming influence which, in an imperceptible, intimate way, makes them similar to the picture. 'We are transformed into the same likeness.' For 'transformed' Paul here uses *metamorphoein*, 'change form'.

Such a transformation can only happen gradually. It is a matter of a process, a development by degrees: 'from one glory to another'. In this way, a delicate soul-process is indicated that is not dependent on whether an authentic portrait has been preserved for us from the turning-point of time, which, of course, it has not. But it is an intimate experience that for those who take the content of the gospels into their hearts, a countenance, at first perhaps more or less dark, then gradually growing clearer, can begin to appear; a face which is unmistakably 'known' to a Christian.

2. Reshaping

Paul approaches the mystery of transformation from another side in his Letter to the Philippians:

> Our home is in the heavens from where we also await the Saviour, the Lord Jesus Christ, who will reshape our lowly body so that it will be of equal form with his body of glory according to the power of working by which he is able to subject all things to himself. (Phil 3:20f)

This time, it is primarily Christ who acts. We await his return from the heavenly worlds where we ourselves originally were at home. The word for transformation or reshaping this time is *metaschēmatizein*, re-schematise. Here it is important to find the right understanding of the word 'scheme'. It has already been used by Paul in this same Letter to the Philippians, before the passage we are now considering, and actually referring to Christ himself: 'He emptied himself and took on the form and appearance of a servant, entering into human likeness, and was found in his *schēma* as a human being' (Phil 2:7f). The Latin translation here renders *schēma* as *habitus (habitu inventus ut homo), habitus,* as it were, 'having had'. The words habit, habitation and habitude are derived from *habitus*. What people are, comes to expression in their habits which they in-habit. *Schēma* as *habitus,* then, is something like an arrangement of life-patterns which is repeated. It is only when actual life goes out of the life-patterns, so that a mere empty, automatic mechanism is left, that the words scheme and schematic acquire unfortunate overtones. In the New Testament, however, the word *schēma* is meant positively, full of vitality. Inhabiting rhythms of 'going out' and 'going in' means reaching into the rhythms of exhaling and inhaling of the breath and the rhythms of the pulsating blood. Christ works into this realm of life and penetrates it with a life of heavenly rhythm.

The world of rhythmically ordered life has always been the sphere of religious practice, and that is also true of Christianity. In the very concept of religious practice, the element of repetitive 'again and again' is inherent; hallowing of morning and evening, regular prayer, the holy year with its continuous sacramental worship. All this is for the service of Christ, who lets the liberations of a higher, heavenly life work into the coarse vibrations of our earth-bound bodily nature, right into pulse and breath.

3. Making completely anew

In the First Letter to the Corinthians it is the theme of resurrection that leads the apostle to the question of transformation. Here he does not speak of altering or re-shaping. Here Paul uses the word *allassein,* 'make different'. *Allassein* is a word of immediate elementary experience, not as thought-based as alteration and reshaping. With surprise and wonder the experience of 'different' is felt, with a nuance of 'quite different'.

This time the point of departure is the possibility of transformation

42. THE POWER OF TRANSFORMATION

of substance as such. Paul draws attention to the different qualities of the flesh, *sarx,* in the bodily natures of human beings and animals.

> Not all flesh [*sarx*] is the same flesh, for that of man is different, that of the animals is different, that of the birds is different, that of the fish is different. (1Cor 15:39)

This continues upwards into the different qualities of the heavenly bodies, where, instead of 'flesh', the *doxa* (glory, radiance) appears. The heavenly bodies show differences in the aura-like light-qualities of their radiance.

> There is a different quality to the radiance [*doxa*] of the sun, a different one of the moon, a different one of the stars, and each different star differs from every other star through its different radiance. (1Cor 15:41)

In between there is humanity. Like the animals, humanity bears a perishable earthly body. Eventually, humanity is to become a bearer of a starry imperishable body of light. This transition is only possible through death and the power of resurrection:

> Behold, I tell you a mystery. We shall not all fall asleep, but we shall all be transformed into something quite different, in the atom, in the twinkling of the eye at the last trumpet. For the trumpet will sound, and the dead will be awakened imperishable, and we will be transformed into what is quite different. (1Cor 15:51f)

The conception of the atom as that which is ultimately indivisible leads to the limits of the spatial and opens the gaze beyond it to the 'super-spatial', which is 'quite different'. Similarly, the momentary blinking of the eye leads to the limits of measured time and gives a glimpse of the super-temporal, which, again, is 'quite different'. Through this total transformation, death, as the last enemy, is overcome. 'Death is swallowed up in victory' (15:54). 'Swallowed up' is *katapinein* in the Greek: 'drunk down', as when the body takes a drink into itself, absorbing it (as in Latin *absorpta est mors*). The same word can be found in the Second Letter to the Corinthians (5:4), where the reference is to what is mortal being swallowed up by life. This nuance of absorption is of great importance. The experience of death is not simply pushed aside. It is to be worked through inwardly, thereby to deepen and augment the higher life even more, just because of having been absorbed.

When we place the three sayings about transformation from three different letters of Paul into this sequence, they harmonise as a triad. In the sentence about reflecting and being transformed there is the breath of freedom of the Holy Spirit, with and through whom Christ works. The sentence about re-shaping in the Letter to the Philippians speaks particularly about the living and working of the returning Christ. In the resurrection chapter of the First Letter to the Corinthians, the contemplation descends right into the depths of the alchemy of substance. It is here that Paul uses the word 'mystery' (15:51). Material substance is the real enigma of the world, not the spirit. The spirit 'explains itself'. Matter remains dark, as long as it is not made plain, 'explained' and ultimately transfigured by the spirit. In matter, the spirit goes beyond itself, 'ex-pressing' and emptying itself. In this chapter, Paul looks towards a distant fulfilment of the world, when the Son shall return a transformed creation to the Father. This saying about transformation, which we have dealt with here in third place, shows the working of Christ in its connection with the mystery of the Father.

43

AWAKEN, YOU WHO SLEEP!

A LOST HYMN FROM THE EARLIEST CHRISTIAN TIMES

EPHESIANS 5:14

For the disciples gathered in Jerusalem, the Pentecost event signified a great awakening. Seven times seven days had passed since Easter. But now, on the fiftieth day, the Easter event came to their full consciousness. Until then they had been unable to reach out beyond their narrow circle – which still remained behind closed doors – to bring others the message of the resurrection. On Maundy Thursday, the sleep of Gethsemane had fallen upon them – not only an ordinary sleep of weariness, but a dimming of awareness, an inner darkening, under the weight of the 'atmospheric pressure' of the extraordinary events that were about to take place. Out of his spiritual perception Rudolf Steiner described how, even after the resurrection, the disciples were not yet able to shake off this strange dreamlike state. They experienced the manifestations of the Risen One in a kind of sleepwalking condition, not yet able to connect their supersensible experiences with their daytime, waking consciousness. This only became possible at Pentecost. From then on, they were able to proclaim the resurrection in a way that enlightened people and spoke to their hearts, because of their own fiery illumination by the Holy Spirit.

Of Paul's letters, none is as infused in so bright and fiery manner by the Pentecost spirit as the Letter to the Ephesians. It is surely not accidental that this letter, especially, which addresses the community in the ancient, sacred temple city of Ephesus, speaks so strikingly of higher knowledge. One instance: 'May the Father give you a spirit of wisdom [Sophia] and revelation [*apokalypsis*] in the knowledge [*epignosis*] of him and enlightened eyes of the heart' (1:17f). The motif of awakening also resounds in a wonderful shaping of words that Paul introduces as a quotation (5:14):

> Awaken, you who sleep!
> And rise up from the dead!
> And Christ will shine upon you.

Every morning the darkness of sleep brightens from the dim, obscurities of dream to the waking consciousness that we regard as normal. But is this so familiar awakening every morning, this transition to the brightness of object consciousness, the only conclusive and ultimate experience of awakening possible for humankind? Or could it find its continuation in a further awakening to a still brighter, still higher reality, which hitherto we have slept or dreamed through? Such a possibility had arisen for Paul since his Damascus experience. He was entitled to call others to awaken, and he does this, as we saw, by citing a phrase sounding as if from the mysteries: 'Awaken, you who sleep.'

In the second line, our failure to grasp supersensible reality is expressed in a still more radical picture as a 'deadness'. The saying 'Let the dead bury their dead' shows that Christ must have experienced earthly human beings, in all their busyness, as 'living corpses'. In *Faust,* Goethe writes, 'Your mind is closed, your heart is dead.' Awakening, we should conquer the death of the soul and become a risen one in the spirit. Just as rising in the morning follows awakening, so the whole human being can rise from a deathlike horizontality into true uprightness. Each time we rise in the morning this bears in it also a promise of resurrection: 'Rise up from the dead!'

Waking up and getting up belong to the rising sun in the morning. Thus the call to awaken and to rise up points to the radiant new day into which we should awaken and be resurrected: 'Christ will shine upon you.' Paul concludes his quotation with these words.

Clearly, Paul could assume that the Ephesians knew this quotation, and so did not need to tell them where it originated. Its source remains unknown.

43. Awaken, you who sleep!

But fortunately, this same text appears again elsewhere in an extant ancient text, written by the early Christian father Clement of Alexandria, who lived and taught around the year 200. He, too, gives no reference to the origin of these striking lines, but he does quote more of them than Paul. Up to 'Christ will shine upon you' his text coincides precisely with Paul's, but he goes on as follows:

> The Lord [*Kyrios*], the Sun of resurrection
> Begotten before the morning star,
> Who mercifully gives life
> With his own bright beams.*

Unmistakeably, this is a continuation of the words of Paul in his Letter to the Ephesians, and displays the same linguistic energy. The Kyrios, shining towards the wakening and rising one, is expressly connected with the sun. As a Christianity that has not yet lost sight of cosmic wisdom, Christ is here invoked as the *Sun of resurrection*. Then comes a further thought that reminds us of the cosmic dimension: *'begotten before the morning star'*. Here the text relates without doubt to a passage in the psalms that a reader of the Bible will not find in modern translations, as it is not in the Hebrew text itself, but figures in the Greek translation of the Old Testament, the Septuagint, as well as in the Latin version, the Vulgate. They come from Psalm 110 (numbered 109 in both the Septuagint and the Vulgate). The psalm begins, 'The Lord spoke to my Lord', and contains a reference to the priest king Melchizedek. In the time of Christ the words were thought to refer to the Messiah. In this sense, too, Christ uttered them to the Pharisees (Mt 21:42). In the third verse both the Septuagint and the Vulgate give a version that is entirely unique and completely differs from the extant Hebrew text. The Greek translation of the Old Testament was made in the third century BC, in the cosmopolitan university city of Alexandria in Egypt. It does not always abide by the Hebrew text, but, in its very different variants, wholly absent from the Hebrew texts available today, it enables us to conceive of more ancient Hebrew books which later vanished, and which must have been available to the translators of the time.

---

* *Protrepticus* IX 84.

Thus in the psalm passage referred to, we find the sentence, 'Out of the womb, before the morning star I have begotten you.' In the Latin this is *ex utero, ante luciferum, genui te*. The morning star, as light bringer, is *lucifer* in Latin. Ancient cosmic wisdom, confirmed by Rudolf Steiner's modern spiritual research, saw a connection between the radiant Venus star and the proud light spirit Lucifer, who rose up in pride against God. 'How you have fallen from heaven, O morning star, son of dawn' appears in Isaiah (14:12) in regard to the fall of the adversarial powers. In the New Testament, on the other hand, a vision appears of the radiant star of Lucifer coming to serve the Redeemer, who, indeed, holds the seven stars in his hand. Lucifer had promised, 'You will be as God.' Christ says, 'You are gods.' He takes up the promise of Lucifer and makes it true – though naturally in a sense quite different from the one the Tempter intended. In the Revelation to John, the star of Lucifer is, as it were, brought home into the service of Christ, who states there, 'I am the radiant morning star' (22:16); or in Latin: *stella splendida et matutina*. And, in the Second Letter of Peter, the hope is uttered that 'the morning star will rise in your hearts' (1:19). Here, in Greek, the morning star is called *phosphoros*, whereas in Latin, again, it is *lucifer: et lucifer oriatur in cordibus vestris*.

In appropriating the words of the psalm that Christ was 'begotten before the morning star' – that is, before Lucifer – the text that Clement quotes expresses the fact that the 'Son born in eternity', whose intrinsic being is love, is entirely free in his I from that self-willed, proud characteristic that Lucifer embodies. After murdering his brother, Cain says, 'Am I my brother's keeper?' In the original text, the word 'I' is especially pronounced here, standing in its great, emphatic form *(anokhi)*. The phrase actually runs, 'the keeper of my brother – *I?*' We can hear in this the voice of Lucifer. How differently it sounds when Christ says 'I'. The Christ-I is creative self-surrender in holy selflessness. And just as Christ said 'before Abraham was, I am,' so he might also say, 'before Lucifer was, before Lucifer fell, I am'.

This divine being *mercifully gives life with his own bright beams*. In Greek the word for 'own' here is *idios*, which plays such an important role in the New Testament, for instance in the Prologue to the Gospel of John (1:11): 'He came unto his own [*idia*] and his own [*idioi*] did not receive him.' The hour of Christ had come when earthly human beings became conscious of their individuality, when they had become I-people. (Rudolf Steiner rendered 'his own', as it is usually translated, with this phrase 'I-people'). Awakened to their own responsible existence and selfhood, they had the capacity to recognise the selfless, holy I that was made manifest in Christ, and to receive it into themselves. Thus they were 'his own'. And yet the quality of egoism in the human I proved disastrous. Alongside the tragedy of their failure to receive him, however, stands the solace of another possibility: 'But to all who did receive him' (Jn 1:12). Only the single, individual human being, who is his 'own person', can receive Christ. And precisely by virtue of taking up Christ into his inner sanctum, the I-person becomes truly capable of social community again. The 'Sun of resurrection', the one 'begotten before the morning star', gives life with his 'own' beams.

Clement of Alexandria once said that even the outer sun does not shine its light 'in general' upon the earth, but that from this sea of light single rays separate themselves and take their individual path – like someone in their room who experiences the sunlight streaming to them through a window as a message of greeting intended quite personally for them. Clement says, 'For, just as the sun not only illumines heaven and the whole world, shining over land and sea, but also through windows and small chinks and sends his beams into the innermost recesses of houses, so the Word (the Logos) diffused everywhere casts his eye-glance on the minutest circumstances of the actions of life' (*Stromata* VII, Ch 3). Thus the life-giving gift of the Christ sun also finds its way in the single, individualised beam, in its 'own' beams, from the I of God to the human I. The same occurs when the Holy Spirit is poured out at Pentecost: the Pentecost fire divides and appears as an individualised tongue of flame over each separate person's head. Let us hear the whole thing once more:

> Awaken, you who sleep!
> And rise up from the dead!
> And Christ will shine upon you.
> The Lord [*Kyrios*], the Sun of resurrection
> Begotten before the morning star,
> Who mercifully gives life
> With his own bright beams.

It seems astonishing that this text has so completely vanished from literature, apart from in Paul and Clement. It may be that the Church, as it grew more narrowly dogma-bound in the first few centuries, found this cosmic hymn uncomfortable, and, like so much else, eradicated it. Perhaps it was one of those ritual hymns which, according to the proconsul Pliny's report to the Emperor Trajan, the early Christians offered to Christ 'as to a God' in the early morning – *ante lucem* – on a particular day (Sunday), thus towards dawn. For the word 'hymn', Pliny uses *carmen*. Here, this not only means simply a poem but something like a 'song of enchantment' full of magical power, an invocation of the gods. In using this expression, the heathen Roman was seeking to convey the information his police had got out of the tortured Christians about their worship. It may be that the text we have been looking at was one of these original Christian *carmen*, truly an invocation, a mighty, spiritual mantra from the days of the first Christian witnesses that once helped awaken sleeping souls to a Pentecost experience of Christ.

44

GOD'S HUMAN NATURE IN CHRIST JESUS

HUMANITARIANISM AND CHRISTIANITY

LETTER TO TITUS 3:4

A transport of prisoners, which includes the apostle Paul, is sailing from Caesarea to Rome and on the way puts into port at Sidon. The transport commander, a Roman captain called Julius, allows Paul leave on land – on his word of honour to return – so that he can be looked after for a while by friends who live in the city. To describe the captain's behaviour, Luke, reporting this as an eyewitness, uses a notable expression in his Acts of the Apostles: Julius, he says, treated the prisoner with *philanthropos,* that is, in a philanthropic or humane way (27:3).

In studying the New Testament, we must repeatedly examine the underlying meaning of the original Greek text. The Latin translation by Jerome often fails to do justice to certain mystery resonances present in the Greek. But here, in speaking of the friendly captain, the Latin version in fact brings us a welcome enlargement. In Latin the text says that Julius treated his prisoner 'humanely' *(humane tractans).* And very soon afterwards, we meet these same words again in the following chapter of the Acts. The ship is wrecked in a storm and the occupants take refuge on an island – Malta, as it turns out. Then, as now, the Maltese spoke their own Phoenician idiom, and were therefore regarded as 'barbarians' by the civilised Greek and Latin world. The King James Bible calls them 'barbarous people' in translation of Luke's Greek word *barbaroi* (though more modern translations call them 'natives' or 'islanders'). It is therefore all the more striking when he goes on to say of them that they 'showed us unusual human kindness' (28:2). This time the noun is used, *philanthropia*, in Latin *humanitas*. These 'uncivilised' island inhabitants display humanity.

It belongs to the distinctive character of the Greco-Roman cultural period that during it the term 'humanity' makes its appearance. It is not as if humane conduct had never previously existed, for assuredly people sometimes encountered others with disinterested human attentiveness. But full awareness of common, uniting human attributes had not yet properly awoken. Members of more ancient cultures still felt themselves embedded in the superordinate life of higher powers that acted through race, nation and tribe. Not until the Greco-Roman era did the individual come to be more self-reliant and independent. The cosmopolitan empires of Alexander and of Rome contributed a good deal to this development.

In the second century BC, a 'pure humanity' first came to expression as *humanitas* in curious, fated circumstances. Rome had conquered Carthage and then sent powerful invading forces into the Mediterranean region. In the year 196 BC, Rome freed Greece from the domination of Macedonia, but only to subordinate it again to its own rulership as the Achaea Province. Following this increasing subjugation of the region, in the year 167 BC a thousand Greek leaders were deported to Rome as civil prisoners. Here, fate intervened in a wonderful fashion. A highly-educated man, Polybius, was one of the thousand and found accommodation in Rome, and soon also human contact, in the house of a respectable Roman. The son of the house became his friend and, at the same time, an eager pupil of Greek culture. This son, Scipio Aemilianus (or Scipio the Younger), eventually went down in history as the final destroyer of Carthage in 146 BC. How strange that of all people this soldier, who was to do so much to expand Rome's power, also bore within him this very different side that sent him on a quest for the higher culture of the Greeks.

Before Scipio attacked Carthage in around 155 BC, the hard-pressed Greeks sent a legation to Rome consisting of three well-known philosophers, one each from the schools of Platonism, Aristotelianism and Stoicism. Nowadays we might call this cultural propaganda. But Cato the Elder, a man of rigid severity, smelled a rat: he thought that good Roman civilisation was under threat here and succeeded in sending the three philosophers back home as 'undesirable persons'. But this did not put a stop to the unfolding events. Soon afterwards, the Stoic Panaetius came to Rome and was enthusiastically welcomed by Scipio, who meanwhile had become the centre of a group with wide cultural interests. It was here, in this destined gathering of Greek and Roman individuals, that the word and the living ideal of *humanitas* – human kindness and humanity – came fully into its own.

The poet Terence (*c.* 195–159 BC) also belonged to Scipio's circle. He, too, had a destiny that guided him towards attributes of a pure humanity. As a slave he had come into the possession of a well-meaning Roman, rather as Polybius had, by whom he was educated and given his freedom. In his comic play *Heauton Timorumenos* (I 1.25) he coined the now famous sentence *homo sum, humani nihil a me alienum puto* – 'I am a human being, nothing human is alien to me'. This idea was received with enormous enthusiasm by its audiences, as if Terence had expressed something that was already in the air and whose time had come, something contemporary in the deepest sense. Half a millennium later, the Church Father Augustine was still relating the striking effect of this sentence at performances of the play: 'This sentence was applauded, as it is said, even in theatres full of foolish and uneducated people' *(Letter to Macedonius).*

Through the Stoic Posidonius, the stream of *humanitas* that had sprung up in the group around Scipio, then found its way to Cicero (106–43 BC). Albeit not a thinker in his own right, Cicero introduced the riches of Greek thought into Latin literature. In his *Dream of Scipio,* which describes experiences of the disembodied soul in the spirit cosmos of the starry spheres, he helped convey ancient knowledge into later eras. But above all, Cicero became the public advocate of *humanitas*. Reitzenstein writes as follows:

> The ideal of humane conduct, of *humanitas,* which at that time filled the noblest minds, as it did in the Renaissance, was regarded by such figures as Schiller and Goethe as definitely Greek in origin, which it is, albeit with a certain proviso. The Greek language never coined a word for it,

and the idea itself remained undeveloped. Only with the Romans do we repeatedly find the words 'true human being' and 'humanity' – *humanus* and *humanitas* ... Latin first elaborates this concept, and does so with a diversity and multiplicity which it is hard to encapsulate in a few words. In Cicero it encompasses, in fact, all mercy, gentleness, equity, reconciliation, charity, good intentions, generosity, friendliness, politeness, in fact all conduct that respects the feelings of others ... In certain circles, the *homo humanus* was intentionally set against the *homo Romanus* as celebrated and urged by Cato ... only in the group around Scipio the Younger could this idea, this ideal, have been developed.

Reitzenstein goes on to show further how this ideal faded after the death of Cicero. And yet this 'humanity' had once shone forth brightly, and when Jerome later translated the New Testament into Latin, he used the idea of *humanus* and *humanitas,* and in doing so he went beyond the original scripture to reproduce what Luke had wanted to say. In Greek usage, the word *philanthropia* employed by Luke did not have the weight and dignity possessed by the Latin word.

In Rome, the *humanitas* stream also belonged to Seneca, Paul's contemporary. From him comes the saying *homo res sacra homini* – man is a sacred thing to man. But Seneca did not become a Christian. In the year 65, at Nero's command, he was compelled to commit suicide. We can regard the rise of the Roman humanism stream in pre-Christian times as a dawn before the sunrise of Christ's appearance. Here what came earlier in time has its source in what would appear later. Seneca was in Rome at the same time as Paul, but to begin with 'humanism' and Christianity stand alongside each other and do not yet flow organically into one another.

The original biblical words about our humanity are contained in the creation story of the Old Testament. The human being is created as image and likeness of the Godhead (Gn 1:26f). The word 'likeness' is repeated there three times. But as the narrative continues, we can have the impression that this high peak has been shrouded again in clouds. No further mention is made in the Old Testament of this motif of man in God's 'likeness'. Only at the beginning of the list of forefathers in Chapter 5 of Genesis does this word 'likeness' resurface, and at the end of the story of the Flood it comes one last time again (Gn 9:6). From the lofty pinnacle of the creation story, a narrative thread leads to the Good Friday account in the Gospel of John. On the Friday, which is the sixth day of creation as Genesis recounts it, the day of the human being, the phrase *ecce homo* resounds – 'see, the human being'. In Jesus, who is filled with Christ, the human being is led to his true likeness to God. The fact that the Son of God could enter fully into the man Jesus shines further upon the whole human race and opens up a new dimension for its evolution.

From the Christ event onwards, the statement by Terence – 'Nothing human is alien to me' – can be understood in a further sense. He does not only mean that we human beings bear with each other in human comradeship with love and understanding of our frailties and faults. Now also intrinsic to what is human, to the *humanum,* is to look 'upward' to our Christ potential, which, since Golgotha, since the resurrection and ascension, is given us as earthly human beings. We only mature into our true humanity when we receive the Christ into us. The ideal that the Roman humanitarians strove for became substantial reality in Christ Jesus.

The confluence of Christianity and humanitarianism was classically formulated by Paul in the letter he wrote to the young Titus:

> But when the kindness and love of humankind [*philanthropia*] appeared of God our Saviour, he saved us, not because of works of righteousness which we did, but in his mercy by the washing of rebirth, and renewal through the Holy Spirit, which he poured over us abundantly through Jesus Christ our Saviour. (Tit 3:4–6)

In the Latin translation of the New Testament, *philanthropia* is again given as *humanitas*. The scope of this statement has not hitherto been fully recognised and felt within Christianity. As in Rome before, Christianity and humanitarianism remained parallel to each other. The humanists of the Renaissance were inspired by the beauty of the upright human form in ancient statues but they did not penetrate to the reality of the resurrection body. They were inspired by the human capacity for speech but they did not get beyond philology to the Logos. They were inspired by the light of reason in rational thinking but they did not work their way through to illumination by the Holy Spirit. In relation to the *humanum,* their knowledge fell short. On the other hand, Christian theology was not yet able to raise itself to the insight that the Christ event signified a continuation of the creation of man, that humankind without the Christ dimension cannot be humanity in the full sense. Christian theology and humanism continued to exist side-by-side. In the Age of Enlightenment, humanism increasingly came into opposition with the Christianity that had evolved until then. Humanism often took issue not only with the Church but with Christianity itself. In the eighteenth century, Herder sought to reconcile humanism and Christianity again. But doing this would have required an insight into the Christian mystery in the sense of a Christian Sophia. In his *Ideas on the Philosophy of the History of Mankind* (1784), Herder wrote lovely words about humanity:

> I wish I could encompass in the word 'humanity' everything I have said in the past about the noble education of the human being to develop individuality and freedom, refined senses and impulses, the finest and most robust health, the fulfilment and mastery of the earth.

In the same year, Goethe began his great poem *The Mysteries* with the central figure of Humanus and the significant sign of the Rose Cross. Yet the poem remained a fragment. In Herder and Goethe, the Christian mystery and the *humanum* strive towards each other but are not wholly united. In the nineteenth and twentieth centuries, humanism repeatedly opposed Christianity. The image of the human being became increasingly informed by the new science whose modes of enquiry cannot actually penetrate the intrinsically human element. On the other hand, a narrow theology considered it necessary to fend off the humanistic outlook. In the twentieth century, the Protestant theologian Ethelbert Stauffer made a notable effort to celebrate the theme of God's 'humanity' once more.* But even here, the new dimension of the Christian mystery that should come to essential life for human beings through Christ did not come fully into its own.

---

* Stauffer, *Die Botschaft Jesu,* pp. 52, 59, 134.

Today it really is high time that we recognised how the Christian mystery and the human being are inseparably interwoven.

Fear of anthropomorphism – the anxiety that we could impermissibly inform our picture of God with our own, all too human nature, has created an unnecessary difficulty for Christian thinkers. This would only be a danger if we did not discern the higher dimension of the human being. As the creation story tells us, we are called to be a 'likeness' of the Godhead. In our higher potential we are, if we can put it like this, 'theomorphic'. This means that higher human nature can serve as a lens through which we can look reverently into the divine. The human being, the *humanum,* enlarged by the Christian dimension, was the foundation upon which Rudolf Steiner gave his modern spiritual knowledge the name anthroposophy. In the same way, the renewed act of worship cultivated in The Christian Community was called the Act of Consecration of Man. Modern Christianity faces the task of increasingly discovering and revealing the full scope and future potency of Paul's words about God's humanity.

45

CHRISTIANITY'S POTENTIAL FOR THE FUTURE

THE LETTER TO THE PHILIPPIANS 3:8–14

The true nature of Christianity is misunderstood by many people, which means that it is generally accepted that being a Christian entails weak passivity and an outlook oriented towards the past. However, if one traces Christianity to its sources, one finds something quite different. The third chapter of the Letter to the Philippians, for example, is a classic expression of the dynamic of the Christian frame of mind and its future potential.

Paul speaks first of all about what had been important for him in earlier years, and how, through his encounter with Christ, a complete change and refounding of his whole attitude to life came about. What was previously significant for him fades before the 'surpassing worth of knowing Christ Jesus my Lord' (Phil 3:8). In our times when church theologians so often play off 'faith' against 'knowledge', it is really a relief to see how unaffectedly and as a matter of course Paul speaks here of knowledge, and how, for him, knowledge *(gnōsis)* and faith *(pistis)* do not exclude one another but work harmoniously together. Without knowing Christ, faith would not be possible, as Paul says on one occasion in the Second Letter to Timothy (1:12): 'I know whom I have believed.' The offering of the heart in faith to what is known leads on to a deepening of knowledge – thus knowledge and faith increase together.

The 'surpassing worth of knowing Christ Jesus' leads to faith in him who gives us true righteousness (3:9). This righteousness 'which is through faith,' so particularly stressed by Paul, is in no way a remote theological dogma but a truth that is more relevant today than ever. If we want to express it in modern words, we could perhaps say: human beings come ever closer to crisis in the human condition. The highly developed intelligence that triumphs in technology and a moral immaturity completely disproportionate to this cleverness are in stark opposition within us. We are on the way to becoming a terrible menace in the life of the world. What we contribute to existence cannot equal what the divine powers of creation have 'invested' in us. The scales are not evenly balanced. According to higher justice, our right to existence in the universe would really have to be denied us; we seem to be something of a failure, a divine 'bad investment'. This negative way of judging our humanity is very much in the air these days. A great deal of the nihilism and the cynicism that fills the lives of our contemporaries comes fundamentally from such conscious or unconscious despair about humanity.

One cannot, however, finally judge of the justification for man's existence if one does not take into account that, since the time of Golgotha, the divine being of Christ has thrown himself into the scales on humanity's side. He has joined himself with the fate of humanity. Everything now depends on whether human beings become aware of this fact and the infinite encouragement and hope it gives, and from their side unite themselves with Christ to say with Paul they 'believe in him'. From such a turning towards Christ the seed of a more exalted humanity of the future begins to grow. Christ thus becomes the guarantor of our true future. If we cling to him, he carries us over the abyss of feeling that we have no right to exist. We can therefore be justified before the divine justice not by looking at what we have achieved hitherto, but rather by looking at the seedlike beginning of the permeation of our being by Christ, which is possible since the sacrificial deed on Golgotha. In this sense, Paul speaks of the righteousness from God that has come to him by faith in Christ (3:9).

This experience of faith now leads on to an enhanced knowledge. Following on directly from Paul's words justifying faith, there are others that emanate from such faith: 'that I may know him and the power [*dynamis*] of his resurrection, and may share his sufferings' (3:10). This knowledge is set out in a threefold way. First of all knowledge of 'him'. But one cannot possibly know 'him' in his true nature without immediately becoming aware of the power that emanates from this being, and which cannot be separated from him – the power of conquering death. This is the second thing. 'The power of his resurrection' is the first decisive and characteristic impression of the being of Christ that one receives.

Thirdly, there follows what is received from the knowledge deepened by faith: 'and may share his sufferings.' How does this third element intrinsically connect with what goes before? For one who knows 'him' and 'the power of his resurrection' the question then arises how to make 'him' and his 'power' one's own in the sense that Paul uses the expression, 'gain Christ'. Knowledge has the answer to this: this 'gaining' can happen only on the path of true sympathy with Christ. 'Sym-pathy', that is, 'suffering with'. If you look at Christ with an open mind as he goes through his fate on Golgotha, you gradually come to feel this suffering with him, even finally to be drawn into it yourself – right to the point of experiencing 'being crucified with Christ' as Paul says in another place. You cannot attain the power of his resurrection if you wish to avoid such suffering.

On the cross Christ certainly took upon himself humanity's burden of sin. To do such a thing was possible only for a divine being; no one else would have been able even to lift this terrible load under which humanity would surely have succumbed. But Christ's deed of redemption can bear fruit only if human beings are willing to help carry their small and modest share of the burden carried by Christ. Paul says that he suffered what Christ, as it were, had left to be suffered (Col 1:24). It is part of this mystery of redemption that human beings do not receive it passively, but that we are considered worthy of sharing in the fulfilment of our own redemption and that of the whole of humanity. The divine help that comes to us in Christ does not make our individual effort superfluous, but works with it. Christians are not to be relieved of all suffering. Rather they are to become acquainted with suffering of a higher grade – and are privileged to do so. They may themselves share in God's suffering for humanity.

So, after he has felt the breath of resurrection emanating from Christ, Paul comes to the profound knowledge of the 'communion with his suffering' now open to man. It leads him on to a personal experience of sharing in the death undergone on Golgotha. Thereby he experiences an inner transformation laying hold of his whole being – *symmorphizómenos,* that is, 'in a similar form' to his death (*morphē,* form).

From the depths of such suffering-with, dying-with, there now emerges the possibility of personally gaining the 'power of his resurrection'. Paul, however, speaks of this with awe and restraint, with a cautious, tentative 'if possible': 'That if possible I may attain the resurrection from the dead' (Phil 3:11).

He sees a mighty though far-distant goal ahead of him, before whose awe-inspiring greatness he feels a deep modesty: 'Not that I have already attained this or am already perfect' (3:12). He is conscious of the fact that he stands within a long-term process of becoming. Elsewhere Paul also speaks of such a gradual progress in inner development when he writes about changing into the Lord's likeness 'from glory to glory' (2Cor 3:18).

'Not that I have already attained this or am already perfect: but I am pursuing this.' Again we find that feeling-of-the-way towards future possibility which could be translated as: 'so that perhaps I may grasp hold of it because I was grasped hold of by Christ Jesus' (Phil 3:12).

Human beings are deemed worthy of partnership by God, free will not excluded. God does not wish all the activity to be on his side; he wants us to work with him. Being 'grasped hold of' by Christ comes first. But this must be followed by the active 'grasped hold' by ourselves. An example may explain this. You hear a symphony and are 'gripped' by it. If, however, you are more profoundly interested and really want to make the symphony 'your own', then you will procure the score and work on it until you can fully grasp what 'gripped' you. It is the same with shaking hands. It is not enough if someone who wants to greet me grasps my hand; I must make a similar gesture on my side.

Paul's modesty is again expressed: 'Brothers, I do not consider myself to have grasped it.' But to one thing he may lay claim for himself: 'but one thing I do, forgetting what lies behind and straining towards what is ahead' (3:13). He feels like a competitor in the ancient games, having only the goal and the victor's prize before his eyes (3:14). In a unique manner these words manifest the forceful, forward-looking nature of the Christian attitude.

'Forgetting what lies behind.' Perhaps it is not superfluous in these times of ours to dwell a little on this statement and make clear in more detail what it says – and what it does not say. It could possibly be understood as a confirmation of that mood so widespread today of wanting to jettison all reflection on the past as troublesome ballast, and to live quite simply for the day. Any feeling for remembrance has got lost in this fast-paced age. The coherence, the continuity of life is in danger of becoming lost, existence is in danger of falling into disconnected, isolated moments.

Paul's words about the great forgetting certainly have nothing to do with this. Other remarks of the apostle show clearly enough how important to him was the connection with the past. Even in his wording of the account of the Last Supper we find the word 'remembrance' in connection with both bread and wine (1Cor 11:24f). It is the consideration of the Christian celebration of the Last Supper in particular that gives us an important clue as to the Christian experience of time and its three dimensions. The three years from the baptism to Golgotha belong historically to the past. The remembrance of the events in the Holy Land is entrusted to the memory of humanity as something that may never be forgotten. Should the remembrance of these events disappear completely from humanity's consciousness, it would face a catastrophe that would correspond – but on a large scale – to the pathological loss of individual personal retrospection. Insofar as it is a 'remembrance' it is first of all the concern of the celebration of the Last Supper to maintain the connection with Christ's deed. But it is just when this remembrance is truly observed that Christ's deed proves not merely to belong to the past. It is not confined within the bounds of merely having been; it breaks through these bounds and proves that it works on in the present. The living Christ is experienced as the Present One. The remembrance of the 'then' enables us to do justice to the present, to truly be 'up to date' with our times.

If we disregard the words that he is 'with us always', we allow the fullness of the present to escape us. And then this rich present, too, breaks its bounds and opens towards the future. The Christ who becomes present in the Communion Service reveals himself as the One who is to come. He comes towards us and offers us our own future. Each time we receive communion, the growth of the future human being is fostered in us. Christianity as it presents itself in the sacrament of the body and blood of Christ, comprises true remembering, real present, and therefore also a genuine future. In contrast there is the opposite picture threatening humanity: the lost connection with the past, the thoughtless living-for-the-day, the anxiety of what is coming.

'Forgetting what lies behind' also certainly does not mean that we should simply let yesterday remain undigested and not deal with it properly. In that case we should not get free from it. Anyone who does not develop a right attitude towards the past is, as experience shows, all the more helplessly abandoned to all the possible ill consequences of a past event. The soul then gets 'hooked' to this and that, very often quite unconsciously; it cannot 'get over it'. If you look back as a Christian, then wrongs done to others in the past can be taken hold of by the transforming forces of Christ's forgiveness. The consequences of the deed are then borne with a soul at peace, the remembrance is certainly painful but is no longer 'galling'. The pain becomes fruitful in that it now proves to be even more of an incentive to do good. Similarly the memory of the wrong that was inflicted on you by another, the gnawing and poisoning of the soul, also fades if you know how very much you are in need of forgiveness yourself, and if it is clear to you that you cannot be a partaker of forgiveness if you are not willing to put it into action yourself.

Or if it is not a case of right and wrong but of the blows of fate, of an irrecoverably lost fortune, of horror and terror that is experienced, even that takes on a different character if it is digested in submission to the wise and ultimately good-intentioned powers of destiny. It is when we take care to remember in the right way that the loved one who has died increasingly becomes like one present who moves on into a higher world, and who remains connected with us in all that is highest and best. Then we overcome what keeps the soul fettered in unfruitfully looking back to the pain, separation and sense of deprivation we have already undergone. Thus we can understand Paul's saying about 'forgetting' as a dismissal of what monopolises the soul from the past in what one might call an unlawful manner, what makes it insensitive for the demands of our times, and shuts it off from the possibilities that press towards it from the future. 'Forgetting what lies behind and straining towards what is ahead.'

46

FATHER OF LIGHTS

THE CHRISTMAS MOOD IN THE LETTER OF JAMES (1:17F)

There is a verse in the Letter of James that radiates the glory of Christmas and makes an indelible impression on our souls: 'Every good gift and every perfect gift is from above, descending from the Father of lights.' (Jas 1:17).

These words express the mystery of giving and making gifts. During the Christmas season we can make it our concern to meditate on this mystery. When someone makes a gift, they have the feeling that it cannot just be handed over as it is; they wrap it up, perhaps in festive looking Christmas paper. This wrapping up is nothing more than a symbol that we ourselves have to turn into reality. The wrapping that really lifts the gift above the 'bare' thing is invisible, and has to be contributed from our souls. It is like an ethereal substance of the soul itself. But it is always at our disposal when we want to make a gift. Where can we find this strength? From where does it come? James's verse gives the significant answer: 'from above'! The donor must make themselves open if something is to flow in from a higher world and bless the giving. If you have realised that, then you may with good conscience tell a child that the gift comes from Father Christmas; it is the deeper truth in comparison with the trivial fact that you have perhaps bought the present in a shop.

The gift from above is the Christ-child. Every true gift is related to this original Christmas gift. The Greek text of the letter uses the word 'descend' *(katabainein)*, the same word that is so often used of Christ in the Gospel of John. Every good gift descends from above.

46. FATHER OF LIGHTS

Translating literally, one should say 'is descending' (Latin, *descendens*) – a continuously happening event, a permanent Christmas.

By careful consideration of the Greek words we can come still closer to James's text. Most translations twice use the word 'gift' – 'every good gift and every perfect gift' – which blurs a fine distinction in the original text. There, the first time it says *dósis;* the second time *dōrēma*. The different endings of the Greek words show that with *dósis* the action of giving is emphasised, whilst *dōrēma* on the other hand emphasises what is given, the gift received.

Correspondingly, the related adjectives are also different. The act of giving is 'good', the gift 'perfect'. 'Good' *(agathós)* is a word applicable to the highest, to the very Godhead. For Plato, the idea of goodness is the sun in the realm of ideas. 'No one is good but God alone' we read in the gospel. The 'good' endowment is therefore a giving from the primary divine source. Just as 'good' indicates the primary source of all creation, so 'perfect' *(téleios)* indicates the final goal, the future perfection. The 'perfect gift' is called perfect not only in view of its faultlessness, but also because it helps the recipient to become perfect. It is not an additional burden to bear through life, but promotes the recipients development, bringing them further on their way.

One could paraphrase the Greek text thus: 'Every act of giving from the primary source of good, and every gift that helps the recipient towards perfection – is descending from above.'

But that is not the end of the verse. As the inner experience moves on, the 'above' turns into a sublime vision of divine being: 'from above, *from the Father of lights*'. This plural, 'lights', refers to the stars. We can see from Paul's First Letter to the Corinthians (15:41) how the stars were once still felt to be living beings. He speaks of every star shining in a way peculiar to itself. People still knew that the shining of the stars – in the same way as the light coming forth from the eyes of people – is the outer manifestation of some inner quality behind them. Human beings saw in the fullness of the stars the visible sign of a fullness of spirits, of the heavenly hosts.

As late as the thirteenth century the works of Dionysius the Areopagite enjoyed the greatest veneration. In them ancient wisdom lived on: not only below the human being are the kingdoms ranged in descending order to the mineral, but above the human being the ladder continues on up into the invisible. Above humanity are the angels, above these the archangels, and so on through three times three hierarchies right up to the exalted seraphim who glow with holy love before the countenance of God. The book, *Celestial Hierarchies*, in which Dionysius the Areopagite deals with the nine angelic realms, solemnly begins with this verse of James, and puts the phrase about the Father of lights as a motto for the whole work.

The verse makes the further step of distinguishing between the world of lights and the Father God himself. The starry heaven appears to comprise manifold movements. There is rising and setting, there are turning points between ascending and descending, there is moving and changing. Exalted above all this variability is the Father. He is bearer and guarantor of what remains the same and keeps its own identity through all change. All change also presupposes such a principle of remaining 'constant'. Otherwise everything would lose itself in continually becoming something else. How different the old person is from the child they once were, and yet through the changes there runs a permanence that preserves the sameness of the person. This all-pervading permanence is ultimately embodied in the Father God himself, of whom the verse from the Letter of James further says: 'with whom there is no variation and no shading off as a result of turning change [*tropēs aposkiasma*].'

The calm constancy of the Father does not, however, necessarily imply a dogma of immoveable rigidity whereby God would cease to be the 'living God'. From the calm of his exalted realm above the stars the all-loving Father bends down and sends the earth his Son. The verse immediately following that about 'the Father of lights' pronounces very explicitly the mystery of Christ's birth. 'He chose to give birth to us with the word of truth, that we should be a kind of first fruits of all he created' (Jas 1:18).

The Greek text uses a word for 'to give birth' that apart from the Letter of James does not appear in the whole New Testament: *apekuēsen*. What is meant is the bringing forth of a being that was previously formed in the womb and now by birth is released into its own independent existence. The Father of lights has given humanity birth – in this image, the Letter of James pronounces the mystery of Christianity.

Originally humanity – or what was to become humanity – was still completely contained within the upper worlds of light like the unborn child in the womb, still carried and protected. Gradually we were released from this divine, cosmic womb for our own independent existence on the earth. But, as we are now, we are still incomplete. We are not yet completely born. We always give the impression of unsatisfactoriness, often appearing quite godless and godforsaken. Friedrich Hölderlin had a feeling for the fact that humanity's nature needs completing from above, when in a perceptive late poem he wrote, 'What we are here, a god can there complete'. Christianity, however, knows that this completion not only awaits us 'there', but that it is gradually to permeate us already 'here' on earth. For through Christ's descending to earth the completion from above has come within our reach as the gift that leads us to perfection.

Through Christ's becoming man the higher part of our being has stepped forth from the womb of heaven, it has in him, for the first time, been brought forth into earthly human form. In Christ Jesus, humanity as a whole has reached the point of being born. It is therefore now a question of this Christ birth also coming about in us as individuals. But in principle the Letter of James is right in saying, 'he chose to give birth to us'. The actual name of Christ is not here used, but the connection with Christ is given by the addition: 'by the word of truth,' for this Word, the Logos, has appeared in Christ. Through the Logos of truth our higher nature, formerly hidden in the womb of heaven, is born into our human nature on earth and is thereby given to us.

We have not yet considered the phrase introducing this sentence. 'He chose'. Translated literally, 'having willed it'. *Voluntarie,* (willingly) is the Latin translation. 'Having willed it, he brought us forth.' The Greek used here for 'will' – Greek has more than one word for it – has the same stem as the noun *boulē,* which means 'decision'. A willing is therefore meant that proceeds from a foregoing decision. Allowing human beings to come forth, with all the risk involved in a nature destined for freedom but also open to seduction, necessitated a unique decision by the Godhead, in which is included from the very beginning the readiness for sacrifice on the cross. Therefore in Christ was seen the 'messenger of the great decision'. The biblical phrase stumblingly signifies in insufficient human language proceedings of the most exalted nature within the Godhead: 'having willed it' – 'of his own will'.

Regarded in the light of evolution, the human being is the highest achievement of the earth's development. Our appearance concluded the creation. The birth of Christ, however, means that the last to appear, the 'lastborn', becomes the 'firstborn' of a world which is renewed by human beings permeated by Christ, and in which also all creatures are to be redeemed and transformed. On humanity's salvation or lack of it depends salvation or lack of it for the lower kingdoms.

'From his own resolve he had the will and brought us forth from the womb of heaven by the Word of truth, that we should be the firstborn of his whole creation.'

47

THE SEVEN BEATITUDES OF THE APOCALYPSE

A PATH TOWARDS RESURRECTION

Less well known than the beatitudes of the Sermon on the Mount, but no less significant, are the seven that are found in various places throughout the Revelation of John. They shine all the brighter against the background of apocalyptic catastrophes. According to St Augustine, the history of Christianity takes its course between the persecutions by the powers of the Adversary and the consolations of God. These beatitudes can shine upon us like bright stars as 'consolations of God'.

I

> Blessed is the one who reads aloud the words of the prophecy and blessed are those who hear, and who keep what is written therein; for the time is near. (Rv 1:3)

This beatitude occurs right at the beginning of the Apocalypse. The Greek word for 'read' *(anaginōskein)* actually means something like 'know upwards'. What appears in the book is the 'sediment' of an original live experience; it is now relegated into dead letters, it is written down. But the one who reads with real understanding brings it to life again. His perception rises 'above' what is written 'down'.

To this enlivening act of spiritual perception is added the full, feeling response of the 'hearing' soul that relates itself in devotion to the word of the spirit; to this in turn is added the 'sustained will' in 'preserving' or 'keeping'. The original text means by that a sort of garden-tending activity, performed regularly, over and over again. Repetition and regularity are indispensable elements of all spiritual life; it is not for nothing that we speak of 'religious practice'.

Perceptive reading, devoted listening of the soul, consequent action through the regular exercise of the will – with these the Apocalypse in its opening lays the basis of a development that finally leads to participation in the resurrection world of the heavenly Jerusalem.

'Words of the prophecy' are all the words of wisdom that have flowed from a true revelation of Christ. In contrast to pre-Christian wisdom all Christian knowledge is directed towards the future, is apocalyptic, is prophecy.

'For the time is near' does not refer to the indifferent flowing on of time through the hour-glass, *chronos,* but to *kairos,* the moment heavy with destiny, charged with decision. With Christ the kingdom of heaven has drawn 'near'. When the soul awakes to this nearness, when it becomes aware of what is brought within its reach, then the decisive hour strikes for it. This moment is 'near' for each one who takes to the path of which the first beatitude of the Apocalypse speaks.

II

We now have to wait a long time when reading the Book of Revelation until the second beatitude appears. What was contained in the first has to last a long time, for there follows the description of catastrophic events, and the Antichrist setting up his rule. Then at last, the fourteenth chapter presents the Christ returning in the clouds. Immediately before, as if already in the light of this coming on the white cloud, stands the second beatitude:

> 'Blessed are the dead who die in the Lord from now on.'
> 'Blessed indeed,' says the Spirit, 'they will rest from their
> labours, for their deeds follow them.' (14:13)

'Blessed are the dead' – a great contrast to the mood of the ancient Greeks who saw the life of the dead in Hades diminished to a grey shadow-existence. 'Blessed are the dead' – nor is this meant in the pessimistically resigned sense of a materialistic age, which envies the dead because they have fortunately left it behind them and have entered into the great nothing. The Apocalypse is conscious of saying something new in this blessing of the dead, something that first becomes real through Christ, and therefore continues 'from now on'. It does not simply bless the dead indiscriminately, but makes the important qualification, 'who die in the Lord'.

The 'rest' they are to find after their great labours certainly does not mean rest in the churchyard, but a profound recovery in the spirit.

What human beings have done during their existence on earth, with all its pain and difficulties, what as apparently transitory beings they have put forth as transitory deeds in a transitory world, is now revealed in its eternal significance. 'Their deeds follow them.' These real consequences of their deeds working on into the supersensible are for the dead a stern judgment. Only those who 'die in Christ' need not fear these consequences.

John then beholds the one who comes on the white cloud with the sickle in his hand. Death has become as it were subservient to Christ as the Lord of destiny.

'Dying in the Lord' is not confined simply to the moment of death. If it is to come about, then it must already have begun during life as an inner 'mystical' process in a soul united with Christ, as a constant sacrifice of the lower self. Paul said, 'I die every day,' and said it, moreover, in his chapter on the resurrection (1Cor 15:31).

The perceiving, hearing and practice of the first beatitude has to deepen into a 'dying in Christ'; then it leads to the mystery of the one who comes again, of the one who comes on the white cloud.

III

> Behold, I am coming like a thief. Blessed is the one who remains awake, keeping his garments, so that he may not go naked and be seen exposed. (16:15)

Christ's coming again, which makes itself felt more and more as a spiritual fact, asks grave decisions of human beings. It does not leave them as they were before. If they sleep through the event, they are inwardly the poorer – this is the point of the comparison in the strange and yet realistic picture of Christ coming 'like a thief'. In comparison with this is the blessing of him who 'remains awake'.

In ancient times the Lord gave to his own in sleep, but human beings have stepped out of the divine dream of the early childhood of humanity; they have begun to wake up – primarily at first to the earthly world. If the wakefulness is limited to the material world, however, the feeling gradually arises, 'Unfortunate are the wakeful'. Humans bear this adult wakefulness like a burden, seek narcotics and opiates in order to escape the desolate reality. Rightly understood Christianity is not opium. It means raising the power of wakefulness beyond the material world into the spiritual. Those who shrink back from the full adult responsibility of sober awakening in order not to lose their childhood faith, do not yet know that all waking and knowing that could be dangerous to Christianity is always only a half-waking and half-knowing. It is precisely within the purpose of Christianity to penetrate to the full awareness and the full knowledge that includes the supersensible. Therefore, 'Blessed is he who remains awake.'

'Keeping his garments.' Everyone knows the sort of dream in which they find themselves not properly dressed. This can reflect deeper things. Humans are beings with a central core surrounded by various sheaths. Besides the physical body we carry still finer supersensible sheaths about us which can be represented as garments – as in fact they are in the priest's vestments. If human beings are not awake, do not 'pull themselves together' with all their innermost core's energy for full awareness, then the sheaths can become estranged from their own centre, and evil things can take up their abode in them. If, for example, we do automatically, indifferently, what we should be doing with our whole being, we allow our sheaths to act independently of us. The same is true if we lack self-control and allow ourselves to be pulled in all directions by our emotions. 'The one who remains awake' should permeate all the members of their human nature from their inner core outwards – then they 'keep their garments together'.

Being 'seen exposed' occurs when human beings without sheaths permeated by spirit and soul, without the 'cloak of Christian love for their neighbour', without the aura of their true spiritual nature, represent themselves only as a material body, when, to put it crudely, they regard themselves and others only as so many pounds weight. Then the depths of human shame are reached.

Those, however, who keep their garments also becomes wearers of the 'wedding garment'.

IV

> Blessed are those who are invited to the wedding feast of the Lamb. (19:9)

Invited, called by name. The true inner being, the individuality, which makes a human being something unique, unchangeable, irreplaceable, is called upon by 'name'. Yet our earthly name holds the place of our hidden, eternal name with which God called us into existence. If human beings hear this eternal name as called by God, then they know they are invited to the wedding feast of the Lamb. For John, it is in the image of the Lamb that the Christ appears as the fulfiller of the great sacrifice of redemption. From the sacrifice of Christ there blossoms forth the great wedding, the marriage of heaven and earth in glorious transformation. In this holy event seen in the image of the 'meal' and the 'marriage' – 'the wedding feast' – the Christian who is fully awake is to share.

V

Towards the end of the Apocalypse the beatitudes follow one another more closely. The calling to the wedding now becomes a 'being chosen'.

> Blessed and holy is the one who shares in the first resurrection. The second death has no power over them, but they will be priests of God and of Christ, and will reign with him for a thousand years. (20:6)

The word 'holy' is now included in the form of the blessing. He who shares in the wedding feast increases in saintliness.

Being able to share in the 'first resurrection' – 'dying in the Lord' was the precondition for this. What is the 'first' resurrection? The writer of the apocalypse also distinguishes between a first and a second death. Neither death nor resurrection can therefore be grasped in a single concept; they are processes, developments that gradually unfold. The 'first death' is obviously the death of the earthly body. The 'second death' is undergone when it becomes clear after the death of the body that the soul has lost its spiritual home through the way it has conducted its earthly existence.

Conversely, the 'first resurrection' is the awakening of the soul that has 'died in the Lord' and is therefore not affected by the second, the soul death. In the wedding garment of the higher, Christ-permeated sheaths, it is able to lead a conscious life after death, in which it can serve Christ as a priest. It lives like a king, in that, with death, it has not had to lay aside the crown of consciously directed will to the spirit. It can carry over into life after death the individual power of the awakened higher I.

The first 'resurrection' happens therefore in the realm of the soul and the more subtle life-forces. It does not yet reach the earthly body so strongly that it can wrest it from the fate of death, spiritualise it and incorporate it into the higher world – that would then be the 'second resurrection' that deals with the 'first death', just as the first resurrection, the inner awakening, renders powerless the second death, the death of the soul.

The first resurrection remains in the realm of Holy Saturday when the body still lies in the grave, but when, as a radiant soul, Christ already brings the light of Easter to the departed souls. The 'saints', strictly speaking, are not only those in the Church calendar of saints, but all the Christ-imbued souls that by virtue of the first resurrection reign with Christ in the invisible world like priests and kings.

In the 'thousand years' this working with Christ in the supersensible world gradually matures towards the 'second resurrection' which then also includes the earthly body and overcomes the last enemy, death. This is described in the Apocalypse as the 'heavenly Jerusalem'. In the sphere of this mighty closing picture we meet the penultimate beatitude.

VI

> And behold, I am coming soon. Blessed is the one who keeps the words of the prophecy of this book. (22:7)

Once the first difficulties are overcome, the stream of redeeming events rushes on with full force. The coming of Christ makes itself felt ever more powerfully.

Like the first beatitude this one again speaks of 'keeping', tending Christianity's wisdom like a gardener for the future. This referring back to the beginning shortly before the end is a reminder that the beginning is not something suspended and set aside by the following stages, but that in principle it already contains the true 'keeping' that leads to perfection. The 'sustained will' of this tending and practice is recognisable in it. The constantly practised enlivening of Christianity's future potential finally reaches its goal.

Separated by only a few verses from the almost disappointingly simple sixth beatitude, which apparently leads so little further, there now follows the seventh and last, which contains the whole Easter mystery of the resurrection.

VII

> Blessed are those who wash their robes, that they may have the right to the tree of life and that they may enter the city by the gates. (22:14)

'Keeping' the garments was spoken of earlier, now 'washing' them. In the life of the first resurrection there occurs a continuous cleansing of the human being from the stains and blemishes of the Fall. In his earlier vision of all the saints, John describes the truly Christian dead as clothed in white robes. 'They have washed their robes and made them white in the blood of the Lamb' (7:14). Their original purity can only be given again to man through the power of the great loving sacrifice emanating from Golgotha – 'the blood of the Lamb'. But human beings must really take hold of this grace, they must 'wash their robes' and make them 'white' in the sacrificial blood. It is in reality an added grace that they may co-operate in this.

By such working of the effects of Golgotha into the finer sheaths of humanity's being, the second resurrection also becomes possible, the resurrection that finally wrests the earthly body, too, from the forces of death. Those redeemed 'have the right to the tree of life'. The Fall with its consequences is overcome. Fallen humanity had once to be barred from approaching the tree of life 'Lest he reach out his hand ... and live for ever' (Gn 3:22). Humanity had to be preserved from having to live eternally in this fallen state, estranged from God. Making the sinner subject to death was the greatest boon of Providence. Only through Christ are we gradually to become mature enough to immortalise our true being, restored and perfected in all its members. Once it was said, 'lest he ... eat', so now it is said of the purified 'that they may have the right to the tree of life'. Now humanity may consciously take up those mysterious, hidden, divine life-forces that no longer allow death its power.

To the picture of the garden of Paradise is added that of the 'city', the resurrection world of which those who are Christ-imbued are to be the rightful inhabitants.

Whilst the first beatitude contained the motif of 'perception' in the word 'read' *(anaginōskō)*, the last contains that of 'life'.

If one looks at these seven beatitudes as a whole, it is also noticeable how singular and plural alternate in them. 'The one who reads – those who hear – the dead – the one who remains awake – those who are invited – the one who shares in the first resurrection – they shall be priests – the one who keeps the words – those who wash their robes.' It is like a rhythmical breathing in and out, a contraction to the realm of the purely individual and then an expansion again into the element of a higher spirit of community that arises from it: a rhythm of 'I' and 'we'. It begins with the singular of the one concerned with knowing the holy book. It ends with the great 'we' of a future humanity – those who 'have the right to the tree of life' and 'may enter the city by the gates'.

48

LIFE AFTER DEATH AND THE BIBLE

Having a philosophy of life is not a luxury to which we treat ourselves away from from the practical demands of life. When someone we love dies, the way in which we adapt ourselves and behave in relation to them is an important part of life's experience, depending very much on our particular view of life. If we are of the opinion that death is the end of everything, then we will behave in quite another way than if we are convinced that the soul lives on. In the first case we shall leave it at nostalgic recollection. We have then, as we think, only to do with our own soul and its emotions, which no longer concerns those who have died for they have ceased to exist. In the other case a systematic care in thinking about the dead will have an objective significance beyond our own feelings. We are then not alone with our own soul, but we feel with a certain responsibility that our inner emotions reach the one who has died, could be burdensome to them – or helpful if we do the right thing. On the basis of such a view of life, we have begun in The Christian Community to build up something like a culture of relations with the dead in connection with the sacramental life.

We are accustomed to the fact that materialism, where it is represented as a conscious philosophy, sees human existence as ending with his bodily existence. But we must regard as alarming the fact that, for some time now, certain influential streams of Protestant theology also take this point of view. Thus even in such circles, which certainly want to adhere to Christianity, the way is prepared for a materialistic view of human nature and its consequences for life. Various theological trends, in other respects not at all united, today agree in the doctrine that all is over for the soul at death – until the Last Day.

In contrast to atheism the existence of God is adhered to, but this God and his act of awakening the dead on the Last Day is quite incongruous with the otherwise accepted materialistic outlook. The idea of a soul continuing to exist after death without a physical body is rejected as Platonism, which is alien to the Bible. These theologians think they should do justice to the Bible by dismissing the idea of the continued life of the soul adhered to by Christianity for the past two thousand years.

Is this really what the Bible means? Should a Christianity orientated to the Bible really dispense with this universally Christian, truly ecumenical idea that has prevailed until now? First of all we must add something on the approach to the topic. It cannot be expected that everything belonging to the realm of supersensible experience and knowledge must be comprehensively contained in the Bible if it is to be taken as true. Nowhere does the Bible lay claim to being *the* complete text book in relation to supersensible truths. It is not a compendium of metaphysics, but a document that testifies to a fact. It is the unique document of a divine activity that culminates in the deed of redemption of Golgotha. In testifying to this fact of salvation, what concerned ideology was mentioned in passing if there was occasion for it. But the great comprehensive world picture, against the background of which the story of salvation occurs, is nowhere described as such. One could assume the elements of such a world picture, in which the supersensible had its place, to be still fairly general among people of those times. They still knew that there were angels, even several orders of angels, devils and evil spirits. They stood much closer to the supersensible realities.

For example, when the priest Zechariah had had the vision of Gabriel and came out of the Holy Place unable to speak, the congregation praying outside was immediately aware that he must have had a supersensible experience during his service there (Lk 1:22). People knew that such things happened. One can certainly not say that of modern day people. If they are again to find a relationship to the biblical record, people must be helped to find an outlook in which the supersensible realities again have their place, as is the case with Rudolf Steiner's anthroposophy. This outlook cannot be built up from the Bible alone for the reasons given – that the Bible is not in this respect complete and does not intend to be. It is therefore not to be expected that everything concerning the supersensible must 'be in the Bible'. The survival of the soul could be a truth even if it were not expressly taught in the Bible.

However, that is certainly not the case. Reference to life after death *does* occur in the Bible. Theologians know that too, of course. They see themselves under the necessity of devaluing the implications of such passages and representing them as intrusions of 'heathen' doctrine that have penetrated no more than the fringes of the Bible. The really central message of the Bible, so they think, proffers the idea of the non-existence of the dead until the Last Day.

Let us see what the Bible has to say about that.

The Old Testament, it is true, is extraordinarily reticent about what concerns the continued existence of the soul. Where it rises prophetically to a hopeful outlook, it looks to the resurrection of the body at the end of days. Is there no indication of anything between?

Not absolutely. There are several places that indicate an existence after death. When Abraham died, he was 'gathered to his people' (Gn 25:8). When this expression appears in connection with the other patriarchs, one could apply it to the burial chambers in Hebron where the bodies rest beside each other. But in Abraham's case it is different, since his forefathers lay buried in Chaldea, in Ur and Haran. Therefore something supersensible is meant. Moreover, the Old Testament speaks occasionally of Sheol as the abode of departed souls. It is a dark region, a shadowy world like the Greek Hades.

Why is the view of life after death in the Old Testament so gloomy? The unique task of the people of Israel consisted in preparing the earthly body of the approaching Messiah. Thus there was a special way of looking at bodily existence on earth in Old Testament religion. The other side to this deeply justified interest was that bodiless existence could not be regarded and appreciated in the same degree. It was certainly known that the soul continued to exist after death, but this existence without the earthly body was felt to be an existence of a subordinate kind.

In yet another but also similar way the Greeks came to their grey Hades. They were so full of the dignity and the beauty of the physical body that the loss of it was bound to weigh very heavily. Sheol and Hades were not just theories, but these pictures correspond to certain factual experiences of disembodied souls who, because of their high estimation of the earthly, did not find it easy after death to make themselves at home in the bodiless world. Homer has Achilles say he would rather be a beggar on earth than a king in the realm of shadows. Plato, who was also a Greek, could speak very differently thanks to the heritage of the ancient mystery schools where the soul became open to the supersensible through exercise and purification. Against the background of such special experience, Plato could glorify the grandeur of souls made free from the body, though he fell into the prejudice of undervaluing the significance of the earthly body by seeing it merely as a grave for the soul. He would not have cared for the Christian hope of a transfiguration of even the physical at the end of days. In his brushing aside the importance of the earthly body, Plato was as one-sided as the Old Testament in its lack of interest in the disembodied soul.

Only in Christianity can the one-sided truths of the Old Testament and Platonism be harmoniously united in one picture of the true reality. Christianity concentrates on the resurrection of the body of Christ on Easter Day. It knows that for Christians the attainment of such a resurrection body may be hoped for at the end of time, and that thereby human beings will, for the first time, be perfected in the God-likeness intended for them. But it is not therefore less aware of the continued life of the soul after death, even if in the New Testament this fact falls more into the background in face of the tremendous event of the resurrection of the body.

By the resurrection of his body, Christ has already achieved what will only be accomplished for human beings on the Last Day. When the Saviour died on Good Friday, the earth shook. On Easter Sunday it shook once more. Between these two dramatically accentuated moments, however, something happened in the silence that also belongs to the total event of Golgotha, and cannot be thought of apart from it. The fact that the dead body rested in the grave is not all there is to be said about the period between death and resurrection.

On Good Friday the crucified Christ spoke to the criminal: 'Truly I say to you, today you will be with me in Paradise' (Lk 23:43). When someone is dying, a loosening and setting free of the soul may possibly already begin so that there are certain clairvoyant moments as it wrests itself from the body. Something like this must have been the case with the dying criminal. He must have perceived something about the one crucified with him, who outwardly looked nothing more than an unfortunate man in the last extremity, that enabled him to see in him the king of a heavenly realm. Christ is able to carry this soul that clings to him through the crisis of death – and in a few moments something of the greatest importance can happen to change a person – and allow him to share in Christ's sunlit spiritual kingdom. As a result, the criminal dies differently and goes towards a quite different kind of experience after death from what would otherwise have been the case. Here the gospel speaks quite openly of an event that happens for the soul separated from the physical body. 'Today' does not refer to Easter Sunday. If one takes what Christ says as it stands, it can mean only the situation directly after death.

This opens for us the door to that mysterious happening that Christian tradition has called the descent to those in the underworld *(descensus ad infernos)* or, not altogether correctly, the descent into hell or the harrowing of hell. It is not a question of 'hell' but of Sheol or Hades. 'I have the keys of death and Hades' says the Risen One in the Revelation to John (1:18). This journey to Hades is clearly mentioned in the First Letter of Peter (3:19; 4:6) and we hear of it in the Letter to the Ephesians (4:9). It is a basic part of the original Christian belief, and was taken up as a separate article in the Apostles' Creed. Christ was not swallowed up by death in the time till Easter Day, but had a real and fully conscious existence as an excarnated soul.

Modern theology regards this biblical statement as the typical mythological way of speaking as conditioned by the times. This is correct insofar as the idea of a kingdom of the dead to be found 'under the earth' has no place in today's scientific world picture. Within this purely materialistic world picture the ancient view of the three-tier heaven, earth, underworld is obviously impossible. But if one speaks of the ancient world picture being 'conditioned by the times', it is not good enough simply then to reject that world picture. One should see that for people of ancient times the purely material experience of the world was still permeated in many ways by experiences of a supersensible kind – the two were interwoven. Today, we can neatly divide them. The 'three tiers' are connected with what was seen by unsophisticated people as an above and a below. However, along with this picture there was an experience of supersensible reality that was 'set in motion' by the related sense impressions. The impression made by the picture of the visible 'heaven' disposed the soul to be touched by a 'higher' world beyond the spatial. The Hades-underworld is the pictorial expression for a supersensible realm that again, as such, is beyond spatiality, where disembodied souls live, as it were, 'in the shadow' cast by their lives on earth. In the experience of the departed soul this earthly life, with all its culpability and estrangement from its divine source, thrusts itself in front of the spiritual sun. The soul finds itself 'in the shadow of the earth'. Thus Hades can be understood as a 'soul-landscape', as a 'soul-place'.

The disembodied Christ-soul entered this world and became as we say in the Creed of The Christian Community 'the helper of the souls of the dead who had lost their divine nature'. Christ was able to do this because in his holy life on earth he had not lost the divine nature, and, as a result, in death his soul could immediately enter 'Paradise', which clearly does not mean something spatial-geographical, just as the 'underworld' or the 'prison' of which Peter's Letter speaks does not.

The truth of the further life of the soul after death is centrally anchored in the New Testament by Christ's descent into Hades.

One should also think of the transfiguration, in the course of which Moses and Elijah – that is, souls living in the other world – appear in glory and converse with the transfigured Christ about his approaching death (Lk 9:30f). Moses and Elijah are therefore by no means 'dead'. They look with great concern at what happens on earth.

Christ taught 'as one having authority, and not as the scribes'. That is also valid for the words with which he spoke of the life of the soul after death. These occur first and foremost in the story of the rich man and Lazarus (Lk 16:19–31). It is not exactly a parable, nor is it called one by the gospel, but tells a story from life. One could speak of a parable only insofar as the fire in which the rich gourmand suffers his torment is no physical fire but an absolutely appropriate picture of the truth, just like 'Abraham's bosom'. The story allows us to see quite clearly how souls have a consciousness after death that extends not only to their own destiny but also to other souls, even indeed those remaining behind in earthly existence. Christ told this story since he had insight into the world beyond. If similar ideas are shown to exist in the Judaism of those times, then Christ has confirmed them as correct by his own words. He also points at times in other contexts to the further life of the soul after death. A man should practise conciliation whilst he is still 'on the way' with another lest he come to prison, which he cannot leave before he has paid the last farthing (Mt 5:25f). One should not be afraid of those who can kill only the body but not the soul (Mt 10:28). The dispute with the Sadducees – 'he is not God of the dead, but of the living' – is primarily about resurrection, but if Christ says that Abraham, Isaac and Jacob, as living souls, already now belong to God and not only at the Last Day, then that also indicates that we are not annihilated when we die, 'for all are alive to him' (Lk 20:38).

The New Testament also speaks of how Christ and the power of his redemptive deed should then be taken up by *individual* Christians. Such solidarity with Christ – 'Christ in me, I in Christ' – bears within it the certainty of overcoming death. And not only in relation to the Last Day. 'He who believes in the Son *has* eternal life' (Jn 3:36). He *has* it already now, even if not in the absolutely final fullness of the Last Day when 'the last enemy', the death of the body, will also be rendered powerless. This is just what John's Gospel says (5:24; 6:54). This 'already now' by no means precludes the fulfilment of the Last Day (6:39f, 44, 54). As far as the soul is concerned, however, death is beaten from the field *before* the Last Day: 'if any one keeps my word, he will never see death' (8:51). The Christ-permeated man will still have to die bodily, but for him death goes no further: 'whoever believes in me will live, even if he dies' (11:25).

The first death of a Christian recorded by the New Testament, the death of Stephen, certainly does not call up the impression of a soul preparing to enter 'the long night of death' until the Last Day. On the contrary, it is an absolutely triumphant crossing into the higher world opening before him: 'I see the heavens opened, and the Son of Man standing at the right hand of God' (Ac 7:56). Therefore, when the expression 'fall asleep' is used for death (7:60), we should consider that the point of comparison does not necessarily lie in the fact that we more or less lose consciousness on falling asleep. It can just as well be seen in the fact that when we fall asleep, there is the slipping out of the soul from its physical body that also happens, though more profoundly, at death. Stephen 'fell asleep' – his soul left his body. Nothing is said there about the kind of consciousness of the excarnated soul, only about the process of leaving the body.

The original Christians certainly did not experience their dead martyrs as unconscious sleepers in the beyond, though these like Stephen had 'fallen asleep'. That they were living and active in the spirit was a fundamental experience. The Letter to the Hebrews speaks of the 'spirits of righteous made perfect' (12:23). From the early Christian experience of the helping nearness of the world of the dead springs the wonderfully comforting picture of being 'surrounded by so great a cloud of witnesses' (Hb 12:1). Nor are the martyrs by any means sleeping spirits according to the Revelation of John – they are conscious and active. Twice the 'souls' *(psychai)* are specifically mentioned (6:9f; 20:4); they have therefore separated their existence from the body before the Last Day. The 'first resurrection' in which these souls participate is an anticipation of the awakening in the spirit, which will be completed only at the end of days in the resurrection that includes the body.

In harmony with this there also stand the direct statements of great Christian personalities in the New Testament who, out of their Christian feeling for life, look towards their approaching death. In the Second Letter of Peter we find the expression: 'as long as I am in this body [tent]' (2Pt 1:13). There is no mention of that indivisible unity of body and soul postulated by modern theology in the wake of materialism. The nearer the soul comes to death and the closer it is united with Christ, the more it feels itself as something independent of the body. The body becomes a 'tent' or 'dwelling' that the soul leaves behind in death. The passage continues: 'I know that the putting off of my body [tent] will be soon, as our Lord Jesus Christ showed me.' It is therefore a supersensible knowledge that he has about his imminent death. 'The putting off' of the 'tent' is indicated in what follows by the word *exodos*, Latin *exitus*, 'departure' (1:15). Still today the expression *exitus* is used for death in medical terminology. One would wish that those who speak of *exitus* in this sense would take the expression quite literally. It clearly does not say that death is the end but that a 'departure' occurs. Is it then ancient superstition or Platonism that intrudes as something alien in the New Testament with these expressions about 'putting off the tent' and 'departing'? Is it not much rather in harmony with the sacred experiences of so many dying Christians throughout two thousand years?

In a similar way Paul faces his approaching death. He feels it already near, but is inwardly torn in two. On the one hand it requires him to 'dissolve' *(analysai)* his union with the body 'and be with Christ' (Phil 1:23). On the other hand his sense of duty urges him to persevere in his body with the communities entrusted to him. Here it is obvious that he is not thinking of the Last Day, but that he expects this being 'with Christ' immediately after death. Thus for him, the revaluation of values can take place. Dying – which for people bound to the material is the essence of 'loss', since it means losing all with the earthly body – turns for Paul into a 'gain'. 'For to me to live is Christ, and to die is gain' (1:21).

Such testimonies of an indestructible awareness of victory over death seem to us to proceed truly from the very centre of a living experience of Christ.

That the hope of resurrection on the Last Day suffers no injury by a continued life of the soul after death we hope has been sufficiently stressed. One does not exclude the other. On the contrary. The true foundation for the hope of a final transformation of even the body actually lies in the fact that the light of immortality already shines forth from the soul united with Christ.

V

SACRED NUMBER IN THE GOSPEL OF JOHN

49

PRELIMINARY REMARKS

Robert Goebel described the composition intrinsic to the Gospel of John as a 'musical' one:

> John, as artist, stands clearly before us in sharply delineated outline: his gospel must be absorbed in its sonority, its rhythms, its harmonies. The motifs in Christ's earthly journey are at the same time musical themes that resound together in the mightiest symphony ... Amongst the evangelists, John is the Christ-devoted musician.*

That we can also call the Gospel of John the gospel of numerical ordering, might well be connected with this musicality. In the 'material' of John's account, patterns, or we might say 'patterns of sonority', repeatedly become apparent which permeate, configure, inspirit it, and which can be discerned as the arrangements of certain numbers. Above all, this involves the sacred numbers three and seven.

Sacred, configuring number is, however, also present in the first three gospels, especially in Matthew, but has nothing like the significance that it does in John. To gain a strong sense of this, we can contrast the Easter accounts in the synoptics with John 20.

Biblical scholars, right up to the modern day, have scarcely remarked on the numerical secrets in the Gospel of John. As far as we are aware, Ernst Lohmeyer has looked into this in greatest detail. Previously, commentators have only occasionally remarked on these numerical patterns. Lohmeyer, who also discovered patterning of three and seven in Revelation and the First Letter of John, says of the division of the story of the Samaritan into seven sections:

---

* *Das Evangelium in den vier Evangelien*, p. 20.

> Scarcely anywhere else does it become so evident that the sevenfold structure is not an external schema imposed on a recalcitrant material, but a profound and intentionally used artistry that permeates the inmost fabric of the text, and as it were makes it into a transparent sheath for the gospel's ultimate religious thoughts.*

The present study seeks to expand on Lohmeyer's work with further observations (some of which have been made also independently of him), but above all also to attempt to examine the question of truth thrown up by this. Lohmeyer, it seems to us, out of his finer intuition, claims that sacred number holding sway in John has nothing 'playful' about it, but is organically intrinsic to the material.

In relation to the number *three,* we can turn to the wealth of insights that Rudolf Steiner offered on the Trinity. By contrast to ecclesiastical dogmas (in their own way historically justified) that sought to lay down ultimate truths for all time, anthroposophy avoids final and watertight formulations about divine nature and instead offers a range of concrete insights within whose multiplicity the mystery of the Trinity is reflected ever and again anew. By working through all these perceptions, to which the number three repeatedly provides a key, a new understanding of the threefold nature of the divine gradually and organically arises.

Of these insights, that of the tripartite human being must be mentioned first and foremost. It was tragic for the pursuit of knowledge that the Church Council of Constantinople in 869 relinquished the division of human nature into body, soul and spirit. This left only the duality of body and soul, although the latter was accorded 'some spiritual qualities'. But the tripartite view was fundamentally destroyed by this, depriving us of the lens that could give insight into the mystery of the Trinity in accordance with the ancient doctrine of man in the 'likeness' of God. Instead of cultivating the trichotomy of the human being (body, soul and spirit) as a living tool of enquiry, human knowledge fell into dualism,

---

* 'Über Aufbau und Gliederung des vierten Evangeliums,' *Zeitschrift für die neutestamentliche Wissenschaft,* 1928, p. 23. See also Stange, *Die Eigenart der johanneischen Produktion,* p. 348ff.

and then imposed upon this dualistic epistemology an abstract, rigid dogma of the Trinity.

Anthroposophy regards threefoldness as a unique key for unlocking knowledge of the human being and the world. This trichotomy is one of its most fundamental insights. In the clear mirror of a truly Christian wisdom about human nature, it brings the divine, Trinitarian secret of humankind closer to us than the old dogma was able to, despite its commendable astuteness.

In the context of this study only a summary outline of the whole of anthroposophy must suffice. In the basic works by Rudolf Steiner (such as *Theosophy, An Outline of Esoteric Science, Riddles of the Soul, Anthroposophic Leading Thoughts),* the Trinity appears in a wealth of aspects, without ever falling into a comfortable schematism. We should not shy away from efforts to work our way towards this theme from ever new angles, and with active patience seek a view of the Trinity that can slowly ripen into something like a comprehensive picture.

How the *seven* is connected with the Trinity, and its importance as an ordering, configuring principle in evolution, is elaborated particularly in *Theosophy* and *Esoteric Science.*

In showing that the triads in the Gospel of John are reflections of the Trinity, we cannot use preconceived, schematic figures. There is no single formula that is universally valid here.

In examining whether and how a triad in John reflects the Trinity, we cannot either, for example, cite the mere 'appearance' of certain terms, even of 'Father', 'Son' and 'Spirit' themselves. The attribution can only arise from a detailed, *meditative* contemplation of each single instance, not from intellectual sampling. It must be sought above all in the dynamic, living play of forces at work in the organism of each context, rather than in the static element of isolated words. Thus a polar tension can develop between the first and third element of a triad, while the second plays more of a mediating role. The play of forces latent in any such triad reveals itself in meditation as a living back-and-forth. Such polarities between 1 and 3 are, for example, past/future, dark/light, will/knowledge. The perspective can sometimes relate more to content, at other times more to form, and both are usually intimately connected in the Gospel of John.

It is also possible that a reciprocal turnaround occurs, giving rise to the reverse sequence. Initially it is a matter of distinguishing the different correlating perspectives. The required gain in flexibility should not lead to a deficit of precision and accuracy of insights thus obtained.

Apart from an indispensable and thorough study of anthroposophy as already referred to, and apart from a meditative occupation with the gospel, participating in the *rituals* of The Christian Community can be an important practice for the reader of the Gospel of John, helping us become aware of its Trinitarian dynamic. The text of the Act of Consecration of Man (and of the other sacraments) is entirely oriented to the tripartite picture of the human being. To live with the Act of Consecration is to be pervaded by the breathing rhythm of the mystery of the Trinity.

Out study makes no claim to identify and illumine all the triads that appear in the Gospel of John. We wish to confine ourselves to a few archetypal phenomena. The latter term signifies a 'higher experience within experience'. In the many triads of the Gospel of John the reflection of the Trinity is more or less apparent. But from the very clear and evidently Trinitarian instances we learn more about the essential, underlying nature of all the triads than we do from the less characteristic ones in which the archetype is veiled. The clear, truly transparent cases are then, indeed, 'higher experience within experience', are archetypal phenomena.

If we should succeed in showing that what seems an arbitrary and playful handling of sacred number by the evangelist, in fact has its ultimate, essential justification in the reality of divine order, then we could fully apply Goethe's phrase about style resting on the deepest foundations of knowledge to John's unique manner of depicting sacred history.

Today we can at least begin to raise this foundation of knowledge into our clear awareness with the help of anthroposophic concepts. The question arises whether the evangelist himself was also conscious of this foundation of knowledge in the same way.

To explore this question let us first consider the example of an artistically creative human being. It can happen that a great artist can reveal wisdom whose scope they are unaware of at the moment of composition, and perhaps even later as well. Only gradually does it dawn upon posterity.

It is part of the genius of a creative artist to utter truths whose profundities they may not have an inkling of. How can this be? It is because, under the threshold of clear, waking soul-life, they are connected in an unusually essential way with great world mysteries. They play into the artist's creative work and in this way give it the stamp of genius. The foundation of knowledge that makes it possible for later generations to draw ever new truths from the work of this genius was certainly present as they produced their work, if not consciously then in the depths of their soul in sleeping or dreaming form.

'Style rests on the deepest foundations of knowledge.' But Goethe does not say that these foundations must always be conscious, since they do, after all, lie so deep within.

John wrote his gospel in a state of 'Inspiration'. This means, after all, that as he wrote, the eternal, God-sustained truth was intimately close to him. It informed his soul and lent his work its fathomless, inexhaustible, shining depths, giving it the divine truth even in small details.

Whether the foundation of knowledge in his soul was a sleeping or a dreaming one, or perhaps, after all, unfolded in waking consciousness, is not so decisive a matter for study of the issues at hand. Answering this question, however it might turn out, cannot cast any doubt whatsoever upon our efforts to discern the profoundest laws in the Gospel of John by drawing on anthroposophic concepts.

Apart from its debt to the foundations provided in books by Rudolf Steiner already mentioned, the present study draws gratefully on Friedrich Rittelmeyer's essays on the Gospel of John. Schooled as he was in anthroposophy, Rittelmeyer offers particular illumination of the subtle organism of threefold and sevenfold qualities in the fourth gospel.*

---

* See, for instance, *Meditation,* or in German, *Briefe über das Johannes-Evangelium; Welterneuerung,* and *Vom johanneischen Zeitalter.* Also on this theme is the detailed study by Rau, *Struktur und Rhythmus im Johannesevangelium,* Stuttgart 1972.

50

THREE IN THE UTTERANCES OF CHRIST

At the beginning of the Gospel of John, Christ is called the 'Logos', the 'Word'. With this, John gives us the key to everything else that follows. In his narrative, nothing 'material' remains spiritually inarticulate. Everything outward, everything seemingly external, becomes utterance, the expression of divine interiority. Despite this expressivity imbuing the gospel right down to its smallest elements, Christ's actual *speech* acquires distinctive importance. Here is Word in a specific sense: not word as deed, as fate, as gesture, but Word as word, where the Logos announces itself in its deepest intrinsic element.

The Logos itself speaks. This thought gives the speech of Christ in the Gospel of John its festive quality. The words of Christ reproduced by John are configured and mantled by sacred number.

Here, the way that Christ's utterances are inwardly structured is not the only important thing (see a few examples of this in Chapter 52) but also *how often* he 'breaks the spell of silence', how often he begins to speak. This breaking of silence is clearly felt by John to be a special event, for otherwise he would not call upon sacred number to accentuate it. The following will show that this indeed the case.

While, from another perspective, it is no doubt important whether the springing fount of speech flows on for a longer or shorter time, the moment where utterance begins is an event in itself.

Every time Christ steps forth into speech from silence is like a reflection of the secret of his being altogether. Each time he opens his mouth, whether for a longer address or to give voice to a comment not seemingly especially important, the mystery that John so festively accords him with the name of the Logos transpires again in more or less real symbolic form.

It is not the case that John calls Christ 'the Word' as a metaphor or figure drawn from human speech. The reverse is true: the human capacity of speech is a true reflection of the mystery that occurs between God the Father and God the Son, as that of 'silence' and 'speaking' or 'self-imparting'. The divine mystery of silence and revealed Word (of *sigé* and *Logos*) has its more or less diluted reflection in human speech, in the power of utterance with which we are endowed. Christ is not called the Word *in comparison* with this endowment. He is, rather, the reality of the Word, a reality of which human words are in fact only a likeness and shadow. Christ is the Word in a sense far more real than the human capacity to express what lives within us can ever be.

The imparting Word proceeds from the silence of the Father-Ground of Being. While this sublime occurrence finds only a dull reflection in human speaking, the reflection is clear and pure when Christ Jesus himself speaks.

With this in mind, we will not regard it as a lesser matter if John in most cases 'counts' the number of times that Christ gives utterance. In the modern era we are too hasty to home in on the intellectual content of words and seek its ordered, logical sequence. We have lost a feeling for what is actually at work when we 'break the spell of silence', when speech springs and flows. Below we will therefore consider these moments and their number.

The healing at the pool

The healing of the sick man at the Pool of Bethesda is an archetypal phenomenon of utterance, which finds its clear counterpart in the Trinity.

Christ speaks three times:

1. 'Do you wish to be healed?' (5:6)
2. 'Rise, take up your pallet and walk' (5:8)
3. 'See, you have been made whole! Sin no more, lest a worse thing befall you.' (5:14)

If we dwell a little on this triad, the dynamic at work in it soon becomes apparent. Between the first and the third we can discern a polar tension: 'Do you wish ?' and 'See!' This is the polarity of *will* and *knowledge*.

In the first, the will forces slumbering in hidden, dark, mysterious depths are invoked.

In the third, what has occurred is raised into the bright light of perception and understanding. The importance of a fact that first resides in the dull constraints of immediate existence and experience is brought to consciousness.

In full accord with the psychological law that to know something a certain distance is needed from an immediate occurrence, this third utterance is isolated from the first two by the intervening scene in 5:9–13. Its context is a sequel in the temple, an 'epilogue in heaven'. Christ, having left the scene of the healing, 'finds' the healed man 'later' at the temple (5:14). In an intimate conversation between the two of them, in the protected sanctuary of the sacred temple area, he makes the man aware of what he has experienced. He reveals to him the connection between sin and illness, which is the direct obverse of the other context, between the holy one and the one who needs healing.

The polarity of 1 and 3, as the polarity of will and knowledge, is at the same time that between Father and Holy Spirit.

In addition, the third utterance, spoken in the temple, again microcosmically encompasses all three aspects of the Godhead.

> See, you have been made whole!
> Sin no more,
> lest a worse thing befall you.

In the first line here, the principle of spirit knowledge predominates, standing over the whole occurrence.

The second line urges the man to shape his destiny aright; this is the realm of the Son's intrinsic manifestation.

The third touches on the implacable necessities and iron laws of karma ('What a man sows, that will he reap.' Gal 6:7), which are ultimately founded in God the Father's deep, dark silence.

Between 1 and 3 stands the second, mediating utterance (5:8). In its three parts, 'rise (resonant of resurrection) – take up – walk', it establishes the picture of the redeemed human being in whom the divine Son is figured. In arising, taking up one's destiny and walking (which intimates transformative progress), the Son principle in particular comes to expression. This triad encapsulates the nature of 'Christ-figured' humanity.

But also where the relationship to the persons of the Trinity is not so palpable and apparent, the Johannine triad gives Christ's utterance the festive quality of a ritual. This is true, for example, of the two 'Eucharistic' miracles of giving *wine* and *feeding with bread*.*

The conversation with Nicodemus

As in some of the miracles, we also encounter threefold utterances by Christ in his conversations and addresses.

In the night-time conversation with Nicodemus, the latter speaks three times (3:2, 4, 9) and Christ replies three times. Characteristically, these three replies are distinct from each other in terms both of form and content. Even outwardly it must be apparent how their scope continually enlarges.

On the other hand, the words of Nicodemus grow ever briefer and more humble. In the decreasing of Nicodemus' words, and in the growing of Christ's words during this conversation, we are already prepared for the Baptist's utterance that follows in the same chapter; 'He must increase, I must decrease' (3:30).

1. The first reply (3:3) is the succinct, oracular, classically crystallised epigram on the necessity of rebirth. 'Truly, truly I say to you, unless a person is born anew, he cannot see the kingdom of God.'
2. The second reply (3:5–8) first takes up this saying again in

---

* At the marriage at Cana, Christ speaks three times: to Mary (2:4) and to the servants (2:7f). This triad is emphasized by an accompanying triad of utterances spoken by Mary (2:3–5) and the governor of the feast (2:10). Similarly the feeding contains three utterances by Christ (6:5, 10, 12), which are likewise accompanied by three different utterances by the disciples (6:7, 9) and the people (6:14). The feeding of the five thousand is described in all four Gospels, but the synoptics only convey two sayings by Christ in direct speech (Mt 14:16, 18; Mk 6:37f; Lk 9:13f).

changed form, but moves it on from insular self-containment into a *human proximity*. The utterance begins to reveal the wealth and vitality of its content just as a root starts to sprout with the strength contained in it.
3. In the third reply (3:10–21) this growth process of opening and revealing continues, bursting the bounds of what was a dialogue until then, and unfolding into a lengthy discourse.

In 1 and 3 a polarity becomes vividly discernible. The first answer expresses a law, a kind of 'spiritual law of nature' rooted in irrevocable divine *imperatives*. The appropriate form for this is that of the pithy saying not primarily accessible and comprehensible but, rather, a rune, a hieroglyph of an eternal mystery.

The third answer, while perhaps also not devoid of hieroglyphic elements, is far more intent on being a *teaching* that seeks to be understood. 'You are a teacher of Israel, and do not know these things?' Here a teacher imparts knowledge, revealing light-filled resolves of the Godhead.

Nicodemus comes 'at night'. The first reply still belongs wholly to the mood of this word. The teaching discourse acts like a gradual illumination of the dark of the night, and at its end come striking reiterations of the word 'light' (3:19, 19, 20, 20, 21). One has the sense of a sunrise by the end.

In the first, monumental, oracular saying, and the third, clarifying discourse, we see the two principles of Father and Holy Spirit at work.

In the natural kingdom, the polarity of night and day, of concealment and opening, is apparent in root and blossom. The root dwells in continuous darkness, while the flower raises itself, reveals itself, in light.

Less terse and night-veiled than the first, less expansive and far-illumining than the third, the second reply occupies a middle position and helps Nicodemus gain human understanding of the first aphoristic utterance: 'Do not wonder that I said to you, "You must be born anew".' It impresses on him how our birth in the flesh needs to be supplemented by a birth in the spirit.

The first reply is directed to the self-assured Pharisee ('Master, we know' 3:2), a 'ruler of the Jews', who greets in Christ a God-sent teacher and miracle-worker of divine authority.

The third is directed above all to the 'master in Israel', answering his question 'How can these things be?' and offering the scholar a different teaching drawn from vision of heavenly things, which is thus also able at last to illumine the ancient, time-honoured pictures of tradition (the raising of the serpent upon the cross).

The second reply most clearly addresses the *human being* within Nicodemus. It relates to the question that touches on a core human problem, 'How can a man be born again when he is old?' (3:4). How can a person grown old find new access to the rejuvenating powers of childhood? How can he knowingly unite with these powers which once formed and imbued him without his knowledge in his mother's womb? As someone whose past now lies behind him, how can he become someone who can live on into the future with strength and energy? In other words, the great question is how can he take the step from the Father to the Son principle? Nicodemus, as one in need of healing, asks about the *Son*. Christ shows him the picture of the one reborn from water and the wind of spirit *(pneuma)*. Where this rebirth occurs, the voice from heaven speaks, 'This is my beloved Son.'

Thirdly, there follows the question of knowledge ('How can these things be?') and the teaching discourse.

Thus, the three replies of Christ relate organically to each other as *root, leaf* and *blossom*.

The Festival of Dedication

In another way, but with equal clarity, the exchange between Christ and the Jews at the Festival of the Dedication of the temple is coloured by the Trinity (10:22–39).

1. Pressed by the Jews on the question as to whether he is Christ, he replies to them that they do not believe he is the Messiah because they are not of his sheep. Those who belong to him are safe, no one can sunder them from his hand and that of the Father. 'I and the Father are one.' At this they wish to stone him (10:25–31).

2. He replies by speaking of the 'good' (or beautiful*) works that he has shown them 'out of the Father (10:32).
3. In the third utterance he counters the reproach of blasphemy, of unjustified self-deification (10:34–38).

This third utterance has an instructing character, one that seeks to convince; it even has a disputatious quality. Here, Christ addresses his listeners' *capacity of knowledge.* He cites the scriptures: 'Is it not written in your law, "I said you are gods?" If he called them gods ... do you say ...?' What was so apodictic in the first utterance, subsisting in itself like a stone memorial that stands unaffected by the understanding or non-understanding of passing generations – 'I and the Father are one' – now appears in modified form, 'that you may know and know ever more that the Father is in me and I in the Father.'

Precisely in the juxtaposition of these two sentences, the differing character of the two passages become apparent. The third utterance – likewise within this triad – belongs to the light-filled realm of the *Spirit.* It invokes the powers of insight and perception. It speaks of sanctification and deification. 'You are gods' is here more than a quotation: precisely at this place in the Gospel of John (immediately before the Lazarus chapter) it allows humanity's spiritual future to shine in. The third utterance has the future perspective of 'ultimate things'.

The first shows a very different tonal quality. There, Christ speaks of his care for his sheep, of their safety in his hands and the Father's great hand. A Fatherly, authoritative element holds sway in these sentences. The statement that 'you are not of my sheep' stands in the darkness of fathomless decrees.

The middle utterance shows the Son in the work intrinsic to him, shaping his deeds out of hidden Father powers. He has shown many 'good' or 'beautiful' *(kala)* works 'out of the Father'. In the phrase 'beautiful works', lies something of the configuring artistry of the *Son* – even if we must remember that *kalos* in the Gospel of John means more than something only aesthetically beautiful. At 2:10 it is given as an attribute of the Cana wine, and at 10:11, 14 as an epithet for the shepherd.

---

* The Greek word *kala* means both beautiful and good.

The Greeks

A similarly threefold context of discourse is elicited by the appearance of the Greeks (12:20–36). This is the last time that Christ speaks to the Jews in public. His words here, as he closes his outward-directed deeds, possess a concluding festiveness.

1. The appearance of the Greeks gives him the certainty that his 'hour has come'. This is the first time we encounter this striking phrase in the Gospel of John.* Struck by the near approach of his death, Christ proclaims the incontrovertible, immutable *law*: 'Truly, truly I say to you, unless the grain of wheat, having fallen into the earth should die, it remains alone. But if it dies, it brings forth much fruit.' Looking into the dark abyss of earth, he is seized by the chill of earthly death. Out of the convulsion of his soul he calls to the Father and wrestles his way through to the words, 'Father, glorify your name.'
2. In the second context (12:30–32) he speaks very specifically of the *death* on the cross, referring to it in veiled terms as 'if I am lifted up from the earth'. ('This he said signifying by what death he would die' 12:33). Overcoming the Adversary and merciful 'drawing' of humanity upward to the heights of the Christ-I are connected with this mystery.
3. The third utterance (12:35f) is characterised by the predominance of the *light* motif. The word 'light' appears no fewer than five times in these brief sentences. 'Whoever walks in darkness does not know where he is going.' His listeners are to know where they should walk, their destination in the light, they should become 'children of light'.

There is a polar contrast between the *dark earth* in 1, into which the grain of wheat must go under, and the brilliant *light* of spiritual existence in 3. (However, the latter detaches itself from 'darkness' and

---

* Lohmeyer draws attention to the triad (the hour has come) of 12:23, 13:1, 17:1 which corresponds to the other triad (not yet come) at 2:4; 7:30, 8:20. In 7:6 (twice), 8, the word *kairos* appears, rather than *hora*.

the first saying begins and ends with the motif of transfiguration. Between these polar contrasts we can often observe such crossovers.)

Between these two utterances, the middle one refers to the redemptive work of the Son on the cross. It stands, on the one hand, against the dark background of the eternal Father law 'Dying to become', as the specific, historical, destined embodiment of this eternally valid necessity. On the other hand it spans a bridge to the bright future of the spirit where spiritualised human beings walk in light, believe in the light and indeed may be called 'children of the light':

Law of death – Golgotha event – light's glory.

Father, Son, Holy Spirit. The third utterance has 'finality' ('so that you become children of light!'), directed towards a future goal.

Words on the cross

Of the seven words on the Cross, John gives us three:
'Woman, behold your son ... behold your mother' (19:26).
'I thirst' (19:28).
'It is finished' (19:30).

These last three utterances upon earth are once again transparent for the mystery of the Trinity.

The founding of the community between the mother and the disciple occurs in the light of the *Holy Spirit*. The community grows forth from knowledge and perception: 'Behold your mother', 'Behold your son.' The Holy Spirit is the loving bond between one person and another, as indeed it is also the 'principle' of the Church. It unites the disciple's striving, illumined will for knowledge with the more unconscious, naturally divine depth of wisdom and magic of the mother.* From whatever perspective we may regard this

---

* Compare Rittelmeyer: 'In Mary, the mother of the Saviour of the world, called Sophia by the Gnostics, ancient Christian reverence saw the motherly, weaving wisdom of the cosmos ... In the image of the disciple and the mother we can behold the new humanity where a human being does not stand isolated in the world but participates in wisdom-sustaining cosmic love that projects through the mother into his life. With these words, Christ really founded the Christian Church ...' *(Christengemeinschaft* II, p. 373) See also Beckh, *John's Gospel,* and Steiner, *The Gospel of St John,* lecture of May 31, 1908, for more on the relationship of Mary to the Sophia.

profoundly mysterious scene, we will sense the breath of the Holy Spirit in it.

The 'thirsting' once again seals the *Son's* full immersion in human nature, which he is able to redeem through such complete incarnation, sparing himself nothing in the process.

The last utterance, 'It is finished', closes the sacred enactment in monumental fashion, allowing it now to 'stand in eternity'. It bears the fulfilled deed of the Son into the *Father's* eternal world.

The resurrection

The account of the resurrection is entirely pervaded by the triad of the Trinity, as by the chiming of Easter bells.

Three appearances of the resurrected one are recounted in Chapter 20:

1. To Mary Magdalene on Easter morning.
2. To the circle of disciples on Easter evening.
3. To Thomas, in particular, the following Sunday.

On each occasion, the Resurrected One speaks *three* times. All this conveys a festive liturgical quality. Often these words, which resound from the resurrection world, in turn possess a microcosmic threefold form.

The first and third appearance of Christ, to Mary and Thomas, bear a polar relationship to each other: 'Do not touch me' and 'Bring your finger here.'

The appearance to *Thomas* is in answer to doubt and stands in the sign of *knowledge*. It leads the disciple to a 'grasping' of the resurrection body, and thereby also to comprehension of the divine I that lives within it as the architect: 'My Lord and my God!'

The appearance to *Mary Magdalene* is veiled in the frisson of unapproachability. *'Noli me tangere.'* This encounter is by the open tomb, still within the spell of the night of death. The last words of this appearance fade away in the mystery of Christ's ascension to the *Father.*

The middle of the three appearances in Chapter 20, to the

disciples, has more of a *Son* character compared to the other two. The Risen One shows his wounds. Yet here it is not a matter of comprehending but of affirming the great deed of life and death that has been accomplished.

This Trinitarian structure is apparent in miniature within each scene.

Christ speaks three times to *Mary Magdalene:*
'Woman, why do you weep? Whom do you seek?' (20:15).
'Mary!' (20:16).
'Do not touch me ...' (20:17)

1. Mary Magdalene stands weeping before the tomb and hears the words of the angels, 'Woman, why do you weep?' (20:13). The angelic words are like a call to spiritual awakening that reaches her soul so full of pain, and opening through pain. By virtue of this she is now able to see the Risen One himself, as yet without knowledge, in the Imagination of the 'gardener'. He takes up the angels' words, 'Woman, why do you weep?' and adds, 'Whom do you seek?' The question requires a reply. It urges the soul, lost in pain, to take hold of itself and become aware of something. To a still greater degree than the angels' words, these words of Christ are a wakening call of the Spirit, reaching the soul caught up in its own dull sorrow.
2. 'Mary!' Christ here calls upon her own, deepest intrinsic being. With this name, with the personal tenor he gives it, he approaches her individuality, her I.
3. The third utterance belongs to the Father. The ascension is announced, and the word 'Father' resounds three times. Likewise the unapproachability of the Noli me tangere – which can continue to be felt in the distinctions of 'my Father and your Father, my God and your God' – invokes the Father mood that prevails especially in this third utterance but also overall in this appearance to Mary Magdalene at the tomb.

On the evening of Easter Sunday, the Risen One appears to the disciples.

1. 'Peace be with you' (20:19). In this instance this is not a greeting of like to like to which the others respond fraternally, but a blessing streaming from above downwards from a higher being who emerges from the mysterious seclusion of his passage to the Father, who appears to them out of the darkness of a mystery sublime beyond all understanding.
2. The middle utterance, that of the Son (20:21), is prepared with a distinctive gesture. The Risen One shows the disciples his wounds, the eternal stigmata of his true incarnation and 'becoming man'.

    'Peace be with you.
    As the Father has sent me
    so I am sending you.'

   The first line repeats the blessing greeting.
   The second touches on the relationship of the Son to the Father, the latter sending the former forth from their primordial union.
   The concluding line is already infused with the spirit of Pentecost, and points towards the third utterance.
3. As the Son utterance is preceded by the showing of the wounds, so the Spirit utterance is likewise prefigured by an equally characteristic action, that of breathing on them.

    'Receive the Holy Spirit.
    Those whose sins you forgive, they are forgiven them.
    Those whose sins you retain, they are retained.' (20:22f)

   The first line belongs in a special sense to the spirit principle.
   The second inaugurates the motif of the redemptive work of the Son: the sin-forgiving capacity, which will stream on through the apostles.
   The 'retention of sins' points to wherever the stream of forgiveness mediated by Christ-filled human beings does not reach, wherever the transformation of evil into good does not take effect, but where, instead, implacable law must

hold sway. Dante assigned his *Inferno,* with its inexorable consequence of misery for all unforgiven, untransformed sins, to the Father God and his punishing justice. In him the great laws of natural and spiritual existence have their foundation.

The third appearance is to doubting Thomas.
1. Here again the *blessing* greeting of peace first comes (20:26), the third time it has figured (20:19, 21, 26).
2. As Christ previously showed his disciples the wounds after the peace greeting, so here, at the corresponding place, he says:

   'Bring your finger here, and see my hands,
   bring your hand and put it into my side,
   and do not be unbelieving, but believing.'

   This second time of speaking, Christ turns most directly and *personally* to Thomas. Within the triad, this is the same position as when Christ uttered the name 'Mary!' And in the same way that she, when addressed in her inmost being, replied 'Rabboni' (my master), so here Thomas answers, 'My Lord and my God.'
3. The third utterance (20:29) first picks up on this personal and intimate mood, but then leads it on into the broad scope and sway of all humanity:

   'Because you have seen me, you have believed.
   Blessed are those who have not seen and yet have believed.'

   This utterance, which speaks of inner powers through which humanity makes the fact and reality of Christ its own, looks beyond the individual Thomas to the developing Church.

This wonderful structure of the Easter accounts has no equal in the other gospels. Its mode and fashion is unique to John. With primary clarity it becomes apparent here how the Trinity is inmost soul breath for John in his celebration of his gospel.

The appearance by the Sea of Galilee

As an appendix to this, we mention here the other Johannine Easter passage, John 21, the appearance by the Sea of Galilee.

In the early morning, the Risen One causes the miraculous draft of fishes. With the seven disciples he celebrates the mysterious dawn breakfast and then turns especially to Peter, distinguishing Peter's mission from that of the 'disciple whom he loved'.

His *three questions* about Peter's love for him (21:15–17) remind us of the disciple's three denials. Peter answers three times, and three times the Risen One gives him a mission.

But otherwise in this chapter the Risen One's speech does not have a threefold pattern: in its entirety it contains *twelve* utterances of Christ. (Apart from the places already referred to, these are: 21:5, 6, 10, 12, 19, 22.) This is surely no accident in this chapter in which sacred number is of such salient importance: the seven disciples as opposed to the five in Chapter 1 (21:2); the 153 fishes (21:11); Christ's 'third appearance' (21:14); the three questions (21:15–17); and perhaps also the 200 cubits (21:8). In the number twelve is manifest the starry resurrection cosmos, from which the sustaining, nourishing powers of the Eucharist spring. As the number of eternity, twelve has the special mission of concluding and encapsulating the whole.

Apart from the triads, a four can also be distinguished within this encompassing twelve: the four utterances as the draft of fishes is caught and during the breakfast.

In John, the significance of the four is above all that, together with the three, it forms the seven, into whose realm we now pass.

51

SEVEN IN THE UTTERANCES OF CHRIST

The first disciples

The very beginning of the Johannine account is in various respects already ordered by the number seven. The calling of the first disciples stands in the context of seven scenes (to which Lohmeyer also refers).

First come three scenes with the Baptist:
1. The questions asked by priests and Levites about his person (1:19–23).
2. The questions of the Pharisees about his work (1:24–28).
3. The Baptist bears witness to Christ (1:29–34).

In a fourth scene (1:35–39), the circles of the Baptist and of Christ engage closely with each other. When instigated by the Baptist, two of his disciples leave him and are the first to follow Christ. In this central, fourth scene the decisive transition occurs.

Now follow three further scenes with Christ and the disciples:
5. Peter (1:40–42).
6. Philip (1:43f).
7. Nathanael (1:45–51).

In the significant middle scene, Christ speaks for the first time in John's account. He turns to the two disciples who follow him and asks, 'What do you seek?' In response to their question about where he is staying, he replies, 'Come and you will see' (1:38f).

Then he says to Peter, 'You are Simon ...' and to Philip, 'Follow me' (1:42f).

Three further utterances follow, directed to Nathanael: See, a true Israelite ...' 'Before Philip called you ...' 'Because I said to you ... you will see greater things' (1:47–51).*

Thus, Christ's utterances are sevenfold, and this ritual, festive quality is also accentuated by the *Baptist's* seven preceding utterances. The first four are statements about himself:

1. 'I am not the Christ' (1:20).
2. 'Am not,' (1:21) when asked if he is Elijah.
3. 'No,' (1:21) when asked if he is the prophet.
4. 'I am the voice of one calling in the loneliness ...' (1:23). This fourth and middle utterance acquires key importance by marking a transition from describing himself to proclaiming Christ: 'Prepare the way of the Lord.'

The three last statements describe the greater, higher being who comes after him:

5. 'I baptise with water, but in your midst stands one ... who comes after me' (1:26f).
6. 'Behold, the Lamb of God ... the Son of God' (1:29–34).
7. In the last statement, the Baptist no longer speaks of himself at all, having previously still spoken of himself as a humble precursor who baptises with water and observing witness. Now he is extinguished entirely. The seventh utterance consists only in the mighty words, 'Behold the Lamb of God' (1:36), which finally separate the two disciples from his side and point them towards Christ.

This seventh utterance stands precisely in the fourth scene that marks the transition from the narrative concerning John to that concerning Christ, with Christ's first utterance following the Baptist's last. At the same time it contains the first words spoken by the disciples, 'Rabbi, where are you staying?'(1:38).

In the same way that the seven first utterances of Christ are preceded by seven sayings of the Baptist, so they are in turn accompanied by seven utterances from the *disciples*. Three of these are directed to

---

* It could be objected that there is an eighth utterance at 1:51 with 'And he says to him'. But this is not a new utterance, one breaking the spell of silence, so much as a continuation and intensification of the previous sentence.

Christ himself: 'Rabbi, where are you staying?' (1:38); 'From where do you know me?' (1:48); 'Rabbi, you are the Son of God' (1:49). Four utterances are spoken between the disciples themselves, and so here, too, we can observe an inner sevenfold structure. Andrew says to Peter, 'We have found the Messiah' (1:41). Philip converses with Nathanael, 'We have found the one of whom Moses wrote' (1:45); 'Can any good come out of Nazareth?' (1:46); 'Come and see!' (1:46).

Thus the three times seven utterances of the Baptist, Christ and the disciples are distributed over the seven scenes. If, as readers of the gospel, we become aware of this patterning, at the same time keeping in mind the fresh, vibrant nature of these scenes, which is anything other than artificially constructed, we can sense how the evangelist's relationship to sacred number arises naturally and self-evidently from his living experience of higher rhythms. Pervaded by sacred number, this account by the evangelist can bring to the correspondingly attuned soul of the reader a delicate experience of something that goes above and beyond what is said in the words actually uttered. Through the way in which the events involving the Baptist and Christ are spread over the seven scenes, through the very mode of description, we can come to feel the organic quality of this historical progress from John to Christ, the heavenly rightness and God-willed nature of this evolution. Furthermore, the three sevenfold utterances convey to the reader a sense that the three worlds – of the precursor, the fulfiller, the disciples – are here expressed in a certain, albeit microcosmic entirety of nuance, and sufficiency of characterisation.

The Samaritan woman

The conversation with the Samaritan woman at the well exemplifies the sevenfold quality of Christ's utterance with primary and archetypal clarity.

The first of the three themes around which the conversation circles is the *well* itself, initially in its earthly reality and then increasingly in its figurative sense. The first utterance of Christ is, 'Give me to drink' (4:7). The conversation starts from the simple reality of the physical plane: the wanderer is tired and thirsty. The second utterance, concerning living water, turns the exchange towards the supersensible and mysterious. 'If you knew who it is who speaks to you' (4:10). The third utterance leads still deeper into underlying spiritual realms, speaking of thirst and the eternal quenching of thirst (4:13f).

With no seeming connection, the conversation now turns to a completely different theme: 'Call your *husband* and come here' (4:16). 'You had five husbands, and the one you have now is not your husband' (4:17f). Given the whole nature of the Gospel of John, it is very improbable that, after the depths plumbed in Christ's third utterance, he would now speak only in an outward way of the Samaritan woman's private life. As *fourth* utterance, this sentence about fetching her husband, has a pivotal position: what is seemingly only private and personal becomes transparent for a mystery. The Samaritan woman asked, 'Lord give me always this water!' But to be able to receive this water, which eternally stills the thirst of human longing, something more is required. The more soulful forces of the feminine must unite harmoniously with the more spiritually active powers of the masculine. Through all ages the union of man and woman has been felt as the most sublime metaphor for the inner harmonisation that is the goal of higher evolution, so that we rise to become truly human. The Samaritan woman should make herself worthy of receiving living water from Christ's mysterious well by informing her soulfulness with the configuring will-power of the I.

As the perfected bearer of this power of the I, Christ is the true bridegroom of the human soul. Thus, at the end of Chapter 3, which directly precedes this scene, the Baptist also gives Christ the mystery name of the 'bridegroom' (3:29). This quietly resonates here. The Samaritan woman has not yet accomplished the mystic wedding of the soul with the true bridegroom. 'The one you have now is not your husband' (4:18). Instead of this she has so far unworthily squandered the devotional power of the soul.

In this context the question of true worship now surfaces, the right manner of devotional prayer. Christ speaks of worshipping in spirit and in truth (4:21–24). He shows that he is entitled to urge this by revealing himself to be the Messiah. 'I am he who speaks with you' (4:26). Here, for the first time, we find the formulation *ego eimi* (I AM) which will then play such an important role in the Gospel of

John (for instance, in the seven I AM utterances*). We can feel it to be the secret name of Christ. Certainly, *ego eimi* also has the ordinary, mundane sense of 'I am he'; but in the Greek this 'he' does not figure, leaving just 'I am', in which the great I AM appears. This first *ego eimi*, spoken in the brilliance of the midday sun, is already accentuated by the fact that it forms the dramatic highpoint and conclusion of the whole exchange. Through its significant position as *seventh* utterance in a sevenfold sequence, it is elevated like a monstrance. Repeatedly we can see how the gospel points beyond what is expressly stated to moments of illumination through the configuring and patterning of particular words and utterances. (Today, mostly, we know only a much balder form of expression in 'dry words' that so easily deadens any sense of subtler meanings.)

In the structure of the exchange, the *three* is also apparent alongside the *seven*. Among other things, this is apparent in the Samaritan woman's use of the reverent word *Kyrie* (Lord) three times in addressing Christ (4:11, 15, 19).

She utters the first *Kyrie* (often translated as 'sir') in wonder and amazement: 'Lord, you have nothing to draw with and the well is deep. From where, then, do you have the living water?' He seems to her like a mysterious magician, 'Surely you are not greater than our father Jacob?'

While the 'Lord' of her first, wondering question springs from the faint and distant intimation of a mystery, the third arises from clear discernment. While the first is addressed to a magician, the third addresses a master of knowledge: 'Lord, I discern [*theōrō*] that you are a prophet.' And now she asks him about the proper way to worship.

The second *Kyrie* is spoken to him in the most directly human way: 'Lord, give me this water!' Here *Kyrie* does not so much address a worker of wonders, nor a master of knowledge, but rather the benevolent giver of sustaining life in whose love we trust.

The spiritual subtleties in the patterning of this exchange at the well can be seen in such 'small' aspects as this, each time colouring the same word *Kyrie* with different nuances and tones.

---

* As far as we know, Friedrich Rittelmeyer was the first to point to the sevenfold nature of these utterances (*Welterneuerung*, pp. 44ff). They are 6:35 (bread), 8:12 (light), 10:7 (door), 10:11 (shepherd), 11:25 (resurrection and life), 14:6 (way, truth, life), 15:1 (vine).

Light and judgment

The great 'I AM' that first appears in the exchange with the Samaritan woman, is above all the content of Chapter 8, the chapter of light and judgment, in which we find the next set of seven utterances. This dramatic and dynamic chapter encompasses three sets of exchanges:
1. 8:12–20.
2. 8:21–29.
3. 8:30–59.

At the beginning of the *first* exchange comes the utterance, 'I AM the light of the World.' The Pharisees object that such self-testimony is invalid. Christ justifies the truth of his testimony by referring to scripture: 'Is it not written in your law?'

Christ speaks three times in this context (8:12, 14–18, 19).

The character of the *second* exchange is marked by the grave utterance concerning 'dying in sins', which awaits human beings if they do not grasp with belief and knowledge the I AM manifesting in Christ.

Christ speaks four times in this exchange (8:21, 23f, 25f, 28).

The *third* exchange brings the great dispute with the Jews about their claim to have Abraham as their father. Here the Father principle succumbing in rigidity to the Adversary stands in contrast to the true Father-Son relationship.

Christ speaks seven times here (8:31f, 34–38, 39–41, 42–47, 49–51, 54–56, 58).

The three and the four of the first two exchanges together form a seven.

The Trinity is reflected in the triad of exchanges.

Firstly, in 8:12–20, we see the *Spirit*. This first section is of special brightness: 'I AM the light of the world.' In Christ's dispute with the Pharisees, it is a matter of justifying this witness and testimony of Christ's self-revelation. He wishes to persuade his opponents. He does not speak apodictically or authoritatively but tries to lead them to *insight:* 'In your law it is written ...' (8:17). In these few sentences the word 'know' plays an important tole (twice in 8:14, three times in 8:19). Christ founds the truth of his self-witness in knowledge, 'For I know where I came from and where I am going' (8:14). His I is the light of the world, it shines out in the brightest deliberation, in the clearest awareness of himself. Without this highest spirit-illumination of knowledge concerning where we are from and to where we are going, there is only a 'walking in darkness'.

In 8:20 the manner of his speech in this first exchange is expressly characterised: 'Jesus spoke these words in the treasury as he taught in the temple.'

Secondly, in the second exchange, Christ appears less as teacher than as *Saviour*. His speech is here determined by his Redeemer will. It is not now a matter of knowledge or lack of it, but of the *death of the soul or salvation*. The utterance 'I AM' stands here like a redeeming island in the midst of a deadly flood of sin. 'I said to you that you will die in your sins; for if you do not believe in the I AM, you will die in your sins' (8:24). In the same way that the I AM in 8:24 is connected with belief or faith, so in 8:28 it is connected with knowledge: 'When you have raised the Son of Man, then you will know that I AM.' This raising, as in 3:14 and 12:32, points to the death on the cross (12:33). The sacrificing death of Christ is what can save human beings from the death of the soul. This death on the cross is, however, a freely undergone death in a quite different sense from that misunderstood by the Jews ('surely he will not kill himself?' 8:22).

This whole section, 8:21–29, is pervaded by the intrinsic *Son* mystery of Christ, through to the last words that he always does those things which please the One who sent him (8:29).

Thirdly, the dispute only intensifies into implacable sharpness in the third passage, 8:30–59, which ends with the Jews picking up stones to force him to leave the temple. The fiercest opposition becomes apparent when the *Father* principle is in dispute. Christ disputes the Jews' claim to Abraham as their father. They wish to remain in the old Father principle and not progress to the Son. But according to a spiritual law, it is not permissible to play off an 'ancient good' against what is real, God-willed progress, for in such instances this 'ancient good' imperceptibly becomes something quite different in the hands of those who piously preserve it. It does not remain what it was, but succumbs to an evil power that enacts evil by its means. Thus the Jews believe they have kept faith with God and fail to see that this same

God is now manifesting in contemporary form in the figure of the Son. The tragedy occurs that the Adversary, Ahriman,* has come to occupy the place of God the Father. The rigid Father principle of the Jews, which has succumbed to Ahrimanic obduracy, and leads them to raise stones against the 'I AM', stands in opposition here to the true Father-Ground of the World who has sent this bearer of the 'I AM'. Abraham is a historical shadow image of this eternal Father: 'Before Abraham was, I AM' (8:58).

The whole, grand scenario of the dispute with the Jews in Chapter 8 begins and ends characteristically with the I AM. The first utterance is 'I AM the light of the world' (8:12); the last is 'Before Abraham was, I AM' (8:58). In comparing these two sentences we can also grasp how the moods of Spirit and Father are distinguished, whereas in the Son section the I AM, spoken twice and strikingly (without the pronoun 'he', 8: 24, 28), appears in connection with the death of the soul and the redeeming death on the cross.

The content of this great dispute in Chapter 8 could be encapsulated in three words that are intimately related to one another: *light – I – judgment*. These are three aspects of one and the same essential being. Friedrich Rittelmeyer has often pointed to the close relationship between light and I. The relationship between light and judgment is also clear, as, for instance in the Grimm fairy tale, 'The Bright Sun Brings it to Light'. The light-bringing I of Christ becomes – inevitably but inadvertently – a judgment upon the world (compare Jn 3:19). Because Christ comes as the true sun, he brings to light whatever is ungodly in humankind.

In all three sections, light, I and judgment are present, and yet they are differently accentuated. We might attempt the following concordance – albeit taken very elastically and unrigidly:

8:12–20	Spirit aspect	Light	(three utterances)
8:21–29	Son aspect	I	(four utterances)
8:30–59	Father aspect	Judgment	(seven utterances)

* As Lucifer is the spirit of the vanity of false light, so Ahriman is the spirit of hardening and petrification. Lucifer is a distortion of the Holy Spirit, and Ahriman of the Father.

Three and seven are interwoven in the structure. The triad of exchanges encompasses twice seven utterances of Christ (Lohmeyer mentions only the seven in 8:30–59), patterned as 3 + 4 + 7. Here too, the Father section appears as the weightiest in this context of crisis, since its seven here is self-contained and compact. The first seven is divided – though again not arbitrarily – into the three and four, in such a way that the higher, heavenly three is assigned to the light principle, and the lower four to earthly fate and tragedy.

The healing of the blind man

Closely related to the light and judgment chapter, is the healing of the blind man. This not only takes up the whole of Chapter 9 but its last scene extends into 10:21. It is a dramatic sequence of seven scenes (see H. Windisch* and Lohmeyer).
 1. The healing itself: 9:1–7
 2. The healed man and his neighbours: 9:8–12
 3. The healed man and the Pharisees: 9:13–17
 4. The parents of the healed man: 9:18–23
 5. The expulsion from the synagogue: 9:24–34
 6. Christ and the healed man: 9:35–39
 7. Christ and the Pharisees: 9:40–10:21

Three scenes (1, 4 and 7) unfold in the presence of Christ and four in his absence.

The healing of the blind as a work of illumination places Christ's deeds with special clarity into the great opposition between light and darkness. The battle between light and dark is the origin of all drama. There is deep justification, therefore, for the dramatic nature of the account of this particular miracle of light within the gospel.

The man blind from birth has received the light of Christ. What first occurred in his outward, bodily nature is ultimately realised inwardly too. The healed man is freed from a further and far more significant blindness towards Christ. His eyes are opened to the Son of God, whom he gradually comes to perceive: first he calls him the 'man whom they call Jesus' (9:11), then 'a prophet' (9:17), a 'man without

---

* 'Der johanneische Erzählungsstil,' *Eucharisterion* 1923 II, p. 181.

sin', a God-fearing man, a man who 'does God's will' (9:31). Then he calls him one who is 'from God' (9:33). To this degree he himself attains knowledge of Christ. This process of dawning realisation is crowned by the grace of Christ's self-revelation as the 'Son of God':* 'You have seen him, and the one speaking with you is he' (9:35–37).

This increasing *light of knowledge* is accompanied by a second process: the *growth of consciousness of self.* The healed man must assert himself against ever stronger resistance and opposition. First he must deal with his neighbours, affirming himself in the face of their doubt about his identity: 'I am he' (9:9). Then the Pharisees interrogate him with increasing hostility. His parents distance themselves from him, withdraw, and let him deal himself with what is happening: 'Ask him yourselves. He is of age. He will speak for himself.' (9:21). The Pharisees try to shout him down him with their overweening authority. When this achieves nothing, they insult him and expel him from the synagogue.

The phrase 'I am he' initiates a process of development of the I. The healed man learns to say 'I' and to stand firm in the face of powers that wish to crush him. We can seek the beginning of this narrative further back: in the healing itself where Christ calls upon the man to exert his own activity (similar to the way in which he says to the lame man, 'Do you wish to be healed?'). He requires the man's collaboration: 'Go, wash in the Pool of Siloam' (9:7). In fact we can see the beginning of this whole process of I development in a still subtler occurrence: in the gift of Christ-light. Because Christ himself is in essence the 'light of the world' (8:12, 9:5) he can implant the eyes as organs of light within the man born blind. He gives of his light being; the man's newly opened eyes are light of this light. In this gift of light lies also, ultimately, the I-awakening power.

There is an intimate connection between *light* and *I.* Light is as it were 'externalised' I, while the I is 'internalised' light.

Along with a false, eye-opening light, fallen Adam received from Lucifer (the light-bearer) also the glittering, false I. What occurred there as a kind of distortion is accomplished in pure, divine truth by Christ. He gives true light and therefore the true I.

And now it is clear why the trajectory of developing knowledge

---

* At 9:35 some ancient manuscripts have 'Son of Man', others have 'Son of God'.

(growing light) coincides with that of personality development (growing I). Both lines of development have their common origin in 'I AM the light of the world'. In both cases the seed of Christ-light germinates in one who was previously blind. And both these processes, the growth of light as well as the growth of the I, unfold in battling encounter with opposition. In fact, they owe their forward progress altogether to such resistance. Without the hostility of the Pharisees, the healed man would have stayed at the level of knowledge embodied in his statement 'a man whom they call Jesus'. If the Pharisees had not expelled him from the synagogue, he would never have become able to experience the loneliness that follows as consequence of the phrase 'I am', which, in exchanges with his neighbours, previously fell so easily and unthinkingly from his lips. It is surely no accident that precisely this man who is 'illumined' by Christ is the only one in the Gospel of John to utter the *ego eimi* (I AM), that festive formulation uttered otherwise only by Christ himself. The phrase here is only the simple, everyday assertion of identity, 'I am he,' (in the Greek the phrase in both senses lacks the pronoun 'he'). John scarcely uses this sacred utterance without it also implying the great 'I AM'.

We saw at the beginning that there are four scenes (2–5) in this drama in which Christ is not present. These are at the same time the scenes in which the healed man has to wage his battle against hostility. He would not have been able to draw upon the powers he needs in this battle, which is what properly initiates processes of increasing light and development of the I, if the Christ had not left him alone. There is significance in his being left to himself – to this self within which the seed of light germinates.

These thoughts give us a foundation for understanding the quality of four in the scenes from which Christ is absent. Four – the number of earthly things, of the cross, of tension, edges and corners, of all things square.

At the end of the four scenes without Christ, the healed man faces the consequences of his 'I am' statement. He is entirely abandoned and isolated, alone with himself.

But the important thing is that this does not mark the end of the story of the I. The lower four of the conflict scenes is the foundation for a *higher three*. These are the three scenes (1, 6, 7) that are filled with the light of Christ's mercy.

In Scene 1, Christ plants the seed of light by healing the blind man. He appears again in Scene 4, 'finding' the lonely man and mercifully revealing himself to him. The healing of blindness is completed in the man's recognition and worshipping of the Son of God: '"You have seen him, and the one speaking with you is he." Then the man said, "Lord, I believe," and he worshipped him.' (9:37f).

Developing knowledge culminates in Christ knowledge. Belief here is not in conflict with knowledge. The word tells us only that knowledge finds its full resonance in the life of feeling and will.

The process of development of the I culminates in the man's willing devotion to the Son of God: 'he worshipped him'.

If we compare the two scenes with Christ, 1 and 6, it becomes apparent that the first unfolds more in the realm of the outward bodily nature, in the public domain. Scene 6 is a much more intimate event that transpires only between Christ and the healed man. The divine Son reveals himself to the human being. This intimate event, since it belongs to a higher level, surpasses the work of illumination first accomplished in the natural, bodily realm. On the other hand, at the same time it consecrates and dignifies the natural realm as a sphere of parable (the 'opening of eyes' as metaphor for insight).

The third scene with Christ, Scene 7, remains fully in the sphere of pure inwardness. Certainly, Christ turns to the Pharisees, and judges their arrogant form of religious practice, which has become malign. But this is not the key thing in this final scene. Christ does not so much battle here with darkness as discern himself, rather, against its background. The darkness here stands only as a foil to light's self-knowledge.

The dispute with the Pharisees culminates in Christ's self-acknowledgement. The Pharisees 'did not know what it was that he was saying to them' (10:6). They remain outside the sublime monologue that the eternal light holds with itself. Christ delves here ever deeper into the light-filled chasm of his own being. 'I AM the door', 'I AM the good shepherd'.

If we survey these three scenes with Christ – first, the bodily healing; second, the Son of God's intimate self-revelation to the healed man; third, the growing self-realisation of the eternal light – we cannot help also observing the Trinitarian quality here.

It may be taken as sublime confirmation of the affinity mentioned earlier between light and I that precisely in these Johannine light chapters, Christ's 'I AM' revelations accumulate. 'I AM the light of the world' (8:12) – this is 'quoted' again as Christ begins to heal the blind man: 'As long as I am in the world, I AM the light of the world' (9:5). After completing the healing: 'I AM the door' (10:7, 9). 'I AM the good shepherd' (10:11, 14).

These three 'I AM' utterances are likewise subject to the Trinitarian law.

The door – the Christ himself is the 'Portal of Initiation', in destined, necessary, implacable inevitability.

The good shepherd – the Christ gives his life for those who are his. He is the self-sacrificing Son who, in all beauty and perfection, realises the consecrated aims of the Father, surrendering his life and taking it up again (10:17f).

The light of the world – the Christ recognises those who are his and offers himself to their recognition, he lives in the brightness of the Holy Spirit.

Within these multiple layers of the narrative of the healing of the blind man, Christ speaks seven times.

In the first scene he says to the disciples who ask him whose fault it is that the man is blind, 'Neither his … nor his parents …' (9:3). Then, to the blind man, 'Go, wash in the Pool of Siloam' (9:7).

Scene 6 contains three utterances: the question to the healed man, 'Do you believe in the Son of God?' (9:35); the self-revelation, 'You have seen him, and the one speaking with you is he' (9:37); and the grave word of judgment, 'For judgment I have come …' (9:39) – light – I – judgment.

Scene 7 shows Christ in his dispute with the Pharisees, which leads him to the sublime 'I AM' proclamations. His speech is structured as two utterances: 'Jesus said to them, "If you were blind" … Jesus spoke this parable to them, but they did not know what it was that he was saying to them' (9:41–10:6). 'Then said Jesus to them again, "Truly, truly I say to you, I AM the door … This command I received from my Father"' (10:7–18).

These seven utterances of Christ give coherence to the whole extensive context from 9:1 to 10:21. (The exclamation by the people at 10:21, 'Can a demon open the eyes of the blind?' again elicits the parable of the good shepherd in relation to the healing of the blind).

51. SEVEN IN THE UTTERANCES OF CHRIST

Centrally amongst these seven utterances stands the fourth, the real healing of blindness, in which the intuitive flash of recognition dawns: 'You have seen him, and the one speaking with you is he.' There is a discernible resonance between the first and seventh utterance. In the first, Christ 'quotes' something he said previously, essentially invoking it again: 'As long as I am in the world, I AM the light of the world' (9:5). In the seventh utterance this 'I AM' sounds once more and reverberates further: 'I AM the door.' 'I AM the good shepherd.'

The passion

In the context of the passion story, Christ makes three times seven utterances:

1. The washing of the feet (13:1–30).
2. The arrest and interrogation (18:1–27).
3. The drama of Pilate and Golgotha (18:28–19:16).

(If we exclude the self-contained Farewell Discourse, the true passion story, beginning at 13:1, contains this three times seven patterning.)

The *washing of the feet* displays the rigorous structure of a ritual. The seven patterning is especially clear here as 3 + 1 + 3, in a symmetry that adheres to the pattern of a seven-branched candelabra.

The fourth utterance of Christ stands dominant in the middle, giving the 'interpretation' roughly in the same way as, in ancient mystery rites, the *legomenon* (words) were added to the *dromenon* (actions). This central utterance stands in the middle between two triads. Three of these are addressed to Peter, and three to the betrayer.

The symmetry is apparent from the scheme below (1 and 7, 2 and 6, 3 and 5). The third and fifth concern the betrayal; the second and sixth both involve, as it were, a sacred action by Christ characterised by very personal attentiveness; the first and seventh both speak of a *doing* whose scope the disciples do not yet discern.

The John passion in the narrower sense begins after the end of the Farewell Discourse and the High Priestly Prayer, with the departure from the room of the Last Supper at 18:1.

The seven utterances at the washing of the feet

1	2	3	4	5	6	7
What I do, you do not know now, but you will understand after these things (13:7)	Unless I wash you, you have no part with me (13:8)	Those who have bathed … You are pure, but not all. (For he knew who would betray him) (13:10f)	Do you understand what I have done to you? … I have given you an example … (13:12–20)	One among you will betray me (13:21)	He it is to whom I shall give this morsel after I have dipped it (13:26)	What you are about to do, do quickly. (But no one at the table understood why he said this to him) (13:27f)

The second seven passion utterances of Christ are contained within the context of his *arrest and interrogation.*

Christ emerges from the Garden of Gethsemane. John does not describe the terrible, prayerful battle he wages, nor his blood-perspiring struggle in abandonment. He describes the majesty of one who remains victorious. The words 'I AM (he)', under whose force his pursuers sink to the ground, would not have the same magical, thunder-and-lightning power without Christ's preceding prayers in Gethsemane.

Twice Christ asks, 'Who do you seek?' (18:4, 7).
Twice he speaks the word 'I AM (he)' (18:5, 8).
These four utterances are joined by three single utterances:
To Peter, who draws his sword (18:11).
To the High Priest (18:20f).
To the soldier who strikes him (18:23).

In the same way that the first utterances of the Logos incarnated on earth in Chapter 1 were festively configured by seven, so also are his last words on earth. Though John only gives three of the last seven words from the cross, these three utterances augment Christ's *utterances before Pilate,* thus making seven.

The account of the interrogation before Pilate is a grandiose drama in the Gospel of John. Seven scenes arise here through Pilate's coming and going. Pilate alternates between negotiating with the

51. SEVEN IN THE UTTERANCES OF CHRIST

crowd standing outside his palace and speaking within to the prisoner Christ. There are four outside and three inside scenes.

The outside scenes:
1. 18:28–32
3. 18:38–40
5. 19:4–7
7. 19:13–16

The inside scenes:
2. 18:33–38
4. 19:1–3
6. 19:8–12

The content of these scenes is symmetrical like the pattern of the seven-branched candelabra.

Scenes 1 and 7, as outer scenes, depict the physical and judicial situation, accusation and judgment.

Scenes 2 and 6 are the two interior ones in which Christ speaks. To the Roman who acknowledges only earthly reality, first he speaks of the nature of the upper world, his kingdom: it is 'not of this world'. Then he speaks about the authority of Pilate's office that is in truth given to him from 'above'.

Scenes 3 and 5, once again outdoor scenes, contrast sinful humanity (Barabbas the murderer; 'Crucify him!') with the guiltless Christ as the truly human being and Son of God. Three times in these two scenes Pilate states 'I find no guilt in him' (18:38, 19:4, 6).

The central (interior) Scene 4, standing alone in the middle, contains the flogging and crowning with thorns as well as the robing in a purple cloak. These events in the form of certain initiation practices, stand at this central point of the organism of seven.

This potent structure of the Pilate drama contains four utterances by Christ, of which three belong to Scene 2 and one to Scene 6:

Scene 2
'Do you say this of yourself ... ?' (18:34).
'My kingdom is not of this world ...'(18:36).
'You say that ... everyone who is of the truth ...' (18:37).

Scene 6
'You would have no authority over me ...' (19:11).

These four, together with the three words from the cross, form the last seven.

52

TRINITARIAN FORMULATIONS AND REITERATIONS

It is clear, among other things from the reiteration of formulaic turns of phrase in the Gospel of John (which theologians have often remarked upon), that it was written out of a sense of the whole. The degree to which this holism of the gospel is an organic configuration is apparent in the fact that such reiterations are almost invariably informed by sacred number. A few specific instances can illustrate this.

'The time of Passover was near'

At the beginning of spring, the sun enters the first sign of the zodiac, Aries. New growth needs to be sanctified by sacrifice. The sacrifice of the lamb (Aries) maintains the connection between new resurgence and the divine.

Golgotha is the epitome of all spring sacrifice. The winter of humanity is overcome and a new, God-united evolution instigated. Everything that 'heathen' peoples celebrated as an annually recurring consecration of nature's new life, and that the people of Israel celebrated as a single historical spring experience (the awakening and liberation of the people from Egypt), was nothing but a prefiguring of the great Passover festival of humanity: the sacrifice of the Lamb at Golgotha.

The whole John Gospel is oriented to this incomparable spring sacrifice. From the mighty gesturing words of the Baptist, 'Behold the Lamb of God', through to the crucifixion, in which ancient words about the Passover lamb – 'You shall not break any bone of it' – were fulfilled, everything circles around this Passover mystery.

Almost the whole Johannine narrative unfolds in the context of festivals. The three years of Christ's working are encompassed by four Passover feasts. Three Passover festivals (2:23; 5:1; 6:4) precede the fulfilment of the last. As Johannes Jeremias credibly suggests, all narrative up to 6:65 can be grouped around these three Passover festivals. What follows in 7:1 to 10:21 belongs to the Festival of Tabernacles of the last, third year. This autumn festival is followed at 10:22 by the Temple Dedication at Christmas time. Then, with the story of Lazarus, we are already approaching the last and final Passover (11:55). The festival context of the gospel, therefore, is: first Passover, 2:23; second Passover 5:1 (while no direct reference is made to Passover, its character is clear from the context); third Passover 6:4; autumn festival 7:2; Christmas 10:22; last Passover 11:55. We can feel how each of the preceding three Passover festivals prefigures the forthcoming Mystery of Golgotha and Easter, how this casts its shadow, or brilliance, backward from the future.

Three times the formulation 'The time of Passover was near' recurs in the Gospel of John: 2:13, 6:4 and 11:55. The number of Passover festivals, as such, would be four. Yet these references are not there to offer chronology but to signify something particular by this triad, which is distributed with a certain symmetry between the seven miracles: the first, the fourth and the seventh.*

The first miracle occurs during the *marriage at Cana*. Christ dispenses wine. Yet his 'hour is not yet come' (2:4). Only after three years, once again at Passover, will it arrive. But in the mood of this first Passover festival, it is prophetically prefigured. Here he dispenses *wine* and three years later he will dispense the true wine that 'has been kept back until now': his *blood*. Thus the sentence 'The time of Passover was near' has a deeper sense than merely chronological. It intimates the 'approach' of the Passover mystery. The blood sacrifice of Golgotha shimmers in the prefiguring wedding wine.

The fourth and middle miracle of the seven is the *feeding of the five thousand*. Here he gives bread. 'The time of Passover was near.' The

---

* The marriage at Cana, the healing of the official's son at Capernaum, the paralytic at Bethesda, the feeding of five thousand, the walking on water, the healing of the blind man, the raising of Lazarus.

dispensing of bread becomes prophetic of the Eucharistic *bread,* as does the great address in Chapter 6 about the bread of life that 'comes from heaven'. The bread that he will give a year later is his *body.* The feeding is a prophetic event at Easter time, hence the 'closeness' of the Passover mystery.

The formulation comes for the third time as the last Passover festival begins, the one of final fulfilment, accompanying the seventh miracle when *Lazarus* is raised from death. The miracle stands in closest proximity to this last Passover, and is already in some way integrated into the Christ events themselves, as Beckh points out. Thus, through the recurring litany of references to the Passover festival, the deep sacrificial context of the miracles becomes palpable.

The closeness of Passover can be felt in a different way in each of these three passages. The identical formulation nevertheless has a different resonance each time it recurs. At the *marriage at Cana,* the far-off peal of bells of the coming mystery chimes quietly but also most prophetically. The wedding of spirit and soul to be celebrated as the perfecting of humanity, is figured here in prophetic image. In the juxtaposition of water and wine is reflected the two kinds of baptism: with water and, in future, with the fire of the spirit. The dispensing of wine at Cana is something like a prophecy of the future outpouring of the *Spirit* in tongues of flame.* 'On the third day there was a wedding ...'

The *feeding of the five thousand* with bread and fish, upon the plentiful green grass (Jn 6:10; Mk 6:39) announces the 're-enlivening of dying earth existence' (words of the Creed of The Christian Community). It is entirely filled with the life-giving 'etheric' forces of the divine *Son.* The Last Supper is 'close' in this feeding narrative. Close, but not yet present in its full reality. With all its proximity to the Last Supper, this feeding is still a prefiguring occurrence. The Last Supper has not yet descended fully to the earth, and is still as if delicately veiled.

Compared to these two events, the *raising of Lazarus* has the character of fully real occurrence. Certainly it is also to a large

---

* This does not contradict the aspect highlighted before of wine as the blood of Christ. To receive the blood of Christ means to experience the fire baptism of the spirit.

degree prophetic: the awakening of a humanity that has succumbed to death. But this prophesy is rooted far deeper in reality than the preceding miracles. In the dispensing of wine and bread, what is thereby prophesied does not yet immerse itself fully in the prophetic occurrence but hovers over it as a far-off intimation. At the wedding at Cana, this 'hovering' quality is clearest. A failure to notice this has led often to the most trivial and mundane interpretations of the story. In the feeding of the five thousand, what is prophesied lives much more strongly in its prefiguring. Here the 'closeness' of Passover is much more discernible. The raising of Lazarus is a fully 'real' symbol, a prefiguring reality. *Est quod significat:* it *is* what it signifies, the overcoming of death. Here the victorious power of Christ is enacted, in the face of gravestone and decay, upon death itself.

Over the wedding at Cana shimmers a fine and delicate *Spirit* future.

The evening feeding with bread and fish is like an intimating, twilit dream of the etheric Christ, of the *Son* who, descending from the heavens, gives life to the world.

From the cave-grave at Bethany comes the silence of the eternal *Father* majesty of death's mystery.

Nicodemus

The Gospel of John speaks of Nicodemus three times. These three passages are:
1. The great night-time conversation (3:1–21).
2. His appearance in the circle of Pharisees (7:50f).
3. His involvement in the burial of Christ (19:39).

The *night-time conversation* and *burial* appear in magnificent polarity. In the conversation, Christ is the sublime *teacher* who instructs the teacher of Israel. At the burial, Christ is the one who has entered the abyss of *silence*. The conversation unfolds in the body-free etheric heights of world-encompassing thoughts; it is an encounter in the Holy Spirit. The burial is hard, dumb, dark, earth reality. Whereas in the conversation we have the sense of a sunrise at the end of it, after the darkness of night (the word 'light' appears with striking frequency towards the end of the conversation), the burial, which occurs in the gathering gloom of the evening, is a prelude to the impenetrable dark night of the grave.

We can put it like this: the conversation is a *Spirit* experience, while the burial is a *Father* experience for Nicodemus. Fine connections play between them. What appeared in the first occurrence as thought – entering the mother's body again, rebirth – becomes bodily reality in the second. The earth is surely, after all, a womb shrouded in night from which the body of light is to emerge on Easter morning.

Corresponding to the intimate relationship between night-time conversation and burial is the fact that at 19:39 the evangelist refers back to 3:2: 'Nicodemus, who had first come to him by night.' It becomes ever clearer as we occupy ourselves more thoroughly with the Gospel of John that such backward references are not memory aids for forgetful readers but fine spiritual bridges.

When Nicodemus is mentioned a second time at 7:50, appearing within the circle of *Pharisees,* we again find a reference to his earlier appearance: '... who had come to him before'. At 19:39 the word is *proton*, or 'at first' and at 7:50 *proteron* or 'earlier'. Thus the second time (7:50) is precisely distinguished from the third (19:39). The evangelist attentively distinguishes between the second and third reference, giving each its own quality.

If the better version of the text at 7:50 is (as is very probable) the one that does *not* contain 'at night', then a subtlety would exist in this seemingly small matter. Mention of that spirit-illumined night at 3:2 has its profound meaning precisely for the burial at 19:39. The conversation – which occurred within the mood of the Passover festival (2:23) – surfaces again three years later. The special relationship between conversation and burial would be more strongly accentuated by omitting a mention of the night motif at 7:50.

At 7:50 the reference back is also not meant in an external sense, and yet it is not as profoundly significant as at 19:39. Here it is a matter of the courage involved in confronting the Pharisees for perhaps the first time. The courageous affirmation of individuality is now more important than a connection with the deeper mysteries, whether articulated in the conversation or silently present in the burial. The division and crisis presaged in the conversation here begins to be realised. In the circle of Pharisees, Nicodemus makes a statement that can be regarded as a deed. His 'deed of truth' comes to light: he emerges from his unspoken knowledge and here, clearly for the first time, breaks the spell of silence of his secret discipleship. In the tense situation that prevails there, his reticent words do have the character of standing up for Christ. This self-sundering from the 'group soul' of the council (to which expression is given at Nicodemus' very first appearance: *'we* know that you are a teacher, sent by God,' 3:2) is for Nicodemus an *I* event, a *Son* experience.

The three references to Nicodemus are thus oriented to the Trinity in the sequence Spirit – Son – Father.

The three prayers to the Father

John recounts three prayers by Christ:
1. At the grave of Lazarus (11:41f).
2. After the entry into Jerusalem, when the Greeks approach him and he is shaken by the premonition of his approaching death (12:27f).*
3. The High Priestly Prayer (17).

(The three words from the cross given by John, like two of the three recounted by Luke, do not as such have the character of prayer.)

At the *grave of Lazarus*, 'Jesus raised his eyes and spoke: Father, I thank you that you have heard me. I knew that you always hear me, but I said this for the benefit of the people standing around, so that they may believe that you have sent me' (11:41f).

This prayer is for the benefit of those witnessing it. This does not mean it is a 'show-prayer' in the disparaging sense, as has sometimes been thought. But it is, in a far higher sense, a 'show-prayer'. Christ

---

* The fact that, on page 339, the prayer to the Father (12:27f) is differently assigned, does not contradict what is described here. Here, these two verses are seen in the context of the three prayers of Christ to the Father as recounted by John, within which they occupy the 'Son' position. But there the question is how the whole section 12:20–36 relates to the context of the address to the Greeks, 12:27f. Within *that* triad, the utterance stands in the 'Father' position. Such assignments hold true only within a living dynamic: they are not 'static' but, indeed, dynamic. Perhaps, rather than speaking of 'position' here, we should use the term 'function'.

allows the people there to witness the relationship that exists between him and the Father. This aims to invoke consciousness in those around him – 'for the benefit of the people standing around, so that they may believe that you have sent me'. This prayer does not create new realities between Father and Son, it is not 'dramatic'. It only expresses and reveals to those who behold it, what already exists. It *shows* them this unclouded, clear view of reciprocal knowledge. Between Father and Son the pure light element of the *Holy Spirit* holds sway here.

This unclouded knowledge is clouded in the *second prayer,* which has often been seen as a Johannine parallel to the battle in Gethsemane. Whereas the first prayer has the undisputed, heavenly, clear tranquillity of knowledge, the second has the character of *struggle.* It therefore does indeed have an affinity with Christ's praying in the Garden of Gethsemane, as recounted by the synoptics.

Christ does not speak this prayer 'for those standing around'. More than ever he prays for his own sake.* It is like an exemplification of the statement 'I sanctify myself for them.'

'Now my soul is shaken, and what shall I say? "Father, save me from this hour"? No, for this purpose I came to this hour. Father, glorify your name!' (12:27f).

Instead of blissful resting in the certainty of mutual knowledge, we have here uncertainty, hesitancy, a back-and-forth. This prayer wrests itself from Christ's entirely personal, truly human life of soul. The words at Gethsemane 'my soul is troubled to the point of death' (Mk 14:34) are prefigured here.

The hour has come, the destined moment of the Son. After this first 'human' hesitancy, he battles his way through to upholding the great, pre-birth resolve; he reiterates his mission: 'But for this purpose I came to this hour.' 'Father, save me' is transformed into 'Father, glorify your name'.

Here the Son prays on his own behalf, battling for the dignity to rightly fulfil his destiny.

The dialogue form is apt for the dramatically dynamic character of this prayer. Only in this second prayer, intrinsically of the 'Son', does the Father's answer follow immediately.

---

* The answer from God (12:30) relates to it becoming audible, not to the answer itself.

'A voice came from heaven, "I have glorified it, and will glorify it again"' (12:28).

Prayer is here, more than usual, a dialogue between I and Thou. Unfolding in address and response, it makes the I and Thou most clearly manifest.

These two prayers, 11:41 and 12:27, are preludes to the third and most sublime, the *High Priestly Prayer,* which Christ prays in direct proximity to death. But his inner struggle in expectation of this end stands in the second prayer, 12:27. Here, in Chapter 17, the victory, the inner certainty of resurrection, ascension and final transfiguration is already prefigured. Although Gethsemane and Golgotha still await him, this prayer is already a retrospective 'epilogue'.

As in the first prayer (11:41) he looks up to heaven. In the first: 'Jesus lifted up his eyes'. In this last: 'He lifted up his eyes to heaven and spoke'. Looking up is common to both the first and third prayer. In the second, significantly, it is lacking at the beginning; for this second prayer, uttered *de profundis,* begins under a heaven obscured. Only through the power of prayer does vision clear, calling down the voice from heaven. In the High Priestly Prayer, the perfected tranquillity of clear-sighted vision holds sway again. Death is now no longer something dramatic and troubling, something that creates inner turbulence. Here, in complete, mirror-like calmness of the soul, it is revealed in monumental *majesty* as 'going to the Father'.* This prayer is entirely spoken to the *Father,* to a greater degree than the other two prayers, though they also call on the Father. For here, the light of God to whom Christ prays shines most vividly upon him as he does so.

And so it may be said that the distinctive character of the three divine aspects is revealed one after another in these three prayers: Spirit – Son – Father.

This Trinitarian pattern also continues within each separate prayer. Each is in turn subdivided in three within itself. Let us look again at the *Lazarus prayer:*

---

* Compare Steiner, *The Gospel of John in Relation to the Other Gospels,* lecture of July 6, 1909.

> Father, I thank you that you have heard me.
> I knew that you always hear me,
> but I said this for the benefit of the people standing around,
> so that they may believe that you have sent me. (11:41f)

1. The word 'Father' at the beginning of the prayer, spoken at the open grave of Lazarus, is of particular vehemence and grandeur. In overcoming death, Christ affirms the utterance 'I and the Father are one', which precedes the Lazarus narrative (10:30). The inner movement in the first line is directed entirely to the *Father*, to whom rises the Son's prayer of thanks *(eucharisto)*.

2. While the first line moves away from the Son towards the Father, and is entirely subject to the word 'Father', the emphasis in the second line lies in the 'I' of the Son. The word 'I', *ego,* is accentuated at its beginning. From moving in thankful surrender towards the Father, the *Son* returns to his own world, to the tranquillity of his intrinsic Son consciousness: 'I knew that you always hear me.'

3. The third sentence of this 'Spirit' prayer, is – if we can put it like this – assigned to the *Spirit,* whose quality announces itself most strongly here. Whereas the praying I joins with the Father at the beginning, then rests within itself, so now it looks to the human beings in whose consciousness something should be engendered. The 'I knew' is now followed by 'so that they may believe'. In this final sentence the 'meaning' of this first prayer is revealed. The I of Christ is the centre around which closes the circle of the people standing around *(peri)*. This 'circle' of people which takes possession of the Son mystery of Christ, is the seed of the Church. Before this portion of humanity, the union of Father and Son is made visible, is 'shown'.

The same triad is clearly apparent in the *second prayer,* which proceeds from the words, 'Now my soul is shaken, and what shall I say?'

> Father, save me from this hour.
> No, for this purpose I came to this hour.
> Father, glorify your name! (12:27f)

1. As in the Lazarus prayer, there is firstly a movement here towards

the *Father*. The one who has descended from heaven trembles before the opening abyss of earth existence. 'If the seed does not fall into the earth and die' (12:24). Christ himself is the light-seed. He is seized by fear at the 'quite other' earthly world that is alien to him. 'Now my soul is shaken.' This is reminiscent of the utterance in Luke, 'But I have a baptism to be baptised with, and how I am constrained until it is fulfilled' (Lk 12:50). The beginning of this prayer is a fleeing to the Father, the search for a refuge.

This prayer has often been trivially misunderstood. The plea, 'Father, save me from this hour' is not there simply to be dropped again and 'corrected'. This first plea has its full justification in the overall dynamic. It is not the brief entertaining of a possibility which is then pushed away. Taking refuge in the Father is the prerequisite for the second line where Christ takes hold of himself once more. The plea is prayed in true earnestness. It is heard, too, but differently. The granting of the prayer consists in the Son finding his way back into his own I out of the Father. He is 'saved' from this hour, not by being lifted out of it but by receiving the strength to go through it.

2. In the 'intermediate space' between the first and the second line, the prayer is heard. The flight to the Father becomes a new grasp of Christ's pre-existence and the great incarnation resolve made then. 'For this purpose I came to this hour.' This is something like a new Son birth, a new, strengthened emergence of the *Son* out of the Father into whom he had cast himself, into whom he had been subsumed, in the first plea.

3. And so now the plea can appear transformed in the third line. It is reborn in the Holy Spirit. 'Father, glorify your name.' Here Christ's reaching beyond himself is achieved. Here all personal soul fear vanishes for the sake of the greater revelation of God. Here is complete self-forgetting: the soul is filled only with one concern: to multiply God's revelation. Here the prayer becomes entirely light. The 'name' of God is the epitome of his revelation. It is both the Godhead revealed and known to himself ('I AM, that is my name') and also the existence of God in the consciousness of those who know him. Through the sacrifice at Golgotha, towards which Christ's whole life of sacrifice moves, the name of God is brought to brighter luminosity. The veil before the holiest inner sanctum is rent, and the inmost

being of the Godhead is divulged. 'Glorify your name' – with this, the prayer immerses itself in the brilliance of the *Holy Spirit.*

Despite its brevity, this second prayer is a wondrous Trinitarian organism that encompasses the secret of transformation. The Son moves from the Father to the Spirit.

The threefold nature of the *High Priestly Prayer* has often been remarked upon:
1. 17:1–5.
2. 17:6–19.
3. 17:20–26.

Friedrich Rittelmeyer speaks in detail about this orientation to the Trinity.* Once again, we find here the sequence Father – Son – Spirit, which we saw to be the same in all of Christ's three Johannine prayers.

Pre-existence

The very first words of the Prologue announce the eternal being of the Logos that existed before the world came into being. The evangelist's testimony is followed by that of the Baptist (1:15–30) and finally by the testimony of Christ. To see how pre-existence unfolds in the consciousness of the Johannine Christ is a divine and exalted spectacle. Following the motif of 'coming down from heaven', which forms a kind of prelude (3:13; 6:33), pre-existent consciousness first comes to clear expression in the prophecy of the ascension: 'Then what if you should see the Son of Man ascending to *where he was before?*' (6:62). Here, however, pre-existence is still couched in very general terms, as an existence previously in the heavens.

In what follows, knowledge of such pre-existence is now expanded into various directions of time and space. This is done in a triad of statements:
1. 'Truly, truly, I say to you, before Abraham was I AM' (8:58).
2. 'And now, O Father, glorify me with your own self with the glory that I had with you before the world existed' (17:5).

---

* Rittelmeyer, *Briefe über das Johannes-Evangelium,* pp. 258ff.

3. 'Father, I want those you have given me to also be with me where I AM; that they may see my glory you have given me because you loved me before the foundation of the world' (17:24).

The words about *Abraham* are spoken in the context of a sharp dispute with the Jews. They seek to crush and destroy the new with the old, and invoke their descent from Abraham to do so. Abraham is the epitome of the time-honoured age of the Patriarchs. Precisely in this dispute, the I AM living in Christ becomes ever more conscious of the depths of its own being, and raises itself in its divine sovereignty. It knows itself to be superordinate to this revered *past* – firstly in as much as it preceded it in time, 'before Abraham was'. But this temporal pre-existence is not the only thing that matters here. The superiority is not one merely rooted in a past that lies still further back in time. Christ does not compare himself to Abraham only in terms of earlier or later but he belongs altogether to an incomparably different level of existence.

Abraham *was*. In the same way, the Prologue says of the Baptist, 'there *was* a man'. The Logos itself by contrast never began, but was 'in the beginning'.* It is existence itself. There is a similar clear distinction here in Christ's words about Abraham: Abraham 'arose' or 'became', whereas 'I AM'. Through his eternal being Christ precedes all evolving existence. The 'before' becomes pre-temporality, super-temporality. This is why Christ does not say, as we might have expected, 'before Abraham was, I was' but 'I AM'.

The words in the High Priestly Prayer about *glorifying* – 'And now, O Father, glorify me' – return to the festive beginning of the prayer: 'Father, the hour has come' (17:1). This time, a consciousness of pre-existence before the world began does not relate to the past but to the *present*. The 'hour' which can in a special sense be called *the* hour, is the great moment when the Son takes his passage through the mystery of death. 'And now ...'

---

* In English translations of the Bible there is rarely a distinction made between *ēn* (was, from *eimi*, to be) and *egeneto* or *genesthai* (became, from *ginomai*, to come into being). In the Prologue 'there was a man sent from God' is literally 'there (be)came a man ...'

This time, it is no longer a question of the eternal being rendering itself different and distinct in all its inherent sublimity from temporal evolution. Having first clearly distinguished 'becoming' and 'being', they can once again be reconciled: for this is, after all, the grandeur of the 'hour' – that eternal existence and temporal occurrence essentially engage with each other. In the same way, the Prologue first keeps separate and distinct the Logos that 'was' *(ēn)* and the man who 'arose' or 'became' *(egeneto)*, but then goes on to bridge this divide in the words, 'and the Logos *became* flesh'. The eternal shines out in time, the imperishable within the transient, when the 'hour' of the Son has arrived. In view of this hour, he reflects upon his pre-existent glory and prays that it may stream into the 'now' with its whole, radiant fullness of light.

The third statement has finality. At the end of the High Priestly Prayer, the visionary gaze of Christ is focused upon the humanity that will belong to him *in future*. 'I want those you have given me to also be with me where I AM' This future union with humankind only becomes reality in the light of the Holy Spirit, which pervades this community in Pentecost fashion and brings to human perception the glory of Christ's revelation: 'that they may see my glory'.

The primary and archetypal divine love that sustains this all was invested in Christ 'before the foundation of the world'. It is pre-existent, pre-temporal, eternal – truly it is 'love in the Holy Spirit'.

The three utterances about pre-existence follow in wonderful succession. In the words about Abraham, about glorifying, and about humanity, we see Christ's consciousness of the originating, pre-existing realm grow and unfold in glorious fashion.

It raises itself royally upright, as Christ becomes conscious of his inherent majesty in opposition to the past.

It consecrates the present hour of destiny as the wedding of time and eternity.

It finds its crowning glory in a vision of the future of humanity, of the great community of love, where the love from primordial beginnings comes full circle in the love of fulfilment.

The unfolding of consciousness of pre-existence in these three utterances occurs in as organic a way as the growth of a flower through the developmental stages of root, leaf and blossom. The reverent, loving gaze of John beholds the wondrous flower of this consciousness grow and blossom in Christ.

'Where I am ...'

Christ says to the 'Jews' that they have no access to the world in which his I dwells: 'You will seek me and not find me, and where I AM you cannot come' (7:34).

To the disciples, however, he accords this entry into the lofty world of his I AM three times, in this way revealing the Trinity.

> Whoever serves me must follow me:
> and where I AM, my servant also will be.
> If anyone serves me, the Father will honour him. (12:26)

1. The disciples appear here initially as 'servants'. Service is the precondition for being raised aloft to the pure heights in which the Christ-I breathes. 'Whoever *serves* me ... my *servant* ... If anyone *serves* me ...'

The server is urged to follow. 'Serving' and 'following' are offered to something that we acknowledge as greater than ourselves, as the bearer of authority. 'Serving' and 'following' spiritually inhabit the life sphere of the *Father* principle that reveals itself wherever a justifiable hierarchy of greater and lesser holds sway. God the Father is the epitome of all superordinate existence, the origin of all true authority. 'The Father is greater than I' (14:28). In the same way, Christ is 'greater' than the disciples and receives from them service and followership.

There is a wonderful order in the fact that the sentence concerning service ends with the words, 'If anyone serves me, the Father will honour him.' The server places himself organically into the life sphere of the Father principle and, if we can put it like this, receives his thanks. He gains the sovereignty and dignity with which the Father God endows all who truly serve. 'The Father will honour him.'

> And if I go and prepare a place for you,
> I will come again and receive you to myself;
> that where I AM, you may be also.' (14:3)

2. Christ speaks of 'I' and 'you' (plural) in very personal, tangible terms here. '*I* go ... *I* prepare a place ... *I* will come again ... *I* receive you to myself.' This I addresses the apostles in an intimately human way: 'if I prepare a place for *you* ... receive *you* to myself ... *you* may be also'.

> Father, I want those you have given me
> to also be with me where I AM;
> that they may see my glory you have given me
> because you loved me before the foundation of the world.
> (17:24)

3. These words belong in the festive context of the High Priestly Prayer. Seeing far beyond the apostles, they look towards a future Christian humanity, towards the Church. 'With me.' This clearly addresses community in the *Holy Spirit*. Those who have inclined in service may now raise their heads to the highest vision, for which their devotion has prepared them, 'that they may see my glory'. Thus they live in worshipping acknowledgement of the pre-existing, eternal glory of light that issues from the Christ-I, whose origin lies in eternal, antemundane love.

The ascension

The ascension is one of the contents of gospel tradition that John does not directly report, but which he places indirectly into a higher light through certain reflective means. Thus, for instance, instead of an account of the Last Supper, John offers the Eucharistic passage concerning the bread of heaven in Chapter 6, and the parable of the vine in Chapter 15. Lack of narration of the event itself is balanced by illumination of the deeper content residing in its imagery. The same is true of the ascension.

Let us for now leave aside the many references in the Farewell Discourse to the ascension as a 'going to the Father' and confine

ourselves to the passages where it is expressly named. Again there are precisely three such passages:
1. In the conversation with Nicodemus (3:13).
2. In references to the bread of heaven (6:62).
3. At Easter, when Christ appears to Mary Magdalene (20:17f).

The first mention of the ascension in the Gospel of John is part of the teaching that Christ imparts to *Nicodemus* as a teacher of Israel.* Christ contrasts his mode of annunciation, as a speech drawn from vision, with the Pharisees' manner of instruction. He knows of 'heavenly things', for 'No one has ascended into heaven except the one who descended from heaven, the Son of Man, who is in heaven' (3:13).

In John, the ascension is not only something unique that occurs forty days after the resurrection, but it is something prepared through inner processes. What 'will be' is, as John conveys it, also 'already now', and this removes from the occurrence its outward, miraculous character, and presents it as the organic conclusion of an inner dynamic.

In the utterance to Nicodemus at 3:13, the ascension appears initially as inwardly pertaining to Christ, as his intrinsic habitus. Ascending and descending is, in a sense, an enduring, rhythmically dynamic condition: a rising and descending of the consciousness of Christ: a rising to divine heights, a descent to earthly conditions, an alternation between divine and human consciousness. The concluding event of the ascension on the fortieth day after Easter, which then encompasses and takes with it the spiritualised resurrection body, has been prepared by the inner ascents of Christ as he still walked on earth. By virtue of this ascension-prefiguring rising *in the spirit,* the earth-walking Christ has the capacity and right to be a *teacher* of heavenly things.

Here, the ascension is first intimated in connection with Christ as teacher.

The second reference is found in the Eucharistic address of Chapter 6, following the *feeding of the five thousand.*

The discourse, which reaches its culmination in the announcement

---

* In 1:51 the ascent and descent refers to the angels and not to Christ himself.

of the Last Supper, 'My flesh is food indeed, my blood is drink indeed', appears 'hard' to the disciples. At this, Christ says, 'What then if you see the Son of Man ascend to where he was before?' (6:53, 62). The 'seeing' of the ascension is therefore a key to understanding those mysteries of the body and blood of Christ, and avoidance of literal Capernaitic* materialism in views of the Last Supper.

In the ascension, Christ attains the Archimedean point where he can raise the earth. Only then, when he has united himself with the ultimate and highest powers of the encircling cosmos, does he have the authority truly to transform the earth. In this sense, the ascension is not a departure but the beginning of a higher coming. We can never understand this transformation only by staring fixedly at the earth itself, but only by looking towards the periphery. What remains a difficult enigma as long as we consider only the earth-confined element of the Last Supper, brightens and lightens as soon as we behold the influx of powers from the cosmic periphery, over which the one who has risen to the heavens now holds sovereign sway.

The first promise of the Eucharist remains obscure to its hearers. Christ prophesies the illumination of the riddle through beholding of his ascension.

The third mention of the ascension, in the conversation of the resurrected Christ with *Mary Magdalene,* is closest in time to the actual ascension itself, and is of special clarity. 'Do not touch me, for I have not yet ascended to the Father. But go to my brothers and say to them, "I am ascending to my Father and your Father, to my God and your God".' (20:17).

In this Easter passage in Chapter 20, the two events of Ascension and Pentecost, which John's account does not extend to (for he ends with the Easter epiphanies), are prefigured as inner processes. Instead of the Pentecost narrative, John reports how the risen Christ, already on Easter Sunday evening, breathes upon the disciples, 'Receive the Holy Spirit'. This is not to diminish the importance of Luke's account of the rushing wind and tongues of flame on the fiftieth day, but to show that this event crowns a process that is already at work.

* Capernaitic eating refers to a misunderstanding by some people in Capernaum of Jesus' words, 'I am the bread ... this bread is my flesh' taking the words literally in a cannibalistic sense (Jn 6:43–59).

Just as John's account of the evening of Easter day prefigures the Pentecost outpouring of the Holy Spirit, so the conversation with Mary Magdalene on Easter morning prefigures the ascension. This is the *process of eternalisation* of the body wrested from the grave, the 'incorporation' of resurrected human existence (with spirit, soul and also 'body') into the worlds of heaven.

If we look at the three Johannine ascension passages together, it becomes apparent that the goal of this ascension is defined differently in each case.

1. In the conversation with Nicodemus, we read the word 'heaven'. This word *(ouranos)* figures three times: 'No one has ascended into *heaven* except the one who descended from *heaven,* the Son of Man, who is in *heaven*' (3:13).
2. At the feeding of the five thousand: 'see the Son of Man ascend to *where he was before*' (6:62).
3. At Easter: 'I have not yet ascended to the *Father* ... I am ascending to my Father and your Father' (20:17).

The first and the third again have a special connection. What is encompassed in the first as 'heaven', the world of light, appears in the third as a being, the Father: the ultimate, personal fount of all heavenly manifestations of light.

In the conversation with Nicodemus, Christ shows that, as *teacher* of heavenly things, he is initiated into the realm of light.

At Easter, the emphasis is more on the aspect of a magic working right through into the *body,* of the power of being, of substance: the *Father.*

Between these two, the second utterance has its place. Here the goal of the ascension is not 'heaven', nor 'the Father', but the *Son's* experience of 'where he was before'.

In both 3:13 and Chapter 6 there is a dynamic of ascent and descent, yet it is different in each case. In Chapter 6 the *Redeemer* is important rather than the teacher. The focus here is more soteriological. The 'descent from heaven' *(katabainein ek tou ouranou)* is announced seven times (6:33, 38, 41, 42, 50, 51, 58). Christ descends not primarily in order to teach but for the 're-enlivening of the dying earth existence', as the bread of life. This sevenfold formulation of descent powerfully contrasts with the ascension utterance at 6:62. The descent has already been accomplished and is palpable and apparent, while the ascent is as yet reserved for the future. The sevenfold 'down' contrasts with the single, as yet veiled 'up'. But it becomes clear how the mystery of the Son is accomplished only in both the downward and upward directions. The feeding of the five thousand is not yet the Eucharist itself, however prophetic it is. We can sense a paradox here: the descended Christ only becomes the true bread of humankind when he has once again ascended. What descended to earth with him is only recognised and appropriated in the glory light of the ascension. Only as the 'Lord of the heavenly forces' and enthroned to the right of the Father, will he truly become omnipresent on earth as the *Eucharistic Christ*.

In the context of this triad of references to the ascension in the Gospel of John, 6:62 is the 'Son' passage proper.

The Adversary

The Adversary is given three names in the Gospel of John. First he is called the *devil,* later the *prince of this world* is predominant, and between these two comes *Satan*. The scheme illustrates the distribution of these three names:

devil	6:70	8:44	–	13:2	–	–	–
Satan	–	–	–	–	13:27	–	–
prince of this world	–	–	12:31	–	–	14:30	16:11

The *devil (diabolos)* passages form an organism together. Three different connections between the human being and the devil can be distinguished.

'One of you is a devil' (6:70). Here the relationship is one of *being*. One of you *is* a devil.

The third passage (13:2), likewise referring to Judas, relieves the all too irrevocably real nature of the first utterance in so far as it speaks not of being but of *consciousness*. It is a matter here of inspiration: 'The devil had already put it into the heart of Judas to betray him.' Here, Judas is not the devil himself, but only inspired by him, albeit at the very centre of his being.

We might feel it to be inorganic that the stronger statement – *being a devil* – comes first, and that precisely where the deed of Judas is enacted, the less substantial, and less irrevocable statement follows, concerning consciousness. The intensification of the narrative from 6:70 to 13:2 would seem to correspond more to the reverse sequence. And yet this decreasing trajectory has its profound and comforting meaning. Precisely where the actual enactment by Judas begins, it becomes clear that the relationship of full identity between man and devil cannot be sustained, but only an – albeit extensive – possession. This modifies the meaning of 6:70, lessening its full and terrible import, 'Have I not chosen you as twelve? And one of you is a devil.' The twelvefold circle of disciples is a sacred image representing the twelvefold powers of the cosmos. The group of twelve 'is' an embodiment of the cosmic twelve, its representation. And just as the destructive powers intrinsically belong to cosmic powers, so Judas 'is' the devil. In the group of disciples he 'is' evil itself, though only in an extenuated, representative sense.

Between these two comes the utterance at 8:44 spoken to the hostile Jews: 'You are of your father the devil'. This stands in the *middle* of the triad, not only outwardly. It is a relationship both of being (you 'are of' your father the devil) and also of consciousness. But both are extenuated. There is no full identity here but a derivative, secondary form of being, the existence of a son relative to his father. There is no inspiration in the sense of the clear content of an idea (as in 13:2, 'put it into the heart of Judas to betray him') but more a dreamlike, dull influence of the devilish world of passions and desires upon the motions of the human soul: 'and you want to carry out your father's desires'.

If we compare these mentions of the devil with the three places where the *prince of this world* is named, we can see that in the latter the Adversary's relationship to the earth is predominant, whereas his relationship to humankind is only more quietly intimated. 'This world' is that of the senses, the sphere of earthly creaturehood. By coming to rule over human beings, the Adversary has been able to make himself lord of a part of the world that he has wrested from the good powers. For this reason also the redemption by Christ is not only a redemption of humankind but, through the human being, the regaining of 'this world' for the divine. Like Christ, the evil power has a cosmic effect. Whereas the utterances with the devil were more in reference to the human being, the later ones concerning the prince of this world – corresponding more to the narrative's approach to the Mystery of Golgotha – invoke the significance of evil for the *world*. They show, as it were in negative, the cosmic character of the Christ sacrifice. Thus the first of these utterances is spoken at the moment when the Mystery of Golgotha first becomes shockingly tangible, when Christ speaks of the 'hour' that has come; when he overcomes the horror of death that first afflicts him and utters the victorious words about drawing all to him from the cross. In this prophetic vision of the Golgotha event as realised in the historical 'now', he cries: 'Now the prince of this world will be cast out' (12:31).

The third passage, part of the Farewell Discourse, and in the context of the promised coming of the Holy Spirit as Comforter, looks back to evil as something whose overcoming has already been 'perfected'. The Comforter will show the world that the prince of this world '*has been* condemned' (16:11). His expulsion from the world is a fact fulfilled. From the perspective of the Holy Spirit, from the viewpoint of eternity, evil is something inherently belonging to the *past,* that has only its allocated time and therefore, as non-eternal, is fundamentally already over.

Once again, the second passage occupies a middle position, also inwardly in terms of its content. It belongs entirely to the *present*. 'The prince of this world is coming. He has no hold over me.' (14:30). An old proverb says that with every step we come closer to God, the Adversary also comes a step nearer to us. As Christ approaches the Mystery of Golgotha, he comes decisively nearer to God the Father, and thus the presence of evil also grows palpable. 'He has no hold over me.' He has no share in the I as it indwells Christ. However much he has rooted himself in the egoistic I of earthly humankind, this sacrifice-filled, Father-surrendered I-hood of Christ is inaccessible and alien to him.

He 'will be cast out' (12:31) – he 'is coming. He has no hold over me' (14:30) – he 'has been condemned' (16:11): future – present – past.

Between the 'devil' and the 'prince of this world' passages, or more precisely in the region where these two triads intersect, is found, once only in the whole gospel, the name that is all the more eerily unique in this context – *Satan*.

When Judas had taken the piece of bread, 'Satan entered him' (13:27). This is the third and last utterance about Judas and the devil. This is followed by Judas' departure from the circle of the sacred meal, concluding with the harrowing phrase, 'it was night'. Like the devil, Satan enters into the closest relationship with the human being, the 'night' here reminiscent of the cosmic meaning of the 'prince of this world'. Satan brings with him lightlessness, he spreads darkness over the world.

The interweaving of the three and the seven is clearly discernible in this Johannine organism of words about the Adversary.

53

THE TRINITY IN THE STRUCTURE OF SINGLE SENTENCES

The sacred triad is manifest in the most intimate way in the Trinitarian patterning of single sentences and interrelated clauses. A few primary examples of this will be cited.

The Prologue

The Prologue is exemplary here. The classical beginning of the gospel provides the archetypal example, the primary Trinitarian patterning in the Gospel of John altogether.

> In the beginning was the Word
> and the Word was with God
> and the Word was God.

This fundamentally Trinitarian form has often been remarked upon. For instance, Frédéric Louis Godet wrote in his commentary, 'The three sentences of John 1:1 are brief, of singular formulation, oracular in quality. The first expresses the eternity of the Logos; the second, in especially profound manner, its personhood. Whereas the second sentence accentuates the distinction of persons, this is resolved in the third sentence into a community of being.'

Friedrich Rittelmeyer conveyed the perspective of The Christian Community as follows:

The first sentence – 'In the beginning was the Word' – allows us to gaze into the world of *being:* that of the Father.

The second sentence – 'and the Word was with God' – reveals the world of *love:* that of the Son.

The third sentence – 'and God was the Word' – shows us the world of *knowledge and insight:* that of the Spirit.

The evangelist did not necessarily have to be conscious of this. But the fact that he wrote these words intrinsically demonstrates that he initiated his gospel in a region where he dwelt within the rhythm of ultimate world secrets; that he felt these ultimate world realities stirring within him, coming to expression in him.*

In the Prologue, other sentences too have a Trinitarian structure. The schema below gives an overview of this.

1:1	1:6	1:7	1:9	1:10	1:18
In the beginning was the Word	There was a man	The same came for a witness,	That was the true Light,	He was in the world	No man has seen God at any time,
and the Word was with God	sent from God	to bear witness of the Light,	which lights every man	and the world was made by him	but the only begotten Son who is at the Father's side,
and the Word was God	whose name was John	that all men through him might believe	who comes into the world	but the world did not know him	he has made him known

These show themselves to be more or less clear reflections of the Trinity, with multiple variations in perspective. This structure is especially clear, no doubt, in verses 1:10 and 1:18.

---

* Rittelmeyer, *Briefe über das Johannes-Evangelium*, p. 138f.

> He was in the world
> and the world was made by him
> but the world did not know him. (1:10)

Here the Trinitarian patterning of *being – creation – illumination* is clearly apparent. The development of the world is the work of the Son (1:3). The spiritual aspect of perception and knowledge follows the Son aspect, albeit here only in a negative ascertainment: that the world did not know him.

> No one has ever seen God,
> but the only begotten Son who is at the Father's side,*
> he has made him known. (1:18)

In this triad, the polarity of *hiddenness* and *revelation* is at play. God the Father is the ultimate mystery. No one's gaze has ever reached him, enthroned in unapproachability. (Even Isaiah did not see the Father but the Logos, Jn 12:41.) 'He who sees God, dies.' This imperceptibility contrasts with his being 'declared'.

Exegēsato (made known) is translated by Rudolf Steiner as, 'he has become the leader [or guide] in this beholding.'† Through the sway of the Holy Spirit, ever more divine nature is to be raised from the dark depths of the Father's being into the bright consciousness of humankind. The Holy Spirit brings about reverent insight and sacred knowledge.

The *mediator* between hiddenness and revelation is the Son. He is initiated into the love mystery of the Father. 'The only begotten Son who is at the Father's side.'

---

* In the Greek text this word, *kolpos* (literally 'bosom') is the same word used at the Last Supper to describe the beloved disciple at Jesus' side (13:23).
† Steiner, *The Gospel of St John,* lecture of May 22, 1908, p. 67.

The conversation with Nicodemus

In the conversation with Nicodemus we read the sentence at 3:14f:

> And as Moses lifted up the serpent in the wilderness,
> so the Son of Man must be lifted up,
> so that everyone believing in him should have eternal life.

This is an invocation, initially, of an image from the *past:* an enigmatically hieroglyphic picture from the obscure and ancient era of Moses, 'And as Moses lifted up the serpent ...'

'So the Son of Man must be lifted up,' spans a bridge to the *present* moment of the conversation. It takes place within the context and mood of the Passover festival (2:23), and each time Passover figures in the Gospel of John we gain an especially tangible sense of how the great Golgotha Passover, which is fast approaching, throws its shadow ahead of it. The crucifixion is intimated in the picture of being 'lifted up'. The Son of Man is now to take the place of the serpent.

'So that everyone' – the beginning of the third line – is entirely *future,* and 'aims' at an ultimate fulfilment. It is a 'final' sentence in more than a grammatical sense. The deed of the Son upon the cross is to take effect within the consciousness of humanity. The divine will for redemption universally encompasses humanity. But, despite being intended for all, this aim of redemption is limited by human conduct – by whether people engage with it or not. 'So that everyone believing in him ...'

The enigmatic symbol of redemption rises within the darkness of past patriarchal times. In a light-filled future, eternal life is to become reality for all believers. The deed of the Son upon the cross makes this future possible.

'As Moses – so the Son – so that everyone': the utterance of Christ makes its way from the Father to the Son to the Spirit.

Some 'I am' sayings

Threefolding also inheres in some of the Johannine 'I AM' utterances of Christ. The overview below reveals the recurring pattern of the four utterances cited there.

6:35	8:12	10:9	11:25f
I AM the bread of life;	I AM the light of the world;	I AM the door;	I AM the resurrection and the life;
whoever comes to me will never hunger	whoever follows me will not walk in darkness,	if anyone enters through me he will be saved,	whoever believes in me will live, even if he dies,
and whoever believes in me will never thirst at any time.	but will have the light of life.	and will come in and go out and will find pasture.	and everyone who lives and believes in me will never ever die.

The *founding* and sustaining aspect of all these triads is, in each case, the actual 'I AM' utterance in its succinct simplicity: 'I AM the bread ... I AM the light ...' This 'I AM' phrase does not speak of evolving development, of the dynamic and drama of a quest, nor of a 'having' that could suggest an outward and perhaps transient relationship. It rests, rather, in eternal being: 'I AM'.

The second line always introduces the element of *motion*, and strikes the note of human destiny. Those people of whom the Prologue said, 'But to all who did receive him,' those who individualise themselves out of the indifferent generality, enter into a personal relationship with this I AM.

The conclusion is then formed by an utterance that is imbued with future fulfilment. It leads into a transpersonal 'life in the Holy Spirit': following the stasis of eternity in the I AM, and the destiny dynamic of becoming Christian, it brings us to *tranquillity in movement* and *movement in tranquillity.*

> 6:35
> I AM the bread of life;
> whoever comes to me will never hunger
> and whoever believes in me will never thirst at any time.

The ever-resting utterance of *being* is followed here by the motion of *destiny* in 'coming' to the Son. Initially, the words speak of bread and hunger; the third phrase aims further in speaking of belief and thirst. 'Belief' and 'never thirsting' have a specially close connection with each other, as, on the other hand, do 'belief' and the 'blood of Christ'. The words referring to the chalice or cup in the mass contain the mystery of faith, which also has parallels in the Act of Consecration. The believer receives the cup in whose pure spirit-flame the fire of impassioned, tormenting 'thirst' is quenched. As bread has a special connection with the Father-Ground of the World and its cosmic substance, so the cup has to the enthusiasm of *kindled spirit.*

Thus the whole of the Last Supper is encompassed in this first of the seven I AM utterances. Besides the bread, there is also a veiled intimation of the mystery of the chalice, in which all yearning finds peace. 'Not hungering' is surpassed by the heightened enthusiasm implicit in 'never thirsting'.

> 8:12
> I AM the light of the world;
> whoever follows me will not walk in darkness,
> but will have the light of life.

The 'coming' to him has here become 'following'. Walking in the darkness of God-alienated consciousness forms the bleak contrast to this mercifully illumined path of destiny in following the higher I. The dynamic of following and transforming is resolved by the triumph of life in the *Holy Spirit.* 'But will have the light of life.' The two trees of Paradise, the Tree of Knowledge and the Tree of Life, are here united. Knowledge in the Holy Spirit is higher than a merely intellectual enlightenment in whose cold gaze everything immediate and present wastes away. This kind of knowledge is a life-awakening, life-nurturing 'light of life'.

> 10:9
> I AM the door;
> if anyone enters through me he will be saved,
> and will come in and go out and will find pasture.

The individual nature of each person's *shaping of destiny* is almost more striking here in 'if anyone enters', than in 'whoever comes to me' and 'whoever follows me'. Walking through the door is a matter of the most personal and individual choice. 'If anyone ...' To pass through the door is a transformative act, a decisive passage from death into life – 'he will be saved'.

This decisive event of destiny is again followed by the fullness and fulfilment of attainment. Once again, a triad marks this fulfilled life in the *Spirit,* this now freely flourishing eternal life: come in – go out – find pasture. Underlying the rhythm of going out and coming in is a cosmic law that can be seen in the mundane secret of waking and sleeping. In falling asleep, our soul and spirit depart from the house of the body and, albeit initially unconsciously, immerse themselves in the ocean of divine life. On awakening, we re-enter the house of the body so as to be able to work upon earth. Similarly, the rhythm of entering and leaving applies to the swing between 'praying' and 'working': repeatedly we must close our earthly eyes, turn inward in seclusion, so that we can, inwardly strengthened, better fulfil our earthly tasks. All this to and fro between heaven and earth is now to pass through Christ – going and returning should happen in Christ. Then we can receive nourishment for our eternal being, both in heaven and on earth; then we can find 'pasture'.

> 11:25f
> I AM the resurrection and the life;
> whoever believes in me will live, even if he dies,
> and everyone who lives and believes in me will never ever die.

The same Trinitarian play of forces also holds sway here. Whoever finds the *Son* in belief, gains a share in the life-and-death mystery of Christ: they will live even when they die. And, as previously, once again the third line of the utterance is imbued by a fulfilment that surpasses destiny. Beyond the struggle between life and death, it leads into a lofty realm over and above such dramatic dynamics, and becomes a triumphant song of 'deathless life', a hymn in the *Holy Spirit*. It is very significant here that 'whoever believes in me' is transformed into 'everyone who lives and believes in me'. In this invoking of 'everyone', a Pentecost hope dawns. It is a word that encompasses all humanity. This spirit hymn is once again inwardly triadic in its microcosmic structure: life – believe in me – never die. Precisely through the negative affirmation of 'never ever die', the mystery of deathless life stands all the more brightly against its dark background. 'never ever die' – here we can recognise the same, spirited ardour as we found in the 'never thirst at any time' at 6:35.

Thirst and the Samaritan woman

> 4:13f
> Everyone drinking of this water will thirst again;
> but whoever drinks of the water I give him will never ever thirst;
> instead the water that I will give him will become in him a fount of water springing up into eternal life.'

Underlying this initially is a *natural fact,* a law of earthly existence. 'Everyone drinking of this water ...' At the same time, this becomes figurative of how a person clinging only to earthly realities can never quench their longing, their 'thirst'.

But now the natural water becomes a metaphor for a higher water given by the *Son:* 'the water I give him'. The law of nature applies to all, to 'everyone'. But coming to the Son is a matter of destiny, distinguished here by the phrase 'but whoever' as opposed to 'everyone'. Those who detach themselves from the indifferent generality and, by coming to the Son, raise themselves to true individuality ('to all who did receive him ...' 1:12) will find fulfilment and peace.

But this is not yet the last thing. It leads to the thought that the perfected human being not only does not thirst but is, rather, to become a source, a spring, himself. We see here the same intensification as in 7:37–39, where the motif of thirsting* and drinking – 'if anyone thirsts, let him come to me and drink' – is followed by the words, 'He that believes in me, as Scripture has said, out of his belly shall flow rivers of living water,' a saying then qualified by the addition, 'He said

---

* In the texts of John there are seven passages referring to thirst: four in the gospel (4:13–15, 6:35, 7:37, 19:28) and three in Revelation (7:16, 21:6, 22:17).

this concerning the Spirit, whom those who believed in him were later to receive.' The human being given peace by the Son grows into life in the Holy Spirit, where he himself can give gifts of solace.

The three stages in this process are clearly distinguished:
1. The human being bound up with earthly existence: thirsting.
2. The human being redeemed by the Son: the peace of quenched thirst.
3. The human being living in the Holy Spirit: himself a spring.

The water whose source is within the redeemed human being himself not only 'springs up' into eternal life but literally 'leaps up' *(hallomenou)*, as if pointing us here to the active inner movement in a person, the 'leaping vivacity' of this life in the spirit.

Before Pilate

As an example of an archetypal phenomenon, let us here also mention an utterance of Christ from the Pilate drama.

> 18:37
> You say that I am a king.
> For this reason I was born and came into the world to bear witness to the truth.
> Everyone being of the truth hears my voice.

As in the I AM utterances,* we first have here a majestic resting within divine *substance*. The second line conveys the dramatic quality of *destiny*, the world of the Son. The third looks towards the Church of those who acknowledge Christ, who hear the inner testimony of the *Holy Spirit*.

The middle line is once more 'microcosmically' differentiated within itself, reflecting again the threefold pattern of the whole:

---

* Here, in 18:37, it is not actually an 'I AM' utterance although it sounds like it in the English translation ('You say that I am a king'). In the Greek text the *ego* (the accentuated I) is missing: it is not *ego eimi basileus* but only *basileus eimi*. Christ specifically does not couch the attribute of kingship in relation to himself in the festive I AM form here; rather this must be perceived and acknowledged by others: 'You say it.'

53. THE TRINITY IN SINGLE SENTENCES

> For this reason I was born
> and came into the world
> to bear witness to the truth.

'Came I into the world' is more conscious, more active than 'being born', which belongs to a naturally given world; it is uttered more in the sense of a free determination of destiny. The third line has finality. The destiny of bearing witness rises into the transpersonal, objective realm of the Spirit. Spirit-enhanced destiny become rune or emblem of the truth, has a manifesting, revealing action. Thus the transition to the world of knowledge of the third line is attained: 'Everyone being of the truth hears my voice.'

54

IN CONCLUSION

It has become apparent that the material of the Gospel of John is to a high degree informed by sacred numbers. Can we draw particular conclusions from this?

Godet, for instance, who upheld the authenticity of the Gospel of John, energetically disputed tentative efforts by his contemporaries to demonstrate that the fourth evangelist had a special preference for triadic patterns. Both those who defended and disputed the gospel's authenticity were trapped in the preconception that such evidence, if established, must cast doubt on the historical credibility of the gospel. 'Real events are not encompassed by systematic patterns of this kind.'

The following considerations aim to show that this is indeed a preconception. Apart from the fact that the life of extraordinary human beings does tend to unfold in 'canonical' ways, as Novalis says, we must ask ourselves this: What do we expect, in fact, of a faithful, authentic account? What conditions must it fulfil? The last words of the Gospel of John express a truth that is of fundamental importance in this regard: that it is actually absurd to try to faithfully record a real, lived human life in the form of a mere transcript: 'even the world itself would not have space for the books that would be written.' An account is always a selection. It records only some things and leaves much out.

If, for instance, all the words in a conversation were faithfully recorded and preserved, even this faithfulness would be only an excerpt of the reality. Lacking still would be gestures, looks, tones of voice, timbre, everything that is imponderable and yet so decisive in the fine back-and-forth of human interplay, all the details of the surroundings, the quality of light, the weather, the landscape, the constellations of stars and planets, what else is happening close by at the time, the mood at that moment and how it stands between before and after, the waves stirring in supersensible worlds. The complete 'totality' of all life actually lived cannot be recorded in a verbatim account, which can offer only a small portion of this singular whole. And this portion might even sometimes convey an erroneous impression, because it is only part of what happened.

An account is always a selection; but *what* and *how* this selection is made is what really counts. The faithful minute-taker is not really aware of the fact that thay are recording only a small part of proceedings and leaving much out. They work in piecemeal fashion in the naive belief that they are reproducing the whole. The evangelist John has a clear *awareness* of this selection process. 'Jesus performed many other signs in the presence of his disciples, which are not written in this book' (20:30). 'There are many more things that Jesus did, which, if every one should be written down, I suppose that even the world itself would not have space for the books that would be written' (21:25). But above all, there is a consciousness apparent in him of how the inspired human being touches what he does with a configuring genius. The little he does select and record he orders into wonderful configurations, into an independent, life-sustaining pattern.

And then he can calmly relinquish much else. 'The world would not have space for the books ...' Thus, instead of an inevitably hopeless attempt to write these books, he composes a brief, succinct gospel, yet one in which the three years of Christ's working nevertheless come to living expression. How is this possible? Precisely because it does not break off a piecemeal transcript from the totality of the whole, living reality. Instead, it responds to the unity of form contained in ungraspable dimensions with a whole that is shaped and rounded according to an intrinsic, inherent order, as a unique work of art. In its larger-than-life quality, it reproduces the inimitable artwork of the life of Christ in a microcosmic form. A whole can only ever be reproduced by a whole, never by a portion or fraction. The macrocosm of a great whole can never be conveyed in a micro-chaos of fragments but only in the microcosm of a small whole. Only what has qualitative affinity with what it reproduces can pertain to its truth. Thus the microcosmic pattern and form of the Gospel of John can testify to the macrocosmic artwork of Christ's life.

Simple observation can show us, therefore, what the account of a lived life can and cannot be. Such reflections have also occasionally been made by the defenders of 'authenticity'.

However, we can go further than this.

The previous train of thoughts would not necessarily dispel a troubling sense that, in the fourth gospel, the utterances of Christ can appear in very altered form due to the stylisation employed, precisely due to the patterns of three and seven with which the material is informed.

At the beginning we mentioned Novalis's saying that the life of great people has a 'canonical' quality. The more significant a human being is, the more they partake of the hidden world with its secret patterns and laws, and the more therefore their life will shed all random or incidental qualities. It is for this reason that we can very frequently discern in the biographies of very great figures a shaping configuration and patterning that appears almost ritual and stylised in nature.

This is true to a much greater degree still in the Son of God himself, who is always 'in heaven' (Jn 3:13). This 'being in heaven' signifies, indeed, a resonating in divine rhythms and harmonies. The saying 'All good things come in threes' contains an inkling of the sacred three, which is the inward dynamic principle of divine life and is repeatedly reflected in creation in so far as this mirror is not tarnished. Through the Fall our conscious existence lapsed from these divine rhythms and fell into the 'prose' of non-organic, intellectual mentality. Re-encountering these rhythms in, say, a truly inspired text or ritual can seem like a memory or admonition. The soul is then breathing 'in heaven'. Precisely because the Son of God appeared in Christ, it is inevitable that this inner life within 'heaven' gave his words and deeds their unique configuration. For this reason his earthly existence unfolded with the strict form of a ritual and could do no other than manifest the patterning of sacred number. We can therefore say, in fact, that the Gospel of John is *more* authentic than the other gospels precisely because it recounts the life of Christ in more thoroughly stylised form.

John, the *beloved* disciple, lay 'upon the Lord's breast'. In the breast dwells primarily our rhythmic being. Surely this expression might also signify that, more than the others, John was able to let his own inner life resonate with the divine breath and pulsing rhythm of his Master?

The synoptics, too, though less characteristically, allow us to intimate this life of Christ in sacred number. We need think here only of the three times three beatitudes of the Sermon on the Mount, and the seven petitions of the Lord's Prayer in Matthew.

Thus, the microcosm of the Gospel of John, precisely also in its numerical patterning, is a faithful and truly authentic representation of the macrocosm, which embodies the life of Christ Jesus in its totality.

Certainly the Johannine account relies on selection and is a structure with its own laws, as are the other three gospels. But as far as the three and the seven are concerned, specifically, these laws 'intrinsic' to the gospel are identical with the laws of the life of Christ himself. This comprehensive accord and resonance with the inner dynamic of Christ distinguishes the fourth gospel from the other three, though these representations are also valid, microcosms of the life of Christ Jesus each in their different way. The fourth gospel most clearly reflects the fact that in Christ the Godhead's Trinitarian fullness of life is uniquely manifest, a sacred patterning of the cornucopia of manifold cosmic being. To the really attentive and devoted reader, this gospel reveals itself – already in its rhythms – as the gospel of the beloved disciple, who was able to hearken most intimately to the breath and heartbeat of the Son of God.

VI

THE I AM UTTERANCES IN THE GOSPEL OF JOHN

55

THE TWELVEFOLD NATURE OF THE I AM UTTERANCES

Friedrich Rittelmeyer was the first to describe the I AM utterances in the Gospel of John as a spiritual 'organism of seven' and to illustrate this from various perspectives. These are the seven utterances by Christ about himself, each of which starts with the words 'I AM': I AM the bread of life, the light, the door, the good shepherd, the resurrection and the life, the way, the truth and the life, the true vine.

If we trace the context of these utterances within the Gospel of John we will notice that some of them figure several times, recurring in a slightly modified form.

There is no I AM utterance before Chapter 6. This chapter recounts the feeding of the five thousand, the walking on the waters of the lake, and the discourse on the bread of life. In the context of the very precise time reckoning given in John, we are at the Passover festival of the year 32 ('Passover was near' Jn 6:4). This is the last Passover before the Golgotha Passover and is already tangibly overshadowed by that forthcoming event. We can have the sense that these coming events were first prefigured, reflected downwards from the clouds to the earthly realm, before finally descending to the hard ground of Jerusalem and becoming historical. They have not yet arrived on earth, but they shine down from higher worlds where they are in preparation. And where better could this descending influx be captured than in the living, etheric atmosphere of Galilee?

Galilee is, indeed, the scene of Chapter 6 in the Gospel of John. All its events take place beside or upon the Sea of Galilee. Could we not see this lake as something like a magical mirror that captures and reflects this light shining downward from the clouds of the future?

In a similar pre-mirroring sense, the discourse on the bread of life prefigures the Last Supper, which will take place one year later. Within this discourse, the first of the seven 'I AM' utterances, concerning bread, appears no less than three times (if we discount the one at 6:41, where it figures only as an echo in the mouths of the Jews).

> I AM the bread of life.
> Whoever comes to me shall never hunger
> and whoever believes in me shall never ever thirst. (6:35)

> I AM that bread of life.
> Your fathers ate manna in the desert yet they died.
> This is the bread that comes down from heaven that
> anyone may eat and not die. (6:48–50)

> I AM the living bread that came down from heaven.
> If anyone eats of this bread, he shall live for ever.
> And the bread that I will give for the life of the world
> is my flesh. (6:51)

In the first version, the words are 'never hunger and thirst'. In the second, 'not die'. The first points to a world of longing and yearning, the 'astral' region of soul stirrings. The second points to the world of physical earth existence that has succumbed to death, and cannot be redeemed by the patriarchal powers of the past.

The third version no longer looks to anything negative that must be overcome, but only to life as such. The word 'life' is repeated in every line. It is now no longer a question of hunger and thirst, or not dying, but of a power of life that issues from the redeemed human being to encompass all life on earth.

And here, as this third formulation comes to an end, appears the phrase 'my flesh', which from now on will become the leitmotif of an ever more intimate discourse about the Last Supper: 'And the bread that I will give for the life of the world is my flesh.' The word flesh *(sarx)* has a special resonance in the Gospel of John, endowed by the Prologue: 'And the Word became flesh.' After the Jordan baptism,

55. THE TWELVEFOLD NATURE OF 'I AM'

Christ had gradually to grow in to the earthly body available to him and entirely penetrate it. A certain period is required for him to truly 'come up against' the sphere of the earthly physical body, and become fully aware of it. Death awaits him within this earthly, physical body, but so too does resurrection. It may well not be accidental that the expression 'my flesh' appears at this particular moment, at the Passover festival of the year 32, when Golgotha is beginning to announce itself. This moment of 'coming up against' physical corporeality is also the moment of the first I AM utterance. The unfolding of consciousness of the I on earth requires the physical body's resistance. Thus a connection may exist here between this developing consciousness of the physical body and the coterminous beginning of the 'I AM' utterances.

The second of the seven I AM utterances appears in only one formulation:

> I AM the light of the world.
> Whoever follows me shall not walk in darkness,
> but shall have the light of life. (8:12)

This recurs at the beginning of the healing of the blind man: 'As long as I am in the world, I am the light of the world' (9:5).

But in the original text, this second occasion does not have the high, festive form of the full *ego eimi* (I AM). The Greek here has only the 'am', directly following the word 'light'. By contrast, at 12:46, the *ego* stands alone with the 'light' as *ego phos* ('I a light'), without the 'am'. In these two instances, the great I AM formulation is as it were divided up so that each of its constituents – first the 'I' and secondly the 'am' – can entirely merge and unite with the 'light'. There is no full repetition of the festive formulation.*

This utterance about the 'light of the world' comes at the time of the Festival of Tabernacles, thus in the autumn. In the same way that the first I AM utterance, about the bread of life, resounded at the time of Easter, so the saying about light belongs in the Michaelic part of the year. The same is true of the third and fourth I AM utterances,

---

* It should be mentioned that in the phrase, 'You say that I am a king' (18:37) only the 'am' figures, and so as such this is not one of the I AM utterances.

concerning the 'door' and the 'good shepherd'. In fact, the whole context of John 7 to 10:21 falls in the autumn of the year 32.

The 'door' utterance has two forms. Firstly, it concerns our access to other people, into whose interiority we should not penetrate like a thief or a murderer. We must seek entry to the hidden sanctum of another individual only through the portal of the Christ-I. This is conveyed figuratively in the words:

> I AM the door of the sheep.
> All who preempt me are thieves and robbers. (10:7f)

But Christ is not only the door into the inner life of the other. He is also the 'portal of initiation' through which we rightly enter the higher world:

> I AM the door.
> Whoever enters through me will be saved,
> and will go in and go out, and find pasture. (10:9)

It is not only a matter of crossing the threshold to the other world. As earthly humankind, we can only do this in a wholesome way if we can then also find the way back into earthly conditions. We cannot 'evaporate' into the higher world, and in doing so dream away from, neglect or entirely forget our tasks on earth. We have to learn to be fully, consciously present both here and there. This is the secret of 'going in and out'. Only then is our entry into the higher world sound and beneficial – as expressed in the image of finding pasture. Christ does not signify a one-sided spiritualisation that takes flight from the world, but a fruitful back and forth, a conscious passage across the threshold in both directions, enabling us to become beneficent mediators between heaven and earth.

In the same way, the next utterance concerning the good shepherd also has two aspects:

> I AM the good shepherd.
> The good shepherd lays down his life for the sheep. (10:11)

55. THE TWELVEFOLD NATURE OF 'I AM'

> I AM the good shepherd,
> and know my own
> and they know me. (10:14)

Here we can see the polarity of will and knowledge. The first version conveys the courageous will for self-sacrifice, the shepherd who throws his own life into play and fearlessly combats the wolf, before whom the hired hand flees. Christ's leadership of humanity is founded on this willingness to sacrifice himself for the sake of his own.

The second version brings an important enlargement. The relationship to the good shepherd of those whom he saves from the wolf through this living commitment, should not be one of blind dependency but of clear-sighted and perceiving trust.

A pre-Christian leader of humanity would also have been able to say, 'I am the good shepherd and I know my own.' But he could not have continued by saying 'and they know me'. This strikes a new tone. The human being should come to self-aware maturity, and acknowledge the leadership of Christ in full freedom.

This relationship of mutual acknowledgement is further exalted by the following sentence, by virtue of which it gains an affinity with the most sacred relationship between God the Father and God the Son. 'Just as the Father knows me, I know the Father' (10:15). The concluding 'and I lay down my life for the sheep' once again unites the perspective of discerning knowledge with the previous aspect of self-sacrificing courage.

The fifth of the seven I AM utterances leads us back again to the pre-Easter springtime, that of the decisive year 33. Golgotha is fast approaching.

At the grave of Lazarus, Christ finally becomes fully conscious of his power to raise from the dead, and thus of his own capacity for resurrection.

> I AM the resurrection and the life.
> Whoever believes in me will live, even if he dies,
> and everyone who lives and believes in me
>   will never ever die. (11:25)

This is said only once and there is no parallel version. The same is true of the sixth I AM utterance, which already leads us into the sacred realm of the Farewell Discourse on Maundy Thursday:

> I AM the way, the truth and the life.
> No one comes to the Father except through me. (14:6)

Also on Maundy Thursday, in continuation of the Farewell Discourse, the seventh and last of the I AM utterances is spoken. It figures twice in different forms:

> I AM the true vine
> and my Father is the vinedresser. (15:1)

> I AM the vine,
> you are the branches. (15:5)

In the phrase following the utterance 'the way, the truth and the life', the motif of the Father appears: 'No one comes to the Father except through me.' Christ stands at the threshold of death, which will unlock for him the deepest secret of the Father. In the same way the words about the vine initially concern the Father: 'my Father is the vinedresser'. The Greek *georgos* really means the 'one who works the earth'. It is he who ensures that the vine, in which the wonderful transformation of water into wine is to be enacted, is rightly rooted in the depths of earth, which are at the same time the dark bowels of the grave. The truth of what the vine 'signifies' in its transformation of earthly bitterness and sourness into ripe, sun-pervaded sweetness is realised in Christ, the 'true' vine.

The second version then looks to the disciples, who can only thrive and flourish in a direct, living connection with this vine rooted in the Father-Ground of Being. 'I am the vine, you are the branches.'

The immediately following words, 'whoever abides in me and I in him' form the bridge back to Chapter 6, where this motif first sounded: 'He who eats my flesh and drinks my blood abides in me and I in him' (6:56). Thus the beginning and end of the I AM utterances, the chapters of the bread and the vine, come full circle.

55. THE TWELVEFOLD NATURE OF 'I AM'

Let us once again survey the whole organism of I AM utterances extending between 'bread' and 'wine'. They all belong to the last year of Christ's mission: Passover 32 – autumn festival 32 – Passover 33.

Before the spring of 32, as we noted above, there are no I AM utterances. The right moment in the life of Christ first had to arrive for this. We do not have the sense that they lay in his consciousness in advance like the content of a prepared sermon which was then gradually conveyed to his listeners. Rather, each of these utterances, in the moment it was spoken, has the air of being 'originally engendered', in the lightning flash of his divine self-discovery. Or perhaps it would be more accurate to speak of a rediscovery – for Christ has to rediscover his divine self-knowledge, previously possessed in heavenly worlds, within the earthly, human context, as it were translated into earthly consciousness.

In the seven I AM utterances he re-engenders his consciousness, which has been transformed from the heavenly into the human dimension. And because this concerns divine, heavenly things, the process is governed by sacred number – initially the number seven.

But if we include all the versions, the similar yet different formulations, then the precise number of the I AM utterances by Christ himself in the Gospel of John is twelve: 6:35, 48, 51, 8:12, 10:7, 9, 11, 14, 11:25, 14:6, 15:1, 5. Thus the seven I AM utterances are at the same time twelvefold. Behind the seven, as revealed in the developing octave of world evolution, in the planetary element, the twelve appears like the background of fixed stars, the zodiac.

Before Christ had assumed human form on earth, his I AM was reflected back to him from the twelve starry regions. In giving voice to the twelve I AM utterances on earth, his heavenly, zodiac consciousness was reborn in a human earth consciousness, and the God truly became man.

VII

Agape – Divine Love in the Fourth Gospel

56

OVERVIEW

John's Gospel is especially concerned with the Word. That is obvious not only from the Prologue, which speaks about the deepest dimensions of the Word, but also in the minute way in which the gospel deals with its vocabulary.

Recent theology has often spoken of the monotony of John's language. The general impression was that the fourth gospel liked to return continually to a limited number of basic concepts. The reader repeatedly confronts certain words and phrases, which are extremely significant but tend to become monotonous through constant repetition.

This impression of monotony is totally reversed when the reader realises that such specific Johannine words and phrases are managed within the whole according to a wise economy. It appears as if the ordering within the whole and the weaving into meaningful contexts were controlled from a mysterious spiritual centre that surveys all the relationships. We need not determine here to what extent this results from the conscious intention of the author, from inspiration, or from both. Initially it is necessary only to notice the fact. Because of the economy we mentioned, each word can be given a multitude of nuances. In various passages the single word stands for this multitude and thus is able to express more than it could in isolation. Thus what first appeared as an absence of richness in colour and perspective in John's Gospel is more than compensated.

The following will attempt to demonstrate this assertion using the word *agapē* as an example. The word *agapē,* love, certainly belongs among the most important in John's vocabulary. A closer look at the use of this word in the course of the gospel will give an insight into what we referred to as this gospel's special way of dealing with the word.

Before going into details we should have a general orientation about the passages within the fourth gospel in which the word *agapē* or the verb *agapan* – to love with agape – are used.

It appears neither in the Prologue, nor in the first chapter (John the Baptist, the first disciples), nor in the second chapter (marriage at Cana and cleansing of the temple).

It first appears in the conversation with Nicodemus: 'God so loved the world' (3:16), and at the end of the conversation: 'People loved darkness' (3:19). This negative use of the word also appears at 5:42 and 8:42, which likewise point out the absence of true agape among people.

The passage 10:40–42, which reflects again on Jesus, beginning with John the Baptist, can be regarded as a division in the gospel. If we take the first ten chapters as the first half of the gospel, then the word *agapē* is spoken within that half only two more times in its positive, divine meaning after the conversation with Nicodemus: the Baptist's speech in which he surrenders his legacy to Christ, 'the Father loves the Son' (3:35), and at the conclusion of Christ's parable about the good shepherd, 'the Father loves me' (10:17).

In all these chapters, whose contents include the talk with the Samaritan woman, the healing of the boy, the healing of the paralytic, the feeding of the multitude and the walking on the waters, the speech about the bread of life, the controversy at the Festival of Tabernacles in Jerusalem, the healing of the blind man, the speech about the good shepherd, and the words about the Festival of the Dedication in winter – in all these chapters there are only three places in which agape is used, and in all three cases it is said about God the Father. The entire section of the first ten chapters recognises no other bearer of agape than the Father.

A new concept appears in the chapter about Lazarus. For the first time agape is given another bearer: Christ (11:5). At the beginning of the chapter about the washing of the feet this motif of Christ's love for his own is resumed more forcefully, and, in the Farewell Discourse, it is as if the isolated sounds of the bell have turned into a powerful pealing. With the preceding occasional use of the word as a background, it is all the more impressive to encounter it repeatedly now. It appears seven times in Chapter 13, ten times in Chapter 14, nine times in Chapter 15, and five times in Chapter 17. In comparison to the preceding chapters that is extraordinary. Both Christ and the Father appear as bearers of agape in the Farewell Discourse; we even notice the transition to a third subject: the disciples, although in this connection it is used only as a commandment, a commission, and a future goal. But we can get an impression of the full pealing from this trio: Father-Son-disciples.

The word nearly disappears during the recounting of the passion. In the conversation of the risen Christ with Peter by the lake, it is spoken a final time in Christ's question to Peter: 'Do you love me?' and in the evangelist's expression for the disciple, 'whom the Lord loved'.

Two observations arise at first, and we simply want to point to them as phenomena.

Firstly, there is a difference between the first and second halves of the gospel; that is, before and after the raising of Lazarus.

Secondly, as bearers of agape there appear in succession Father, Son, disciples.

This alone makes it obvious that the word 'agape' is not used in John's Gospel with indiscriminate monotony.

In treating the various passages we will follow the order that is followed in the gospel: firstly, the agape of the Father; secondly, the agape of the Christ; and thirdly, the agape of the disciples.

57

THE AGAPE OF THE FATHER

In the initial overview we were concerned only with the bearer of agape, its subject. Another division arises when we consider the object of love. Once again we will follow the sequence observed in the gospel: the first use of agape, in Chapter 3, speaks of the Father's love for the world.

1. The agape of the Father for the world

'God so loved the world …' This is probably the most sublime revelation during the conversation with Nicodemus at night. Christ had told him that no one can ascend to heaven who has not descended from heaven. What he said to Nicodemus about God's decision to redeem man is derived from an inner ascension to heaven, an elevation to the highest mysteries of the Father. Golgotha is predicted first in the symbolic parable of the serpent lifted up by Moses, and then totally from within as if right from God's heart.

The synoptic gospels report that, at the moment of Christ's death on the cross, the curtain of the temple was torn. The Holy of Holies was no longer hidden. These words of John's Gospel in the conversation with Nicodemus can make a similar impression. During this unique hour of revelation in the night, what happens here, in truth, is symbolised by the torn curtain on Good Friday, when the Holy of Holies was revealed.

> For God so loved the world that he gave his only begotten Son, so that everyone believing in him shall not perish but have eternal life. (3:16)

57. THE AGAPE OF THE FATHER

There is no other passage in which John makes the 'world' the object of God's love. No one else is said to have 'loved' the world except God the Father.

A good way to envisage the uniqueness of this passage is to realise that, for John, 'love of the world' is reserved for the Father.

John's Gospel gives us a sensitivity for the incomparable sublimity of the Father. The Logos creates the world (1:3) while the Father remains hidden; he is more like the silence, the nocturnal ground, out of which the Word emerges. On the other hand, since the enlightening Word is the true proclaimer and worthy interpreter (1:18) of the Father, his darkness is caused by the blinding unapproachable light that first becomes perceptible and accessible to human eyes in the Son. His darkness is an excess of light and his silence an excess of sound. He is beyond our comprehension and is reached only in his Son.

On the one side it is true: 'No one has ever seen God.' But on the other side, we have: 'He who sees me sees the Father' (1:18; 12:45).

He conveys himself totally in the Son, and yet the Son says, 'The Father is greater than I.'

It may be part of this 'being greater' that the Father alone is said to love the world.

'World' *(kosmos)* in the New Testament does not mean quite the same as what we call cosmic or cosmos. It has the connotation of being unredeemed and solely created and transitory, of having fallen out of the divine relationship. Human beings could not love the world in the Johannine sense ('do not love the world or the things in the world' 1Jn 2:15) since we ousevles are much too much a part of this world, and participates in its transitory nature. First of all, we must free ourselves from it and grasp something within us that 'is not of this world', that is eternal instead of transitory ('the world and its desires pass away, but whoever does the will of God lives forever' 1Jn 2:17). In other words, we must overcome the world or else the budding power of love within us will turn into love of darkness. In the same context of the conversation with Nicodemus, remarkably the passage about God's love for the world is followed by the words, 'but people loved darkness instead of light' (3:19). Darkness – that is the world seen without its divine foundation, the epitome of the non-eternal, human existence that has been sundered from the divine and become vain and meaningless in this isolation. The love of those not yet aware of the eternal within them becomes caught up in this morass. 'If anyone loves the world, the love of the Father is not in them' (1Jn 2:15). In view of the conversation with Nicodemus, one could alter that to say, 'Only if someone had God's love in them could they love the world with true agape.'

People's 'love of darkness'* is not only insufficient love of the light, but even a 'hatred of the light' (3:20). In the same conversation during the night in which the mystery of divine love is proclaimed, one finds these words about 'hatred'.

Insofar as Christ loved the world for its salvation, he did it in terms of John's Gospel, in that the Father and the Father's love were 'in him'. It is never said of him as the Son that he loved the world – that is reserved for the Father. 'The Father is greater than I.' The Son is called redeemer of the world (4:42, 3:17, 12:47), who surrenders himself to give it new life. But in order to redeem it, he must 'overcome' it. This is the keystone in the arch of the Farewell Discourse: 'I have overcome the world' (16:33).

This power to overcome must now enter into his disciples. As long as they regard themselves simply as a component part of the world, they cannot redeem it. For that reason one may not interpret it as cold indifference to the fate of the world when Christ, in the Farewell Discourse, says: 'I pray for them; I am not praying for the world, but for those you have given me' (17:9).

In the process of overcoming the world and transforming humanity, Christ becomes the redeemer of the world. In this simple yet monumental way, it is only about the Father that John says, 'He so loved the world.'

The ultimate simplicity of the following proclamation is just as magnificent, 'that he gave his only begotten Son'. The New Testament usually speaks of the Father sending the Son; this is the sole passage in John's Gospel that speaks of the Son being given. The foregoing

---

* Out of the five passages in John's Gospel that use agape negatively, there are two that speak of humanity's predisposed love going astray or being diverted. One is here: 'love of darkness' (3:19); the other is: 'they loved human praise [*doxa*] more than the praise [*doxa*] of God' (12:43). In the second case, humanity's natural love is not consumed by the darkness but seduced by the glitter of a false light. The love for light is distorted into a love for appearances, which are the nonappearance of the divine. Rudolf Steiner recognised these opposing forces in the polarity of the Luciferic (false appearance) and the Ahrimanic (darkness).

prophecy of the cross on Golgotha, formulated in the image of the elevated serpent, clearly shows the sacrificial character of this 'giving'.

'Giving' is one of John's basic concepts. Everything which in the further course of the gospel the Father is said to give is included in this one sentence as in its root: he gave his Son. Here two of the basic concepts of John's Gospel meet: 'agape' and 'giving'.

The night is the appropriate setting for this revelation. The night of the conversation with Nicodemus is not the night of Judas Iscariot. Judas' night is darkness, the absence of light. The revelatory conversation with Nicodemus penetrates the curtain of darkness to the hidden light that radiates from the sun that 'shines at midnight'.

The only passage about God's love for the world is followed by the only passage in John's Gospel about the 'anger' of God. It is John the Baptist's final word: anyone who refuses to believe in the Son will not see life: the wrath of God remains on them (3:36). This relation of the Father to the world as it is distorted by the Fall is described with the form of wrath, which had been preached by the last representatives of the Old Covenant. It strikes one as the outer shell of a deeper mystery that was preached not by the Baptist but by God's only Son: the mystery of God's love for the world. This mention of anger serves not only as contrast but is like a shell around the words about love; it serves as protection against a cowardly, sentimental understanding of love that lacks austerity and awe in the face of God's holiness.

2. The agape of the Father for the Son

The Father loves the Son

This consideration of the Baptist's final words leads immediately to the second mention of divine agape.

> The Father loves the Son and has given everything into his hand. (3:35)

The Father 'surrendered' his Son for the salvation of the world because he is at one with him. This giving is a sacrificial act of love because he is not simply giving an external possession, but something intimately bound up with him.

At the baptism at the Jordan, the synoptic gospels report how the heavens opened, the dove descended, and a voice was heard from heaven: 'You are my beloved son.' Such a report is missing in John. His account begins at a later point, when the baptism is already regarded as a past event.

The absence of just such events, which one would have thought were particularly close to the heart of the fourth evangelist, is altogether surprising. Not only is the baptism 'missing', but also the transfiguration, the Last Supper and the ascension. On closer inspection, however, one may discern that the events missed are still contained in the gospel in some way, albeit in a finer, more 'atmospheric' form, as it were. It seems that the 'body' of a concrete event-related narrative has been sacrificed, liberating in its place something of the inner essence of the event in question, permeating the text like a fragrance.

Thus the first chapters especially give the impression of having had something of the *substance* of the event at the Jordan poured into it. This is confirmed by such passages as 'you will see heaven open' (1:51) or 'coming from above' (3:31), not to mention the Baptist's direct testimony in 1:32–34. Thus the words 'you are my beloved [*agapētos*] Son' have their echo in what the Baptist, who witnesses the baptism at the Jordan, says: 'The Father loves the Son.'

Here again agape is bound up with 'giving'. The sentence quoted is flanked by two others that speak of the Father's giving: 'The one whom God has sent speaks the words of God, for God gives him the Spirit without measure,' and he 'has given everything into his hand'.

The divine ground of the universe shows his love for the Son by giving him words of wisdom from the Holy Spirit and power from the Father.

The Father loves me

The evangelist leaves a significant gap of time before he has Christ himself express his consciousness of being loved by the Father with agape. This gives rise to the impression that it was only gradually that the event at the Jordan developed within Christ's consciousness.

57. THE AGAPE OF THE FATHER

The sentence in 5:20, 'the Father loves the Son and shows him everything he does himself,' serves as a transition from the words of the Baptist, 'the Father loves the Son,' to the passage where Christ says it himself, 'The Father loves me.' But in 5:20 the word used is not *agapa* but *philei*.

Philéein is the other Greek word for 'to love'. To anticipate the result of our subsequent treatment of John 11:5 and 21:15, *philéein* stands beneath *agapē* in the hierarchy of Johannine words. It expresses more personal friendship and affection, whereas *agapē* points to a high, majestic form of divine love, which does not exclude this more personal 'liking' but does express something higher. In any case, the word *agapē* is not in question in 5:20.

A great deal has yet to happen before Christ's perception of the voice from heaven has sufficiently matured to be expressed in words. Between the baptism at the Jordan and these words lies nothing less than the greatest portion of Christ's public service, six of the seven miracles that John mentions: the marriage at Cana, the healing of the boy, the healing of the paralytic, the feeding of the five thousand, the walking on the water, and the healing of the man born blind. We are standing between the sixth and seventh miracles, between the healing of the blind man and the raising of Lazarus.

It is the time of the last autumn Festival of Tabernacles before the Passover of Golgotha. The words are spoken towards the end of the parable about the good shepherd. The words of Christ spoken in Chapter 10 spread over the autumn (10:1–21) and winter (10:22–39) periods (the Festival of the Dedication of the Temple took place around mid-December) and they receive their peculiar character by standing in this interval between the sixth and seventh miracles. On the one hand, they refer to the healing of the blind man. As opposed to the loveless treatment shown to the man by the Pharisees, who were appointed as shepherds of the people, Christ shows himself to be the good shepherd. On the other hand, the approaching raising of Lazarus also casts a special light on these words in Chapter 10. In a very specific sense Christ will show himself as a shepherd to Lazarus. The raising of Lazarus also stands in the closest proximity, both chronologically and in its essential nature, to the death and resurrection of Christ.

Thus the parable about the good shepherd is partly inspired by what is about to come and already contains thoughts about Jesus' free and sovereign sacrificial death. It is in this context that Christ speaks for the first time about the agape of the Father for him:

> The Father loves me, because I lay down my life so that I may take it up again. (10:17)

He then speaks of the sovereign freedom with which he goes out to meet his death: 'No one takes it from me; I lay it down of my own accord, I have authority to lay it down, and I have authority to take it up again. This command I received from my Father' (10:18). The word 'command' *(entolē)* here must intend something beyond its Old Testament connotations. It must be something like 'a goal to which he has been consecrated' or 'a goal he strives towards spiritually' that the Father has shown him. It is similar to the passage, which speaks, in place of charge or commandment, about the Son's looking towards the Father who 'shows' him what he himself is doing (5:19f). The 'commandment' that the Father gives Christ is such a goal-image that is 'shown' to him.

Dying and rising, self-surrendering and receiving anew, is a law of life grounded in the divine. Through Golgotha and Easter, the Son reveals a mystery within the realm of what human beings can conceive – a mystery that would otherwise be lost in the depths of the divine brilliance in the night of the blinding light which no one can penetrate.

When Christ speaks of the good shepherd who gives his life for those entrusted to him, he realises with special clarity that he is the Son of the Father.

The importance of the phrase: 'to lay down one's life'* is brought out through repetition:

> I AM the good shepherd: the good shepherd is one who lays down his life for the sheep. (10:11)
> And I lay down my life for the sheep. (10:15)
> The Father loves me, because I lay down my life. (10:17)

As is so often the case with John, the order within the Trinity is revealed within the development of the thought: the thought first

---

* Most English translations use 'life' for the Greek *psychē,* soul.

appears as objective knowledge in the third person (10:11). Then it is expressed personally in the first person (10:15), and finally it is related to the Father (10:17).

Christ is about to fulfill this 'commitment' in an overwhelming intensification now that he approaches the mystery of his death: first, through the raising of Lazarus and, second, through his own resurrection. This drawing closer to death is a progression within John's Gospel and is designated by the reference to the Father's agape for Christ. The Son, who is preparing himself 'to go to the Father', grows towards a constantly increasing similarity with the Father. 'I am going to the Father' is not only the most sublime interpretation of the death that he is approaching. It also means that in freely taking upon himself this sacrificial death, Christ is drawing decisively closer to the Father. The passage we already mentioned is being fulfilled here:

> The Son can do nothing by himself; he can do only what he sees the Father doing: and whatever the Father does, the Son does too. For the Father loves the Son and shows him everything he does. And he will show him even greater works than these, so that you will marvel. (5:19f)

In carrying out and realising what has been shown to him, he experiences the Father's love.

This first mention by Christ of the Father's agape for him is the presupposition for the overwhelming revelation that 'I and the Father are one' (10:30). While a quarter of a year lies between the shepherd parable, which was told at the autumn festival, and these words, which were spoken at the winter Festival of the Dedication of the Temple, there is a thread uniting the two. This can be seen in the resumption of the shepherd motif in 10:27. Therefore this statement about being 'one' stands within the light of the statement about agape. This statement is remarkable in that Christ for the first time combines himself with the Father in a 'we' *(esmen,* 'we are', the first person plural), even though the emphatic 'we' *(hēmeis)* is reserved for the High Priestly Prayer (17:11). His consciousness of the Father's agape being poured out over him enables Christ to say this.

Our attention might be drawn to the appearance of the 'oneness' motif immediately preceding the statement about agape (10:17): 'one flock, and one Shepherd' (10:16). 'Oneness' for John is not merely numerical but connotes a kind of mystical yet personal union. In the immediate vicinity of the agape passage it appears in three different forms: one flock, one shepherd, one *(mia, heis)*.

With this consciousness Christ approaches the mystery of his death. The first step is the raising of Lazarus. This sentence, 'The Father loves me,' sets the tone for the whole new portion of the gospel, which begins with Chapter 11.

The motif is carried on within the Farewell Discourse. In the conclusion to his parable about the vine, Christ says:

> As the Father has loved me, so I have loved you. Remain in my love.* (15:9)

Christ's love for his disciples (which we will discuss in the next chapter) presupposes the Father's love for Christ. Unlike 10:17, the Father's love is not the only thing expressed here. 'The Father loves me' is now woven into a larger context through the Johannine 'so' or 'just as'.

It appears within the same context in the following sentence:

> If you keep my commandments, you will remain in my love, just as I have kept my Father's commandments and remain in his love. (15:10)

Here too, 'just as'. Christ applies to himself the same words as to his disciples: keep the commandments, remain in love. We have already spoken about the word 'commandment' *(entolē)*. 'To keep' is more than an external obedience. It is a careful watching and a watchful carefulness; it points to a nurturing of the interior life. It is much more living than a rigid observance of ordinances. Its connotations include faithful 'meditation' and correct action. It designates a reception into the rhythmic course of one's daily life of the divine goal to which one has been consecrated. Inseparable from it is the endurance of pious fidelity and persistence.

In accepting this goal as he does, Christ goes out through his own

---

* In the Greek 'I' and 'my' appear in the emphatic form.

activity to meet the love being given him. This gives the passage its special character. This time it does not say merely: 'The Father loves me,' but, 'I remain in his love.' It is impossible in a personal relationship for one member to be 'merely an object'. Therefore, Christ relates himself consciously through his activity to the highest gift of grace being given him. In this way it becomes fully his own.

'Remain' belongs among the unfathomable Johannine words. Its meaning stretches from the simplest literal interpretation to the most hidden mystical interpretation. It can mean remain, abide, dwell, persist, be eternal.

Its imperative use, 'Remain!' (15:9), shows that it is bound to an inner activity and, contrary to the first impression, does not refer to something stationary and passive as opposed to the dynamic of movement. Its antonym is not active movement but inactive coming to an end (1Jn 2:17).

In order to remain in John's sense it requires the expenditure of a powerful inner energy, a putting of oneself in motion. It is similar to the word 'keep' or 'observe' *(tērein)* – both words point to a process of life in which one is rhythmically 'breathed through'. One is moved and yet calm within this movement.

In relation to 10:17 and 15:9, this is an important expansion: the Father loves the Son, and the Son makes himself worthy to remain permanently in this state of being loved through constant interior movement and careful observation of the divine goals. In this being loved, he possesses the eternity of his own essence. 'I remain in his love.'

You loved me

The High Priestly Prayer gives a final form to the thought, 'the Father loves the Son.' At the conclusion of this magnificent text the love of the Father for the Son is expressed three times.

> I have given them the glory [*doxa*] that you gave me, that they may be one as we are one. I in them and you in me, that they may be completed in unity [oneness], so that the world will know that you sent me and loved them [the disciples] as you have loved me. (17:22f)

The most intimate and personal formulation is reached here. Let us look back at the previous passages: 'The Father loves the Son'; 'the Father loves me'; 'I remain in his love'; 'you love me'.

Thus, at the conclusion of Christ's earthly life, the perfect reflection is attained of the words spoken at the baptism in the Jordan: 'You are my beloved Son.' This occurs in the third part of the High Priestly Prayer. After Christ first prays for his own glorification and for that of the apostles, he broadens his scope and prophetically includes the growing Church, the future Christian humanity.

As in Chapter 10, the chapter about the good shepherd, the notion of 'one' (a neuter in Greek, *hen; unum* in Latin) reappears here and is once again placed in relation to the divine plural 'we'; here, however, it stands as a climax.

This 'one' (in Greek *to hen,* 'the One') has a special intonation in John's Gospel. The word is a neuter, an 'it'. Through a transition from the personal, which corresponds to the dignity of the human being, to the nonpersonal 'it', language can express descent in the hierarchy. For example, one might point with scorn to a person, by using the words, 'that thing'. There is, however, the reverse possibility. One can also say of someone that they are 'something very great'. Then the neuter expression intends something very high that is not beneath but above that which we usually refer to as the personal language. This is the case in the Annunciation to Mary in Luke's Gospel (1:35): 'The holy one to be born will be called Son of God.' This 'holy one' (neuter in Greek) pushes language to its limit and tries through this neuter to intimate something unspeakably high. Thus the Johannine 'one' is also to be placed beyond the everyday personal.

The 'one' motif appears for the first time in John's Gospel during the Festival of Tabernacles. Christ has given light to the man born blind. The repeated appearance of the words 'see', 'know', and 'recognise' within this chapter that encompasses the Festival of Tabernacles indicates that something more is being spoken of than eyesight (9:1–10:21). Gradually the eyes of the healed man are opened so that he can see his healer. The man must then hold fast to his understanding in the face of doubts and resistance from the people around him, and even in the face of the enmity of the Pharisees who are supposed to be his pastors or shepherds of soul. This insistence on his personal experience can be maintained only at the cost of total isolation. He is turned out of the synagogue. In view of this isolation Christ begins to speak of the new community of those who have become free through knowledge and over which he will be the 'Good Shepherd'. His relation to those who follow him, he expresses as follows: 'I AM the good shepherd; I know my own and my own know me, just as the Father knows me and I know the Father' (10:14f). The presupposition for the new community Christ is founding is the opening of eyes, knowledge, and the freeing of the individual. It is not until then that the words *one* flock, and *one* shepherd' are spoken.

The first 'one' in 10:30 refers to the relationship between God the Father and God the Son. In 11:52, the evangelist allows this 'one' to fall from above to our level and to be applied to human beings. After that it appears in the sacred context of the High Priestly Prayer. If we follow the apparently more reliable reading, according to which it appears only once in 17:21, it is used five times in the prayer: 17:11, 21, 22, 22, 23. Therefore, together with 10:30 and 11:52, it becomes one of those phrases that John uses seven times.

The words in 17:21, 'that all may be one' (*Ut omnes unum sint* in Latin), do not intend the 'one' to apply to an external organisation and have nothing to do with what would be called in the language of power politics a 'monolithic block'. Because of its connection to the relation between God the Father and God the Son ('just as'), the 'being one' becomes something infinitely sublime and of a divine character; human beings will not achieve it before their future 'perfection' (17:23).

In the High Priestly Prayer, the two series of passages about 'oneness' and 'love' are definitely fused.

'That they may be one like us' (17:11) appears in the second part of the prayer. The main passage, however, is in the last part: 'that they all may be one ... may they be in us' (17:21), 'that they may be one as we are one' (17:22), 'that they may be completed in unity [oneness]' (17:23).

In contrast to 10:30, the divine plurality is expressed with unusual force in that the emphatic form of 'we' *(hēmeis)* is used. It appears here three times with reference to God (17:11, 21, 22). This is without parallel in the rest of the gospel. The 'I' is surpassed here by the 'we'. Once again, the key to the 'one' and to the 'we' is agape.

Seeing the Trinitarian love between the Father, Christ, and the Church (17:23), the world is to be brought not only to faith in the mission of Christ (17:21), but to a knowledge as well: 'so that the world will know'. The world will know not only that Christ has been sent by the Father but also 'that you ... loved them as you have loved me' (17:23).

The veil that has hidden the divine from the world until now will be removed in the future. The appearance of the Trinity, which breaks into the human realm in the Church, causes the presence of the divine on earth to become so obvious that it can be known – even by 'the world'. This must, however, be preceded by a powerful realisation of the divine in man. By the way in which Christians manifest their 'being loved by God', a window is opened for the world so that it can actually know something of that transcendent mystery within God 'as you have loved me'.

The next sentence shows this love to have existed before creation:

> ... that they may see my glory that you gave to me *because you loved me before the foundation of the world.* (17:24)

John causes us to look through the words spoken at the baptism in the Jordan and see an eternal mystery. Christ had already spoken (17:5) of his 'glory [*doxa,* a revealing, radiating brightness] that I had with you before the world began'. When *doxa* is spoken of again in 17:22 and 17:24 the phrase, 'that I had' is replaced by 'you gave to me'. Friedrich Rittelmeyer often pointed out how, in the High Priestly Prayer, 'my' is for the most part replaced by *'which you gave me'.* He drew attention to the way in which 'my' was transfigured. 'The work that you gave me' (17:4); 'the people you gave me' (17:6); 'the words you gave me' (17:8); 'the glory that you gave me' (17:22). It is significant that in the final reference to the *doxa* of Christ (it is the last within John's Gospel), the word 'my' should nevertheless reappear. The way in which 'my' and 'that you gave me' are combined with one another in this passage is unique. The key to this is agape: '... that they may see *my* [emphatic form in Greek] glory that you have given me because you loved me before the foundation of the world' (17:24).

'My' is purged of all egotism and made selfless and transparent by means of this reference to its original 'givenness' by God. On the other hand, 'you gave me' becomes clear in all its seriousness in this 'my': it is a thoroughly real giving in which the giver divorces himself totally from his gift in order that it may fully belong to the receiver.

This is the ultimate conquest over Lucifer: radiant glory combining the two qualifiers 'my' and 'you have given me'. As in 3:16, the agape motif is here again joined with that of giving in a fundamental relationship.

Just as the Johannine agape-context in the High Priestly Prayer is brought into contact with the other contexts of 'one', 'we', and 'giving', so too, as we have seen, with the *doxa* context. Doxa is one of the most important Johannine words. The history of this concept of the *doxa* of Christ in the fourth gospel stretches all the way from the Prologue ('we saw his glory,' 1:14) to this passage ('so that they may see my glory,' 17:24). This final passage resounds together with the first.

The final passage in this series is the concluding sentence of the High Priestly Prayer.

> I have made your name known to them, and will continue to make it known, so that the love with which you loved me may be in them, and I in them. (17:26)

Even here, at the conclusion of the prayer, the truth of the Father's agape for the Son does not stand in isolation. The way it was woven in to the 'just-as' sentences (15:9f; 17:23) has already shown that it does not want to stand alone. This not-standing-alone is intensified in this final passage, even though the thought 'you loved me' is placed in a modest relative clause. This construction is by no means intended to relativise the reality.

It shows that this agape is in the fullest sense not to remain 'exclusive', but rather, in the receiver's opinion, ought to be mediated. This again reveals the contrast between Christ's essence and Lucifer's. He regards this highest gift as something he cannot keep to himself. The emphasis in this sentence is on the desire of the Father's love to be in the disciples. His own reception of this love serves only as a background. For that very reason, this passage is the apogee of the series of passages we are now able to survey. It is precisely in its stepping back, in its unwillingness to be a final goal sought for its own sake, that this agape reveals its dignity.

3. The agape of the Father for the disciples

The Father's agape is directed towards the world, the Son, and the disciples. In the order in which they are mentioned the disciples are the third object of the Father's love.

The entire first part of the gospel does not give them this honour; the first reference is in the Farewell Discourse. It is also significant that in all these passages about the Father's love for the disciples, it is always spoken of as something future, as something that has yet to be brought to them. Obviously the reference here must be to a special meaning of agape. The Father's general love for the disciples does not need to be realised in the future. We are here concerned with a special kind of agape. If the disciples have not yet received it, it can only be because they have not yet developed sufficiently to participate in it. The love given them up until now is the one mentioned in 3:16 ('loved the world'). Not until they have been awakened can they raise themselves above this world.

Chapter 14

The first passage is in the fourteenth chapter. In 14:16 Christ has promised, for the first time, the coming of the Holy Spirit as a consoler. He then spoke of his own return, and of the higher life to which the disciples are called, but which they have not yet begun: 'you will live' (14:18f).

> Anybody who receives my commandments and keeps them will be one who loves me; and anybody who loves me *will be loved by my Father*. (14:21)

One is struck by the passive form, 'will be loved'; it is the only one in John's Gospel. This unusual mode of expression, occurring precisely at the point where a new thought is introduced, is bound to have a special significance. It could mean 'will be able' (in this higher, special sense) to be loved by the Father. Through their disposition they are enabled to absorb the rays that up until now more or less passed over them. Because their love for Christ has proved itself in action, they have made themselves worthy objects of this highest agape.

57. THE AGAPE OF THE FATHER

Immediately after this passage the thought reappears but in a different formulation:

> If anyone loves me he will keep my word, and *my Father will love him.* (14:23)

Once again, an active love for Christ is presupposed. This time the active form is used, 'my Father will love him.' Here, the future experience, also mentioned in 14:21, is more God's. It expresses something unusual. God the Father, who is the first beginning from eternity, will make a new beginning. His eternity is not stagnant. It does not exclude but specifically includes the possibility that God will move on to new possibilities – because of the maturing of en-Christened human beings. This can be illustrated by an example: one shows a different love towards a child from what one does towards an adult. In order to receive the love that an adult is capable of receiving, a person must first have matured to adulthood. Likewise there is a special kind of divine love for mature human beings, but God must retain it until they are ready for it. This is a human comparison, but anthropomorphism is not false in principle; after all, humanity's fundamental direction is 'theomorphic'.

The passive form in 14:21 had more the meaning: when they become aware of it, human beings will open themselves to something that may already be present but which they are unaware of until now. The active form in 14:23 brings a new nuance: God will do something new, something that previously did not exist. (The present-tense verb in 16:27, 'for the Father himself loves you,' is not a contradiction because it is *philei,* not *agapei).* Perhaps, however, we are being too rigid to talk of such a delicate matter in this way. Perhaps the sensitivity needed to perceive this love cannot be expressed in words.

These passages (14:21, 23) end as they began, with a promise of the Holy Spirit: 'the Advocate, the Holy Spirit, whom the Father will send in my name' (14:26). Thus, this promise that the Father will show humanity a special love that he could not show previously is enclosed by two promises to send the Holy Spirit, who will be active among Christians. Within the Godhead, the Holy Spirit represents the future aspect.

The High Priestly Prayer

Turning from Chapter 14 to the High Priestly Prayer, we find that the concluding sentences of the prayer also lead into the sphere of the Holy Spirit, the future Church:

> That the world will know that you sent me *and loved them* as you have loved me. (17:23)

Looking out beyond the present apostles, Christ prays for those who will come to believe in him through the preaching of the apostles. The glory *(doxa)* of Christ is to radiate from them in such a way that the world can perceive that the Father's agape is being poured out upon them. The concluding 'as' places the future Christians alongside the Son. The words spoken at the baptism in the Jordan apply to them as well. What John intimated in his First Letter will be fulfilled: 'what we are to be in the future has not yet been revealed; we know that when it is revealed we shall be like him' (1John 3:2).

As unbelievably bold as the prophecy in 17:23 is, it is surpassed in the concluding sentence of the High Priestly Prayer:

> *So that the love* with which you have loved me *may be in them* and I in them. (17:26)

This surpasses the 'as' insofar as it expresses a total identity of agape. The very same love with which the Father loved Christ should be 'in them'. This is an absolute climax. 'In them' means that the Father's agape is no longer something that comes from without and merely externally touches humanity's essence; it is fully received and made a part of man; it will become one in a final communion with man's self *(en autois,* 'in their very selves').* This is the mystical, Johannine 'in'

---

* The passage 5:42 is the 'negative side' of this crowning conclusion of the High Priestly Prayer: 'I know you too well: you have no love of God in you [*en heautois*].' The two passages are related as *emptiness* and *fulfilment.* Without the in-pouring of divine agape, the human personality remains an empty cup. It is not only in their contents that 5:42 and 17:26 stand in a polar relation to one another. The noun *agapē* appears seven times in John's Gospel and it appears that these passages, aside from being in the larger contexts that we have already pointed out, also combine with one another to form a sevenfold organism, listed here:

that appears for the last time in John's Gospel at the end of the High Priestly Prayer. The series of agape passages converges here with the high point of another Johannine series, which is characterised by the mystical 'in'.

It is certainly no accident that John on the one hand is the evangelist of the 'I AM' statements and, on the other hand, so frequently uses the word 'in'. The self-contained character of the personality is inseparably bound up with the 'I AM'. The personality powerfully comprises itself within itself and is distinguished from all other beings. If the personality succumbs to egotism, the character of self-containedness becomes one of isolation, of being caught and imprisoned in oneself. If the I, the self, makes itself into a bearer of love, it is capable of selflessly and yet personally living into another's being with full consciousness. Likewise, it can invite another being into its interior and receive it within. The self-contained character of the person is not a goal in itself, but the presupposition for free disposition over oneself. Only those who fully possess themselves can fully give themselves. The 'I' that is capable of living in the other and of taking the other into itself is capable of intimacy.

It is important to notice how 'knowledge' and 'love' are united with one another at the conclusion of Chapter 17. The Father's agape will be able to be in the disciples because Christ reveals the Father's name to them more and more clearly. This emphasis on knowledge also leads into the realm of the Holy Spirit.

In comparing passages 17:23, 26 and 14:21, 23, one notices, among other things, that Chapter 14 speaks of the *individual* who opens himself to the Father's agape through active love for Christ. 'Anyone who receives my commandments and keeps them ... anyone who loves me.' The transformation begins in the individual. The individual Christianised I is then allowed to recognise itself more

---

1. You have no love of God in you. (5:42)
2. If you have love for one another. (13:35)
3. Remain in my love. (15:9)
4. You will remain in my love. (15:10)
5. And I remain in his love. (15:10)
6. No one has greater love. (15:13)
7. That the love with which you have loved me may be in them. (17:26)

The words about emptiness and fullness stand in the first and last of these seven passages. In this sevenfold series is also a crowning conclusion (17:26).

and more in the great 'we'. The High Priestly Prayer, as distinct from Chapter 14, speaks of the many who will become one community ('unity'): 'that you ... loved them ... that the love ... may be in them'. This community of inwardly awakened individuals is also ruled over by the Holy Spirit.

58

THE AGAPE OF THE SON

1. The agape of the Son for his own

In the survey at the beginning we saw that in the first ten chapters only the Father is said to practise true agape. To declare the Son a bearer of agape as well shows his increasing transfiguration. This is done for the first time in the story about Lazarus.

Lazarus

It is to some extent prepared in the previous chapter, where Christ says for the first time that he knows he is loved by the Father with agape (10:17). These words at the end of the first half of the gospel serve as a transition to the word at the beginning of the second half:

> Jesus loved Martha and her sister and Lazarus. (11:5)

The beginning of the new division at Chapter 11 is indicated by the concluding verses of Chapter 10 (40–42), which recall the activity of the Baptist near the Jordan. On the other hand, one could also rightfully claim that the major division, which divides the gospel into clearly distinct parts if not into two 'halves', lies between chapters 12 and 13. The conclusion to Chapter 12 resembles an epilogue, and the beginning of Chapter 13 a prologue, which introduces the washing of the feet and the sacred realm of the Farewell Discourse. That in turn puts us in immediate proximity to the Mystery of Golgotha.

Nevertheless, it is still not wrong to place the major division before the Lazarus chapter. The difficulties one has in trying to assign the raising of Lazarus to either the first or second part of the gospel indicate the twofold role of the chapter.

It belongs to the *first half* insofar as the raising of Lazarus concludes and crowns the series of the seven miracles reported in John's Gospel. It is the conclusion of Christ's externally directed activity.

It belongs to the *second half* insofar as the raising of Lazarus stands in the narrower realm of the Mystery of Golgotha. Just looking at the external chronological aspect, it is necessary to see this event as quite close to Easter. It is also closely related to the death of Christ in that the Sanhedrin was moved by reports of the event at Bethany to make the final decision to kill Jesus (11:50). In John's Gospel, the exaltation of the people during Christ's entrance into Jerusalem is motivated by their knowledge of his raising of Lazarus (12:17).

But the relation is even more intimate. Through the raising of Lazarus, Christ becomes aware of his own power to rise from the dead – a power hidden in the depths of his being. He experiences the power of Easter at the grave of Lazarus: 'I AM the resurrection and the life.' Thus the awakening of Lazarus belongs intimately to the events of Golgotha and Easter. Friedrich Rittelmeyer once said that Christ needed to raise someone from the dead in order to be able to rise up himself, in order to approach his own death with a consciousness of having overcome death. In this respect, the story of Lazarus belongs more to the second than to the first half of the gospel. This is true also from the point of view of John's statements about agape.

The sisters have sent their message, 'Lord, see, the man you love [*phileis*] is sick' (11:3). Christ answers with the overwhelming interpretation: 'This sickness will not end in death'. This is followed immediately by the evangelist's comment: 'Jesus loved [*ēgapa*]'. The two words for love, *philein* and *agapein,* are placed right next to each other. The order of precedence cannot be overlooked. The sisters speak of 'having affection' [*phileis*], just as the Jews do at the grave: 'See how much he loved him' (11:36).

It is as if the evangelist wanted gently to correct what the sisters said. He knows that Christ loves Lazarus in an even deeper and more divine way than the sisters can intimate. They appeal to his *philein* but in reality he was already showing *agapē* above and beyond their desire and understanding.

The key to the transition from *philia* to *agapē* lies in the words of

Christ that unite the two passages: 'This sickness will not end in death, but is for the glory [*doxa,* renown, manifestation] of God, through which the Son of God may be glorified [*doxasthē*]' (11:4). This may not be interpreted in the superficial sense to mean that Lazarus has to die in order for Christ to have the opportunity to show his miraculous power. To put it bluntly, there were plenty of other dead people for Christ to awaken. It was not a question of just anyone, but specifically of Lazarus, for whom he 'had affection', whom he called 'Our friend [*philos*], Lazarus' (11:11). Lazarus had to be someone for whom this dying and being raised would have a very special meaning. There were other dead for whom relatives and friends mourned, but Christ did not raise anyone else after four days. This is one consideration that could help us to appreciate Rudolf Steiner's interpretation of this as a 'death of initiation'. The words spoken at the graveside, 'I AM the resurrection and the life; whoever believes in me will live, even if he dies,' show that he is speaking not of an external revivification, but of a rebirth from the dead (11:25).

This would remove our indignation at Christ's strange, seemingly callous delay after receiving the message. When he heard that Lazarus was ill, he stayed where he was for two more days, before saying to his disciples, 'Let us go to Judea' (11:6f). He did not delay in order that his miracle might appear all the more wonderful because he raised up someone dead for several days, but in order for the three and a half days of the death of initiation to pass. The attempt has been made to see in this delay a psychological proof for the falsity of the Johannine Christ: How could that be the merciful Saviour if he ignores the pain of the sisters and is concerned only with proving his divinity through the most spectacular miracle possible? All of these accusations would be justified if we were concerned here only with the revivification of a dead man; they are refuted, however, if we look at the event as an initiation. This could happen not to just any dead man, but only to someone who was close to Christ.

If Christ had only *philia* for Lazarus and his sisters, he would have spared them the death and the sorrow – but in so doing, he would have withheld the mystery of the resurrection from them. He allowed Lazarus to die and raised him because he loved him with *agapē,* with a love that was concerned with Lazarus' eternal life and its development. *Agapē* reveals here its magnificent austerity and majesty.

This clarifies the short sentence (11:5) inserted by the evangelist. It makes Christ's seemingly callous behaviour understandable and places the right sign before the entire event.

The agape sequence merges here with the other Johannine sequence of *doxa*. The sickness was not intended to end in death but to provide the occasion for a greater revelation of the divine; it was 'for the *doxa* of God'. It is put even more explicitly, 'through which the Son of God may be glorified [*doxasthē*]'.

The raising from the dead brought greater glory to the Son of God, not only in the person of Jesus of Nazareth but likewise in Lazarus. Shortly afterwards John writes that he sat at the same table with the Lord (12:2), which is to be interpreted in the sense of 'and in them I have been glorified' (17:10).

We have already referred to the transfiguration as an account that is 'lacking' in John's Gospel (p. 418), but which constitutes the delicate atmosphere of the entire gospel. What in the synoptics is a single isolated event on Mount Tabor, has been developed in John to the grand sequence of *doxa* passages, which begins even in the Prologue ('we saw his glory'). In John's view, Christ had his divine glory from the very beginning of his activity. After the first miracle at Cana, John writes: 'He revealed his glory' (2:11), but this glory is more hidden in the beginning. Its full majesty appears more and more fully as Golgotha and Easter approach. Thus, in spite of the statement at Cana, the evangelist writes in the seventh chapter, 'because Jesus had not yet been glorified' (7:39), and likewise in 12:16.

The statement in 11:4 that through the sickness 'the Son of God may be glorified', introduces something new into John's Gospel. The transfiguration and glorification that will occur at Golgotha and Easter begin here with the raising of Lazarus.

It should be noticed that in 11:4 John speaks of the glorification of the Son of *God,* and in 12:23 and 13:31 of the glorification of the Son of *Man*. The glorification comes from above and penetrates into the earthly more and more deeply. First the form of the Son of God begins to radiate more brightly and, later, Christ's human nature becomes more luminous.

The mystery of Bethany glorifies the Son of God and the Mystery of Golgotha the Son of Man.

John's first reference to Christ's agape (in 11:5) is made more meaningful by this context. It follows immediately the words about glorification: 'but is for the glory of God, through which the Son of God may be glorified'.

The sequence 'Jesus loved Martha and her sister and Lazarus' contains an intensification. Martha has the most distant relation to the event, Mary is more sensitive to his agape, and Lazarus experiences it most decisively of all. This likewise interprets the sequence of scenes at Bethany: the first meeting is with Martha (11:20), the second with Mary (11:32), and the third with Lazarus.

Perhaps it is also worth noticing that the Father's love is first referred to by the Son (3:16) and the Son's love by the evangelist (11:5).

The motif of Christ's love for those who belong to him and whom he wants to lead to a higher life develops in the second part of the gospel.

At the beginning of the washing of the feet

At the beginning of the thirteenth chapter, where the account of the washing of the feet leads to the inner sanctuary of the Farewell Discourse, the evangelist speaks of the agape of Christ with great solemnity:

> Now before the Passover feast, Jesus knew that his hour had come for him to depart from this world to the Father. *Having loved his own who were in the world, he loved them to the end.* (13:1)

Looking back, the author places all that Christ had done under the radiance of the word *agapē*. 'Having loved his own who were in the world.' This is a continuation of the sequence begun in 11:5. But the following is immediately presented as an intensification, in that the word 'love' is united with the expression *telos* (in the mysteries, *telos* meant the final stage of initiation): 'he loved them to the end,' to the end of the initiation. *Telos* is also contained in the word spoken from the Cross: *tetelestai*, 'it is accomplished' (19:30).

This 'love to the end' is related to his departing from this world and going to the Father, to his being fully consecrated by his free surrender of himself into the bosom of the Father.

The sentence in 13:1 is not only a solemn introduction to the washing of the feet, but also a significant prologue to the Mystery of Golgotha. It is the heading for the most important part of John's Gospel, which begins here.

From the thirteenth chapter on, it is possible to distinguish two different continuations of the newly begun sequence of Christ's agape for his own.

On the one hand, we find this agape spoken of as before by the evangelist in the third person. These four passages about the beloved disciple, added to the three references already mentioned in 11:5 and 13:1 (twice) all add up to a sevenfold sequence.

On the other hand, a second sevenfold sequence begins after the washing of the feet, and in it Christ expresses his love for his own in the first person. We will begin with the words about the beloved disciple.

The beloved disciple

The first mention of the 'disciple whom Jesus loved' appears at a very dramatic moment.

The washing of the feet has been completed. In deep agitation,* Christ said, 'One of you will betray me.' This sombre background highlights the first reference to the beloved disciple.

> On of them, *the disciple whom Jesus loved,* was reclining at Jesus' side. (13:23)

The word for 'side' is *kolpos* (literally 'bosom') and is also used in the Prologue (1:18): 'the only begotten Son who is at the Father's side' *(kolpos)*. *Kolpos* is the sphere of the heart's inspiration. Just as God's only Son came from his Father's heart, as one consecrated to reveal the Father's most intimate love, so the beloved disciple was allowed to receive the inspiration of Christ's heart and become his most prominent herald.

---

* 'He was troubled in spirit' (13:21); this is the third and last time that John uses *tarassō* in reference to Christ. The word is much stronger than 'disturbed', meaning 'troubled, agitated, shaken'. Previously it appeared in 12:27, 'Now is my soul shaken'. Its first use was in 11:33, at Lazarus' grave, 'convulsed himself'.

58. THE AGAPE OF THE SON

The communion of the beloved disciple with Christ contrasts glaringly with Judas' communion with the Adversary. Like a stroke of lightning, this scene reveals the two ultimate possibilities for a human being: either union with Christ or possession by Satan. 'Satan entered' into Judas (13:27).

At the beginning of the thirteenth chapter is written: Christ loved his own with agape. And suddenly a specific one of the Twelve is to be specially characterised as 'the one whom Jesus loved'. If the verb *philein* had been used here, the statement would not be so unusual. In that case it would simply refer to a special, personal friendship for one person, in addition to his general agape for all. In 20:2 we are told that such a special friendship did also exist, for the reference is to the disciple for whom he had affection *(ephilei)*. But how can it be that precisely Christ's agape should explicitly single out the disciple from the others? Once again, the word must have a special meaning here, too. It is similar to 14:23, 'my Father will love him,' which apparently refers to a special love that humanity generally is not yet capable of receiving. We have already seen that the more a recipient ceases to be a mere 'object' of agape, and the more they become an active subject, the more intensely divine agape can encounter them. For example, human beings have an endlessly deeper appreciation for God's agape for them than a stone does, which is also an object of God's agape. Likewise, there are various degrees of openness among people. John was the most *awakened* among the apostles; Christ's agape had to be a different experience for him than for the others who, in comparison, were 'sleeping' disciples.

The fact that the expression 'the beloved disciple' does not appear until after the raising of Lazarus is, among others, an intimate confirmation of Rudolf Steiner's explanation. He claims that John, the author of the fourth gospel, hides himself behind the figure of Lazarus who has undergone the mystery of death and resurrection. This would enable John to become a specially initiated herald of Christ.

The master's agape was given to everyone (13:1), but John alone received it as one who had been awakened. For that reason it meant so much to him that he could justifiably be distinguished from the others as the disciple whom Jesus loved. Christ could reveal to him the depths of his person. John alone would record the Farewell Discourse.

John was the only disciple to stand under the cross on Golgotha:

> So Jesus, having seen his mother and *the disciple he loved* standing nearby, he said ... (19:26)

The awakened disciple beholds the mystery of death for the sake of love. He recognises the sacrifice of the cross as a deed of agape. It produces the agape of the Father who surrenders his only Son (3:16); it produces the agape of the Son who loves both his Father (14:31) and his own to the end (13:1).

Just as he recognised the nature of the crucified Christ, so too does he recognise the risen Christ before the other disciples. After the miraculous catch of fish, he sees the risen Christ standing on the shore of the Sea of Galilee. He speaks the first words of recognition.

> Then *the disciple whom Jesus loved* said to Peter, 'It is the Lord' [*ho kyrios estin*]. (21:7)

This story of the catch of fish and the meeting in the morning on the shore, strikes one very much like a dream, and that is what constitutes its unique fascination. If one removed John's words of recognition, the scene would pass before us like a marvellous morning dream, which definitely moves the soul in an unusual way yet leaves behind an uncertainty as to whether it is a fabric woven of remembered images or a factual, real meeting with a being out of the supersensible world. When John speaks his words of recognition, a flash of intuition breaks through the obscurity. The fabrication of dreams reveals itself as a true image. In the glimmer of this obscure, early morning experience an absolutely certain truth is grasped.

Friedrich Rittelmeyer pointed out that this sentence, 'It is the Lord,' which in the original has the connotation of 'the Lord *is*,' occurs three times in the story of the catch of fish. The second time is 'As soon as Simon Peter heard him say, "It is the Lord"...' (21:7). The third time: 'None of the disciples dared to ask him, "Who are you?" They knew it was the Lord' (21:12). This knowledge originated in John. Peter heard it first and in the end all the disciples realised it. This is followed by the eating of bread and fish (21:13). The account is stylised like the feeding of the five thousand and thus like the words of the Last Supper.

As we see the beloved disciple in a special relation to the crucified

Christ (19:26) and to the risen Christ (21:7), so the last of these passages, after the meal on the shore of the lake, relates to the return of Christ. (As was said earlier, 20:2 uses *ephilei*.)

> Peter turned and saw *the disciple whom Jesus loved* was following them. (The one who had reclined at Jesus' side, and said, 'Lord, who is it who will betray you?') Having seen him, Peter said to Jesus, 'Lord, what about him?' Jesus answered, 'If I want him to remain until I come, what is it to you? You must follow me.' (21:20–22)

The last mention of the beloved disciple refers to the first one. It recalls again the scene at the Last Supper, his reclining close to Jesus and his question about the traitor. The gospel text does not mention the scene a second time simply to refresh the memory of the forgetful reader. By means of the repetition it illuminates the great mission that has been assigned to John – 'I want him to remain until I come.'

This already refers to the Apocalypse. The 'remaining'* refers to a level of inner life that John had now reached, to a light that has been enkindled in him, that has not been obscured by denial (Peter), nor extinguished by treason (Judas). John's task is to carry this light through a darkened world until the sunrise of Christ's return. In a way, he has anticipated its light and represents the future form of Christianity.

The words spoken in the 'first person'

After the washing of the feet, during the course of the Farewell Discourse, Christ expresses his agape for his disciples in direct address. This occurs seven times between chapters 13 and 15.

The washing of the feet has been completed. The traitor has disappeared into the night. Jesus now devotes himself to his disciples with a special intimacy. Indicative of this devotion is the unique use in John's Gospel of the word *teknia*, 'little children' (in 21:5 the word *paidia* is used). He uses this word to express to his disciples something germinal, something underway, something to be fulfilled

---

* A superficial misunderstanding of 'remain' is explicitly corrected in 21:23.

in the future. In spite of all their imperfection, he sees in them a beginning of their new birth out of God, by which they will become, as the Prologue says, children of God (1:12). The use of the diminutive 'little child' expresses how tender and in need of care this seed in them still is. A little child needs warming love without which it cannot grow.

Immediately after Judas' exit, Christ's glory shines forth majestically. 'Now the Son of Man has been glorified' (13:31). Clothed with the radiant cloak of his glory, Jesus gives his 'commandment of love' and confirms it with a reference to his own agape for the disciples:

> As *I have loved you*. (13:34)

He also refers to the other form of agape, which is given not to the little child but to the mature. We spoke of this passage in another context.

> Anybody who receives my commandments and keeps them will be one who loves me; and anybody who loves me will be loved by my Father, and *I will love him* and reveal myself to him. (14:21)

This is not said about the agape he has already given; it is prophecy, apocalyptic. The appearance of a new Christian humanity will give both the Father and the Son a new possibility – a future experience for God. He will be able to communicate himself to those who have sufficiently matured by means of an agape that has not yet been manifested in the course of the world's development. In regard to this passage, we said earlier that it is significantly placed between two promises of the Holy Spirit (14:16, 26).

Corresponding to this future epoch of the Holy Spirit, the prophesied revelation of love is something bright and visible, enlightening and revelatory. 'I will love him and reveal myself [emphatic *emauton*] to him.' This prophecy has already begun to fulfil itself in regard to John.

The other five passages are in Chapter 15. They are all closely grouped together in reference to the image of the vine and the branches. The

58. THE AGAPE OF THE SON

mood of the fifteenth chapter is that of the Last Supper: it is filled with the mystery of the Eucharist. The following words are condensed out of this atmosphere of communion:

> As the Father has loved me, so *I have loved you.* Remain in *my love.* (15:9)
> If you keep my commandments, you will remain in *my love,* just as I have kept my Father's commandments and remain in his love. (15:10)
> This is my commandment: love one another, as *I have loved you.* (15:12)
> *Greater love* has no one than this: to lay down his life* for his friends. (15:13)

One should recall that in the entire first half of the gospel there are not more than three references to true agape, and then only to the Father's love. Keeping that in mind, one can better appreciate the uniqueness of this context where the agape of Christ is spoken of again and again and placed in relation to the agape of the Father and the disciples.

This love for his own is like the inner aspect of what the other evangelists describe as the institution of the Eucharist.

Christ's love for his own was presented as the standard for the disciples' love for one another (13:34), and is itself measured by the standard of a 'just as': 'just as the Father loved me'. This 'just as' applies also to the subsequent 'remaining in love'. The 'remaining in me',† spoken in connection with the vine (15:4, 5, 6, 7), is transformed into a 'remain in my love'. As we have already seen, this is a formulation that grants to the 'object' of agape an activity of its own and thereby elevates it above being a mere object.

Christ speaks here twice of 'remaining in his love'. That occurs in 15:9 in the form of the imperative, 'Remain!' which expresses the

---

* Most English translations use 'life' for the Greek *psychē,* soul.

† This 'remaining in Christ' is spoken of for the first time in the chapter about the feeding with bread in addition to the chapter about the vine from which wine is produced: 'remains in me and I in him' (6:56). Bread and wine. The evangelist uses the formulation 'remain in Christ' specifically in the Eucharistic contexts of chapters 6 and 15. In addition, one might mention that this motif, which occurs first in 6:56, develops into a sevenfold sequence in Chapter 15 (15:4, 4, 5, 6, 7, 9, 10).

active work aspect of this remaining. In 15:10 this activity is then further defined as 'keeping the commandments' and assuming the sacred goals of Christ with great perseverance. It is only through this activity that the disciples can hope to maintain themselves in the reception of his love.

A further difference between 15:9 and 15:10 is the emphatic 'my love' *(emē)* in 15:9. This emphatic 'my' is difficult to translate into English. It appears frequently in John's writings, for instance, 'my peace' and 'my joy'. He expresses the thorough relation of something to Christ's 'ego'. The emphatic 'my' corresponds to the emphatic 'I AM'. Thus 'my peace' is the peace that is not to be expected from without, from the world, but gives itself from within, from the ego of Christ. Thus the personal character of Christ's agape is especially emphasised in 15:9. This has nothing to do with any kind of egotism; rather, in the way in which Christ's I lives, lies the complete victory over egotism. The I does not withdraw selfishly into itself, but in full, sovereign freedom makes out of itself a grail of divine love.

Precisely because this agape emerges out of the 'I *am*,' it desires to be received by the disciples in the sphere of the conscious, active, 'lasting' I. Thus in 15:10 it is simply, 'Remain in my love' (*agapē mou*, without emphasis).

In 15:12, the phrase from the account of the washing of the feet reappears. This is not a merely monotonous external repetition, but has a specific sound to it after 15:9 preceding it: 'As the Father has loved me'. Thus the links of the chain mesh together in the chapter with the vine metaphor: 'As the Father has loved me, so I have loved you.' The series of passages about Christ's agape for his disciples reaches its climax in 15:13, 'Greater love has no one than this'.

In the ancient sacred texts the word 'great' usually has more or less 'magical' connotation (in the sense of a force that comes from the spiritual and 'moves the world'). The greatest love is simultaneously that which is most effective, which has the highest potency of 'white magic'. Black magic acquires its potency through the sacrifice of another's life. White gives its own life.

'To surrender one's life [*psychē*]' – this formulation is familiar to us from the chapter about the good shepherd where it is significantly repeated by Christ, the third time in relation to the Father's agape (10:17). Here, in 15:13, it is related to agape in an ultimate, classical way. Christ interprets his death as a deed of the 'greatest love'.

It is unjustifiable to compare this sentence with the exhortation to love one's enemies, in the Sermon on the Mount, and to declare that love 'even greater'. The attempt has been made to prove in this way that the 'Johannine Christ' is a constructed form and does not attain the stature of the true synoptic Christ. The 'greater' in 15:13 does not refer to the object of the love, to the friends. That definitely could be surpassed. It refers to the way in which the love is shown: through the sacrifice of one's own life. No form of love can surpass that which reveals itself through self-sacrifice.

2. The agape of the Son for the Father

We see repeatedly that John does not place the divine persons in an 'equality' as abstract dogma does. As unequivocally as the divinity of Jesus is proclaimed, just as clearly is the Father said to be greater.

To bring out the incomparable character of the Father's majesty, the reader should realise that in no place – to anticipate for a moment – does John speak of the disciples' love for the Father, not even as a possibility or as a command, as is the case with their love for the Son. With John's Gospel (but not in his other writings) the word *agapē* is so highly esteemed that human agape for the Father cannot even be remotely envisaged.

The Father loves the disciples, first insofar as they are members of the world that is in need of redemption, and then, in a higher sense, as 'disciples' who become 'fully mature with the fullness of Christ' (Eph 4:13). The latter, however, is a future possibility; but the possibility of the disciples' answers does not even appear on the horizon.

This silence is a powerful witness to the transcendent majesty of the Father. His agape for the world remains unanswered, also his love for the disciples. Even the best possible human answer would be no answer, would not merit being called 'mutual agape'. The source of the Fatherly love lies on an inaccessible mountain peak.

When one has concentrated on this impression of silence, this silence of the evangelist, in regard to human agape for the Father, one is all the more impressed by the magnificent conclusion to Chapter 14:

> The prince of this world is coming. He has no hold over me,

but comes so that the world may know that I love the Father, and that I do as the Father has commanded me. Rise up, let us go from here. (14:30f)

Christ senses the enemies' approach. Is not 'prince of this world' a bold, almost divine, title? It states not only that Satan has managed to find a place in souls, but in so doing has gone on to take possession of a part of the world, of creation. Out of the great, unified universe that God penetrates, a certain province seems to have been sundered, in which God's omnipresence and omnipotence have lost their dominance. This realm of existence has become so thoroughly blinded to, and walled off from, the original divine that intelligent beings can act and think in it as atheists. (Naturally, this disregards the fact that even this 'fallen' province could not exist for a moment if God the Father did not keep it in existence. What we said is not intended absolutely, but relatively. God is definitely omnipresent, but there is more or less of this presence, which accounts for the dramatic fluctuation of the human history of rebellion and salvation.)

Christ came not only to save souls but, through them, the world as well (3:17, 4:42, 6:33, 51, 12:47). When he once again accepted his death in spite of the horrible consternation in his soul, he knew that this dealt a decisive blow to the prince of this world, and that through his sacrifice on the cross the prince of this world had been, in principle, dethroned. 'Now the crisis comes upon the world. Now the prince of this world will be cast out' (12:31).

As when he underwent his temptation, so too on the eve of Good Friday, Jesus experienced the sinister presence of the Adversary. At the last moment, when he is about to take the final steps of his return 'to the Father,' the Evil One approaches once again. 'The prince of this world is coming' (14:30). Since his temptation, Christ's spirit has taken increasing possession of his human nature and increasingly sanctified it. There is no longer a point where he is open to attack from him who is evil. 'He has no hold over me.'

That is the unique situation out of which the unique words about Christ's love for the Father are spoken. If we may express it like this, Christ needed to feel Satan's breath before he uttered these words out of the depths of his being. If it had not been for this 'provocation', they probably would have remained unspoken and never brought to this final stage of consciousness.

One senses, remotely, how the powers of evil have been given in some way a mission to 'call forth' this highest revelation of divine agape.

With the same breath Christ speaks of both his love for the Father and his readiness for action, 'that I do' *(poiō)*. This love expresses itself in action, in a deed that will dethrone the 'prince of this world' and reorder the development of the world so that the Father will become 'all in all'. The drive to action vibrates in the dynamic conclusion to the chapter, 'Rise up, let us go from here.'

59

THE AGAPE OF THE DISCIPLES

1. The agape of the disciples for one another

Due to the unusually exalted concept of agape in John's Gospel, it is not until after the thirteenth chapter, when certain presuppositions have been established, that the disciples can even be thought of as loving with agape.

After the washing of the feet

John's Gospel contains an intensely dramatic conflict between light and darkness. Perhaps the most ingenious revelation of the evangelist's artistic use of black and white lies in the dramatic moment of conflict, in the transition from Judas' expulsion to the Farewell Discourse. There is the darkness that consumes Judas and then the shining forth of a radiant glory in the room of the Last Supper.

> Having received the morsel, he immediately went out. And it was night. When he had gone out, Jesus said, 'Now the Son of Man has been glorified and God has been glorified in him. If God is glorified in him, God will also glorify him in himself, and will glorify him at once.' (13:30–32)

Through the unusual repetition of the word 'glorify' *(doxazein)* five times in the short text, one acquires the impression that an immeasurable radiance broke out. In the attempt to understand the text more fully, it becomes apparent that this radiance is derived from not one but three sunrises.

There is a threefold glorification:

1. The Son of Man is glorified.
2. God is glorified (revealed) in him.
3. God will glorify the Son of Man now in himself, in God.

The Son of Man – God in the Son of Man – the Son of Man in God. That is the hierarchy of glorification. The third and final one has yet to happen. It is completed in the ascension, when human nature is freed from death and the devil and given its place in heaven, when not only soul and spirit but the body as well receives eternal life.

As mentioned earlier, before the raising of Lazarus, Christ speaks of the glorification of the Son of God (11:4), and only when the Greeks approach and Christ feels the proximity of Golgotha does he speak for the first time of the glorification of the Son of Man. 'The hour has come for the Son of Man to be glorified' (12:23). This will be continued and powerfully intensified in 13:31.

The essential being of humanity, darkened through the Fall, becomes luminous again. In its weakened condition it obscured the divine foundation of the world, but now it begins to become transparent for the light of God. Humanity, which was about to succumb to dead matter and the prince of this world, becomes a rightful member of the heavenly world through the resurrection and ascension of Christ.

This is the threefold glory of which 13:31 speaks. This illumination, transfiguration, and glorification of humanity's essential nature is the presupposition for calling on humanity, for the first time in John's Gospel after the washing of the feet, to be bearers of agape. This is a counterbalance to Judas' 'mystical union' with Satan and his disappearance into the kingdom of the night (13:30). To the divine potentiality of man is opposed his diabolic one.

> I give you a new commandment, that you love one another. As I have loved you, so you also should love one another. By this all will know that you are my disciples, if you have love for one another. (13:34f)

The commandment of love is spoken solemnly in a threefold form according to its Trinitarian aspects:
1. A command, or task, 'I give you a new commandment.
2. Dependence on their imitation of Christ's example, 'As I have loved'.

3. The promise of a knowledge that 'all' will derive from it, 'By this all will know'.

The first sentence expresses authority (the principle of the Father). The second brings a human closeness to the commandment for the disciples by pointing to the example of the Logos become flesh (the principle of the Son). The third points to a knowledge that is intended for all (the principle of the Spirit). The assembly of Christianised people, the Church, should take on a radiance that seeing it, this knowledge will be enkindled for 'all'. We saw this same chain of thought in the High Priestly Prayer.

One should not overlook the nuance of the 'giving'. As in the other passages where John speaks of 'giving', it has a very full resonance here, too. We encountered this important Johannine context of 'giving' the first time in 3:16 ('he gave his only begotten Son'), where it is united with the agape sequence. In order to hear the passage (13:34) properly, it is necessary to realise that it belongs to the series of passages that deal with giving, and specifically with Christ's giving.* We pointed out earlier that 'commandment' is not to be understood in the Old Testament sense. This will become clearer in the following.

The image of the vine

Following the image of the vine, the commandment of love appears once again in the Eucharistic fifteenth chapter:

> This is my commandment: *love one another,* as I have loved you. (15:12)

As opposed to the formulation in 13:34, one notices that here John wrote 'my' instead of 'new' commandment. *New – my.*

'New' *(kainos,* not *neos)* does not mean anything superficial like

---

* Here are a list of all the passages in John's Gospel where Christ *gives* something: authority to become children of God (1:12), living water (4:14), bread (6:11, 6:51, 21:13), fish (6:11; 21:13), food for eternal life (6:27), his flesh (6:51), eternal life (10:28; 17:2), his example (13:15), a new commandment (13:34), his peace (14:27), the words *(rhēmata)* of God (17:8), the Word *(Logos)* of God (17:14), his glory (17:22).
In addition Christ is 'given' a command by his Father in regard to his speaking and acting: 'the Father who sent me, gave me a commandment, what I should say and what I should speak' (12:49); 'I do as the Father has commanded [given] me' (14:31).

'an eleventh commandment in addition to the other ten', but has a more qualitative significance. As in many other passages in the New Testament, it points to something 'specifically Christian'. One might say that the newness was not 'formal' but 'material' – newness in content. With Christ's 'I AM', the epitome of all sources and origins appears on earth. When this 'I' expresses its life, one sees that it emerges immediately from the sphere of the divine Creator. Everything that comes in contact with this 'I' receives the character of divine originality; it is 'renewed'. This is expressed by such phrases as 'new creature', 'new heaven and earth', and 'behold, I make all things new'.

We would misunderstand Christ if, when he spoke of the 'new commandment', we were to search anxiously through the history of religion to see if perhaps someone else had given the commandment of love before him. As many others as may have given it, it is 'new' because Christ gives it, and in his 'I' he bears the power to transform and renew the world. Its 'newness' lies in the saying, 'as I have loved you', and 'by this all will know that you are my disciples', disciples of my I (emphasised in the Greek: *emoi mathētai*). Earlier we explained that this emphatic 'my' in John's Gospel is to be understood in the light of the Johannine 'I AM' statements.

Thus it is not surprising that, in the repetition of the commandment of love in the fifteenth chapter, 'new' can be replaced by the emphatic 'my': 'This is my commandment' – the sentence sets a goal for the disciples that emerges from the 'I AM' of Christ.

The fifteenth chapter, more than any other, is filled with 'mysteries of the I'. It is introduced by the seventh and final Johannine 'I AM' statement: 'I AM the true vine.'* After it follow all the passages about 'I' and 'my' in which the vine of Christ glows and the mystery of the chalice of his blood radiates. 'Every branch in me' (15:2), 'remain in me, and I in you' (15:4), 'unless you remain in me' (15:4), 'I AM the true vine' (15:5), 'apart from me you can do nothing' (15:5), 'if anyone who does not remain in me' (15:6), 'if you remain in me' (15:7), 'you will be my disciples' (15:8), 'so I have loved you' (15:9), 'remain in my love' (15:9), 'as I have kept my Father's commandments' (15:10), 'so that my joy may be in you' (15:11).

---

* Bread (6:35), light (8:12), door (10:7), shepherd (10:11), resurrection and the life (11:25), the way, the truth, and the life (14:6), the vine (15:1). Rittelmeyer was the first to point out this sevenfold organism.

'My commandment' in 15:12 must be seen in this context.

Before the transition is made from the theme of mystical unity to that of the hatred the disciples will undergo, Jesus summarises his proclamation about love in the brief pregnant sentence:

What I command you is to *love one another.* (15:17)

Here the noun 'commandment' is replaced by the verb 'command', becoming a more personal, immediate address to the disciples.

All of these passages have in common the reference to the setting of a goal, to a 'command'. This agape 'for one another' does not yet exist. It is still pre-existent in the Spirit of Christ.

2. The agape of the disciples for Christ

The promises

Love of Christ is not a 'commission' like brotherly love. According to the strict, factual, sober understanding of John's Gospel, the latter can only be a later fruit of Christian development. But the agape for Christ, which has been placed before the eyes of Christians in all its divine and human glory, is expected to be the basic disposition of the disciples.

Thus it is simply stated in the fourteenth chapter, 'If you love me'.

If you love me you will keep my commandments. (14:15)

True Christian activity originates in love for Christ. The 'keeping of the commandments', the 'goals', includes the activity of consistent, faithful meditation as well as the right exterior deeds. All other motives for activity, such as the fear of hell, are beneath the Christian standard. Love for Christ is the driving force behind the development of a Christian personality. It leads into the kingdom of the Holy Spirit by creating the proper presuppositions for the proper knowledge of the truth. The quoted sentence continues: 'And I will ask the Father, and he will give you another Advocate [*paraklēton*] to be with you forever, the Spirit of truth.'

The following passages no longer say 'you'. The promise in 14:15 is general and applies to all Christians. Now we see more clearly how the treading of this path is the concern of each individual. Thus the plural is replaced by the singular. The transition is not from plural to singular 'you' but to the distant 'third person'. There are numerous sentences in John's Gospel that begin this way, 'of anyone' or 'whoever (does this or that)', a participial construction in Greek: 'the one doing this or that'. For example: 'I AM the living bread that came down from heaven. If anyone eats of this bread, he shall live for ever.' (6:51). Or: 'I AM the light of the world; anyone who follows me [the one following me] will not walk in darkness' (8:12). This form of speech has a specific person in mind, a certain 'somebody'. The hearer is not immediately exhorted to do this or that; it is left entirely up to him whether or not he wants to be this 'somebody', this 'whoever'. Christ communicates merely a higher law, a propriety of the higher world. The hearer must decide on his own whether or not to apply it to his own person. Even this tender reverence for human freedom is related to the 'I' character of John's Gospel.

> Anyone who receives my commandments and keeps them,
> will be *one who loves me*. (14:21)

With all possible emphasis, Christian activity is presented as the hallmark of those who truly love Christ. It is given the emphatic position at the end of the sentence: 'he [in the original the strongly emphatic *ekeinos*, 'that one'] it is, who loves me.'

The sentence in 14:15 allows the deed to proceed from the love; 14:21 leads again from the deed to the love. Perhaps not only in the sense that the confirmation of love through action is once again strongly emphasised, but also that Christian activity continually deepens one's love for Christ. The way in which heaven opens up in response to such striving is described in the very next sentence.

> And *anybody who loves* me will be loved by my Father, and I
> will love him and reveal myself to him. (14:21)

This flowing of the agape of the Father and the Son is finally intensified to a full experience of *Communion*.

Judas, 'not the Iscariot', had asked why the revelation of Christ was not to take place before all the world. He failed to see that Jesus could reveal his glory only to loving eyes. Just as in ordinary life someone cannot reveal themselves unless another shows openness and receptivity, so too, and even more so, in the world beyond the senses. There is no disinterested looking that simply sees everything that is visible. Vision is given only to the eyes of those who love. In the realm of the spiritual, love is not blind but opens the eyes.

Judas still lacked this intimate knowledge. In response to his question Christ concludes the chain of thought begun in 14:21:

> If anyone loves me he will keep my word, and my Father will love him, and we will come to him and make our home with him. (14:23)

In response to Judas' concern about world opinion, Jesus emphasises that he is first of all concerned with the individual and his inner experience. The redemption of the world must begin in the interior of the individual. 'If anyone.' This time, the keeping of the 'commandments' is replaced by the keeping of 'my word' (Logos). This transfers even more the notion of Christian activity into the inner and spiritual realm. This strong emphasis on the 'meditation on the word' returns even more directly to the root of proper outward conduct. Now Father and Son are combined in a divine 'we'. It is the plural of the divine fullness and, at the same, time the plural of the community of love within God. Heaven's mystery of love reveals itself on the level of communion ('make our home with him'). The mystical union of man with God permits simultaneously the experience of the inner-Trinitarian 'we', which includes the mystical union of the Father with the Son. 'We will come to him' and 'make our home with him'.

This is a reversal of the sentence at the beginning of the fourteenth chapter, 'There are many rooms in my Father's house' (14:2). The one verse speaks of the multitude being given roots and protection in the one divine ground. The other speaks of the fullness of the divine dwelling in the individual. The Greek middle form also says, 'we will make him [*autō poiēsometha*] our dwelling'.

The lack of agape

These passages, 14:15, 21 and 23, have shown how agape for Christ consecrates the disciples even to the point of communion, where humanity becomes the dwelling place of the divine fullness. The Greek word for 'dwelling' is *monē*, which is the noun derived from the verb meaning 'to remain'; we have already shown this important Johannine concept. Thus it means here 'a lasting abode' or 'a lasting place to remain'.

But the sketch of this line of development has passed beyond the reality of the moment. The disciples cannot yet be said to have agape for Christ. This is shown not so much by 14:24 ('Whoever does not love me does not keep my words'), for this verse expresses merely a general possibility without specifically applying it to the disciples.* But it can be seen clearly in the same speech:

> If you loved me, you would have rejoiced that I am going to the Father. (14:28)

These words sound resigned. This is the counter to the positive 'If you loved me', that is to say, 'but actually you do not'. Christ acknowledges the disciples' *philein* for him (16:27) 'for the Father himself loves you, because you have loved me'. This love is not to be scorned, since it is said of God the Father himself. The comparison with 16:27 gives us an idea of how exalted the concept of agape is in John's Gospel.

---

* It shows 'negatively' the meaning of agape for Christian activity. It is the driving force along the way of consecration that leads to the rebirth of man.

The relation of agape and rebirth is shown from another perspective in 8:42. Jesus challenges the Jews in Jerusalem, 'If God were your father, you would love me.' This is a 'negative' indication of the importance of rebirth for the life of agape. (It is only through the rebirth as described in 1:12 and 3:3, 5, 7 that the Jews, who believe their relation to the world of heaven to be guaranteed by their descent from Abraham, will in truth receive God as their Father.)

Does this not leave us with a circle? First rebirth through love and then love through rebirth. We are, however, dealing with two vital processes that occur simultaneously and foster one another; they cannot be definitely classified in the categories of cause and effect. According to the perspective, either the origin of love in rebirth or of rebirth in love is emphasised. It is easy to see why rebirth is emphasised to the Jews, who boast of their descent from Abraham; and agape, to the disciples.

The disciples' agape for Christ should have shown itself in their joy over his return to the Father. As divine love, agape is concerned above all with the salvation of the beloved and the suffering that is involved in attaining this high goal; and as long as he is moving towards it, he lives in the most interior joy despite all pain. We encountered something similar in the story of the raising of Lazarus.

Chapter 14:28 shows more shockingly than any other the heroic and austere side of the agape.

The resigned 'if' – 'if you loved me' – is a transition to the two final passages in our series, which likewise point to the absence of agape.

In the conversation by the lake, the risen Christ asks Peter if he loves him.

This is the only time that agape is spoken of in the form of a question. Let us look at the context. It is preceded by the miraculous catch of fish, during which John spoke the words of recognition: 'It is the Lord.' After the catch comes a meal. The mood pervading this meal on the shore of the lake in the early morning dawn is one of mystery. The disciples see a charcoal fire burning, as well as bread and fish – bread and fish as at the feeding of the five thousand. Likewise, this early meal has the character of a Eucharistic mystery.

About the feeding of the five thousand, John writes: 'Then Jesus took the loaves, gave thanks [*eucharistēsas*], and distributed to all who were sitting; so also the fish' (6:11). About the early morning meal, he writes: 'Jesus came, took the bread and gave it to them, and the same with the fish' (21:13).

Both descriptions are obviously stylised according to the words used to describe the institution of the Eucharist. There are a few minor differences: nothing is said about 'blessing' at the early morning meal, and it begins with the 'coming' of Jesus: 'Jesus came, took'

The feeding of the five thousand took place before the death and resurrection of Christ, and thus before what John calls the 'glorification' of the Son of Man. It is a prophetic event.

The early morning meal takes place after the 'glorification'. It clearly transpires in the sphere of the resurrection, of the realm beyond the senses. This renders superfluous the special Eucharistic blessing that, in consecrating the earthly, elevates it beyond the senses. The world of the miraculous and of the heavenly blessing is simply presupposed to be open. The important point is that the realm beyond the senses draws sufficiently close to human beings on earth and is experienced vividly enough as a reality. Therefore, the taking and giving of the bread is introduced with 'Jesus came'. The risen Christ had already called to the disciples, 'Come and have breakfast.' If we considered only the external situation, it would be hard to understand this emphasis on 'coming'. This is changed as soon as we realise that John is describing delicate events here that surpass the senses. There are degrees to which we experience a being we cannot sense. The impression from this meeting can be stronger or weaker, more or less conscious. The being that reveals itself can appear either 'farther' or 'nearer', whereby 'far' and 'near' do not refer to quantitative space, but to the greater or lesser reality the being seems to have. The disciples should 'come': they should set themselves in motion with their own activity towards the event. The risen Christ 'is coming'; the disciples consciousness of his nearness is intensified. This awareness of his greater nearness is then combined with the actual Eucharistic event: 'He came up, took the bread, and gave it to them.'

A similar intensification of an experience that surpasses the senses and is expressed in terms of a spatial drawing-near occurs in Matthew 28:17. The risen Christ appears but some of the disciples 'doubt'. Their 'seeing' is so weak that it cannot give them the certainty that they are confronting a reality. 'Jesus came up and spoke to them.' The encounter becomes more intense and has within itself the evidence of a real experience. One can also detect an uncertainty among the disciples in our text (Jn 21:12). Looking at the passage purely from the viewpoint of formal logic, we have to admit that it contains a contradiction, but psychologically it expresses perfectly a simultaneous knowing and yet not-knowing: 'None of the disciples dared to ask him, "Who are you?" They knew it was the Lord.' This recognition that the beloved disciple first expressed, 'It is the Lord' (21:7), is adopted unquestioningly by the others because of the sacred meal. Jesus' coming to the meal is a more clearly resounding 'I am', and for the disciples a clearer and clearer 'He is'.

All of this provides the necessary preparation for the question addressed to Peter.

> When they had eaten, Jesus said to Simon Peter, 'Simon son of John, *do you love [agapas] me more than these?*' (21:15)

The first word that breaks the 'ban of silence' – the event of the meal took place in the silence of a mystery; the first word spoken out of the presence of the risen Christ, as it becomes more and more real, is this question about agape.

It is well known how intimately the early Christians associated 'meal' and 'agape'. In giving them to eat, Christ reveals most fully the mystery of his agape, of the surrender of his being – the mystery that is therefore repeatedly proclaimed in the sacrament of the altar.

The experience of Christ's substantial, nurturing agape in his 'third' appearance before the disciples (21:14) prepares Peter to hear and be struck by this threefold reproachful question.

The question is definitely reproachful; it has often been recognised that this threefold question called to mind Peter's threefold denial.

On the eve of Good Friday, Peter had spoken generously, 'I will lay down my life for you' (13:37). These words, which we saw to be intimately related to agape (10:17; 15:13), Christ repeats, 'Will you indeed lay down your life for me?' as if he wanted to make Peter fully aware of what he had said. He then predicts the threefold denial after the crowing of the cock.

If Peter at that time had had the right to say what he did, he would have been able to answer the question of the risen Christ: 'Yes, I love you with agape'. As it is, he must forgo the use of this exalted word and restrict himself to *philia:* 'Yes Lord, you know that I love you with affection [*philō*].' He felt he had the right to say that (compare 16:27: 'because you have loved [*philein*] me'). In his answers he does not mention the 'more than these' and thus it is dropped in the second question:

Simon son of John, *do you love [agapas] me?* (21:16)

Christ asks him once again for agape. Peter answers again: 'Yes Lord, you know that I love you with affection [*philō*].' Once again he forgoes using the exalted word and assures Christ of his philia.

Thus it is all the more painful when Christ himself, in the third question, descends to the level of *philia* with the words: 'Simon son of John, do you love [*phileis*] me with affection?' and thereby places even that kind of love in question.

60

SUMMARY

The fundamental threefold division that we noticed in the first survey – agape of the Father, agape of Christ, agape of the disciples – was further subdivided when we asked about the object, the 'whom' of agape in addition to the subject, the 'who'. This resulted in various relations of agape:

1. The agape of the *Father* that applies to the world (3:16). The agape of the Father that applies to the Son (3:35, 10:17, 15:9, 10, 17:23, 24, 26). The agape of the Father that applies to the disciples (14:21, 23, 17:23, 26).
2. The agape of the *Son* that applies to the disciples (11:5, 13:1, 23, 19:26, 21:7, 20 and 13:34, 14:21, 15:9, 10, 12, 13). The agape of the Son that applies to the Father (14:31).
3. The agape of the *disciples,* which should apply to one another (13:34, 35, 15:12, 17); which should apply to Christ (14:15, 21, 21, 23, 28, 21:15, 16).

Thus we see that there are seven such relationships of agape in John's Gospel. Even the individual passages are ordered according to sacred numbers. The seven reappears frequently (the love of the Father for the Son; of the Son for the disciples, in two sevenfold series; of the disciples for Christ); in divisions 1 and 3 it is increased by five to make twelve.

In all of these what remains unsaid is, as we have seen, just as important as what is said. What agape is in John's Gospel becomes clear only when the various passages have been assembled. Only that agape is the subject of our study. Agape is something different in the other books of the New Testament, even in the First Letter of John, which is closest in content and language to John's Gospel. Agape appears there both as a noun and as a verb more often than in all twenty-one chapters of the gospel. But in the Letter, agape is not conceived of so strictly and exclusively, which can be seen for instance in the unquestioned presupposition of the disciples' agape for God. The five negative passages – 3:19; 5:42; 8:42; 12:43; 12:25 – were not highlighted in the survey, but have been discussed in the appropriate contexts.

As was just said, what agape in John's Gospel is, becomes clear only when the various passages are viewed. It is a very special concept of agape which, with this meaning, belongs only to the fourth gospel. It is not a thought that one can easily master at the first try. Rather, one is dealing with a living organism. This study has pointed out the various functions, in detail, but it cannot be concluded without reminding the reader that these various functions are the expressions of the life of a unified whole.

VIII

THE TRANSFIGURATION

61

PRELIMINARIES

In theological circles today, it is taken as self-evident truth that the wondrous stories found in the gospels belong to the realm of the mythical or legendary and thereby stand outside reality. For a long time now, theology has accepted the perception of the world currently held by the natural sciences, as if there were no alternative at all.

Does it have to remain like this? So much is clear in any case that, within the framework of the only worldview scientifically accepted today, the gospels can only fall victim to corruption and disintegration. All the intelligence brought to bear on them can only destroy them. There is, however, the possibility of this intelligence advancing with insight to the point where it becomes conscious of its own limitations in relation to reality, where it becomes aware of its own relativity, where it perceives that an essential part of reality simply slips through the much too wide-meshed net it has cast. Then this intelligence can, without losing face, develop the inclination to look more closely at certain philosophical concepts as they exist in Rudolf Steiner's anthroposophy. To begin with, they can serve as working hypotheses.

There, one comes across the view that the idea of evolution so vigorously promoted by the newly emerging scientific studies of nature, is also applicable to science itself, to human consciousness and to its potentialities in general. Modern scientific methods are given their due, but they, too, show their relativity inasmuch as their achievements – grandiose as they may be – reveal their one-sidedness. Only one plane of reality is being dealt with. But there are several such planes and, corresponding to them, several forms of human consciousness. Without the hypothesis that there are other methods of establishing reality, one can only see ignorance and fantasy in the old religions of a bygone humanity, although the cultural creations left behind by these 'unenlightened' people must make a deep impression. A different aspect presents itself the moment one considers the possibility that myths and fairy-tales are echoes of a clairvoyance that was originally inherent in human beings and gave them direct knowledge of the existence of supersensible worlds and beings. As long as the question is 'How did religion come into being?' one gets nowhere. The question must be, 'How did it get lost?'

Anthroposophy speaks of a form of consciousness that is clearly defined as *imagination*. Images appear clairvoyantly, beheld directly as such, which must not, however, be made to relate to material matters. Rather, they should be seen as windows through which something supersensible can be glimpsed, something that has created in just this image an appropriate expression of itself. Visions of this kind were known in the old religions. They immediately become absurd if applied to material matters; if, for example, the hammer of Thor is taken for a material object. The fact that the idea of God held by different peoples varied considerably, does not mean that what they perceived was not reality; for the realms of supersensible beings should be thought of as a manifold abundance of hierarchically graded spirits who worked in different ways in the various cultures and religions.

The old way in which supersensible reality was perceived had something instinctive. It was lost to the degree to which humanity 'landed' with its consciousness on the material earth and developed a one-sided natural science based on sensory observations and the intellect. This consciousness works with enormous efficiency towards wakefulness and independence of the human being, but it completely loses sight of the supersensible reality and is therefore quite incompetent to deal with religious contents. The necessary progress will be made only if the 'lost provinces', which had lain shrouded in twilight long before total darkness fell, are recovered for the knowledge of reality in a new way, by means of the newly-acquired wide-awake consciousness. In this direction – and not by looking back and reaching into the past for old practices – does anthroposophy wish to be understood. By making clear distinctions between the various stages of consciousness, and the spheres pertaining to them, it is in a position to do full justice to the old religions as well as to science. Such a distinction was not possible in former times.

Anthroposophy also presents us with the unique opportunity to comprehend Christianity. It is not one of the old religions depending on diminishing archetypal revelations. Here, an event of the very highest order bursts into the history of humankind. To the question, 'What new reality was it then that the Christ brought?' the answer would have to be: himself. He brought himself, a divine being who, through the deed of Golgotha, transposed himself into the sphere of earthly humanity in order to help it by his supersensible presence to enter now, in freedom and independence, into the New Covenant with the world of its origin. Christ is not one of the founders of a religion, and his deed of redemption can stand only beside the creation of the world itself as the next continuing chapter, as the Prologue to John's Gospel shows.

The gospels tell of this Christ-event, which unfolds between the baptism in the Jordan and Golgotha. Interwoven with these events are major and minor supersensible elements, and the gospels can only be understood against a background of a philosophy that restores to the supersensible its rightful place as a reality.

In the field of gospel research, modern science has gathered together any number of items that, under the heading of background, were intended to assist comprehension. But absent was expert knowledge in the true sense, a knowledge that enables one to approach the question of truth.

For example, modern theology accepts that the question of 'heaven opening' at the baptism in the Jordan has now been finally demythologised and 'disposed of' by modern astronomy, not to mention astronautics, because 'in reality' there is only a black void. Similarly, the 'descent' of the dove is lost. From where is it supposed to have descended? And, anyway, what do 'above' and 'below' mean? If one can accept that 'imagination' exists, then these images found in the gospels can stand as statements of truth. They are visions. Made to relate to the material plane, they become absurd. But as visionary images they are a legitimate expression of the fact that by taking possession of Jesus, a being from the supersensible world entered the earthly world. Superstition only arises where reference is made to the wrong plane; then it is easy to demolish such images.

And when in the narrative of the Jordan baptism a heavenly voice sounds forth, it is worth listening to what anthroposophy has to say about a second state of consciousness beyond that of imagination, known as *inspiration*. Just as imagination is related to seeing, so inspiration is related to hearing: it opens to the soul's devoted listening – a hearing that is able to surrender completely to its object. In the same way as the visionary image can be clothed in pictorial forms that exist already in the inventory of the soul (such as 'heaven', or 'dove'), so inspiration, appearing as inner persuasion, can be clothed in language available at any given time, and use words that are already waiting in the soul.

This type of study should satisfy the need for 'interpretation' that found voice in the demythologisation theory. An abstract philosophy that does not consider the possibility of a consciousness extended to encompass the supersensible, cannot accomplish the interpretation demanded here. It can only eliminate all that does not conform to the materialistic view of the world. Instead of interpreting, it can only 'dispose of'.

Included in these 'disposed-of' subject matters is the transfiguration narrative, which we shall look at more closely in the following pages.

The transfiguration on the mountain

The great German theologian Rudolf Bultmann has no doubt that the transfiguration narrative is a 'legend'. Although – and this should be food for thought – it is chronologically bound up with another important event in all three gospels, namely the confession of Peter. With a stroke of the pen, Bultmann simply shifts it to an entirely different point in time. According to him:

> Peter's confession, like the transfiguration of Jesus, is an Easter story projected back into the life of Jesus by Mark (9:2–8). The account of the baptism of Jesus (Mk 1:3-10) is a legend, and this is as certain as that the legend rests on the historical fact of the baptism of Jesus by John. It has not been told in the interest of biography but in the interest of religious faith, and it is an account of the consecration of Jesus as the Messiah.

It dates from the time when the life of Jesus was already regarded as Messianic while the transfiguration, being the original resurrection story, dates his Messiahship back from the resurrection. The story of the temptation is also a legend.

The appearance of the Risen One before Peter 'is reflected in the narratives of Peter's acknowledgement of the Messiah, of the transfiguration'.*

Because there are certain suggestions reminiscent of the Easter narratives, it has simply been decreed that Peter's confession and the transfiguration are 'backdated Easter stories'. Before embarking on such enormous changes, one really ought to begin by taking the gospels as they present themselves, look at the phenomena and see where the actual text leads us.

The idea of the transfiguration being a legend does not accord very well with the fact that it appears to be connected with the striking event of Peter's confession by a very accurate chronological statement. Except for the account of the Holy Week, the synoptic gospel writers use no such built-in chronology anywhere. A legend floats in a chronologically indeterminate space, whereas the transfiguration is expressly tied to the course of events at a specific point in time. Of course, according to Bultmann, Peter's confession, too, would have been 'backdated', belonging in reality to Easter. This is contradicted, among other things, by the fact that according to Matthew and Mark this confession is, in its turn, tied to a place specifically identified: Caesarea Philippi. Nowhere else is this place mentioned in the New Testament; it lies far to the north in the Holy Land, close to Mount Hermon. Nowhere is it said that this place was of any importance at the time of the manifestations of the Risen Christ. Neither has the name any symbolic significance that could have led to Peter's confession having been shifted to just there. There is no reason to doubt this positive identification of a place. Nor has the narrative any legendary features and nothing miraculous happens. And it is precisely into this event that the transfiguration is locked, chronologically.

Incidentally, the chronological link also applies to the following. All three synoptic gospel writers, immediately after the descent from

* *Theologie des Neuen Testamentes,* pp. 28, 48.

the transfiguration mountain, have their report of the possessed boy whom the disciples staying behind were unable to heal. According to Luke this occurred 'the next day' (9:37).

The transfiguration narrative exists in three versions, as does Peter's confession recorded by the synoptic gospel writers, Matthew, Mark and Luke.

For specific reasons the following study will begin with the last of the three texts, that of Luke.

Luke shows a special sensitivity to the spiritual significance of an event. More than Matthew or Mark, he gives us the psychological points of contact for an initial understanding of the supersensible events described. While Matthew, in speaking of the transformation of Jesus into a glorious sunlike being, simply includes it in his text, Luke speaks of the praying of Jesus, out of which develops what follows. He hints at what the disciples feel, so that through his account we can gain a much more intimate insight into the whole incident.

We are thus in a much better position to approach the more cosmically attuned account of Matthew, which provides a certain polarity to Luke's report (like inside-outside). Then we can also deal with the less obvious characteristics of Mark's version.

62

ACCORDING TO LUKE

As already mentioned, the transfiguration is preceded by the confession of Peter. In Luke we do not read anything about the scenery, geographically so distinctive. He does not mention the walk to the north or the name Caesarea Philippi. Instead he gives an indication of the inner situation from which develops all that follows.

The question put to the disciples

> And it happened that when he was praying alone, his disciples were together with him and he asked them, 'Who do the people say that I am?' ... 'And who do you say that I am?' (9:18, 20)

This momentous question represents a turning-point. From here on the course of events flows ever faster towards the Mystery of Golgotha.

It is characteristic of Luke's account that he speaks of the Christ's solitary praying out of which the question arises. 'He was praying', meaning an extended period of time.

From being deep in prayer, the Christ turns to the disciples and asks the question. In this question, then, there is nothing incidental or accidental. It arises out of deeper connections. Peter answers with his confession to the *Christ of God* (9:20).

The Christ gives to this great word the concrete content belonging to it: the *first announcement of the passion*. The synoptic gospel writers agree that there were three such specific, solemn predictions of the Golgotha mystery, and that the first one was made immediately after Peter's confession. For the first time Christ speaks openly and directly of his approaching violent death and subsequent resurrection.

Luke omits the protest of Peter who would keep the suffering from the Christ, and immediately proceeds to Christ's *invitation to follow him*. It is a characteristic feature of the redemptive deed of Golgotha that those to be redeemed should be included in its dynamic as suffering, dying, resurrecting with Christ. Finally, the vision extends to the Second Coming: 'when the Son of Man shall come' (9:26).

The transition to the transfiguration

After the word of the Second Coming, the Christ begins to speak once more, 'Truly I tell you' (9:27). Then follows the saying about 'some standing here will not taste death before they see the kingdom of God'. (In Matthew 'the Son of Man coming in his kingdom', and in Mark 'the kingdom of God having come with power'.)

Faced with such a prediction, one may be quick to point out that in fact it did not come true. One is inclined to regard it as an apologetic explanation when some of the early Church Fathers positively identified 'some standing here' as the three disciples whom the Christ took with him to the transfiguration event. In their vision of the transfigured Christ the promise was fulfilled. Thus Ephrem the Syrian says in his *Sermon on the Transfiguration:* 'The men whom he said would not taste death until they saw the image of his coming, are those whom he took and led up the mountain and showed them how he would come on Judgment Day in the glory of his divinity and in the body of humanity.'

In order to do justice to such an assertion one must take into account a spiritual law of progression, which John expresses in the sentence, 'An hour *is coming* and *has come*' (Jn 16:32). In spiritual perception a series of future events widely spaced in their 'real' progression can appear contracted into a single image. The gospels mention 'the day of the Son of Man', but Luke has a passage where this 'day' is segmented into a series of days: 'The days will come when you will desire to see one of the days of the Son of Man' (17:22). Thereby the Second Coming assumes space in time, and one can imagine the coming supersensible perception of the Christ already present, occurring in stages of gradually intensifying illumination of consciousness. What the disciples are allowed to see on the mountain is already in line with the events of the Second Coming. They anticipate something that shines into their souls as an 'is coming and has come'.

Moreover, it should not be overlooked that all three synoptic gospel writers have the sentence about 'some standing here' followed immediately by the naming of the disciples whom the Christ takes with him to the mountain. Such a sequence expresses something. That certain perceptions can be expressed 'without words' by these means is readily observable in the gospels.

Eight days later

> Now about eight days after these sayings he took with him Peter and John and James and went up on the mountain to pray. (9:28)

The 'six days' Matthew and Mark speak of, and Luke's 'about eight days' do not necessarily contradict each other. Six days it is, if only the days between events are counted; eight, if the day of Peter's confession and the day of the transfiguration are included. So it works out the same. And yet, the number eight preferred by Luke adds another nuance. Observation shows that Luke pays particular attention to the progress of events in time. In both his childhood chapters he mentions the period of growth from conception to birth (1:57; 2:6). He speaks of Elizabeth's fifth and sixth month (1:24, 26), of the forty days of purification (2:22), of the twelve-year-old Jesus in the temple (2:42), and the anxious three-day search for him (2:46), of the thirty-year-old Jesus (3:23), of the forty days in the desert (4:2) and later, in the Acts, of the forty days to Ascension (1:3) and the fifty days to Pentecost (2:1). He speaks of the crippled woman's eighteen years of infirmity (13:11, 16) and of Hannah's eighty-four years (2:37). In the childhood chapters we also come across the number eight. On the eighth day after birth, the circumcision and naming is celebrated for John (1:59) and Jesus (2:21) as 'octave' to the event of their birth. After conclusion of the seven-day week, the recurring event of a time-octave occurs, just as later the octave of the Easter day was experienced every Sunday, beginning with the first Sunday after Easter when the resurrected Christ appears before Thomas (Jn 20:26). Similarly, Luke makes the connection of the 'octave' at the beginning of the transfiguration narrative, between the day of 'these words' and the later day when they were confirmed by the vision.

Christ's praying

Luke is, in a special sense, the evangelist of prayer. The first image Luke's gospel presents is of the priest Zechariah making the incense offering in the interior of the temple, while the devout community outside accompanies the deed with their prayer. It is as if this incense prayer was permeating the entire gospel of Luke's which, at its conclusion, leads us back into the temple. 'And they worshipped him and returned to Jerusalem in great joy, and they were continually in the temple praising God' (24:53). In relation to the Jordan baptism, Luke – and only Luke – mentions the praying of Jesus, which here, too, is of crucial significance. 'When ... Jesus also had been baptised and *was praying*, the heaven was opened' (3:21). Soon after Jesus had begun his public activity, it says: 'He withdrew into the wilderness and prayed' (5:16; also Mark 1:35). Another episode, solely in Luke, is the ascent to a mountain to pray, prior to the choosing of the twelve disciples. 'He went to the mountain to pray, and all night he continued in prayer to God' (6:12).

Some time later it says: 'Jesus was praying in a certain place, and when he paused, one of his disciples said to him, "Lord, teach us to pray"' (11:1). Then the Lord's Prayer, in a shorter version than we know it from Matthew, is given to the disciples. Matthew has built it into the great edifice of his Sermon on the Mount, still early in the gospel. Luke tells, at a later point in time, of a specific situation when this prayer was given to the disciples in answer to the request of one of them. Viewed merely historically, this version would seem to deserve being given preference. But both have their value: the way of Luke, to leave the words of Christ within the framework of the particular situation as it occurred, and, on the other hand, the way of Matthew who makes larger compositions of connected sayings. Luke has preserved for us the situation surrounding the gift of the Lord's Prayer: once again, Christ was in one of his prayer seclusions. But through Luke we learn that such a sustained contemplation could also be interrupted by a 'pause', and in one of those intervals an unnamed disciple, apparently under the deep impression of this prayer, voiced the request that was granted so wonderfully. Christ gives them the Lord's Prayer in its first form; the fully expanded, sevenfold version that we know from the Sermon on the Mount (Mt 6:9–13), would have been developed later.

The transfigured countenance

The transfiguring process began *while* he prayed, *through* the act of praying. Luke thereby gives an important clue to a possible, at least rudimentary understanding, that the transfiguration is not a miracle to be accepted 'from outside'. General inner human access to insight is available – in prayer. Initial experiences in this area are within the scope of what is, in general terms, humanly possible. It is only that the Christ has in an infinitely heightened measure what anyone who really prays can experience intuitively as inner illumination. But before Luke speaks of something like a higher light-substance bursting forth, he speaks of the Christ's countenance.

> And as he was praying the appearance of his face became different ... (9:29)

What we describe as 'appearance' is in Greek *eidos*. This is a word that even in those days had already had a long history. In Plato *eidos* stands for 'idea', next to the Greek *idea*. *Idein* is 'seeing'. Hence, our idea is something one sees, something seen; but looked at closely, seeing not with the physical, but with the spiritual eye. The 'idea' is grasped in the beholding. Aristotle did not want to think of the idea as floating above things; as 'entelechy' he tried to link it more intimately with the world of the physical. Inasmuch as entelechy gives form to matter, he also called it *morphē*, 'form', or else *eidos*: that which 'imagines' the form for matter. The shape in which the forming power of the spiritual is revealed, discernible to the outer as well as the inner eye, is for Aristotle the *eidos*.

And now, at the transfiguration, it is the *eidos* of the face which is seen. A human face is something very special for the eye to behold. It is the strongest manifestation in the physical world of an inherently supersensible quality. Something of the spirit and of the soul can be looked at with the physical eye, as it were. Physical eye and spiritual eye come together almost completely. The 'visage', visible to the physical eye, is at the same time 'vision' to spiritual perception. The human visage is truly a vision.

Of this *eidos* of the countenance of Jesus, Luke says that it became 'different' – *heteron* – while he prayed. One might wonder at this expression, which apparently says so little. Could it be something like a deliberate understatement – the use of all too modest a word because, in any case, even eloquent speech cannot come close to what has to be said. Or how else could it be understood? For 'different' there are two Greek terms: *allos* and *heteros*. *Allos* is a more general term for change. There are also versions of the text which use the verb *alloioō* here: 'the appearance was altered.' But the reading 'became different [*heteron*]' is still preferable, one would think. In *heteros* can be divined the significance of the difference, of the strangeness created by the difference. In comparison, one could perhaps think of impressions created by the sight of a dying person. Suddenly, something hitherto unknown mingles with the familiar features, something alienating infusing them with unapproachable majesty. We feel, here is not only the human being as we knew him or her in everyday life. The unselfconscious familiarity bred by daily contact gives way to a solemn feeling that divines the eternal being, which up to this moment has been hidden in the physical substance. An experience of this kind, a groping for distance-creating majesty, would be at the back of Luke's word 'different', which sounds so reserved.

The possibility would also have to be considered that the transfiguration on the mountain is indeed connected with something like an approach to the threshold of death. If this be accepted as a possibility, then much that is enigmatic in the gospels appears in a new light. One can begin to perceive why Christ goes towards his death in Jerusalem with such certitude, why he 'wanted to die at the Passover'. He wanted to accomplish his death, awaiting him in any case, in the form of the Golgotha mystery as death on the cross, as had been intended in spirit. He wanted to 'fulfil what had been written', not only in old books but, above all, written in the stars according to destiny's divine necessity. Hence the 'must' in the first announcement of the passion – the Son of Man 'must' suffer and die. In Luke this 'must' reappears in the Emmaus narrative: 'Did not Christ *have to* suffer these things to enter into his glory?' The events of the Holy Week, in particular from Maundy Thursday to Easter morning, are governed by the inner necessity of the 'must' to be fulfilled in freedom. At Golgotha, history and ritual coincide. The task that stood before Christ was to celebrate in this sense his last days, suffering and in full awareness. He had to retain his body, which was already under attack from death, until he would be free to say from the cross, 'It is accomplished.'

Seen like this, the wrestling at Gethsemane appears in a new light. It is not that he flinches from the cross at the last moment, but that death threatens to carry him off before the appointed hour. The transfiguration would then represent an important stage in the course of the confrontation with death. It is not accidentally flanked by the first and the second announcement of the passion (9:22 and 9:44). Such an announcement is not only the communication of a thought: it springs from a real presentiment of death. In his call for followers, the Christ speaks for the first time of the 'cross' that has to be taken up (9:23; Luke adds 'daily'). There is no previous mention of the cross. Matthew has the word of 'the cross to be taken up' in an earlier passage (10:38), but it should be considered that he gathers specific sayings into large compositions, and in this case, too, a later saying was put into the earlier address when sending out the twelve. At any rate, Mark as well as Luke has the word 'cross' appear for the first time here. And it does not yet refer directly to the cross of Golgotha arising, as it does, out of the Christ's own experience: that from now on he will 'daily' have to 'take upon himself', with great conscious effort, the cross of his earthly body dedicated to death, and carry it towards the conclusion of the mystery to be accomplished.

Thus the transfiguration also shows a touch of the experience of being close to death. On the mountain top, far removed from the world, Christ enters into a spirit conversation with other souls dwelling 'in the beyond', as if he were already dead. He could now 'pray himself out' of his body, as it were, and cross over to his divine spiritual home. The transfiguration would then have been the beginning of a sublime dying process. Christ contained his heavenly light-being just once more in his earthly-human form and came down from the mountain in order to accomplish his true, great mystery at Golgotha.

The radiant garments

> ... and his clothing flashed forth white. (9:29)

For Luke this bursting forth of inner light is also the result of praying. The praying soul gathers and condenses what lives in it as inner light. The more powerfully this process works, the better this soul-light can penetrate the delicate life-organism, finally showing its reflection even in the physical body.

'The light in you' is also spoken of in the gospels. Matthew has included it in the Sermon on the Mount (Mt 6:23). Luke has left this saying of Christ in its actual original position, not at the beginning, but only after the event of the transfiguration. 'Take heed then lest the light that is in you be darkness' (11:35). In this very passage Luke, going beyond Matthew, has passed on something else, something very strange: 'Therefore, if your body is full of light [*phōteinon*] and no part in darkness, it will be wholly lightlike, as when a lamp shining flashes its rays on you' (11:36). This saying quite obviously rests on the fact of the transfiguration having preceded it – indeed, it all but arises from it. The inner source of the light illuminates *(phōtizei)* like a flash of lightning *(astraptō)* the whole human being, penetrating to the very body.

Looking at the whole gospel with an ear for consonance shows that this term, 'flash of lightning', is reminiscent of Luke's description of the garments beginning to shine as part of the transfiguration process. The garments turned white, 'flashed forth' *(exastraptōn)*. Luke also speaks of the garments 'dazzling like lightning' of the two Easter angels at the tomb (24:4). What is the specific note that thereby comes into the description of Luke?

A 'lightning flash' is 'light in motion'. Not a light in repose, but one creating itself in activity. The radiance that emanates from the two angels at the tomb is of this nature; the light that emanates from the praying Christ is of this nature, penetrating his garments, as it were, and completely enveloping him. It is a light alive in itself, a light of a higher order that cannot, at any other time, be experienced in an earthly context.

In connection with the transfiguration, this 'flashing' is now combined with 'forth' – 'flashing forth' *(ex-astraptōn)*. In all of the New Testament it is found only here, in Luke's gospel. In the description of the two Easter angels it is not used, although their light, too, alive with spiritual creativity, is called a 'flashing' one. The 'forth' points indirectly to an 'inwardness' that is the source of the phenomenon – the inwardness of the Christ become human, gathering his inner light in prayer.

The two spirit figures

While Matthew and Mark introduce Moses and Elijah without any preparation, simply saying 'there appeared to them ...' and immediately calling them by name, Luke does it differently. Again, we notice in him a sensitive awareness of the manner in which a supersensible experience takes shape, step by step, in the souls of the disciples. He does not immediately speak of Moses and Elijah.

> And behold two men began talking with him, who were Moses and Elijah. They appeared in glory ... Peter and his companions ... saw his [Christ's] glory. (9:30–32)

'Behold' points to a perception unexpectedly presented to the spiritual eye. But what is revealed to this eye is initially only 'two men' who apparently have been talking with the Christ for some time ('they talked with him' is, in Greek, the imperfect tense). Roused by the jolt of the 'behold', the disciples become conscious of something that is already under way. By adding only now 'who were Moses and Elijah', Luke allows us to experience the next step: the two figures are recognised as Moses and Elijah. In a kind of inspiration the disciples become aware of the two names.

Only now does Luke say, 'They appeared in glory'. In recording Christ's words about the return of the Son of Man, which precede the transfiguration, all three synoptic writers speak of the 'glory'. But only Luke takes up this word again in the transfiguration narrative, mentioning it twice. Moses and Elijah 'appeared in glory'. Immediately afterwards the disciples saw Christ's 'glory'. The glory belongs to all three participants in this spirit conversation. By the process of dividing the glory of the Second Coming in a triune way – as glory of Christ, of the Father and of the holy angels, Luke creates a delicate relationship, weaving back and forth between the two sets of trinities.

In the Old Covenant Moses re-establishes the connection to the beginning. He beholds the creation and accepts the law designed to keep the world on course as envisaged by creation. In contrast, Elijah was felt to be the genius of prophecy around whom blazes eschatology and apocalypse. He points to the future. Thus the light-aura of Moses contains something of the glory of the Father, that of Elijah something of the glory of the Holy Spirit, whose angel-messengers very much include Elijah. Between these two figures stands the Christ, the Son, in the glory of himself, even though that glory will not be exalted to its full majesty before the great Mystery of Golgotha has been accomplished.

The spirit conversation

The fact of these three holding a 'conversation' is perceived straight away. When the two with Christ are recognised as Moses and Elijah in their glory, the supersensible perception expands once more, in that something of the content of the conversation becomes intelligible.

> They spoke with him of his departure which he was to accomplish in Jerusalem. (9:31)

The first announcement of the passion had preceded the transfiguration. Here it is being confirmed out of the higher knowledge of the illustrious departed. These inhabitants of a higher world apparently look down with great interest to see what is happening to the one who has become flesh. They follow from above the course of his life on earth and are able to foresee prophetically the events taking shape at Jerusalem. They speak to the Christ of the 'departure' that signifies the end of his earthly path. The structure of what was to come, decreed by destiny, is already discernible to the consciousness of these spirits. And what has been foreseen must soon be fulfilled through earthly human experience and suffering.

There can be no doubt that Luke believes the two spirit beings to be the real individualities of Moses and Elijah who, after their departure from earth, continue to live in a higher world. He does not subscribe to the view that, until the time they are raised on the Day of Judgment, the dead are non-existent and simply 'quite dead'. This also becomes apparent from Luke's account of the story concerning the rich man and Lazarus (16:19–31), where after-death experiences of discarnate beings are described quite concretely to show how they may vary, depending on the life on earth that went before. There it is shown that discarnate beings can recognise each other, remembering events experienced together on earth, and are able to communicate with each other. Between the rich man and Abraham a 'spirit conversation' develops. The term 'parable' is not used at all for this story, it being a description of after-death conditions, taken from real life. Further, it is Luke who has the very word from the cross that presupposes a continuing life of the discarnate soul, 'Today you will be with me in Paradise' (23:43). In like manner, the appearance of Moses and Elijah as spirit beings of a higher order, manifesting themselves in 'glory' in the radiant light of a halo, are accepted as spiritually quite realistic.

The spirit conversation that has become perceptible to the disciples has the 'departure' as its subject. Departure – *exodos* – is an important word. It combines *ex* with *hodos* – way. In the New Testament it is found only twice more, and in the gospels only here. In the Letter to the Hebrews (11:22) it describes the departure from Egypt, that is, the classical Exodus, and, in the Second Letter of Peter (1:15), Peter's impending death is defined as 'departure' from the 'tent of this body'. The death of Golgotha would also be what first comes to mind on reading Luke's words: 'accomplishing his departure from Jerusalem'. After all, 'accomplishing' is a bringing to an end. What was intended in the spirit becomes historical fact. To that extent *exodos* is here, in the spirit conversation, the 'end of the way'. But not quite. The way on earth has run out, but opening up at the same time is the 'way out'. Thus, the end is given a new beginning. Exodus, then, is the departure from an existing condition, an emerging and entering new territory. Exodus, as defined here, can almost be termed a biblical leitmotif, starting with Abraham's departure from Chaldea and the exodus of the tribes of Israel from Egypt (which is the subject of the Book of Exodus), to the call for God's people to depart from the fall of Babylon in the Apocalypse (18:4).

When the Christ's two heavenly interlocutors interpret the approaching Golgotha event as exodus, then surely the tragic death motif also contains a promising hint of new beginnings. It is the reference to the new territory, which the Christ, passing through the gate of death, will enter. As one who has died, who has risen from the dead and ascended to heaven, he will continue to be on the move. The Departed One wanders through the realm of the dead (1Pt 3:19). The Risen One says of himself: 'I am ascending to my Father' (Jn 20:17). The Emmaus narrative of Luke who, in a special sense, is the evangelist of 'being on the move', shows the Resurrected One as a wanderer. Nor does his ascension put an end to this movement the Christ is engaged in. The image of 'sitting on the right of the Father' does not necessarily exclude movement and activity. There can exist a lively activity that springs from an inner core of stillness. The Apocalypse contains both images: the Christ sitting on the throne (3:21), and the Christ walking (2:1). He wants those who belong to him to 'walk with me' (3:4), to be on the move with him towards the far goal, which is envisaged at the end of the Apocalypse as 'heavenly Jerusalem'.

In the spirit conversation, the name of *Jerusalem* is heard also as the place of impending accomplishment. Surely this cannot be an accidental place reference known in advance by prophetic spirits. The mystery to be accomplished cannot take place at any arbitrarily chosen locality. Jerusalem is a providential place. Jesus carries the certain knowledge in his soul that he will not die anywhere else but in Jerusalem (13:33). The third and most concrete announcement of the passion begins with: 'Behold, we are going up to Jerusalem' (18:31).

Again it is necessary to look at Luke's gospel as a whole in order to see in its true light the name of Jerusalem as spoken by spirit mouths in so solemn a context. Of the three synoptic gospel writers, Luke is the one to have a certain affinity to John, in that he develops a much stronger 'Jerusalem consciousness' than either Matthew or Mark. Jerusalem has a certain importance for Luke. It is very obvious in the two childhood chapters where three of the seven stories told unfold in the temple of Jerusalem. Quite some time before Palm Sunday we hear the call: 'O Jerusalem, Jerusalem, how often I have wanted to gather your children' (13:34). 'How often ...' For this Christ must have entered Jerusalem before, not only at the end in Holy Week.

In the narrative of Simeon and Anna mention is made of a circle of apocalyptically minded people 'who were waiting for the redemption of Jerusalem' (2:38). In the Little Apocalypse, the destruction of the city is prophesied in concrete images (21:20–24). Christ weeps for the city as he enters (19:41), and on his death-walk he laments for the 'daughters of Jerusalem' (23:28).

Above all, however, it should be noted that Luke places the whole rich content from 9:51–19:28 within the framework of the 'journey to Jerusalem', thereby placing it under a specific sign. This walk begins with the solemn sentence: 'When the days drew near of his ascending, he set his face to go to Jerusalem' (9:51). In two further passages (13:22 and 17:11) we are specifically reminded that whatever was recorded happened on the way to Jerusalem, in other words that it represents the sequence of stations along a 'path'. Luke is the one evangelist who, in his Easter narrative, takes account only of Jerusalem (Emmaus not being far distant). He alone has the Risen One mention the name of Jerusalem (24:47; also Acts 1:4, 8). The disciples are to wait 'in the city' for the Pentecostal Spirit (24:49). Finally, one of the last sentences of the gospel says: 'And they returned to Jerusalem' (24:52).

In the consonance of all these passages, the name of Jerusalem is to be heard when it rings out in the spirit conversation at the transfiguration. It is the earthly place for the Mystery of Golgotha, the end of the road on earth for the One incarnated in the flesh, while above the earthly city there shines the apocalyptic gleam of the heavenly Jerusalem to which the Risen One is on his way.

The changing consciousness of the disciples

Luke is not concerned only with the conversation of the exalted three. He has also something to say about the state of soul the disciples experience during these events.

> Now Peter and those with him were heavy with sleep, and when they were becoming awake, they saw his glory and the two men standing with him. (9:32)

The heaviness of sleep is reminiscent of Gethsemane. Doubtless more is involved than mere physical drowsiness. At Gethsemane, the inner forces of vigilance fail the disciples when they are confronted with an extraordinary task that arose then. The 'agony' of Christ has already been mentioned, and so has the task of the disciples to help him, who was prematurely threatened by death, to hold on to his failing physical body until the mystery could be accomplished. The disciples did not rise to the occasion as the hour demanded. They were not able to prevail against the superior force of the numbness and darkness that rose up out of the, as yet, untransformed earthly heaviness of their being. The 'power of darkness' of which the Christ speaks when he is taken prisoner (22:53) also has the effect of oppressive 'heaviness'. Matthew says that 'their eyes were heavy' (26:43), and Mark 'weighed down' *(katabarynómenoi,* 14:40). Except in Luke, this word 'make heavy' *(barynō)* does not appear anywhere else in the gospels. In the Little Apocalypse on the Mount of Olives the Christ unfolds the eschatological perspective in relation to his return, exhorting the disciples at the same time: 'Take heed to yourselves lest your hearts be weighed down, be it with dissipation and drunkenness and the worries of life' (Lk 21:34). The heart as a sunlike Christ-organ should be spiritually awakened, but opposing this is the darkening power of 'heaviness'.

The Christ took the three disciples up the mountain of transfiguration because the elevation of the mountain predisposes towards the experience of light and spiritual 'lightness'. As darkness and heaviness belong together, so too do light and lightness.

The failure of the disciples, here on the mountain, is not as total as that at Gethsemane. Luke uses quite a unique, concretely spiritual expression: *diagrēgorēsantes,* which would have to mean 'awakening in between'. Obviously it is a question of moments of wakefulness flashing into the heaviness of sleep. In such bright moments of higher consciousness which the disciples manage to achieve, 'they see his glory'. That we are dealing with supersensible perception is shown also by a passage in the Second Letter of Peter. There the mountain of transfiguration is called the 'holy mountain' *(hagion oros),* and for the disciples the technical mystery term *epoptai* is used, which is known from the Eleusinian mysteries (2Pt 1:16–18).

The disappearance of the two spirit figures

> And it happened in their parting from him, Peter said to Jesus, 'Master, it is good for us to be here; let us make three tabernacles, one for you, one for Moses and one for Elijah,' not knowing what he was saying. (9:33)

Luke then describes how this image begins to dissolve 'in their parting from him'. The parting is not something purely spatial and physical in a context like this one. When in the Easter narrative of Matthew the Risen One 'approaches' the disciples 'but some doubted' (28:17f), this manifestly points to a heightened intensity of his making himself known. He makes an effort to reveal himself still more clearly to the limited visionary powers of his disciples. He makes a movement 'towards them'. Here, in the transfiguration, the opposite happens. The spirit event with Moses and Elijah has passed its zenith and the opposite movement ensues, a fading of the impression. Thus, Moses and Elijah are engaged in a movement that takes them from the sphere of manifestation back into the depths of the world of God. They distance themselves and the distance grows.

This special feature of Luke's account can also assume still more eloquence for us if we take note of the consonance once more. It is not the only time that Luke, when writing about a supersensible event, describes the way it concludes. Thus, Gabriel's annunciation to Mary ends with: 'And the angel departed from her' (1:38). And in the Christmas story: 'And when the angels were departing from them into heaven, the shepherds said ...' (2:15). At the Emmaus manifestation, the Risen One becomes invisible at the moment of being recognised (*aphantos egeneto,* 24:31). Ascending to heaven, Christ 'removes himself' *(diéstē)* from the disciples while blessing them (24:51). This vanishing from sight Luke describes in even more detail in the Acts (1:9). Occasionally, the departure of an angel who had appeared is also described in the Acts (10:7; 12:10).

In this manner, Luke describes how the two figures begin their retreat from visibility. And for Luke this is exactly the 'psychological' moment when one of the disciples, Peter, utters his words, 'Master, it is good for us to be here; let us make three tabernacles, one for you, one for Moses and one for Elijah.' Peter feels the bliss connected with a spirit encounter. Peter wants to hold what is about to vanish. There comes to him the image of 'building a tabernacle'. It could have been the time when the Festival of Tabernacles was approaching. Peter would like to provide a place to stay for the three, wanting to transform 'being' in a higher world into 'staying'.

We shall return to Peter's words more fully in Matthew's account.

Entering the cloud

The words of Peter, not spoken out of an alert consciousness, are soon overtaken by a further progression of the supersensible event.

> While he was saying this, a cloud came and overshadowed them; and they were afraid as they entered the cloud. (9:34)

That a cloud forms around a mountain peak is a natural phenomenon. However, there is something special about this cloud. In the Old Testament, the cloud concealing Mount Sinai carries the presence of God. A cloud takes away the Christ ascending to heaven. In the clouds of heaven, it is said, the Second Coming will occur. The cloud appearing at the transfiguration is also a phenomenon of a revelation. All three synoptic gospel writers speak of the disciples being 'overshadowed' by the cloud. Luke's account in particular is reminiscent of 'Mary being overshadowed by the Holy Spirit' (1:35). Luke's account immediately resumes its own direction: 'and they were afraid as they entered the cloud'. If the text were referring to the disciples entering, one would have to imagine that they themselves were touched by the descending cloud. Since the cloud is the vehicle of a divine presence – it is from the cloud that the voice is heard later on – the 'fear' of the disciples, as they entered the cloud, would have had its origin in the shock experienced by earthly human beings coming into direct contact with a higher reality. They would feel their own inadequacy and would be alarmed at the approaching threshold of a higher existence.

This being afraid, however, would also make sense in our text if it meant: 'as they – Moses and Elijah – entered the cloud'. The 'fear' of the disciples would then be the devout awe with which they witnessed a 'communion' of human spirits with the divine. The witnessing of such happenings is enough to bring the threshold-shock before the soul of the disciples still incarnated in the physical body. Moses and Elijah had come out of their life 'in God' into a manifestation directed towards the earth, and now the hour has passed and they returned to their state of 'communion' with the divine.

The voice of heaven

> And a voice came out of the cloud saying, 'This is my Son whom I have chosen. Hear him!' (9:35)

In the original text 'came' is *egeneto* – 'it happened'.* This turn of phrase favoured by Luke in other passages as well, returns with conspicuous frequency in the transfiguration narrative. It lends emphasis to the character of the event, the progression of happenings as they come into being (9:28, 29, 33, 34, 35). The voice from the cloud 'happens'. As the voice of God from above it represents the climax of the whole series of events. It is reported by all three synoptic writers, although their accounts differ slightly. However, the reference to the voice heard by Jesus and John at the Jordan baptism is unmistakable in all three accounts. 'You are my beloved Son, this day have I begotten you' (3:22).

This great begetting formula as told in Luke's version, enhances even further the significance of the Jordan baptism. What happens 'this day' of eternity between Father and Son as you and I, radiates into the temporal 'this day' of the Jordan baptism. The process of begetting the Son descends into Jesus of Nazareth. Distinctly at variance with this is the word spoken out of the cloud at the transfiguration. This time it is not a direct begetting event. It is not directed at the Son. It is not framed in the second person of the 'you'. Rather, speaking in the third person, it is directed as a kind of 'demonstration' to the disciples, as at 'third parties' who now have their share of perceiving the mystery. Hence, this time it does not say: 'you are', but 'this is'. Peter's confession of the week before – a sensing but not yet a knowing – finds its full divine confirmation here. At the Jordan baptism John the Baptist, too, heard the divine word in a kind of 'attendant consciousness' from

---

* In English this word is variously translated, depending on the context.

the perspective of earthly humanity. Now the disciples enter into this attendant consciousness.

Luke's version of the word out of the cloud addressed to the disciples differs from that of Matthew and Mark. With Luke it is not 'beloved' Son, but 'chosen', *eklelegménos.* In the word *eklegō,* however, we may also hear the *legō,* the speaking, the Logos. It is the Son 'pronounced' by the Father in a very deep sense. Here, too, a certain closeness to John is noticeable in Luke.

The concluding words also assume additional depths. 'Hear him!' Surely, this is not only an exhortation directed at faithful pupils to listen to the sayings of their teacher. It was hardly something that had to be recommended to pupils of a Jewish rabbi of that time. Attention and retention were strongly cultivated. The 'hearing' is not so much aimed at the individual sayings, as at 'him'. They should be open and receptive in their devotion to him as the Logos himself in the revelation of his very being.

Luke is the evangelist of 'hearing'. This has to do with the fact that, in a special sense, he could also be called the evangelist of the soul. In its highest potential the soul takes its image from Mary who, as the handmaiden of the Lord, devotes herself to the divine and becomes the Mother of God. The devoted hearing becomes an impregnating process on the highest level. The relationship of hearing to being mother is clearly recognisable with Luke. It is underlined once more by the episode where a woman from the crowd calls the mother of Jesus blessed for being the mother of such a son, and receives the reply, 'Blessed rather are those who hear the word of God and keep it' (11:28). The Christ says in effect, 'You too can become my mother, inasmuch as I am the Logos of God. Your soul, too, can become Mary.'

This consonance gives the mighty 'hear him!' at the transfiguration a particular power.

The silence

With this climax of divine inspiration out of the mysterious cloud, the whole series of supersensible events has reached its conclusion. In the echo of that 'Hear!' the transition to everyday consciousness is completed.

> And when the voice had happened, Jesus was found alone, and out of themselves they kept silent and told no one in those days anything of what they had seen. (9:36)

He stands before their eyes again as the rabbi of Nazareth. Only Luke says that the disciples were silent 'of their own accord' *(autoi)*. Here, he uses the solemn word *sigaō*. In the New Testament 'to be silent' is expressed with *sigaō* or *siōpaō*. The latter means more generally that speaking is suspended, that nobody talks. The first means to keep silent, not only with the lips but with the whole soul, a silence coming from inside. The noun *sigē* as mystery word is well known – for example in the Mithras liturgy *(Sigē! Sigē! Sigē!)*. At the end of the Letter to the Romans (16:25), Paul very solemnly speaks of the 'unveiling [*apokalypsis*] of the mystery, which has been kept secret for aeons'. In the Apocalypse a 'silence lasting for half an hour' precedes the sounding of the seven trumpets (8:1).

In Luke's gospel, the involuntary silence of Zechariah after his encounter with the angel is expressed with *siōpaō*. However, this silence, initially imposed from outside, becomes in the course of nine months, equalling the pregnancy of Elizabeth, an essentially holy silence out of which was born, parallel to the birth of the boy John, the song of praise (1:68–79). In the Acts, Luke uses *sigaō* or *sigē* as solemn silence (12:17; 15:12; 21:40). Paul speaks of the silence of the community during divine service (1Cor 14:28, 30) and there, of course, *sigaō* is used.

Luke thus authenticates the transfiguration as the supersensible experience of a mystery by the silence of the disciples before descending from the holy mountain. There is nothing else immediately following the transfiguration report in Luke. He says nothing of the important conversation about Elijah and the Baptist which, according to Matthew and Mark, took place during the descent from the mountain. He allows the transfiguration to flow into the silence and dissolve in it. He only takes up the thread of his narrative, 'On the next day when they had come down from the mountain' (9:37).

63

ACCORDING TO MATTHEW

Caesarea Philippi

While Luke speaks of the Christ's solitary praying that precedes the momentous question he puts to the disciples at an unspecified locality, Matthew, as well as Mark, mention the name of Caesarea Philippi. Thereby a location is given, unusual, if not unique, in the gospels. It lies high in the north of the Holy Land, near the snow-covered Mount Hermon which rises to a height of 2 800 m (9 200 ft), near the spring of the Jordan that gushes forth as a great waterfall in the valley below. The snow-capped Hermon closes off Galilee towards the north.

Matthew gives the most comprehensive account of the events that took place at Caesarea Philippi. He has much to say about Peter. Peter's confession is given the widest exposure here. 'You are the Christ, the Son of the living God' (16:16). Calling Peter blessed, the Christ replies with the word about the rock ('You are Peter – the rock – and on this rock I will build my church') and the handing over of the keys of the kingdom of the heavens. Then follows, as with the other synoptic gospel writers, the first announcement of the passion. Peter dares to object. The fact that the Christ also talks of the resurrection slips past his soul unnoticed. But the prospect of the Christ having to suffer elicits his immediate protest. 'Lord, far be it for this to happen to you This must not happen to you' (16:22). Whereupon he, who had just been singled out as blessed, is rebuked in the strongest and sharpest terms as a seducing 'Satan' who is a stumbling block *(skandalon)* to the Christ. All this is completely missing in Luke. Matthew is more radical than Mark in describing both the positive and the negative aspects.

The ascent

> 'Truly, I say to you there are some standing here who will not taste death before they see the Son of Man coming in his kingdom.'
> And after six days Jesus takes with him Peter and James and John, his brother, and brings them up alone to the top of a high mountain. (16:28–17:1)

Luke prefers the past tense for his narrative. Mark, with his inclination for the dramatic, the present, and Matthew, most of the time but not always, the past. By jumping into the present on certain occasions, he can lend emphasis to an event and give his narrative something like a jolt. It happens here, at the ascent up the mountain. Christ 'takes with him' the three disciples (in contrast to Luke, Matthew as well as Mark puts James before his brother) and 'brings them up' – *anapherei* in Greek – literally, 'he carries them up'. The same with Mark. The expression is strange. However, the nuance of such an unusual word ought not to be lost. The Luke version shows how the disciples, although chosen specifically in their trinity from the total circle of twelve, and no doubt equipped with special qualifications, were nevertheless able to cope with the event only imperfectly and had to wrestle with the dulling earthly heaviness of their being. The unusual *anapherei* may point to the same state of affairs in a different way. We are familiar with the linguistic usage of carrying someone in our heart. Maybe there is a hint that, in wanting to lead the only three of the twelve disciples who could be considered, Christ had to add 'carrying power' of his own, in order to bring the disciples to something approaching the level of what was to come.

The word, taking on special significance, appears also in the Letter to the Hebrews. There, mention is made both of the Christ as the great high-priest and of his sacrifice. The Letter to the Hebrews says that the high-priest of the Mosaic Covenant must 'carry up' sacrifices again and again for his own sins and those of his people, but that the Christ, as high-priest in the tradition of Melchizedek, 'carried himself up' in a single offering sufficient once and for all (Hb 7:27). Subsequently, the *anapherō* appears in connection with the sins of humanity. Christ 'offered up once in order to carry up the sins of many' (Hb 9:28). Here, it has the meaning that by taking them upon himself, Christ alleviates the consequences of sin that exist objectively in the spiritual world.

Is it not possible that the significance of the sacrifice also pulses softly in the *anapherei* of the transfiguration narrative? In 'carrying up' the three disciples to an initial vision of his divine being, the Christ brings at the same time something like a first gift from a new humanity to the heavenly world.

He leads the disciples up the mountain by themselves, *kat'idian*. The 'alone' *(kata) monos,* mentioned at the end of Luke's account, points to the inner permanent core of the I. *Idios* points to one's own. Removed from the world, the disciples are expected to enter their 'own' sphere, their own essential nature. Matthew uses *kat'idian* frequently: for the prayer solitude of the Christ before the feeding of the five thousand (14:13), and again afterwards (14:23). For the rest, it appears in connection with teaching in the inner circle (17:19, 20:17, 24:3).

The high mountain

According to all three synoptic gospel writers, the transfiguration takes place on a mountain. With Luke, it is simply the mountain as the place of inner elevation. With Matthew and Mark it is a 'high mountain' and, according to some versions, a very high one. In Matthew, this high mountain assumes a special significance, as there is a whole sequence that runs through his entire gospel. In total there are seven mountains.

First, the mountain of temptation to dominate the world. Matthew seems to make a point of placing this temptation in third place: 'And the devil takes him up a very high mountain' (4:8). (Luke has this temptation in second place and there is no mention of a mountain, only: 'The devil led him up'.) On this very high mountain, the Tempter shows Christ all the riches of the world, 'All this I will give you.'

This first mountain of Matthew is balanced at the other end by the mountain in Galilee – and we read this only in Matthew – on which the Risen One reveals himself to his disciples (28:16). He has not accepted world domination from the devil. He has walked the path of sacrifice and may now say: 'All authority in heaven and on earth has been given to me.' The Easter mountain is the last of the seven mountains. It is as if a great arc connects the first mountain and the seventh one.

The second mountain is the scene of the disciples' basic instruction. 'When he saw the multitude he went up into a mountain and when he had sat down his disciples came to him and he opened his mouth and taught them' (5:1f). This is Matthew's Sermon on the Mount. Rising physically to the top of the mountain and reaching for the highest and ultimate goal of perfection – 'be perfect as your Father in heaven is perfect' – this is harmony. In the Sermon on the Mount, a reference to the 'heavenly Father' is heard for the first time – the 'Father in the heavens', so characteristic of the gospel of Matthew. Incidentally, the Sermon on the Mount also contains a reference to the 'city on the mountain' (5:14).

This mountain of the sermon, the second in the series of seven, is mirrored by the sixth mountain, which is also a mountain of spiritual instruction. On Tuesday evening of Holy Week, the Christ sits down on the Mount of Olives (24:3) and the disciples question him about his *parousia,* his coming, and the conclusion of the aeon. He gives them the Little Apocalypse and concludes with the image of the Last Judgment. Within the sevenfoldness an arc stretches between these two mountains of teaching, the second and the sixth.

The three middle mountains are in the specific area of prayer and meditation and are connected with marvellous manifestations of power. Matthew mentions – in third place within the series of seven – the Christ's ascent 'up on a mountain by himself to pray' (14:23). Out of this mountain prayer he allows himself to be seen by the disciples in supersensible form, coming to them as one walking on the lake, as they in their boat battle wind and waves. This manifestation is not unconnected with the praying on the mountain.

In fourth place stands the mountain they ascend as a prelude to the feeding of the four thousand: 'He went along the Sea of Galilee, and he ascended a mountain and sat down' (15:29). Such a sitting down on the mountain is without doubt an indication of meditation. The mountain force flows into the event taking shape, with the Christ praying down forces of heaven onto the bread and fishes. John's gospel also has a sitting down on the mountain preceding the feeding (6:3), giving it crucial significance.

Matthew's fifth mountain is the high mountain of the transfiguration (17:1) with its supersensible occurrences. Here, too, the sweep of an arc is discernible between the third and the fifth mountains. The walk on the lake, which has the solitary mountain meditation as an essential prerequisite (Mark says that the praying figure on the mountain 'saw' the disciples in their boat battling the wind, and came to them), and the transfiguration on the mountain have this in common; out of the prayer on the mountain a special opportunity arises for the Christ to manifest his supersensible being before the disciples.

The fourth mountain, with the feeding of the four thousand, then comes to stand in the middle of the series of seven.

One could wonder if Golgotha, too, should not be included in this series of Matthew's mountains. Golgotha, however, is not described as a 'mountain' in any of the gospels, it being only a rocky hill. With Matthew, the sevenfoldness is certainly no more accidental than the seven parables of the lake. Mark mentions only four of the seven mountains: the mountain of the choosing of the disciples (3:13); the mountain of prayer before the walk on the lake (6:46); the mountain of transfiguration (9:2, 9); and, in the Holy Week, the Mount of Olives (13:3) with the speech about last things. Luke speaks of three mountains: choosing of the disciples (6:12), transfiguration (9:28, 37) and Mount of Olives, the last one also being called the overnight stopping place (21:37, 22:39). John limits himself to the mountain on which the Christ 'sat down' (6:3) and to which he retires again after the feeding of the five thousand before the walk on the lake (6:15). He also mentions the Mount of Olives as the overnight resting place during the autumn festival (8:1). Seen against the other gospels, Matthew's special relationship to mountains becomes obvious.

With the motif of the holy mountain, Matthew also continues the line of the Old Testament – Moriah, Sinai-Horeb, Nebo, Gerizim, Carmel, Zion. In each case the mountain is the place of 'higher' experience. It shows up distinctly in the Sinai experience of Moses. On the mountain he accepted the law. On the mountain the ritual for Israel was revealed to him. On the mountain, finally, Moses was granted a a manifestation of God: although not permitted to see God's countenance, he was allowed, nevertheless, to 'gaze after him' as he passed. Outer and inner elevation were inseparably joined for the people of old. On ascending a mountain one experienced a change in the state of soul, an opening up to the supersensible. The holy mountain is actually an archetypal, religious and spiritual experience common to all humanity.

Metamorphosis

> And was transformed [*metemorphōthē*] before them. (17:2)

Matthew's report now passes straight on to the transfiguration event. The verb *metamorphoō* – metamorphose – is used in the gospels only here and in the parallel passage of Mark (9:2). Apart from that, it appears in the New Testament only twice more, in the letters of Paul: 'You will be transformed by the renewing of your mind [*nous*]' (Rom 12:2), and 'We all ... are being transformed into this same image, from glory to glory' (2Cor 3:18). This metamorphosis comes about through us 'with unveiled face beholding as in a glass the glory of the Lord,' exposing ourselves to the streaming-in of his image in order that it may form and transform us. Paul also speaks of a gradual metamorphosis occurring step by step 'from glory to glory'.

In the same letter, Paul says: 'God who commanded the light to shine out of darkness, shone into our hearts to give us the light of knowledge of the glory of God in the face of Jesus Christ' (2Cor.4:6). In the countenance of the One become Man shines the glory of God, and Christians will share in this glory in progressive metamorphosis. Paul describes the gradual transformation that took place through the en-Christing of the human being who looks with cognition towards the glory of the countenance of the Christ. The gospel describes the precondition for such a process. First, the glory of God had to shine 'in the countenance of the Christ Jesus' in archetypal perfection. Matthew is the portrayer of this happening. His account contains the singular reference to the metamorphosis of an earthly human face into something sunlike – the quintessential metamorphosis.

The sun

> And he was transformed before them, and his countenance shone like the sun. (17:2)

People of former times associated quite different experiences with looking at heavenly bodies than do people of our scientific modern times. The worldview of former times was a 'physiognomical' one, as it were. When we look at a human face we are not primarily interested in the physical side, but in something non-physical, spiritual, that is expressed in the face in a recognisable way. Anatomical, biological or chemical research would be an entirely different matter that would depart from interpreting the essence of a face. Similarly, for people of ancient times, sun, moon and stars were primarily an expression of their inherent spirituality. Paul still speaks of the different glories of the sun and the moon, and the specific individual glory of each single star (1Cor 15:41). Just as a personal psyche shines out of every human eye, so a different cosmic spirituality shines out of every heavenly body.

In ancient times, the state of consciousness would not even have allowed a separation of research methods. While the soul was turned towards beholding the cosmos, perception with the physical eye slid imperceptibly into visions of clairvoyant imagery. Thus, in the varying light of the heavenly bodies, one could discern the emergence of various supersensible qualities. The physically visible starlight triggered perception of the 'aura' of the star in question, the 'glory', in Paul's words. One cannot do justice to the old star wisdom if one does not concede perceptions of this kind, at least as far as their origins are concerned. Beyond the cosmic physicality of sun and moon there is something else, a strange qualitative characteristic, something sunlike and moonlike, which has its representation in the respective heavenly body, but which can also be found elsewhere in the world. For instance, Van Gogh was able to substitute the sun for the figure of Jesus in his copy of Rembrandt's *Raising of Lazarus*. He had the sensitivity for what is 'sunlike'.

Only if there is renewed recognition of such things can Christianity regain its 'cosmic dimensions'. To bring together the Christ and the sun would be an absurd beginning as long as one thinks of a Jewish reformist rabbi on the one hand, and a glowing ball of fire on the other. But, according to Matthew, what the disciples perceive on the mountain is precisely this, that what is sunlike in Jesus lives in a human way. Only if one arrives again at the ability to see something 'countenance-like' in the physical sun, in the sense of a 'physiognomic' worldview, can one accept the full impact of the idea that the sun now shines again from a human face. On reading the sentence 'his countenance shone like the sun', one will then no longer be satisfied with a poetic comparison. This passage, unique in the gospels, has its equal only in the Apocalypse of John. John beholds on the 'day of the Lord', a Sunday, the day of the sun, the Risen One in his greatness. 'His countenance shone like the sun in his strength' (1:16).

Cosmic aspects in Matthew's writing

In Matthew's gospel one is frequently reminded of the spirituality of the cosmically disposed Zoroastrian religion.

There are certain other sun-words. Mindful of the consonance, one may observe the fact that only in Matthew – in the Sermon on the Mount – is a reference found to the royal 'giving virtue' of the divinity who generously 'makes his sun rise on evil and good' (5:45). Equally, only Matthew has preserved the saying of 'the righteous who will shine forth like the sun in the kingdom of their Father' (13:43).

The moon, too, plays a certain role for Matthew. He shares with the other two synoptic gospel writers an account of apocalyptic changes that will befall the sun, moon and stars (24:29), even though, in his case, the superficially 'identical' statement is given an inner enrichment through the consonance with other passages. The transfiguration is followed, after the descent, by the healing of the possessed boy, whom the remaining nine disciples had tried in vain to help. Only Matthew provides for this boy the diagnosis of *seleniazomai* (17:15). This does not necessarily mean 'moonstruck' or 'lunatic' in the narrower sense. It means that the boy is under the one-sided influence of forces which, coming from the night-side of the soul-life, out of the dark lower strata not controlled by the I, throw the sufferer from one extreme to another. These unbalanced soul forces have, for Matthew, a moonlike quality. Christ brings a sunlike healing that subdues these uncontrolled forces. This is how close 'sun' and 'moon' are here. By virtue of the confrontation between sun and moon, the sequence of these two stories, which is the same in Mark and Luke, assumes a cosmic aspect in Matthew's account. Precisely through this sequence it becomes evident that comparison to the sun in relation to the transfiguration is more than just incidentally poetic. Once more, in another passage, Matthew speaks of *seleniazomai,* of 'moon-sufferers'. They are mentioned, along with other categories of sickness, at the beginning of the Christ's healing work (4:24).

In this connection, it should also be noted that Matthew was the only one to speak of the *star* of the magi (2:1–12). 'Magi' were the Persian priests. There is a curious legend from history: when in the year 614, the Persians devastated Jerusalem, they spared the Church of the Nativity in nearby Bethlehem, because the magi were portrayed wearing the Persian garb of Zoroastrian priests.

If one looks more deeply into the references to 'sun, moon and stars' in Matthew's gospel, then the fact that 'heaven', 'the heavens' and 'heavenly', are favourite words of Matthew, appears in a new light. While Luke speaks of the 'kingdom of God', Matthew always says: 'the kingdom of the heavens'. Equally, he speaks several times of the heavenly Father. It has been said, by way of explanation, that devout Jews preferred to speak of heaven rather than of God. That may also play a part. However, a special interest in the cosmic heavens and its manifestations are unmistakable. Behind the plural, 'the heavens', stands the old perception that the supersensible world, which expresses itself 'physiognomically' in astronomical phenomena, is in itself variously graded.

Another peculiarity of Matthew is that he repeats several times the formula 'heaven and earth' (5:18, 5:34f; 6:10; 11:25, 16:19; 18:18f; 24:35, 28:18), from the Sermon on the Mount to the revelation of the Risen One on the mountain in Galilee. In his version of the Lord's Prayer, Matthew preserves the contents with a cosmic ring, a Persian Zoroastrian note, which are missing in Luke. Going beyond Luke, Matthew says in his address: Father 'in the heavens'. The third petition is missing in Luke. It is directed towards the will of the Father, which is done in heaven, but must yet be made truly effective on earth. Heaven is the realm of light where the will of the Father is done. The earth has been darkened by the forces of the Adversary and is yet to become the scene of activity for the divine will. Accordingly, the seventh petition, not found in Luke, says: 'Deliver us from the evil.' The Persian view of the world appreciated the dualistic element in the world, the battle situation that exists between light and dark, the necessity to conquer the earth for the realm of light. Wherever Matthew goes beyond Luke in the Lord's Prayer, there is this particular ingredient.

Thus the 'earth' is also placed into cosmic context. The word *gē*, earth, can otherwise often mean simply 'land'. But it has to be meant in a telluric sense, when Christ says that the Son of Man will 'dwell in the heart of the earth' (12:40) – a truly unique formulation. The same applies when 'salt of the earth' is mentioned (5:13). In the account of the Good Friday darkness that spread 'across the whole land,' *gē* means, first of all, the land around Jerusalem, Judea, *erez Israel*. But, at the same time, 'land' also stands for 'earth' here. And if, after death has occurred, 'the earth shakes', it is the earth as special cosmic body, as 'cosmic individuality' as it were, which reacts as such to the events of Golgotha with the rending of rocks and the opening of tombs (27:51f), just as on the morning of Easter the earth again accompanies the resurrection with a 'great earthquake' (28:2).

From these observations on sun, moon and stars it follows that the gospel of Matthew must be credited with a certain world-embracing cosmic interest. It also gives the description of the transfiguration its peculiar tinge.

Moses and Elijah

Christ was 'transformed before them'. 'Before them' or 'in front of them' shows that the event has its beginning in ordinary perception and, as it progresses towards the supersensible, the consciousness of the disciples also develops towards visionary beholding. The appearance of Moses and Elijah, both of whom no longer belong to the earthly world, quite decidedly comes within the sphere of a purely clairvoyant perception and has no beginning in the earthly visible. It is introduced by the rousing 'behold!'

> And behold, there appeared to them Moses, and Elijah talking with him. (17:3)

'There appeared' is not a plural as one would expect, since two names are involved. Against all expectations the singular is used and relates therefore to Moses only, with Elijah being added somewhat superficially with an 'and'. There can be no doubt that for Matthew the stronger accent is on Moses.

Not only in the selection, but also in the arrangement of the scriptures that together make up the New Testament, especially the gospels, there is a good deal of wisdom. So Matthew was allotted his rightful place. He is the 'liaison' between the Old Testament and the New. Not only is he, as the first author of the New Testament, visibly closest to the Old Testament, but he is also the one who most frequently refers back to the Old Testament. Again and again he points to prophecies being fulfilled. 'This took place to fulfil what had been written ...' It is used much more frequently by Matthew than by any of the other evangelists. To a higher degree than the other evangelists, Matthew shows a retrospective interest. Now the Old Testament, although not yet finally delineated at the time of the Christ, was seen in the duality of 'Law and Prophets', with Moses again gravitating towards the past, while Elijah was felt to be the genius of prophecy, pointing to the future. So it accords with the nature of Matthew that he should develop, within the Old Covenant, a stronger relationship with Moses who, proclaiming the law with paternal authority, was orientated towards the beginnings. For him Moses stands 'to the fore', and not only in a superficially historical sense.

In dealing with the Luke text, we said that in the spirit-radiance of the figure of Moses there was something of the 'glory of the Father', and in that of Elijah something of the 'glory of the Holy Spirit'. In speaking of the sunlike quality of the Christ, Matthew established a special reference back to an important statement in the Old Testament. In the final chapter of the Book of Malachi, the very last of the prophets of the Old Testament, Christ is heralded as 'the Sun of Righteousness'. Following the announcement of the angel who prepares the way, the text says: 'But to you who are in awe of my name, the Sun of Righteousness shall arise with healing in its wings' (Mal 4:2). And immediately afterwards: 'Remember the law of Moses my servant, which I commanded him at Horeb ... Behold, I will send you Elijah the prophet before the coming of the great and awesome day of the Lord' (4:4f). To Moses belongs the retrospective memory, while Elijah is connected with the preview of apocalyptic catastrophes and the eschatological conclusion. This Book of Malachi reads like a testament, like a summary of the Old Covenant. In the first book of the New Testament, Matthew shows the fulfilment. Christ as Sun of Righteousness become human, standing between Moses and Elijah.

Peter

In keeping with his quick-tempered personality, Peter feels an impulse to take an active part in the event on the transfiguration mountain. Matthew and Mark say specifically that he 'answered'.

> Peter answered and said to Jesus, Lord, it is good for us to be here. If you wish, I will build three tabernacles here, one for you, one for Moses and one for Elijah. (17:4)

Luke has Peter address the Christ with *Epistata,* something like 'Master' with the connotation of a leader of an esoteric community. In Mark we find the humanly unselfconscious 'Rabbi'. As he does elsewhere, Matthew uses the most reverential address, 'Lord' *(Kyrie).* In keeping with this reverence is also the 'if you wish'. A further peculiarity is the singular: 'I will build' rather than 'we'. This shows the person of Peter to be more prominent as a special individuality.

Already in the scene at Caesarea Philippi we had occasion to notice how, in Matthew's version, more space is given to the person of Peter than Mark gives him, let alone Luke, who only records the word of confession but is silent about the rest. The hard word 'Satan' is found also in Mark, but Matthew, in addition, shows Peter having to cope with the reproach that he gives offence to the Christ.

Peter's protest against the announced suffering and death must be seen in a wider context. On the mountain of temptation to dominate the world, the Christ, only recently incarnated into the earthly body, encounters the endeavours of the Adversary to divert him from the path of sacrifice, which means earthly failure and violent death. The

Adversary wants to prevent the Mystery of Golgotha. By rejecting the temptation, the Christ restates his resolution to go through with the sacrifice, a decision that was made already in the higher world before his descent and taken with him into his incarnation. He sends the Adversary away and thereby signs his own death warrant.

But the Adversary has not given up yet. After the first announcement of the passion he makes use of Peter who, owing to his lack of spiritual wakefulness, unintentionally serves as his mouthpiece: 'Lord, far be it for this to happen to you' (16:22). The Christ immediately recognises the real speaker, namely 'Satan'. He recognises that the temptation not to tread the road to Golgotha is here again in a different guise. At this moment, Peter's reaction to the reference to the passion is to him the 'affront' that would like to cause his downfall. Looked at from this vantage point, the words on the transfiguration mountain spoken by Peter with less than full consciousness, as Mark and Luke stress explicitly, appear in a strange light. It is then not only a naive expression of bliss connected with the higher experience to the extent that, being in a state akin to euphoria, he completely forgets the misery prevailing down in the valley, and desires to be and to remain only 'up here'. His spiritual delight is tinged with a selfish element. A Luciferic nuance is noticeable in 'It is good for us to be here'.

Rudolf Steiner drew parallels between the transfiguration of Christ and the death of Buddha and his entry into nirvana, stressing that for Christ the great mystery really only begins in earnest when, once more, he gathers his divine being into himself for the final descent into the passion. Christ is indeed quite close to the threshold of death on the mountain. He appears already to belong more to this other world that is home to him, whose air he breathes as it were on the mountain retreat. And, once more, he must confirm his resolve to embrace the sacrifice that had been decided. An indication that the descent into the valley was a sacrifice can be found in the succeeding story of the healing of the 'moonstruck' boy.

Immediately after the descent, Christ encounters anew, down in the lowlands, all of humanity's misery, not only in the form of the affliction but also, and not least, in the spiritual impotence of his disciples. He utters words then that, coming from his lips, might sound almost strange to us, words in which something like annoyance is expressed. 'O unbelieving and perverse generation! How long shall I be with you? How long shall I put up with you?' (17:17). After having breathed again the air of higher worlds, the effluvium of human souls hits him like a suffocating wave. 'How long?' But in an instant this moment of despair is conquered, and with renewed will he turns lovingly to earthly needs, 'Bring him here to me!' This 'how long' is also found in Mark and Luke, but Matthew strikes a special note inasmuch as he gives more prominence to the temptation, and it is he who has the word of the Risen One at the end of his book: 'Behold, I am with you always, even to the end of the age' (28:20). This answers the question: 'How long shall I be with you?'

Christ does not allow the transfiguration event to turn into a premature, light-induced, blissful dying-away. The descent from the mountain is followed by the second announcement of the passion (17:22), and, according to Luke (9:51), this is the beginning of the road to Jerusalem. Peter, however, had 'answered' to the transfiguration in a direction that ran contrary to the scheme of salvation, even if this time the temptation is more hidden than it was in the blunt protest at Caesarea Philippi.

The luminous cloud

> While he [Peter] was still speaking, behold, a luminous cloud overshadowed them. (17:5)

Matthew introduces the phenomenon with 'behold', the second 'behold' in his report. It is one of Matthew's well-known characteristics that he makes frequent use of this 'behold', beginning with the first appearance of the angel before the dreaming Joseph (1:20), to the mighty behold of the very last sentence – 'behold, I am with you always, even to the end of the age'. Mostly, it is a call to be aware of something supersensible approaching. The first 'behold' was aimed at the appearance of Moses and Elijah, the second at the cloud (the latter only in Matthew). He says of the cloud that it is 'lightlike' *(phōteinē)*. This gives the phenomenon an even stronger accent towards the supersensible. It is a luminous cloud, similar to the 'white cloud' in the Apocalypse that carries the returning Son of Man (14:14).

The cloud-space, mediating between heaven and earth, yet still belonging to the earth, represents an area of earthly existence that has not entered the solidifying process but remained pliant. Looking at the clouds one can observe, taking place in a delicate medium, a coming into being and a dissolving, a shaping and a reshaping. It is a realm of possibilities that washes around the solid earth. Gazing into the clouds could stimulate the soul and trigger clairvoyant perception. The ascending Christ, as well as the Returning One, appears 'in the clouds' – since the ascension, the Christ is active in that part of the earth-being that is still pliant and upwardly open, offering new possibilities, and, if by gazing at the clouds the spiritual eye can be opened to higher perceptions, he can be beheld in this state of being. There is nothing to demythologise in the statement of the 'coming in the clouds'. It only needs an understanding of this picture-language, which lives on the border of 'real' and 'unreal', of 'sensible' and 'supersensible'. It is still valid today.

The luminous cloud of Matthew is reminiscent of the auric fabric which hides as well as reveals the deity whose presence is felt at ritual worship. The Old Testament speaks of a cloud which, at the inauguration of the ritual, enveloped the tabernacle, which was filled with the glory of the Lord (Ex 40:34). When the temple of Solomon was consecrated, 'the cloud filled the house of the Lord, so that the priests could not stand there to minister because of the cloud, for the glory of the Lord filled the house' (1K 8:10f). This light-cloud showing itself inside the temple is something perceived supersensibly. At the transfiguration, the vision may have been aided by an atmospheric cloud formation such as might occur around the peak of a mountain.

Out of this light-cloud the voice of God is heard. In Matthew it is preceded by his third 'behold':

> And behold, a voice from the cloud saying, this is my beloved Son in whom I am well pleased. Hear him. (17:5)

It would be easy to suspect Matthew of literary 'preference' being obviously unaware of the fact that the optical word 'behold', used by him so frequently, does not really fit the auditory experience of the voice. Reading Matthew's account of the Jordan baptism, one finds a similar sentence. While Mark and Luke do not have 'behold' in their account of the baptism, Matthew uses it twice over. 'And behold, the heavens opened ... And behold, a voice out of the heavens' (3:16f). As it was at the transfiguration, there first came an impression of light (the heavens opened) and then something is heard (the voice). Both times have 'behold'. Before charging Matthew with literary carelessness for not staying with the image, one should try to gain an insight into these two descriptions of his relating to the baptism and the transfiguration respectively. First of all, there is the lightlike quality where 'behold' is organically quite appropriate. One can detect in Matthew altogether a certain enthusiasm for light and seeing when, for example, he speaks of the star of Bethlehem: *'Behold,* magi from the east ... we have *seen* his star ... and *behold,* the star which they *saw* in the East ... when they *saw* the star they rejoiced ... and entering *saw* the child' (2:1–12).

One could imagine that, for Matthew, the ringing revelation of the word, belonging to a still higher spiritual region, passes through the sphere of the lightlike and is tinged by it. Thus, the heavenly voice, as it first rings out, is for him still more of a light-experience. We too speak of the light and dark of a voice, and we can express tone qualities through light qualities and vice versa.

In Matthew, the word of the transfiguration accords with the word of the baptism, both times in the third person saying: 'He is ...' The close relationship between the two events is underlined by this parallel, just as at other times Matthew shows a tendency in his gospel to duplicate certain terminologies. But on the other hand, the event-like character of the baptism ('you are') is not so clearly distinguished from the descriptive character of the transfiguration ('this is').

The fear of the disciples

> Hear him! When the disciples heard this, they fell on their face and were greatly terrified. (17:5f)

According to Mark and Luke, the fear originated with the appearance of Moses and Elijah (Mk 9:6), or rather their entry into the cloud (Lk 9:34). With Matthew it is the overwhelming experience of the voice of God that throws the disciples down in fear. They were 'greatly terrified'. Matthew is the one who puts the greatest emphasis on this; he alone speaks of the disciples' 'falling on their faces'. Just as he, of all the evangelists, could best relate to the divine Father-principle, so also could he relate to the element of divine authority to which human beings respond with awe and worship. With Matthew, Christ, too, has a share in this majestic dignity commanding reverence. The Christ-image of Matthew's gospel is like an icon's solemnity. We have already noted a preference for the address *Kyrie,* Lord, which can reach right into the divine.

This gesture of worship and prostration runs through all of Matthew's gospel, from the magi in Bethlehem, who fall to their knees and worship the child, to the disciples on the Galilee mountain after Easter.

It is usual, when speaking of such worshipful prostrations, to take into account the established theophanic narrative and the 'court-style' of oriental potentates. The petitioner who was granted an audience threw himself down in front of the great king and waited until it was indicated that he might rise. However, the mere comparative reference to such ceremonies does not satisfy. Surely we must ask where the real origin lies. Falling down and being picked up is not without significance in relation to the religious archetypal mystery of death and resurrection. When someone is granted a visible manifestation of the divine, then the whole inadequacy of their own being vis-à-vis the divine is brought home to them with shattering force. Their whole being is challenged. 'He who sees God dies.' The way they lived up to this moment dies. They die in this encounter. But what makes them die, also awakens them to a higher life. Human beings who walk away from this experience are not the same as before. As ones born anew, they have risen from death.

Therefore, we do not do justice to a scene of the disciples falling on their faces at the transfiguration by pointing to theophanic style and court ceremonial, and leaving it at that. We cannot attempt to derive and 'explain' the gospels from such habits and customs. In fact, the opposite is true – the court ceremonial is a reflection of the divine manifestation.

The disciples experience what John on Patmos lived through with even greater intensity. He saw the elevated Christ whose 'countenance is like the sun shining in its full strength. And when I saw him, I fell at his feet as though dead. And he laid his right hand on me and said: "Fear not".' (Rv 1:17f). And at the transfiguration:

> And Jesus came close and touched them; he said, 'Rise up, and do not be afraid.' (17:7)

On other occasions, we only hear about the Christ touching people in relation to healing, or to the children he blessed. The touch was no mere symbol. Something enlivening emanated from the Christ's hand. The scene at the conclusion of the transfiguration is unique in the synoptic gospels; nowhere else does the Christ 'touch' the disciples, except at the washing of feet described by John. He does for them what later on he will do for John on Patmos. He awakens them back to life from dying into the divine.

The fact that the word of comfort 'fear not' is used in many of the narratives dealing with the appearance of a supersensible being, cannot simply be dismissed with a reference to style of 'majestic appearance'. We should ask what experienced reality may be hidden behind it.

> And when they lifted up their eyes, they saw no one but Jesus himself alone. (17:8)

The lifting of eyes, at other times often an expression just before having a vision, is explained here by what went before, namely that the disciples had fallen 'on their faces'. There is something reverential in this expression. The disciples become aware that the supersensible experience of a 'partial' mystical death has come to a conclusion with this event. The ordinary everyday consciousness has returned. Once more they see in front of them Jesus of Nazareth in familiar guise.

'Do not speak to anybody about this'

> And as they were descending from the mountain, Jesus commanded them, saying, 'Do not tell anybody about this vision until the Son of Man has been wakened from the dead.' (17:9)

The Greek text shows a minor unevenness here: when they were descending 'out of' *(ek)* the mountain, Mark and Luke use the expected 'from' *(apo)*. Although the 'out of' is linguistically inappropriate, the text was faithfully handed down in this form. Sometimes, in a linguistically and logically incorrect formulation, an attempt may be hidden to express something that is difficult to put into words. Thus, the 'out of' might express a certain nuance of the experience the disciples had: that while they were on the mountain they felt themselves to be 'inside something' that embraced them until they stepped 'out of' it again on descending. They are not only 'going down' but, at the same time, 'going out'.

The concluded supersensible experience is, according to Matthew, described by Christ as a vision, something visually perceived *(hórama* in Greek, from *horaō,* seeing).

About this vision the disciples are not to speak with anyone. Luke showed the other side. The disciples themselves 'were silent'. In Matthew and Mark the silence is imposed on them as an explicit command. These two aspects do not necessarily contradict each other. They complement each other. In Christ's command an important principle is involved that goes beyond the text of Luke. Supersensible experiences are of a delicate nature and must be handled with care. If they are communicated, they are in danger of being 'talked to pieces'. They must therefore be protected by a wall of silence.

Here at the transfiguration, the issue was not only that the secret of the nature of the Christ Jesus should remain within the circle of twelve, as had been impressed on the disciples after Peter's confession at Caesarea Philippi: 'Then he charged the disciples that they should tell no one that he is the Christ' (16:20). The renewed command to keep silent in the wake of the transfiguration, restrains the three witnesses in relation also to the rest of their fellow apostles. It does not refer to the knowledge that in Jesus lives the Son of God, this having been pronounced by Peter in the hearing of the disciples and accepted by the Christ. Now the command refers to the supersensible experience, the 'vision'. In accordance with esoteric law, proper 'follow-up' is required, that is, it must be enfolded in silence. This enables it to work all the better in the souls of the disciples until, after a certain time, it reaches the maturity necessary for it to be pronounced. As children develop in the secrecy of the womb until they are allowed to see the light of day, so also should the experience that is wrapped in silence pass through a stage of development 'until the Son of Man has been wakened from the dead'.

The transfiguration, having been absorbed into the meditative silence of the disciples, becomes itself the starting point for a future path at the end of which waits the resurrection. Just as the first signs of an inner light initiate an understanding of the body's possibilities to undergo a spiritualising process, so the transfiguration opens up a further path at the end of which penetration by the spirit will have led to total spiritualisation. But this is the crescendo that leads from transfiguration to resurrection. The transfiguration beheld by the three disciples is, in the following months, expected to mature in their souls to the point where, when the time comes, it can to a certain extent facilitate some understanding of the Easter events.

The appearance of the resurrection motive at the conclusion of the transfiguration narrative, prompts us to return once more to Bultmann's thesis, mentioned at the beginning, asserting that the transfiguration account is a 'backdated Easter story'. Although the connection between transfiguration and resurrection was felt, the very obvious difference between the accounts had not been taken seriously enough, thus giving rise to an incorrect interpretation of the relationship. The 'and is already now' of the transfiguration preceding the Easterly 'it will be', is misunderstood. At the Damascus vision of Paul and the apocalyptic Patmos vision of John, this glory of the Risen One whose body had undergone a further spiritualising process through his ascension, shone forth in full splendour. The ascension is conclusion and crowning of a process through which the resurrected body has passed during the forty days – and, of course, it is the ascension narrative that provides the bridge to the Second Coming in the clouds (Ac 1:11). The Second Coming is connected with becoming aware of the 'great glory' (Mt 24:30). We mentioned earlier that the words spoken by Christ eight days before the transfiguration anticipate the future as far ahead as 'the coming of the Son of Man in his glory'. The transfiguration, with its glorious light-revelation, mirrors a far-away future which, pointing beyond the Easter Day itself, will have grown out of the resurrection event from where it had taken its origin.

The conversation about Elijah

The admonition to keep silent is followed, during the descent, by a conversation about Elijah. The disciples have beheld him as one of the two spirit figures, and now they wonder what to think of the prophecy that Elijah would have to come before the Messiah. The Christ confirms the prophecy and shows that it has already been fulfilled. Elijah has already accomplished his precursor mission in the guise of a personality whom his contemporaries did not recognise as the Elijah individuality. Here Matthew – and only Matthew – follows up with a momentous sentence:

> Then the disciples understood that he had spoken to them of John the Baptist. (17:13)

Thereby, a reference is made to something that happened earlier. The Christ had once talked about the Baptist, and in this context made a statement that again we know only from Matthew: 'And if you are willing to accept it, he is Elijah who was to come. He who has ears, let him hear.' (11:14f). Nowhere else in the gospels is it said with such clarity, 'he is Elijah'. This statement of an instance of reincarnation is presented to the consciousness of the listeners with the addition: 'if you are willing to accept it'. Since that time the disciples had carried the word in their souls. Now, after the transfiguration event, the point in time for this 'accepting' has come. '*Then* the disciples understood ...'

Maybe it is not entirely accidental that this insight comes after a transformation experience. The word 'metamorphosis' was used in connection with Jesus. The metamorphosis of the rabbi Jesus into a radiant sunlike figure is the preview of ultimate perfection accomplished in the resurrection. The Risen One accomplishes in his person, now, what will not be within reach of humanity before Judgment Day. With his wholly spiritualised body that is no longer subject to death, the Risen One puts the ultimate great metamorphosis of the human being into the present cosmic age 'already now', as a piece of future instilled into the present, impelling it towards its coming conclusion. On Easter Day, Christ attains for himself, with the giant, divine strides, what for humanity is still a faraway goal. The road to Judgment Day is a long one and reincarnations have their place on it as comparatively minor metamorphoses, which – step by step – finally lead Christian humanity to the ultimate great metamorphosis, 'From glory to glory' (2Cor 3:18).

So, too, the further transformation of Elijah of the Old Testament into John the Baptist serving Christ, is illumined by the light of the transfiguration metamorphosis of the Christ Jesus. The disciples perceive it in this light. *'Then* the disciples understood ...'

Again, Matthew emerges as the liaison between the Old Testament and the New. Again and again we see him concerned to preserve continuity from the preceding salvation story of Israel on to the present. This continuity cannot be expressed more strongly than by showing that there is a connection by reincarnation. A leading individuality of the Old Covenant has, at the close of an age, reappeared as John the Baptist, and through his own person he binds, in a living way, the Old Testament to the New.

64

ACCORDING TO MARK

Inspiration

We began with the transfiguration as presented in the third gospel because Luke, by his more intimate psychological description, makes more accessible a kind of experience which, initially, is foreign to present-day consciousness. The quite different presentation of Matthew stands in sharp contrast. The characteristics of these two evangelists become clearly perceptible in their divergence in the transfiguration narrative in particular.

On reading the transfiguration of Mark, one may well first gain the impression that it is almost identical with Matthew's account, though certain important features of the latter are omitted, and also that it hardly adds anything of note that is not yet known from the gospels of Matthew and Luke. A widely held theological opinion has it that Mark's gospel was written first and was already known to Matthew and Luke who worked it into their accounts. This view, however plausible it may appear at first glance, has also had its opponents and, we believe, with justification. In detail, a good many observations do not fit this hypothesis. Looking at the actual text, one would do well to consider that various streams of oral retelling flowed into the gospels, with some features being identical even though the streams were independent of one another. The power of memory was incomparably stronger in former times than it is now.

The fact that there is a connection to oral traditions is no contradiction to the gospels being truly inspired. In our era when concrete perceptions of the supersensible have ceased to exist, a completely unrealistic, mechanistic inspiration doctrine was developed that eventually led to the baby being thrown out with the bath water. Nobody wanted to hear anymore of 'inspiration' and the gospels were treated as quite ordinary literature. To this rigid doctrine of inspiration it made no difference whether Mark, as a pupil of Peter's, may still hear his tutor's narrating voice or not, it being thought irrelevant to inspiration. A living interpretation of inspiration will include such references. Just as the fact that inspiration makes use of available words is no argument against it, so too it is feasible that it can incorporate, organically, what has been spoken into more comprehensive word structures.

To begin with, let us put Mark's text before us:

> And he said to them, 'Truly, I tell you there are some standing here who will not taste death before they have seen the kingdom of God coming in power [*dynamis*].'
>
> After six days Jesus takes with him Peter and James and John and brings them up a high mountain alone by themselves. And he was transformed before them. And his garments began to shine exceedingly white as snow, as no fuller on earth can make them white. And there appeared to them Elijah with Moses, and they were talking with Jesus. And Peter answered and said to Jesus, 'Rabbi, it is good for us to be here; so let us build three tabernacles: one for you, one for Moses and one for Elijah,' because he did not know what he said for they were beside themselves with fear. And there came a cloud overshadowing them and there came a voice out of the cloud, 'This is my beloved Son. Hear him!' And suddenly, when they had looked about them, they no longer saw anyone except Jesus alone with them.
>
> And as they came down from the mountain he charged them that they should tell no one what they had seen until the Son of Man had risen from the dead. And they retained this word among themselves, questioning one with another what the rising from the dead should mean. And they asked him saying: 'Why do the scribes say that Elijah must first come?' (9:1–11)

The fact that we first turned our attention to the presentation by Luke and Matthew resulted in us having already dealt with individual features of the report. However, a closer look at Mark's text will reveal some peculiarities in spite of the apparent similarities, especially with Matthew.

Unearthly light

Mark desists from commenting on the countenance of the Transfigured One. Like Matthew, he uses the word *metemorphōthē* – 'he was transformed' – and then turns his attention to the garments. 'And his garments began to shine exceedingly white as snow, as no fuller on earth can make them white' (9:3). To the light-describing words of the other evangelists he also adds *stilbō* (shining, glistening), a word that can also describe the sparkle of heavenly bodies. It appears only here in the New Testament.

'White' *(leukos)* is common to all three synoptic gospel writers. Mark underlines it with 'exceedingly'. Like Matthew, he also speaks of 'snow' – hinting with a geographical reference to Mount Hermon and the region around Caesarea Philippi. But Mark adds his own comparison for the special quality of this snowy light: the fuller who is not able to make anything so white, 'no fuller on earth'.

This comparison was sometimes felt to be somewhat childish. Ernst Lohmeyer, to whom we are otherwise indebted for some sensitive observations, speaks of the 'village-horizon' of such a picture.* At the same time, the term 'on earth' is of great importance here. It plays a major role in all three synoptic gospels.

'On earth' – this is how Matthew refers to that region of the world that has its opposite in the regions of the heavens. In the heavens the will of God is done, while the earth is fought over and has yet to be regained for the light. Through Christ's incarnation, heaven and earth enter a new relationship to each other. The 'as in the heavens, so also on earth' is also subject to reversal. Christian earth-impulses may also weave into the heavenly worlds, 'as on earth so also in the heavens' (Mt 16:19; 18:18; 18:19). The Risen One holds both worlds in his hand, he has authority 'in heaven and on earth' (28:18).

In Mark's gospel, too, this 'on earth' that seems to appear so

---

* Lohmeyer, *Das Evangelium des Markus,* p. 175.

casually in the transfiguration narrative is not unique. Earlier, there was the healing of the man suffering from palsy when the Christ tells the scribes that the Son of Man has authority to forgive sins 'on earth' (2:10, also Mt 9:6, Lk 5:24). For pre-Christian perception, authority for forgiving sins could only be found in a world that lay beyond anything human, that was purely heavenly. Now, this authority became effective at the divine-human level through Christ Jesus in human form – 'on earth'. Christ Jesus has brought down into the earthly human world what previously had been heavenly only. With him something quite new comes towards the earth and humanity. This new element is felt by Mark when, with his 'fuller' comparison, he tries to express that with Christ a light enters the earthly world that is absolutely 'not of this earth'. The white garment has at all times had an obvious pictorial meaning. The washing of a soiled garment and the inner cleansing of the soul's tarnished sheath, became interchangeable in the perception of people of old, when inwardness and outwardness were not yet divided so abstractly. The white garment was the goal of all cleansing endeavour of the old religions, to which all who strove came closer to a greater or lesser degree. But only Christ Jesus makes recognisable what is meant by this ideal, what the 'white garment' is in truth. Beyond all that which earthly 'whitening' endeavours can achieve, the Christ brings down to earth his light which has the purity of snow.

It is a light 'not of this earth' and yet, at the same time, 'for' this earth. It is, of course, not so that it appears from outside once only, illuminating an outstanding figure, only to allow earthbound humanity to sink back into darkness more hopeless than ever. It is no heavenly mirage but the announcement that this heavenly substance is about to communicate with earthly humanity. However, the only way to reach human beings is through death and resurrection of Christ who, through his suffering a human death, has so transformed his heavenly being that it becomes accessible to humans, that it becomes communicable.

The transfiguration is very soon followed by the second announcement of the passion, just as it was preceded by the first one at Caesarea Philippi. This second announcement of the passion has a unique form. It alone contains the motif of the 'Son of Man will be delivered into the hands of men' (Mk 9:31; Mt 17:22; Lk 9:44). In fact, Luke omits any other prediction of the passion or resurrection, having only this one – 'the Son of Man is about to be given into the hands of men.' It is most certainly a prediction of the passion. The One, who is without sin, wearer of snow-white garments spun of light, will be delivered into the killing hands of the sinners. But at the same time, behind this strange formula – 'the Son of Man is about to be given into the hands of men' – there appears, as from afar, another interpretation of meaning, in accordance with the 'paradox' of the Mystery of Golgotha, which hints at a positive aspect that can only come into being at the cost of the passion. The Apocalypse of John sees en-Christed human beings of the future who have washed and 'whitened' their garments in the blood of the Lamb (7:14). The same verb *leukainō* (to whiten) is used as in the transfiguration text of Mark.

Elijah and Moses

With Matthew we noticed that, for him, Moses is apparently more important than Elijah. 'And behold, there appeared to them Moses, and Elijah talking with him' (17:3). 'There appeared' is in the singular. It is exactly the opposite in Mark, 'And there appeared to them Elijah with Moses' (9:4). Here, too, the singular is used, that refers to only one of the spirit figures. But with Mark it is not Moses, but Elijah.

Mark shows in his whole gospel that he is not interested in the past to the same degree as Matthew. He does not present a genealogical tree, be it the one according to Matthew that leads back to Israel's beginnings, or the one according to Luke that reaches to the beginnings of humanity in Adam. He does not relate childhood stories. He begins with the point in time of the baptism in the Jordan, and puts at the front of his book the absolute word *archē,* 'beginning'. It is not the beginning of the world that is meant, nor the beginning of Israel, or even the beginning of the life of Jesus, but what is done to the adult Jesus through John the Baptist. This is for Mark *the* new beginning, once more in the grand manner of a beginning of creation. What had been before this remains unmentioned.

Mark is first and foremost concerned with a happening that begins with the Jordan baptism and strives forcefully in a series of deed-inspired events towards the mystery of death and resurrection. The bare essentials having been said about John the Baptist, verse 9 of the first chapter already brings us to the Jordan baptism. In connection with it, the word *euthys,* 'immediately', enters the narrative for the first time, a word that is so typical of Mark and his impetuous will-orientated character, appearing as it does no less than 41 times in his gospel. 'And immediately, coming out of the water, he saw the heavens breaking open' (1:10). 'And immediately the Spirit drives him out into the wilderness' (1:12).

This emphasis on will can be seen by the fact that Mark brings so much less teaching content than the other evangelists. For him, the teacher is less important than the doer. So it is that Elijah, with his spiritual fire-nature that drives him forward towards decisions and the future, is closer to him than Moses. Certainly, Moses too was in the highest sense a 'doer'. But in the consciousness of his people he was, first and foremost, the great teacher, 'learned in all the wisdom of Egypt' (Ac 7:22). Matthew has the word of the *kathedra,* the seat of Moses (23:2). There could be no question of a 'seat of Elijah'. Elijah, 'the burning and shining lamp' (Jn 5:35), is all blazing will. He has to prepare what is in the future and is always a 'coming one'. Fiery, future-orientated will is also Mark's element. For him it is important that the kingdom of God come 'with power' (9:1). He alone describes the Easter angel as a 'young man' (16:5). Easter is for him the youth-restoring beginning of the world.

Out of this upward and forward striving impulse, Mark, in the transfiguration narrative, puts Elijah before Moses.

The share of the three disciples

An apparently unimportant aspect at the beginning of the transfiguration narrative can attract attention. As in Matthew, Christ 'takes' the three chosen disciples 'with him' and 'brings them up' the mountain, Matthew adding *kat'idian,* 'apart' (17:1). We have already mentioned that in *idios* lies the reference to the 'essence' and the 'essential', to a value that is of significance to the human being as an individual ego-being. Mark also has this *kat'idian* but he adds *monous* (9:2), the plural of *monos* (in the accusative mode). This word has a certain dignity-denoting quality. Any other time it is reserved only for

Christ himself. *Monos* – the unique one, the one who carries the secret of the one-ness of the eternal 'I' within himself.

We could perhaps see a long-term effect of the Christ-event in Plotinus' concluding words of *The Enneads*. This third century mystic, who regarded himself as a non-Christian, wrote, 'The unique only one seeking refuge with the unique only one' *(phygē monou pros monon)*. The one-ness principle in the human being tends towards the great one-ness principle of the world. Only in that which is Christian could these words find total fulfilment, the human I taking refuge with the great sheltering I, protecting from egotism, which has appeared in the Christ: 'You in me.'

With his formulation, then, Mark gives the disciples too their share of being *monos*. It should not be necessary to point out once more that he also wanted to establish that only these three disciples were taken up the mountain and no one else. But beyond that, it cannot be ignored that in the gospels the word *monos* is apportioned to the disciples only here.

The overshadowing

We read of the overshadowing cloud in all three synoptic gospels. It is an almost undetectable peculiarity of Mark that he does not construct 'overshadowing' with the expected accusative, as do both the other reporters, but with the dative. He does not say, in effect, the cloud cast a shadow 'over' them, but it cast a shadow 'to' them (9:7).

Luke also constructs overshadowing with the dative once, although not in connection with the transfiguration, but with the angel's message to Mary: 'The Holy Spirit will come upon you and the power of the Highest will cast a shadow *to* you' (1:35). No natural phenomenon is meant here, no external effect of which the human being is a mere 'object'. The dative does not show up the object-character in a onesided radical way as does the accusative. Mary, for her part, must put herself at the disposal of the Holy Spirit – 'behold, I am the handmaiden of the Lord. May it happen to me according to your word.' In this 'may it happen to me' she opens herself to the heavenly influence. A little of this nuance lies in Mark's formulation, albeit not as expressly conscious as in Mary's annunciation. The disciples are not merely passive objects like earthly things on which a shadow falls. They carry something in themselves that meets halfway the event that is coming 'to' them and is intended to happen 'to' them.

The question of rising from the dead

Mark brings the Christ's command not to talk about their experience in the same way as Matthew, except that he does not speak of a 'vision' *(hórama)*, and that instead of 'has been wakened [*egerthē*] from the dead' he uses 'rises [*anasthē*] from the dead' – 'until the Son of Man had risen from the dead' (9:9). The verb *egeirō* means to waken, to arouse, as well as to raise up. The different nuances in the two words are distinctly discernible in the saying Paul quotes in his Letter to the Ephesians (5:14): 'Awaken, you who sleep! And rise up from the dead!' Waking is the precondition. It is, of course, a well-known fact that a human being can stand erect only when conscious. The Easter message delivered by the angel – also according to Mark – says: 'He has been raised [*egerthē*] from the dead.' Paul uses the same expression in his First Letter to the Corinthians (15:4). But for the rest it should be said that *anastēnai* is a particularly important word for Mark. It is in keeping again with his will-powered drive. 'Rising from the dead' – in Greek also 'rising' in a wider sense – gives a strong indication that the one who has been raised adds his own force.

Comparing the three passion-announcements as formulated by the three synoptic gospel writers, one can observe that Matthew uses 'be awakened' on all three occasions (16:21; 17:23; 20:19), Luke once each, 'be awakened' (9:22) and 'rise' (18:33), the Easter motif being omitted by Luke from the second announcement (9:44). Mark has *anastēnai* in all three instances (8:31; 9:31; 10:34). Closely connected to these announcements, with the thrice-repeated 'rising from the dead', is the prominent resurrection motif at the conclusion of Mark's transfiguration narrative. What follows 'until the Son of Man had risen from the dead,' is one of the passages peculiar to Mark. His 'unique material' may be quantitatively insignificant, but is outweighed qualitatively. Mark – and he alone – relates how Christ's word of the 'Son of Man rising from the dead' strikes a chord in the disciples. 'And they retained this word among themselves' (9:10). One could also translate it with they 'seized' or 'held fast to' the word. The Greek *krateō* is a word conveying will-power. Stronger than in Matthew or Luke, the activity on the part of the disciples finds expression here.

This active attitude is further apparent in the fact that the disciples, in whom the resurrection-word had sparked the desire to make it the subject of a communal effort towards knowing perception, questioned 'one with another what the rising from the dead should mean.' (9:10).

It is strange that immediately afterwards they address the question concerning Elijah to the Christ. 'And they asked him saying: "Why do the scribes say that Elijah must first come?"' (9:11). They turn to Christ with this question, without any inhibitions. They do not do so with the much weightier question, 'What is the rising from the dead?' It is as if something held them back from asking Christ – whom they had just seen transfigured – about this mystery with which he was so closely involved. So they remain among themselves with their question and together they seek to find an answer. The word 'questioning' (*syn-zēteō*, literally 'seek together') is known to us from the Emmaus story: Luke describes how the two wanderers wrestle with the riddle of the death on the cross (24:15): 'And it happened that they talked and sought together ...'

It is this consonance with the other passages, which are all Mark's 'speciality', that gives weight to the statement that the disciples, having taken hold with spiritual energy of the word 'rising from the dead', now seek to comprehend through the joint endeavour of their 'selves'.

It could be argued that nothing was ever said about the disciples having taken up the resurrection motif following any of the three passion announcements, which all conclude with the *anastēnai,* and that, quite to the contrary, their total incomprehension had to be noted. From a purely logical point of view there seems to be a contradiction. But the soul-life has a logic of a special kind. It is true that the disciples have already 'with a jolt' made the transition to everyday consciousness on conclusion of the series of supersensible events. But this transition which, in principle, has been accomplished may also include the possibility that even within 'normal consciousness' a great variety of things can happen.

The allusion to the resurrection that fired the interest of the disciples did not occur until after they had begun descending the mountain. 'And as they came down from the mountain' (9:9). The descent had not yet been completed. It is still in progress. We remember the strange expression Matthew uses: while they were descending 'out of' the mountain (17:9). Precisely in its strangeness it suggests a getting 'out of' a special kind of world in which one has previously stood. For example, we wake up in the morning, the transition to day-consciousness has already been completed; nevertheless, we linger spiritually a little while longer in this strange world of the dream just dreamt, from which we only gradually emerge. In the same way, the disciples are spiritually still 'in' the mountain experience, they are still under its spell. They have not yet arrived back 'in the valley' where they revert again to being people who may occasionally forget what they once knew. While the descent lasts, the condition of the disciples' consciousness was still 'unstable', as it were, and during this state of transition they are still transported beyond themselves. As witnessed by the fact that, according to Matthew, they were able to grasp that Elijah has returned in the person of John the Baptist – 'then the disciples understood' (17:13). And in the ebbing away of their mountain-entrancement, the word 'rising from the dead' shines powerfully into their souls.

Once more, Mark uses the word *anastēnai,* namely in the story of the healing of the possessed boy down in the valley that immediately follows this passage. In this story, Mark's literary individuality comes strongly to the fore. His dramatic narrative gives a wealth of lively detail, his account being twice as long as that of Matthew or Luke. According to Mark, the people who gathered around the boy in the valley were 'awe-struck when they saw him' (9:15). Being awe-struck or beside oneself is mentioned on other occasions only in connection with somebody witnessing an extraordinary deed of the Christ. Here, the deed has not yet been done. It is the mere sight of him who has just descended from the mountain. It seems the crowd must have perceived in the countenance of the Christ something like majesty reflected from the transfiguration.

In the narrative of the healing of the boy that now follows, Mark has once more woven into it the great motif of death and resurrection. Matthew says: 'And the boy was healed from that hour' (Mt 17:18). Luke has: 'And he healed the boy and gave him back to his father'

(Lk 9:42), emotionally human, just as the Christ 'gave the youth of Nain to his mother' (Lk 7:15). Mark, on the other hand, dwells in detail on the process of healing. With a loud cry the spirit leaves the boy, but in departing he once more shakes him with terrible convulsions.

> And he became as if dead [*nekros*], so that many said that he was dead. But Jesus took him by the hand, raised him up and he arose [*anestē*]. (9:26f)

The words of the great mystery, here they are all gathered together: dead – died – arouse *(egeirein)* – rise *(anastēnai)*. The Greek *anastēnai* means 'rise' as well as 'rise from the dead'. The crowning 'and he rose' is *anéstē*. Of course, in the case of the boy, it is not a 'rising from the dead' in the true sense, but his lying ill like one dead, and his rising through the Christ's uplifting impact, acquires a pictorial significance that can in no way be misunderstood. The event, notwithstanding its quite concrete reality, becomes transparent for still greater things to come.

We are well aware of the fact that the word *anastēnai* appears several times in the gospels without there necessarily being such a strong and transparent connection to the resurrection as such. Occasionally, it can just mean 'arising' or 'setting out'. But the identity of the term does have its effect. The reflection of the resurrection may be noticeable to a greater or lesser extent. It cannot be overlooked when Mark (5:42) and also Luke (8:55) say of the daughter of Jairus, *anéstē*. Nor can it be overlooked when Mark weaves, in the vicinity of the transfiguration event, this *anéstē* of the healed boy (9:27) into the tight succession of resurrection words (8:31, 9:9, 9:10, 9:31), all of which relate to the great mystery in the full meaning. Once again, one is confronted by the phenomenon of consonance.

The unique quality of Mark's report

At first it appears that in Mark's report on the transfiguration very little is purely in his account. However, closer inspection shows Mark's 'speciality' does indeed exist; not so much as something distributed evenly throughout, but as an all the more impressive will-powered emphasis – a 'resurrection emphasis'.

In addition there is something else. The characteristic aspect of a gospel, the specific and the unique, cannot be clearly discerned by just looking at specific individual contents. To compare the synoptic gospel writers with one another only 'horizontally' would seem to be the obvious thing to do. It will reveal where the 'parallels' are, where each evangelist has his empty spaces, and where each has his 'speciality'. This 'horizontal' comparison of the three adjoining texts is undoubtedly justified, but one has to be aware of the danger of a certain atomising, and of the fact that one can easily lose sight of the individual gospel as a literary whole. To complement the *horizontal* comparison, *vertical* reading must be cultivated, allowing each gospel to stand by itself, *kat'idian monon,* to have its effect as a whole without the distraction of sideways glances to its synoptic neighbours. Then it becomes clear that the individual and specific characteristics of an evangelist are found by no means only in his 'speciality'. One and the same event, described in like manner by all three synoptic gospel writers, assumes a different place value, depending on its position within that particular whole, and assumes a specific tone, depending on possible 'consonance'.

As mentioned earlier, Mark, for ever driven by his will to forge ahead, confines himself in the main to describe the deeds of the Christ. With him it is not so much his 'special property' that is characteristic, but rather his 'special gap' – what he does not say in order that he can hurry towards the resurrection. As a consequence, the relatively few contents of his choice assume a heightened importance of their own. There is now an empty space around them, and in his gospel they are compressed and together form the whole. The Jordan baptism as the great beginning shows up in quite a different light when allowed to open the chapter without childhood or John the Baptist stories. It stands out more prominently as the one pillar of the true events surrounding Christ Jesus, balancing the other pillar of his death and resurrection. And between the two, the transfiguration has its place.

Mark places it in the *centre* of his gospel. It actually is the exact centre. The number of chapters (the arrangement of the chapters dates back to the thirteenth century) obscure this as the chapters are of very different lengths. Contemplation of Luke's and Matthew's texts has already shown that, by their subject matter, they refer back to the Jordan baptism (the heavenly voice) as well as forward to the resurrection. But in Mark's text, this median and mediating position becomes even more markedly obvious by the transfiguration being placed exactly in the centre of the whole: between the Jordan baptism at the beginning and the resurrection at the end. This centre is not intended to be a chronologically biographical one; purely externally, more time elapsed between the Jordan baptism and the transfiguration than between the transfiguration and Golgotha. But measured by the inner value of the event rather than according to the exterior calendar, the transfiguration stands in the centre.

To regard the transfiguration as 'backdated', in other words as an Easter legend put into the narrative without any justification, is to misunderstand the unique significance of the transfiguration in its role as connecting link. It is in the right position.

65

CONCLUSION

Looking at the Gospel of John

'And we beheld his glory, the glory of the only begotten of the Father full of grace and truth' (Jn 1:14). Judging from this passage of John's Prologue one would expect the transfiguration story to play a significant role in the narrative of the fourth gospel. The words quoted – 'we beheld his glory' – almost sound like a personal echo confirming Luke's sentence 'they saw his glory' (9:32). But reading on, one searches John's gospel in vain for the transfiguration story.

John's account describes the feeding of the five thousand as having taken place at the time of the Passover, making it the beginning of the last year before Golgotha. Then he jumps immediately from spring to autumn and gives a description of events connected with the autumnal Festival of Tabernacles (7:1–10:21). In between lies a span of six months. To this period of time, ignored by John, belongs the transfiguration on the mountain. Tradition gives as its date August 6. But when John takes up his narrative again at the beginning of Chapter 7, it is with the Festival of Tabernacles. Nevertheless, there is in John's text the suggestion of an echo of the transfiguration that had gone before. The Christ, whose countenance shone like the sun, now says at the conclusion of the Festival of Tabernacles: 'I AM the light of the world' (8:12). We also come across the word 'glory'.

As the transfiguration theme is further developed by John, the question why exactly the transfiguration narrative was omitted becomes even more pressing. In Chapter 57 on the agape of the Father, we spoke about the Jordan baptism, also omitted by John:

> The absence of just such events, which one would have thought were particularly close to the heart of the fourth

evangelist, is altogether surprising. Not only is the baptism 'missing', but also the transfiguration, the Last Supper and the ascension. On closer inspection, however, one may discern that the events missed are still contained in the gospel in some way, albeit in a finer, more 'atmospheric' form, as it were. It seems that the 'body' of a concrete event-related narrative has been sacrificed, liberating in its place something of the inner essence of the event in question, permeating the text like a fragrance.

This applies particularly to the transfiguration. What the synoptic gospel writers have enclosed and contained in a relatively narrow frame of a narrative, John has detached from the specific event, allowing it to become an element that pervades his whole gospel. What the synoptic gospel writers describe is an episode, a bright moment in the life of the disciples' consciousness. 'Peter and those with him were heavy with sleep, and when they were becoming awake, they saw his glory' (Lk 9:32). Some moments later, darkening consciousness again fills the souls of the disciples; only deep down does that which they had seen continue to work towards the moment when the Son of Man would rise from the dead.

Something very special attaches to the fourth evangelist. His writings are the life-testimony of one who has been awakened and who, in describing the destiny of Lazarus, speaks of his own Christ-inspired death and resurrection experience. He is the disciple whom the Lord loves, to whom the Lord can reveal himself in a very special way. As one who has been awakened in the spirit, he has discarded the 'heaviness of sleep'. He was privileged to perceive the secret of the nature of Christ Jesus, not only in a few sudden flashes of inner illumination, but in quiet contemplation.

As far as John is concerned, the light of the transfiguration spreads throughout the entire work of Christ Jesus. He has come down to earth, relinquishing the full brilliance of glory he has shared with the Father in eternity before the world existed (17:5). Nevertheless, he brings something of the original shining magnificence into the earthly incarnation of Jesus. When, after the Jordan-baptism, he worked his first miracle at Cana, 'he revealed his glory' (2:11). However, its full splendour can only come into being through the deed of Golgotha.

At the time of the Festival of Tabernacles, 'Jesus had not yet been glorified,' according to John (7:39). Even on Palm Sunday the 'not yet' is still valid: here the evangelist makes the comment that, at the time, the disciples did not grasp the secret behind the entry into Jerusalem and understood only later, remembering 'after Jesus was glorified' (12:16). This *true* transfiguration can only be accomplished through the Mystery of Golgotha and its continuing effect. The Christ is again granted the glory of archetypal light that was his before the world existed (17:5, 24); in renewed form it arises out of the accomplished deed. We are already close in time to this real transfiguration when, at the grave of Lazarus, the Christ speaks of the glorification of the Son of God (11:4), and again at the beginning of the Holy Week when, at the encounter with certain Greeks, he speaks of the glorification of the Son of Man whose hour has now come (12:23, see also 17:1).

The Son's original glory is with the Father before anything else exists. Nearing incarnation during cosmic and historic ages he already had the glory which Isaiah beheld (Jn 12:41). He manifested his glory at the beginning of his earthly work at Cana (2:11) and also on the occasion of the last of the Johannine miracles at the grave of Lazarus (11:40). And yet, prior to Golgotha, he is 'not yet glorified'.

In Luke, who is closest to John, and not only by virtue of the arrangement of the four gospels, we notice something similar. With him, too, the real glory is only realised through the Mystery of Golgotha. 'Was it not necessary that Christ should suffer these things and enter into his glory?' (24:26). But even earlier than that, on the mountain of transfiguration, the disciples saw 'his glory' (9:32). And earlier still, at Bethlehem in the Holy Night, the shepherds see the 'glory of the Lord, shining around them' (2:9), a glory that does not yet live in the body of Jesus as it does later at the transfiguration, but still floats above the child coming from pre-existence and only now striving towards earthly destinies.

With his eyes on the real transfiguration that comes to realisation only through Golgotha, the fourth evangelist can pronounce what was granted to him as Christ-experience and Christ-knowledge, with the words: 'And we beheld his glory, the glory of the only begotten of the Father full of grace and truth.'

In conclusion

The German New Testament scholar Günther Bornkamm says that the gospel narratives like the Jordan Baptism or the Temptation, in which the supersensible plays a part:

> ... are not historical reports, but ... in the form of illustrative tales, explain Jesus' mission and person. We do not deny that the tradition here attaches itself to scenes whose historicity certainly need not be contested, starting with the baptism and continuing on to his crucifixion and resurrection. The possibility, however, of finding a historical kernel in these stories varies greatly in each case, and is generally slight. Any such attempt is purchased as a rule at the expense of cheating oneself out of the real meaning of the text. Anyone may see this more clearly in the description, say, of the story of the transfiguration of Jesus, which really only begins to speak to us when we cease to ask after the 'historical facts' behind it.*

We hope to have shown that, regarding the transfiguration story, such a sacrifice is not called for. It is just that the concept of 'historical facts' must be clarified. The fact that mention is made of supersensible factors having had a part in a certain event does not entitle anyone to deny its historical reality. Rather, it is possible that an event in which specific spiritual beings are involved may, for that very reason, become part of the fabric of events known as 'history', with enhanced significance and range of consequences. Christianity is precisely about such dynamic facts. Christ becoming human in Jesus of Nazareth is not primarily a demonstration of timelessly valid truth that exists in any case; rather, it shows that something is *done,* something that, reaching into the future, triggers further and more distant work.

Surely it is also worth noting that the Second Letter of Peter (1:16) claims actuality in particular for the transfiguration, in marked contrast to 'cunningly devised fables'. *Sesophismenoi mythoi* are probably myths allegorised by the awakening intellect. The events surrounding Christ Jesus have the meaningful content in common

---

* Bornkamm, Günther, *Jesus of Nazareth,* p. 173.

with the myths, but they have the advantage of actuality over the latter.

We also hope to have shown that this particular way of looking at things does not result in 'cheating oneself out of the real meaning of the text'. In conclusion, let it be said that we are convinced that a narrative like the transfiguration story demands to be viewed in the light of 'expert knowledge', which includes the supersensible, and that only then will be revealed 'what the text wants to convey'. Only then will it really begin to speak to us.

Günther Bornkamm says in his book Jesus of Nazareth in which the supersensible plays a part

BIBLIOGRAPHY

Beckh, Hermann, *John's Gospel: the Cosmic Rhythm – Stars and Stones,* Anastasi, UK 2015.
Bock, Emil, *The Three Years,* Floris Books, Edinburgh 1980.
Bornkamm, Günther, *Jesus of Nazareth,* Hodder & Stoughton, London 1960.
Bultmann, Rudolf, *Theologie des Neuen Testamentes,* Tübingen 1977 (English: *The Theology of the New Testament,* Baylor University Press, USA 2007).
Frieling. Rudolf, *Christianity and Reincarnation,* Floris Books, Edinburgh 1977.
—, *The Essence of Christianity,* Floris Books, Edinburgh 2011 (available as free pdf download).
—, *Hidden Treasure in the Psalms,* Floris Books, Edinburgh 2015.
—, *Old Testament Studies,* Floris Books, Edinburgh 1987.
Godet, Frédéric Louis, *Commentary on the Gospel of John,* T & T Clark, Edinburgh 1880.
Goebel, Robert, *Das Evangelium in den vier Evangelien,* Urachhaus, Stuttgart 1929.
Goethe, Johann Wolfgang von, *Italian Journey,* Penguin Classics 1962.
Heidenreich, Alfred, *Healings in the Gospels* Floris Books, 1980.
Jeremias, Johannes, *Das Evangelium nach Johannes,* Max Müller, Chemnitz & Leipzig.
Kelber, Wilhelm, *Der Menschensohn,* Urachhaus, Stuttgart 1967.
Lagerlöf, Selma, *Jerusalem* (tr. V.S. Howard) T Werner Laurie, London 1916.
Lauenstein, Diether, *Der Messias,* Urachhaus, Stuttgart 1971.
Lohmeyer, Ernst, *Das Evangelium des Markus.*
MacGregor, John, *The Rob Roy on the Jordan, Nile, Red Sea and Gennesareth,* J Murray, London 1904.
Meyer, Rudolf, *Die Wiedergewinnung des Johannes-Evangeliums,* Urachhaus, Stuttgart 1962.
Rau, Christoph, *Struktur und Rhythmus im Johannesevangelium,* Urachhaus, Stuttgart 1972.
Reitzenstein, Richard August, *Werden und Wesen der Humanität im Altertum* 1907.

Rittelmeyer, Friedrich, *Briefe über das Johannes-Evangelium,* Urachhaus Stuttgart 1954.
—, *Meditation,* Floris Books, Edinburgh 2012.
—, *Vom johanneischen Zeitalter,* Urachhaus, Stuttgart 1927.
—, *Welterneuerung,* Urachhaus, Stuttgart 1925.
Stange, Erich, *Die Eigenart der johanneischen Produktion,* Dresden 1915.
Stauffer, Ethelbert, *Die Botschaft Jesu damals und heute,* Bern 1959.
—, *Jesus: Gestalt und Geschichte,* Bern 1957.
—, *Jesus war ganz anders,* Hamburg 1967.
Steiner, Rudolf, *Anthroposophic Leading Thoughts* (CW 26) Rudolf Steiner Press, UK 2012.
—, *The Gospel of St John* (CW 103) Anthroposophic Press, USA 1984.
—, *The Gospel of St John in Relation to the Other Gospels* (CW 112) Anthroposophic Press, USA 1983.
—, *An Outline of Esoteric Science* (CW 13) Anthroposophic Press, USA 1997.
—, *Riddles of the Soul* (CW 21) Mercury Press, USA 1996.
—, *Theosophy* (CW 9) Anthroposophic Press, USA 1994.
Thomson, W.M. *The Land and the Book,* Nelson, London 1872.

SOURCES AND TRANSLATORS

Chapters 1, 7, 11, 17, 19, 24, 26, 36, 37, 45, 46, 47 and 48 originally published in German under the title *Bibel-Studien* by Verlag Urachhaus in 1963 (some originally published in German as essays in *Die Christengemeinschaft),* translated by Margaret and Rudolf Koehler.

Chapters 14 and 15 originally published in German as essays in *Die Christengemeinschaft,* translated by Conrad Mainzer, first published in the *Threshing Floor.*

Chapter 16 originally published in German as an essay in *Die Christengemeinschaft,* translated by Jon Madsen, first published in the *Threshing Floor.*

Chapters 56 to 60 (Agape) was originally published in German under the title *Agape: die göttliche Liebe im Johannes-Evangelium* by Verlag Urachhaus 1935, third edition 1967. First published in English by St Norbert Abbey Press, Wisconsin in 1969. Translated by Jeffrey Kay.

Chapters 61 to 65 (The Transfiguration) was originally published in German under the title *Die Verklärung auf dem Berge* by Verlag Urachhaus in 1969. Translated by Hilde Stossel (slightly abridged).

Above chapters were published as *New Testament Studies* by Floris Books, 1994.

All remaining chapters were originally published in German as essays in *Die Christengemeinschaft,* translated by Matthew Barton.

INDEX OF BIBLICAL REFERENCES

Old Testament

Genesis (Gn)
1:26f	292
1:26	48, 279
2:1f	114
3:22	314
4:9	20
5:1	29
5:3–5	26
5:6–8	26
5:22	26
5:24	26, 126
5:25	27
6:9	26
9:6	292
14	261
17:1	26
19:17	206
25:8	317

Exodus (Ex)
22:8	83
33:11	277
34:29–35	277
40:34	502

Ruth (Ru)
3:9	237

1 Kings (1K)
8:10f	502

Psalms (Ps)
2:7	62
8:4	49
16:8	260f
22	111
31	114
31:5	275
34:8	241
82	83
95:7f	64
110	285
110:1	261
115:16	50
126:1	267

Isaiah (Is)
14:12	286
64:1	38
65:17	53
66:22	53

Joel (Jl)
2:28f	258, 261

Malachi (Mal)
4:2	498
4:4f	499

Wisdom of Solomon (Ws)
14:6	206

1 Maccabees (1Mc)
4:36–59	79

New Testament

Matthew (Mt)
1:1–17	25–31
1:16	28
1:20	501
2:1–12	496, 503
3:13	492
3:16f	503
3:17	40
4:1	95
4:3	41
4:6	41
4:8	490
4:10	44
4:13	35
4:24	496
5:1f	491
5:13	227, 497
5:14	491
5:18	496
5:25f	321
5:34f	496
5:45	495
5:48	70
6:3	492
6:9–13	473
6:10	496
6:12	492
6:15	492
6:23	476
6:46	492
7:28	157

– Matthew (continued)

8:1	492
8:22	138
8:23–27	57–60
8:27	41, 156
8:29	41, 60
9:1	35
9:2	492
9:6	513
9:9	492
9:27–31	176
9:28	492
9:37	492
10:28	321
10:38	475
11:2	160
11:14f	508
11:20	158
11:25	496
11:28–30	66–74
11:28	241
12:40	75, 497
12:49f	204
13:3	492
13:23	203
13:43	495
14:13	490
14:14	501
14:16	335n
14:18	335n
14:23	98, 490f
14:33	42
15:29	98, 491
16:16	43, 87, 488
16:19	496, 512
16:20	506
16:21	517
16:22	44, 87, 488, 500
16:23	44
16:28–17:1	489
17:1	492, 515
17:2	493f
17:3	498, 514
17:4	499
17:5f	503
17:5	45, 501f
17:7	505
17:8	505
17:9	505, 519
17:13	508, 519
17:15	495
17:17	500f
17:18	519
17:19	490
17:22f	45
17:22	87, 501, 513
17:23	88, 517
18:18f	496
18:18	512
18:19	512
19:27	226, 228
20:1–16	226–31
20:4	228
20:7	228
20:8	229
20:14	230
20:15	229f
20:17	490
20:19	88, 517
20:29–34	176
21:15	69
21:33–46	232–39
21:33	232
21:34	234
21:37	237, 492
21:38	237
21:41	238
21:42	285
22:1–14	213–19
22:12	229
22:39	492
23:2	515
23:4	71
23:48	151
24:3	490f
24:27	152
24:29f	48
24:29	149, 495
24:30	150f, 507
24:35	496
25:1–13	245f
25:12	249
25:14–30	246f
25:31–46	247f, 250–54
25:31	53
25:34	247
25:40	238, 250
26:33–35	103
26:36	100
26:43	482
26:50	229
26:63	45
26:64	261
26:69–75	104
27:1	105
27:40–42	46
27:44	110
27:46	111
27:51f	37, 497
27:54	47
28:2	497
28:16	491
28:17f	483
28:17	23, 457
28:18	124, 496, 512
28:20	29, 125, 501

Mark (Mk)

1:3–10	466
1:9	515
1:10	37, 515
1:12	96, 515
1:33	96
1:35	472
2:1–12	162–64
2:10	513
3:34f	204
4:20	203
4:35–41	57–60
5:7	60
5:9	57
5:42	156, 520
6:31	97
6:37f	335n
6:39	364
6:51	157
7:32–37	165–70
7:34	166
7:37	82, 157, 170
8:12	167
8:22–26	177
8:31	517, 520
9:1–11	511
9:1	515
9:2–8	466
9:2	493, 515
9:3	512

INDEX OF BIBLICAL REFERENCES

– Mark (continued)
9:4	514
9:6	503
9:7	516
9:9	517, 519f
9:10	517f, 520
9:11	518
9:15	519
9:26f	520
9:27	520
9:31	513, 517, 520
10:24	163
10:32	88
10:34	517
12:1–12	232–39
12:6	237
13:25	150
14:29–31	103
14:34	368
14:37	103
14:40	482
14:71	104
15:1	105
15:32	110
15:34	111
16:5	515
16:9	205
16:14–18	123

Luke (Lk)
1:22	316
1:24	471
1:26	471
1:35	424, 484, 516
1:38	483
1:57	471
1:59	471
1:68–79	487
2:6	471
2:9	525
2:11	61
2:15	483
2:21	471
2:22	471
2:35	111
2:37	471
2:38	481
2:42	471
2:46	471
2:48	157
3:21	472
3:22	30n, 62, 485
3:23	471
4:1	95
4:2	471
4:13	46
4:14	96
4:16	62
4:20	63
5:1–11	133–37
5:1–9	35
5:4	58
5:16	97, 472
5:24	513
5:26	63
6:12	97, 472
6:23–38	27
7:14	128
7:15	520
7:36–50	205
8:2	205
8:4–15	201–7
8:10	88
8:11	202
8:15	88, 203
8:18	88, 203
8:21	204
8:22–25	57–60
8:28	60
8:55	520
9:13f	335n
9:18	87, 99, 469
9:20	469
9:22	475, 517
9:23	475
9:26	21, 470
9:27	470
9:28	99, 471, 485
9:29	99, 473, 476, 485
9:30–32	477
9:31	478
9:32	481, 523–25
9:33	483, 485
9:34	484f, 503
9:35	485
9:36	487
9:37	468, 487
9:42	520
9:43	157
9:44	87, 475, 513, 517
9:45	88
9:51–19:29	128, 481
9:51	145f, 481, 501
9:62	206
10:22	212
10:39–42	193
10:39	204
11:1	99, 472
11:27	205
11:28	88, 205, 486
11:35	476
11:36	476
12:16–21	240–44
12:17	487
12:50	34, 143, 371
13:11	471
13:16	471
13:22	481
13:32f	63
13:33	480
13:34	480
14:15	221
14:16–24	220–25
15:1–7	209
15:4	209
15:5	209
15:6	209
15:7	209
15:8–10	210
15:8	210
15:9	210
15:11–32	210f
15:12	487
15:24	211
15:32	211, 242
16:19–31	320, 479
17:11	481
17:22–18:8	206
17:22	470
17:32	206
18:31	88, 480
18:33	517
18:34	88f

– Luke (continued)		John (Jn)		2:20	80
19:37	158	1:1	384f	2:23	363, 366
19:41	481	1:2	165	3:1–21	365
20:9–19	232–39	1:3	386, 415	3:2	335, 337, 366f
20:9	234	1:6	385	3:3	335, 455n
20:13	237	1:7	385	3:4	335, 337
20:16	239	1:9	385	3:5–8	336
20:38	321	1:10	385f	3:5	455n
21:7	272n	1:11	110, 286	3:7	455n
21:20–24	481	1:12	287, 391, 442,	3:9	335
21:28	152		450n, 455n	3:10–21	336
21:34	482	1:13	195	3:13	141, 372, 377,
21:40	487	1:14	427, 523		379, 396
22:14	222	1:15–30	372	3:14f	387
22:31f	103	1:18	385f, 415, 438	3:14	352
22:33	108	1:19–23	346	3:16	412, 414, 427f,
22:34	64	1:20	347		437, 440, 450,
22:39–41	101	1:21	347		459
22:43f	101	1:23	347	3:17	416, 446
22:45	269	1:24–28	346	3:19	336, 353, 412,
22:53	482	1:26f	347		415, 416n, 460
22:58	105	1:26	116	3:20	336, 416
22:61	104	1:29–34	346f	3:21	336
22:63	105	1:31	33	3:23	387
22:66	105	1:32–34	418	3:29	349
23:28	481	1:34	22	3:30	335
24:34	23, 109, 275	1:35–39	346	3:31	418
23:8f	156	1:36	347	3:35	412, 417, 459
23:42	272n	1:38f	346	3:36	321, 417
23:43	64, 110, 141,	1:38	347f	4:7	348
	275, 318, 479	1:40–42	346	4:10	349
23:46	114, 275	1:41	348	4:11	350
24:4	476	1:42f	346	4:13–15	391n
24:15	127, 518	1:43f	346	4:13f	349, 391
24:17	127, 131	1:45–51	346	4:14	113, 450n
24:19	160	1:45	348	4:15	350
24:26	525	1:46	348	4:16	349
24:27	122	1:47–51	347	4:17f	349
24:28	131	1:48	348	4:18	349
24:31	483	1:49	348	4:19	350
24:36–43	123	1:51	22, 172, 347n,	4:21–24	349
24:41	269		418	4:26	349
24:44f	260	2:3–5	335n	4:42	416, 446
24:47	481	2:4	335n, 339n, 363	4:54	160
24:49	481	2:7f	335n	5	171–75
24:50	144	2:10	82, 335n, 338	5:1	363
24:51	145, 483	2:11	160, 436, 524f	5:6	333
24:52	481	2:13	363	5:8	333f
24:53	472	2:19–21	132	5:9–13	334

– John (continued)		7:8	339n	8:59	81
5:14	333f	7:14	118	9:1–10:21	181–88, 358, 424
5:17	50, 161	7:30	339n	9	179f
5:19f	420f	7:34	375	9:1–7	181–83, 354
5:20	82, 160, 419	7:37–39	391	9:1	182
5:24	138, 321	7:37	113, 391n	9:3	358
5:35	515	7:39	436, 525	9:5	182, 355, 358f, 403
5:36	161	7:50f	365		
5:42	412, 430n, 431n, 460	7:50	366	9:6	76
		8:1–11	72–77	9:7	355, 358
6:3	98, 492	8:3	118	9:8–12	183f, 354
6:4	363, 401	8:5	81	9:9	180, 183, 355
6:5	335n	8:6	75	9:11	184, 354
6:7	335n	8:7	76	9:13–17	184f, 354
6:9	335n	8:8	75	9:15	184
6:10	335n, 364	8:9	118	9:16	184
6:11	450n, 456	8:10	76	9:17	185, 354
6:12	335n	8:12–20	351, 353	9:18–23	185, 354
6:14	335n	8:12	180f, 350n, 351, 353, 355, 358, 388f, 403, 407, 451n, 453, 523	9:21	185
6:15	98			9:21	355
6:26	159			9:24–34	185f, 354
6:27	450n			9:27	186
6:33	372, 379, 446, 113, 350n, 388, 391, 391n, 402, 407, 451n	8:14–18	351	9:31–33	186
		8:14	351	9:31	355
		8:16	112	9:33	355
		8:17	351	9:35	186, 355n
6:38	379	8:19	351	9:35–39	186f, 354
6:39f	321	8:20	339n, 352	9:35–37	355
6:41	379, 402	8:21–29	351–53	9:35	358
6:42	379	8:21	351	9:37f	357
6:44	321	8:22	352	9:37	358
6:45	68	8:23f	351		
6:48–50	402	8:23	76	**9:38**	**187**
6:48	407	8:24	352f	9:39	358
6:50	379	8:25f	351	9:40–10:21	187f, 354
6:51	379, 402, 407, 446, 450n, 453	8:28	351–53		
		8:29	112, 352	9:41–10:6	358
6:53	378	8:30–59	351–54		
6:54	321	8:31f	351	10:1–21	419
6:56	406, 443n	8:34–38	351	10:6	357
6:58	379	8:39–41	351	10:7–18	358
6:62	372, 377–80	8:42–47	351	10:7f	404
6:65	363	8:42	412, 455n, 460	10:7	350n, 358, 407, 451n
6:70	380f	8:44	380f		
7:1–10:21	72, 78, 363, 404, 523	8:46	73	10:9	358, 389, 404, 407
		8:49–51	351		
		8:51	321	10:11	82, 338, 350n, 358, 404, 407, 420f, 451n
7:2	363	8:54–56	351		
7:6	339n	8:58	351, 353, 372		

– John (continued)		11:35	195	13:15	450*n*	
10:14	82, 338, 358, 405, 407	11:36	434	13:21	360, 438*n*	
		11:38	195	13:23	197, 386*n*, 438, 459	
10:14f	425	11:40	525			
10:15	405, 420f	11:41f	367, 370	13:26	360	
10:16	421f	11:41	369	13:27f	360	
10:17f	358	11:42	196	13:27	380, 383, 439	
10:17	412, 420–23, 433, 444f, 458f	11:43	195	13:30–32	448	
		11:44	195, 197	13:30	449	
10:18	420	11:50	434	13:31	436, 442, 449	
10:21	354, 358	11:52	425	13:33	163	
10:22–39	78, 337f, 419	11:55	363	13:34f	449	
10:22	78, 363	12:2	436	13:34	442f, 450, 450*n*, 459	
10:23	79	12:13	450*n*			
10:25–31	337	12:16	436, 525	13:35	431*n*, 459	
10:27	421	12:17	434	13:36	103, 108	
10:28	450n	12:20–36	90–94, 339f, 367*n*	13:37	458	
10:30	370, 421, 425			13:38	103	
10:31	81f	12:20	90	14:2	454	
10:32	82, 161, 338	12:23	339*n*, 436, 449, 525	14:3	376	
10:33	82			14:6	350*n*, 406, 451*n*	
10:34–38	338	12:24	90, 371	14:15	452f, 459	
10:34	183	12:25	460	14:16	428, 442	
10:36	83	12:26	375	14:18f	428	
10:38	84	12:27f	367f, 367*n*, 370	14:21	428f, 431, 442, 453–55, 459	
10:40–42	412, 433	12:27	90, 369, 438*n*			
10:9	388	12:28	93, 369	14:23	429, 431, 439, 454f, 459	
11	189–97	12:29	93			
11:3	193, 197, 434	12:30–32	339	14:24	455	
11:4	192, 435f, 449, 525	12:30	368*n*	14:26	429, 442	
		12:31	94, 380, 382, 446	14:27	450*n*	
11:5	197, 412, 419, 433, 436f, 459			14:28	375, 455f, 459	
		12:32	94, 352	14:30f	446	
11:6f	435	12:33	339, 352	14:30	46, 380, 382, 446	
11:7	196	12:35f	339			
11:11	435	12:41	386, 525	14:31	440, 450*n*, 459	
11:14	196	12:43	416*n*, 460	14:6	407	
11:15	196	12:45	415	15:1	350*n*, 406f, 451*n*	
11:20	437	12:46	403			
11:21	193	12:47	416, 446	15:2	451	
11:22	194	12:49	450*n*	15:4	443, 443*n*, 451	
11:23	194	13:1–30	359	15:5	406f, 443, 443*n*, 451	
11:25f	388, 390	13:1	339*n*, 359, 437–40, 459			
11:25	139, 141, 194, 321, 350*n*, 405, 407, 435, 451*n*			15:6	443, 443*n*, 451	
		13:2	380f	15:7	443, 443*n*, 451	
		13:7	360	15:8	451	
		13:8	360	15:9f	427	
11:26	141	13:10f	360	15:9	422f, 431*n*, 443f, 443*n*, 451, 459	
11:32	193, 437	13:12–20	360			
11:33	195, 438*n*					

– John (continued)	
15:10	422, 431n, 443f, 443n, 451, 459
15:11	451
15:12	443f, 450, 452, 459
15:13	431n, 443–45, 458f
15:17	452, 459
16:11	380, 382
16:27	429, 455, 458
16:32	19, 110–12, 470
16:33	416
17	367
17:1–5	372
17:1	339n, 373, 525
17:2	450n
17:4	426
17:5	372, 426, 524f
17:6–19	372
17:6	93, 426
17:8	426, 450n
17:9	416
17:10	436
17:11	421, 425
17:14	450n
17:20–26	372
17:21	425f
17:22f	423
17:22	425f, 450n
17:23	425–27, 430f, 459
17:24	373, 376, 426f, 459, 525
17:26	427, 430f, 430n, 431n, 459
18:1–27	359
18:1	359
18:4	360
18:5	360
18:6	101
18:7	360
18:8	360
18:11	360
18:15f	106
18:17	105
18:18	106
18:20f	105, 360
18:23	360

18:24	106
18:25	105–7
18:28–19:16	359
18:28–32	361
18:33–38	361
18:34	361
18:36	361
18:37	93, 361, 392, 392n, 403n
18:38–40	361
18:38	361
19:1–3	361
19:4–7	361
19:4	361
19:6	361
19:8–12	361
19:11	361
19:13–16	361
19:18	119
19:26	110, 197, 340, 440f, 459
19:28	112, 340, 391n
19:30	114, 340, 437
19:35	22
19:39	365f
20:2	197, 439, 441
20:13	342
20:15	342
20:16	342
20:17f	377
20:17	125, 136, 342, 378f, 480
20:19–23	123
20:19	119, 343f
20:21	344
20:22f	343
20:26	120, 344, 471
20:28	123
20:29	344
20:30	395
21	124
21:2	345
21:4	137
21:5	136, 163, 345, 441
21:6	345
21:7	137, 137n, 197, 440f, 457, 459

21:8	136, 345
21:9	107, 136
21:10	345
21:11	136f, 345
21:12	137, 137n, 345, 440, 457
21:13	137, 440, 450n, 456
21:14	345, 458
21:15–17	345
21:15	419, 457, 459
21:16	458f
21:19	108, 345
21:20–22	441
21:20	459
21:22	108, 125, 345, 441n
21:25	395
22:27	119
23:46	119

Acts of the Apostles (Ac)

1:2	145
1:3	471
1:4	481
1:8	143, 481
1:9	144f, 483
1:10	146
1:11	145–47, 507
1:22	23
2:1	471
2:14–36	257–62
2:14–21	257f
2:14	261
2:22–28	258–61
2:22	155, 259, 261
2:24	29, 259
2:29–36	261f
2:29	261f
2:31	261
2:36	261
27:3	289
28:2	290
4:31	264f
4:32	264
5:12	80
6:3	270
6:5–7:60	270–76
6:5	270

– Acts (continued)
6:14   271
6:15   272
7:10   272
7:22   272, 515
7:30   272
7:35   272
7:38   272
7:53   272
7:54   274
7:55   274
7:56   274, 321
7:58   275
7:59   275
7:60   275, 321
9:7   128
10:7   483
12:1–17 263–69
12:5   264
12:6   264
12:7   265
12:9   266
12:10 267, 483,
12:12 265, 268
12:14 269
13:33 29
16:26 267

Romans (Rom)
2:4   70
5:17   28
8:22   168
8:26   169
12:2   493
16:25 487

1 Corinthians (1Cor)
11:24f 300
14:28   487
14:30   487
15:4   517
15:26   140f
15:31   309
15:39   281
15:41   281, 303, 494
15:50   140
15:51f 281
15:51   282
15:54   281

2 Corinthians (2Cor)
3:7   277
3:17   278f
3:18   278, 299, 493, 509
4:4   52
4:6   278, 493
5:4   282
12:4   169

Galatians (Gal)
1:15f 117
3:19   272
6:7   226, 334

Ephesians (Eph)
1:17f 284
4:9   319
4:13   445
5:14   283–88, 517

Philippians (Phil)
1:21   323
1:23   323
2:7f   280
2:8   69
3:8–14 296–301
3:8   296
3:9   296f
3:10   297
3:11   299
3:12   299
3:13   299
3:14   299
3:20f 279

Colossians (Col)
1:15   52, 279
1:24   298

1 Timothy (1Tm)
5:21   21

2 Timothy (2Tm)
1:12   296

Titus (Tit)
3:4–6 293
3:4   289–95

Hebrews (Hb)
1:2   237
2:2   272
3:7f   65
3:15   65
4:7   65
5:7   101
7:27   489
9:24   53
9:28   490
11:22 479
12:1   322
12:23 322

James (Jas)
1:17f 302–6
1:17   302
1:18   304
5:16   265

1 Peter (1Pt)
3:19   319, 480
4:6   319

2 Peter (2Pt)
1:13   322
1:15   322, 479
1:16–18 482
1:16   526
1:19   **286**
3:13   53

1 John (1Jn)
2:15   415f
2:17   415, 423
3:2   430
3:9   84
3:14   138

Revelation (Rv)
1:3   307
1:16   495
1:17f 504f
1:18   319
2:1   480
3:4   127, 480
3:12   74n, 236
3:18   252
3:21   53, 66, 480

– Revelation (continued)

5:6	53	14:13	308	20:4	322
6:9f	322	16:5	171	20:6	311
6:11	218	16:15	309	21:1	53
7:14	313, 514	18:4	479	21:6	113, 391*n*
7:16	113, 391*n*	18:10	216	22:7	313
7:17	139	18:15	216	22:14	313
8:1	487	18:17	216	22:16	286
		19:9	311	22:17	113, 391*n*

INDEX

Abraham 317, 373, 479
adultery, woman taken in 72–77, 118
Adversary, the 380–83, 499f
agapa and *philéein* (love) 419
agapē, meaning of word 411
Ahriman 353
Andrew (disciple) 348
angel(s) 19–21
— at tomb 23
— at transfiguration, two 477
— —, disappearance of 483f
—, hierarchies 273
—, two 146f
Annas (former high priest, father-in-law of Caiaphas) 105f
Antiochus Epiphanes 78f
Arimathea, Joseph of *see* Joseph of Arimathea
Aristotle 473
arrest and interrogation of Christ 360
Ascension (festival) 124f, 143–47
ascension of Christ 376–80
Ask and Embla (in Edda) 178
Augustine 291, 307

baptism of Jesus in Jordan 34, 36f, 40, 62, 418, 514f
— and crucifixion 35, 37
—, dove at 465
baptism, 'second' 34f
baptism, water rites 32–34
Barabbas 361
beatitudes of Apocalypse 307–14
beautiful, good *(kalos)* 82
Beckh, Hermann 340*n*, 364

begetting 485, *see also tholedoth*
behold (word in Matthew) 501–3
Bethesda, Pool of 172f, 333
Bethlehem, Church of Nativity 496
birth of Jesus 61
Bismarck, Otto von 50
Boaz 237
body as tent 322, 479
Bornkamm, Günther 426
bread, breaking 132
— from heaven 377
— of life, I AM the 388, 402
Buddha 113, 130f
Bultmann, Rudolf 466f, 507

Caesarea Philippi 43, 87, 467, 488
Caiaphas (high priest) 106
Cain 286
Cana, marriage at 335*n*, 363–65
Capernaitic eating 378n
Carthage 290
Cato the Elder 291
Chanukah 79
Christ, countenance transfigured 473–75, 494f, 504f, 512f
—, garments at transfiguration 476f
— praying 92f, 472f
— — in seclusion 95–101
— — to Father 367–72
chronos (time) *see* time *(chronos)*
Cicero 291f
Clement of Alexandria 285, 287f
clothing, garments, vestments 251f, 310, 313
cloud 147, 484f, 501–3

coin 230
communion 300
comrade *(hetairos)* 229
Constantinople, Council of 328
cross, seven words on 109–15, 340f
crucifixion 109–15
— and baptism 35, 37

Damascus, Paul's experience at 128, 507
darkness, love of 416
David's grave 261
death
—, circumstances of 139f
—, life after 315–23
—, second 312
Dedication of the temple, Festival of 78f, 337f
denarius 230
devil 380f
Dionysius the Areopagite 303f
disciple whom Jesus loved 197, 438–41
disciples 346f
door, I AM the 358, 388f, 404
dove as image 465
doxa (glory) 426f
drink 113

earth, ends of the 143f
Easter evening, Christ's appearance on 123
eat and drink, giving to 251
Ebionites, Gospel of the 36
Edda 178
eleusis 272
Elijah 320, 347, 508f, 518f
— and Moses at transfiguration 477f, 497–99, 514f
Elohim (judges) 72f, 83
Emmaus, Christ's appearance at 121f, 126–32
Enoch 26f, 127
Ephrem the Syrian 470
eternal now *(nunc eternam)* 61

faith and knowledge 296f
Farewell Discourse 413, 416
Father of lights 302–6

fear of disciples at transfiguration 503–5
feeding of five thousand 97f, 363f, 377f, 456
feet, washing of *see* washing of feet
fishes, miraculous draft of 107, 133–37
flame, tongues of 364
Flood 206
friend *(philos)* 229

Galilee
—, mountain in, Christ's appearance at 124
—, Sea of 57–60
— —, Christ's appearance at 124, 345, 413, 440f
garments *see* clothing
genealogy in Luke 27f
genealogy in Matthew 27–29
generations *see tholedoth*
Gennesareth, Lake *see* Galilee, Sea of
Gerasa, possessed man of 57
Gerhardt, Paul 112
Gethsemane, garden of 22, 482
—, Christ praying at 368, 370–72
—, Christ's struggle with death in 100f, 103
—, disciples asleep at 45
gift 302
giving 450
glory *(doxa)*, radiance of 278, 281, 525
Godet, Frédéric Louis 193, 384, 394
gods, you are 82–84
Goebel, Robert 327
Goethe, Johann Wolfgang von 57, 76, 128, 284, 294, 330f
good, beautiful *(kalos)* 82
Greek pilgrims at Temple and Christ 90, 94, 339f
groaning 167–69, 195

Hades 317–20
Hanukah *see* Chanukah
Hauch, Theodor 49
healing
— of blind man in Bethsaida 177–79
— of deaf and mute man 165–70

— of man born blind 179f, 181–88, 354–59
— of paralytic at Pool of Bethesda 171–75, 333–35
— of paralytic lowered through roof at Capernaum 63, 162–64
— of possessed boy 468, 495f, 500f, 519f
— of two blind men at Jericho 176f
heart, hardening of 64f
heaven, new 53
Heidenreich, Alfred 176, 180
heir (kinsman-redeemer) 237
Herder, Johann Gottfried 294
Hermes (Mercury) 130
Hermon, Mount 488
Herod Agrippa 264, 268
High Priestly Prayer 93, 369, 372f, 426f, 430–32
Hölderlin, Friedrich 305
Homer 318
humaneness 289–95
humble 68f
hunger 251

I AM *(egō eimi)* 184
— sayings 349f, 388–91, 401–7, see also bread, light, etc.
—, where 375f
initiation in mysteries 189–91

Jacob and heavenly ladder 172
Jairus' daughter, raising of 156, 189, 520
James, son of Zebedee 264
—, at transfiguration 471
Jeremias, Johannes 363
Jericho 88
Jerome 292
Jerusalem 480f
—, destruction of 148f
—, new 38, 216, 314, 480
—, Persian conquest of
Joel (prophet) 258
John the Baptist 22, 33, 347, 508f, 519
John the Evangelist 110, 137, 327, 438–41
—, at transfiguration 471

Joseph (son of Jacob) 272
Joseph of Arimathea 114
Josephus, Flavius 79f, 267
Judas 383, 448
Judas, not Iscariot 454
judges *see* Elohim (judges)
Julius, Roman captain 289
Justin the Martyr 36

kairos (time) *see* time *(kairos)*
kalos (beautiful, good) 82
Kelber, Wilhelm 52
Kleist, Heinrich von 91
knowledge and faith 296f
Küng, Hans 189

Lagerlöf, Selma 54, 60
Last Day 317
Lazarus, raising of 189–97, 364f, 412, 433–37, 524
—, Christ praying at grave of 367–70
Lazarus (poor man) 240–44
light 355
light of the world, I AM the 180–82, 351, 353, 358f, 388f, 403, 523
Lohmeyer, Ernst 327f, 339*n*, 346, 354, 512*n*
Lord's prayer 64, 99f, 472f
Lot's wife 206f
love *(philéein* and *agapa)* 419
love, question to Peter *see* Peter's love
Lucifer 286, 355
Luke 201
— as physician 102
— as seafarer 58f

MacGregor, John 58
Magdeburg, destruction of 216
magi (Persian priests) 496, 503
Malta, inhabitants of 289
Martha 193, 204, 433, 437
Mary, mother of Jesus 110, 201, 211
—, annunciation to 484, 516
—, as mother 201
Mary, mother of John Mark 265, 268
Mary of Bethany (Magdalene) 121f, 193, 204, 341f, 377–79, 437
materialism 315

meek 68f
Melchizedek 261, 285
memory, power of 510
Messiah, Christ reveals himself as 349
Meyer, Rudolf 33
Mithras mysteries 487
morning star 286
Moses 272, 277, 320, 387
— and Egyptian wisdom 515
— and Elijah at transfiguration 477f, 497–99, 514f
Mount of Olives *see* Olives, Mount of
mountain in Galilee *see* Galilee, mountain in
mountain of transfiguration 489
mountain, high 490–93
mountains of Old Testament 492f
mountains, seven in Matthew 490–93
mystery centres 189f

Nain, raising of young man at 128, 189
nakedness 253
Nathanael 346–48
Nazareth, Christ's reading in synagogue 62f
Nero 292
Newton, Sir Isaac 150
Nicodemus
—, conversation with 335–37, 365f, 377, 387, 412, 415f
— and burial of Christ 366
—, with Pharisees 366f
Nietzsche, Friedrich 71
night 417
Noah 206
Novalis 276, 394, 396
nunc eternam (eternal now) 61

Odin (Norse god) 167f
Olives, Mount of 125, 143, 147f
Olivet Discourse (Mount of Olives Prophecy) 206
one, oneness 422, 424f
overshadowing 484, 501, 516f

Panaetius (Stoic philosopher) 291
parable
— of great banquet 220–25

— of Last Judgment 247f, 249
— of prodigal son 210f, 242
— of rich man and Lazarus 240–44
— of shepherd and lost sheep 209
— of sower 202f
— of talents 246f, 249
— of wedding banquet 213–19
— of wicked tenants 232–39
— of wise and foolish maidens 245f, 248f
— of woman and lost coin 210
— of workers in vineyard 226–31
Paradise 314
passion, the 359–61
—, first announcement of 467, 469
—, predictions of 86–89
—, second announcement of 513
Passover festival 362f
Patmos, John's vision 507
Paul (apostle) 168, 275, 277, 284f, 292, 296–300
—, as prisoner 267, 289
—, experience at Damascus 128
Paul, Jean 116
Pentecost 23
Peter (apostle) 42–45, 87, 133–37, 226, 345f, 348, 440f, 524
—, at transfiguration 471, 481, 499–501
—, confession of 466f, 469, 488
—, Pentecost address 156, 257–62
—, rescue from prison 263–69
—, denial of 64, 102–8
— —, prediction of 102f
—, love, question of his 107f, 456–58
Pharisee(s) 184–86, 221, 357
philéein and *agapa* (love) 419
Philip (disciple) 82, 346–48
Pilate, Pontius 360f, 392f
Plato 318
Pliny 288
Plotinus 516
Polybius 290
Posidonius (Stoic philosopher) 291
power 158f
prayer 264f
pre-existence 372–75
prince of this world 381f

prisoners, visiting 253f
Prologue of John's Gospel 384–86

rainbow 155
Raphael (artist) 266f
refresh, rest 67, 69f
Reitzenstein, Richard August 291f
remain (Johannine word) 422f, 443
Rembrandt van Rijn 494
resurrection 23, 341–44
—, personal 299
—, proclaiming 258f
resurrection and the life, I am the 194, 388, 390, 405, 434
Rhoda, maid at house of Mary 268f
rich man and Lazarus 240–44, 320, 479
rich man and prodigal son 242
Rilke, Rainer Maria 192f, 237f
rising from the dead 517–20
Rittelmeyer, Friedrich 137*n*, 167, 195, 331, 340*n*, 350*n*, 353, 372*n*, 384f, 426, 434, 440
robes *see* clothing
Ruth 237

Sadducees 321
saliva 166, 177, 185
salt of the earth 227
Samaria, woman of 113, 348–50, 391f
Sanhedrin 272
Satan 383
Saul *see* Paul
Scipio the Younger 290
Sea of Galilee *see* Galilee, Sea of
Second Coming 148–52, 206
Seneca 292
Septuagint (Greek translation of Old Testament) 285
Sermon on the Mount 157
Seth 26
seven 346–61
shepherd, I am the good 358, 404f, 419f
sick, visiting 253f
Sidon 289
sighing 166–69
signs 159f
— in heaven 150f

Silas in prison 267
silence 486f, 505–7
Siloam, Pool of 183
sin 164
Skerst, Hermann von 80
sleep 283f, 321f, 482, 524
Socrates 254
Sodom and Gomorrah 206
Solomon's Portico 79–81
Son of God 40–47
Son of Man 48–53
Sophia (higher wisdom) 211f, 270
spittle 166, 177, 185
stars 149
Stauffer, Ethelbert 73, 111, 114*n*, 253, 294
Steiner, Rudolf 36, 46, 49, 55, 77, 100, 116, 119, 129, 131, 139, 176, 189–91, 283, 286f, 295, 316, 328f, 331, 340*n*, 369, 386, 416*n*, 463, 500
Stephen (martyr) 139, 270–76, 321f
storm 54f, 57
—, stilling of 41, 57–60, 156

Tabernacles, Festival of 175
temple in Jerusalem 148
—, destruction of 271
temptation, the 41, 95f
tent, body as *see* body as tent
Terence (Roman poet) 291, 293
Thaumas (Greek god) 155
thief at crucifixion 110, 141, 318
thirst 112f, 251, 391f
tholedoth (begettings, generations) 25f
Thomas (apostle) 123f, 341, 344
Thompson, W.M. 58
three 328, 332–45
Tiberias, Sea of *see* Galilee, Sea of
time *(chronos)* 234, 308
time *(kairos)* 234, 308
Trajan, Emperor 288
transfiguration 44f, 87, 98f, 320, 466–97
— as backdated Easter story 466f, 522
—, Christ's countenance at 473–75, 494f
—, Christ's garments at 476f
—, metamorphosis at 493

transfiguration, mountain of 489
transformation 277–82
trees, seeing people as 178
Trinity 328
twilight of the gods 55, 208

veil over face 277f
vestments *see* clothing
vine 450–52
vine, I AM the true 406
Vulgate (Latin translation of Bible) 292

wakening from the dead 517–20
waking (up) 284, 309f
walking 126f
— on water 42, 157
washing of the feet 359, 437f
water rites, baptism 32–34
water, angel troubling 171

way, the truth and the life, I AM the 406
wedding feast (in Apocalypse) 311
wedding garment 217f
Windisch, H. 354
winepress 233
woman of Samaria *see* Samaria, woman of
woman taken in adultery *see* adultery, woman taken in
wonders 155–58
works 160f
writing, Christ 72–77

yoke 67, 70

Zechariah 316, 472, 487
Zion, Mount 261
Zoroastrian religion 495

You may also be interested in...

The New Testament
A Version by Jon Madsen

Many translations of the New Testament tread a challenging line between scholarly accuracy and living, spirit-filled words which will inspire a general reader.

This unique version balances the two in such a way that something of the Holy Spirit, working in the early church, can become part of a reader's experience.

Madsen draws on other translations, including Emil Bock's seminal German translation, as well as the sacramental language of The Christian Community, to present a singular version which uncovers the living wisdom of the Gospels. Beautifully bound in hardback with eye-catching dust jacket, this gift edition will remain a wise companion for years to come.

Also available as e Book

florisbooks.co.uk

Paths Into the Book of Books
New Biblical Translations through the Festivals of the Year

Elsbeth Weymann

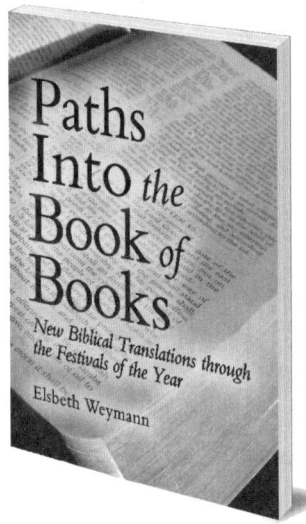

In this insightful book, Elsbeth Weymann, an expert in Greek and Hebrew, has selected biblical passages which take the reader through the festivals of the year – from Advent and Easter to Pentecost and Michaelmas. Each passage has a fresh translation and in-depth commentary. For instance, in the story of Pentecost, she highlights the use of the unusual feminine form of the word 'spirit', which points to a feminine aspect of the Holy Spirit.

Weymann's study of specific words and grammar also shows how the living presence of the Old Testament is evident in the New Testament. This book is for anyone looking for deeper meaning in the Bible.

florisbooks.co.uk

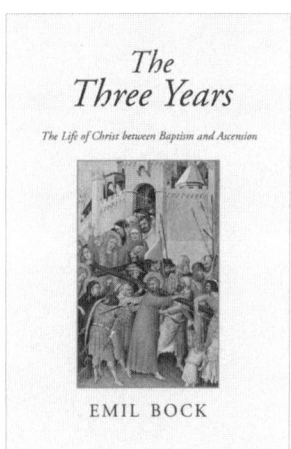

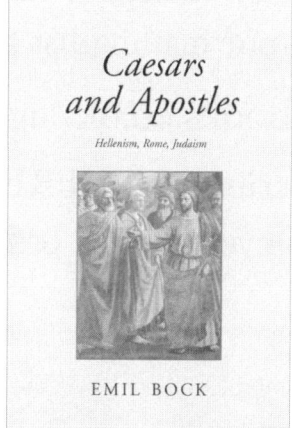

florisbooks.co.uk

For news on all our **latest books**, and to receive **exclusive discounts**, **join** our mailing list at:

florisbooks.co.uk/signup

Plus subscribers get a FREE book with every online order!

We will never pass your details to anyone else.